SELECTING MATERIALS FOR LIBRARIES

SELECTING MATERIALS
FOR
LIBRARIES

ROBERT N. BROADUS
PROFESSOR OF LIBRARY SCIENCE,
UNIVERSITY OF NORTH CAROLINA
AT CHAPEL HILL

THE H. W. WILSON COMPANY
NEW YORK
1981

Library of Congress Cataloging in Publication Data

Broadus, Robert N.
    Selecting materials for libraries.

    Includes index.
    1. Book selection. I. Title.
Z689.B36 1981   025.21   81-650
ISBN 0-8242-0659-2   AACR2

Printed in the United States of America

To Elizabeth Carter Broadus

PREFACE

As the novice librarian looks toward the responsibility of selecting materials, what qualities do we ask this beginner to cultivate? First of all, an appreciation of the infinitely varied interests of other human beings who may use the library; then an awareness of the multifarious works available for library collections and some sense of how interesting so many of these materials are. We expect the librarian to learn quickly the methods, techniques, and tools for evaluating materials for potential purchase; to make distinctions according to format and subject; and finally to take up the long-term challenge of thinking out viable and consistent views on the responsibility of selection as a whole, without overlooking the need for careful attention to the details of the process.

Having tried to convey something of this approach to selecting materials, I hope this book will be useful in connection with first courses in the topic as offered in schools and departments of librarianship, and that practicing librarians also will find here some stimulation.

Anyone who attempts to deal with all types and sizes of libraries has to face the fact that their problems, conditions, and purposes vary tremendously. This book takes as its major focus the small to medium-sized general library, but a fair proportion of the observations are pertinent to university and other large libraries, as well as to some of the more specialized ones. It is assumed also that selectors in small libraries have access to bibliographic tools in large collections, as in fact they often do.

For each subject I have indicated some of the better sources of information which lend help in selection but have not presented exhaustive bibliographies, by any means. Where I have mentioned one title in a series, I have felt no compulsion to list its fellows elsewhere. Knowing representative examples, the student or librarian may be encouraged to ferret out other guides, and, more important, to be on the alert for new information, some of which will have appeared by the time this book comes from the bindery.

In the further interest of brevity, I have set arbitrary limits to the scope of the book. Such important topics as materials for children, library organization for selection, acquisitions procedures, discarding, and censorship are touched upon only as they border closely on the central theme. The book focuses, then, on selection as a part of the slightly larger topic, "Collection Development."

Bibliographic details are given in a footnote for each work cited for specific substantive information. Where a work is used as an example (such as a typical guide to literature or a work that represents a certain kind of publication), the publishing details are included in the text. I have given complete bibliographic information where I thought it of possible use to the reader and have erred, I suspect, on the side of completeness.

I think of numerous persons who have in some way helped with this edition. Special thanks go to Frances Holt, a doctoral student in the School of Library Science, The University of North Carolina at Chapel Hill. She checked references and told me what ideas in the manuscript needed clarification. Other students who verified details of one sort or another are Susan Artiglia, Jane Belsches, Julie Haydon, and Karen Measell. I owe a great deal to the stimulation of my colleagues on the faculty of the School of Library Science. Especially helpful have been Dean Edward G. Holley, and Professors Lester Asheim, Budd Gambee, Haynes McMullen, Mary Kingsbury, Ray Carpenter, and Marilyn Miller. My able typists were Bobbie Lee Holley and Billie Smith. The editorial staff of The H. W. Wilson Company have been wonderfully helpful—especially Bruce R. Carrick and Norris Smith. My wife Eleanor was a help throughout. I appreciate the remarks made by critics (most of them) about the first edition. None of these people are accountable, of course, for any of my follies.

Robert N. Broadus
November 1980

CONTENTS

PART I

THE PROBLEM AND
THE BASIC APPROACH

In practice, the selection of materials for a library means making, from day to day, small decisions, each involving numerous bits of information. It may be helpful, however, to construct a frame for these decisions by defining the overall limits of the problem of selection. The librarian needs to develop general principles and policies to use as guides in selecting individual books, periodicals, films, and recordings. Although these principles must be hammered out over a period of years, the suggestions that follow in the first part of this book ought to provoke discussion and perhaps debate.

1. INTRODUCTION

Take a look at your public or college library. Roam through the book stacks. Pull some of the books from the shelves. Note their ages, bindings, kinds of paper, title pages; the topics they cover. Try reading a little to sample the various styles. Examine the range of audio-visual material — films, recordings, slides, etc. Imagine the kinds of people who must have written and produced these materials — the skills of typesetters, printers, and camera operators that went into their manufacture.

Do you know what a small fraction of the world's total output is represented in this one library? Why is the collection made up of this particular assortment, different from all others? Each item was purchased (or accepted as a gift) because someone considered it a good choice in view of the available funds. How capable were those selectors? What advice did they use? If you took time enough, you could tell a great deal about the kinds of people who, over the years, built this collection: how intelligent they were; how fair-minded; what ideas they valued; how they looked upon the people they served; even perhaps their theories of selection. Librarians inevitably and justifiably impose a little of their own personalities on the collections they develop. They have here a chance for immortality, by leaving an impression on the minds of the people who read or view or listen to the materials they have gathered.

Although selection of materials has always been considered a major responsibility, in the 1960s some librarians began to question the effort necessary to do the job well. Acquisition budgets were substantial, and it seemed somehow wasteful to expend staff time trying to stretch such easy dollars. The many lists of "best books" seemed to provide absolute answers on what to buy. It was inevitable that someone would take it upon himself to announce "The Death of Book Selection," and indeed the *Wilson Library Bulletin* for December 1968 carried an article with that title. Some librarians argued in a rather pious tone that less time spent in selection would mean more time available for serving the public. Even as late as 1976, one commercial firm was publishing an advertisement depicting a contented librarian in a rocking chair, and implying that since the company had made selection and ordering easier, librarians could devote their time to "important" things.

What a travesty of the concept of library services — as if selection were not one of the chief contributions a professional librarian could make to clientele!

The no-need-for-selection approach won't do, as we learned (or rather re-learned) in the seventies. If the library is to add materials in a variety of formats that appeal to a diverse population with changing interests and needs, selection is going to require more time and knowledge than ever before. In any event, choice of some kind has to be exercised, for good or ill. There simply are more materials than any one library can handle. Even if they were offered free and stacked on the library's receiving dock, they could not all be processed, nor would the necessary millions of cubic feet be available to store them. Furthermore, users would be so overwhelmed by the mountains of books that they would despair of finding the works most pertinent to their needs.

But most materials are not offered free, and where is the library that has ever had more than a small fraction of the money it would like? Even large systems, such as the Harvard University libraries, which spend over three million dollars a year for materials, must use care in their choices. In the small or medium-sized library, selection is all the more important, since the budget may be so tight that even some excellent books, periodicals, films, and recordings have to be rejected.

More serious, the current reductions in library budgets have made dollars (already shrunken by inflation) a scarce commodity. As libraries are forced to cut subscriptions to serials, care in choosing new materials becomes even more urgent. The concern with the financial pinch can be seen in the title of a recent (and none too satisfactory) work published in Great Britain: *Book Selection in a Siege Economy*.[1]

Really, the building and shaping of the collection is very close to the heart of librarianship, involving, as it does, the essential philosophy of the profession. Not only is book selection one of the most fascinating tasks in the intellectual world, but it is also "the most important, most interesting, and most difficult of the professional librarian's responsibilities."[2] True, "canned" lists of the "best books" need not be ignored, but like other materials they must be evaluated thoroughly and used only so far as they prove helpful.

Librarians have to decide also on the number of additional copies to order for each title. Generations ago, the great pioneering librarian John Cotton Dana advocated that a public library have "few titles, carefully chosen for the community's needs, and freely duplicated,"[3] but for some reason the notion has been accepted that if the catalog lists a certain title, then the library's obligation regarding that work has been fulfilled. From the standpoint of service, this idea doesn't make sense. Whoever knew "an empty-handed reader who left the library deliriously happy with having found a catalog entry"?[4] In the case of a valuable and popular book, the library needs extra copies. The second, fifth, or even sixtieth copy may represent a wise expenditure of funds. To determine the precise number of additional copies needed requires the application of some intelligence.

Large libraries use blanket-order plans, obtaining, say, all books issued by certain publishers with specialized lists, or all books written in English in certain fields, but there is an increasing awareness that such plans must be examined with some caution. For huge libraries, it is entirely feasible to obtain large blocks of material automatically from jobbers (wholesalers) or other agents. This method is economical for roughing out the collection, but the final polishing, which fits the library to the needs of its clientele, must be done by the local library staff. Many decisions have to be made by librarians in close contact with users. Individual titles must be weighed with care before being selected or rejected; otherwise the library simply cannot give its best service.

There is another important aspect of the selection process: The selector learns a great deal about the materials that ultimately will be placed in the hands of patrons. The information gained from reviews and bibliographies will be essential to the librarian's other functions, aside from book selection, especially in a small or medium-sized institution. How can one advise readers without knowing why the library has selected the particular titles it offers? Books and related materials are the librarian's stock in trade, and no librarian can know too much about them. Augustine Birrell (1850–1933), English essayist and member of Parliament, was speaking of personal collections of books when he declared, "It is no doubt a pleasant thing to have a library left you. . . . But, good as it is to inherit a library, it is better to collect one. Each volume then . . . has its own individuality, a history of its own."[5] The same is true of collecting by librarians.

To further illustrate the importance of selection for libraries, let us focus for the time being on the book.* The significance of the printed word in the shaping of the modern world need not be reviewed here. The rise in functional illiteracy and the increased use of television have led many people to say that print will be less influential in the future, and even to predict the "death" of the book. (Not that this kind of talk is new: As far back as 1895 the prediction was being made that phonograph records would supplant books, on the grounds that people would find it easier and more pleasant to listen than to read.) Other prophets have declared that electronic devices such as computers and television screens will replace print and similar media. On the other hand, the production and sale of books and periodicals go on at a high rate. In the United States, book sales continue strong year after year, and industry receipts are approaching the mark of six billion dollars annually.[6] In 1970 it was predicted that the book industry in the United States would grow from sales of about three billion dollars in 1970 to some thirteen billion in 1990 — a rate of growth considerably higher than that predicted for the Gross National Product.[7] In the same year, Daniel

---

*Sometimes (though not here) I shall take the liberty of using the term *book* to cover all types of materials collected by libraries, because the book is typical of items that libraries collect. (When farmers say *head* of cattle, they include necks and rumps.) The term *generic book* is used in this sense by some librarians; see Louis Shores's *The Generic Book: What It Is and How It Works* (Norman, OK: Library-College Associates, Inc., 1977), 164 pp.

Bell, Professor of Sociology at Harvard University and Chairman of the Commission on the Year 2000 of the American Academy of Arts and Sciences, spoke of our postindustrial society as being primarily concerned with knowledge and information, adding: "In a knowledge society, education and books clearly play a central role. Over the next thirty years the communication industry, and along with it book publishing, obviously will be expanding."[8] Allowing for the factors of inflation and other economic difficulties, both predictions are holding up reasonably well. Moreover, there is evidence that people are reading more books now than formerly. A special Gallup poll in 1975 found 56 percent of those questioned reporting that they had read "all or part of a book in the past month."[9] Another poll in 1978 discovered that 55 percent of the population had read one or more books in the previous six months.[10] Recent suggestions that reading receive more emphasis in schools raise the possibility (a slight one, though) that future adults will consume books at a faster rate. Even if books were used solely as repositories of ideas (they do have many other uses), their future would be assured. After all, the printed page is efficient as a device for storing information, and retrieval of that information from a bound book is relatively uncomplicated.

Books provide a picture (or perhaps a mirror) that represents what we think, imagine, investigate, and hold dear. True, many publications are simply junk or worse (at least to people other than the authors and publishers), but if most of humanity's bad qualities are reflected there, the best ones are shown even more clearly. William Saroyan wrote many years ago, "I am about to place language, my language, upon a clean sheet of paper, and I am trembling. It is so much of a responsibility to be a user of words."[11]

THE BASIC PROBLEM

The world of potential library materials is an immense area for exploration. Knowing something of its extent, we are brought to the question, Of all the books and related materials that have ever been published, which ones are best for a given library? This is not quite the same as the question, What are the best books? for each library has to deal with a certain clientele, and the basic problem is to choose the materials that are best for those people. Selection is not made in a vacuum; it is practiced by an expert (relatively speaking) who wrestles with the question of what books are most needed by a definite group of readers — readers with differing interests, capabilities, and needs; readers who consume books for many and varied reasons.

Look at the dimensions of this problem as indicated by a few statistics on the numbers of publications available. Each summer, *Publishers Weekly* gives the number of new titles issued by American commercial publishers during the previous year. For 1979 there were 36,112 new books and 9,070 new editions for a total of 45,182 titles.[12] (In these tabulations, a multi-volume set with a single title is counted as one. The survey does not include government documents and certain "minor" publications, such as pamphlets under forty-nine pages in length. Many paperbacks simply are not reported.) A 1952 prediction that the annual number of conventionally published titles might drop from 10,000 to 3,000 now seems a bit pessimistic.[13]

The United Kingdom, France, Germany, and other highly literate countries publish almost as many books as the United States, although their populations are smaller. Canada, with far fewer people, publishes about 6,000 titles a year. The USSR often has claimed a very high rate of book production — approximately 80,000 titles per year — but counts pamphlets, brochures and other small items, and perhaps reprints.

Since, for the Western world, these statistics represent only commercially produced books (and just those listed in the regular book trade), what of other materials collected by libraries? The United States Federal Government issues each year perhaps 300,000 separate items, of which about ten percent could be termed interesting to the general public. There are also publications of state and local governments, plus those of foreign jurisdictions. It would be safe to say that altogether (counting all languages) more than 600,000 new books are issued in a typical year, though reports from some countries are hard to interpret.[14]

There is more to the story. The *Ayer Directory of Publications* lists over 11,000 newspapers and over 9,000 periodicals currently issued in the United States alone. Even then, several thousand magazines are omitted — those for employees of companies (house organs), regional church bulletins, publications of primary and secondary schools, etc. Again, other major literate countries boast similar numbers. Back issues as well as current ones may be important. Many periodicals which once flourished and later were discontinued are still useful enough to be bought by libraries from antiquarian book dealers or from reprint houses. Added to these totals are the thousands of maps, films, slides, recordings, tapes — not to mention pamphlets and advertising brochures, and all those other forms that most libraries now take the responsibility for collecting.

One of the pressing needs in the philosophy of librarianship is the development of a rational policy on what *forms* or *types* of materials to gather. As yet there is no clear statement on just where libraries should set the limit and where other agencies should take over collection, preservation, and circulation, but it seems reasonable for libraries to have the responsibility for "graphic" records — those printed, written, or otherwise marked on any surface.[15] Not all librarians share the enthusiasm of one public library trustee who boasted about his institution's loans of lawnmowers to week-end gardeners, nor is the domain of live animals expanding rapidly in the typical library.

So far, I have discussed the torrent of materials currently flowing from the producers. What of the books published in past years? A 1963 article in *Science* estimates the sum of different titles held by libraries of the world as upwards of 75,000,000, including books, pamphlets, and volumes of periodicals.[16] (The same writer, discussing the problem of translating this information into binary bits for storage on computer tapes, gives the number of such bits as 2,000,000,000,000,000.) The next year, another method of estimating the total produced a much higher figure: a whopping 200,000,000 volumes.[17]

It is noteworthy also that whereas the world's population is growing at roughly 1.7 percent per year (though the rate fluctuates), the growth of recordable information each year is about two percent; some peg it higher. This is not to say that real, useable knowledge grows at such a rate; knowledge can't very well be divided into units and counted. But the problem for libraries is the amount of publication.

We may summarize the dimensions of the selection problem: possibly 200,000,000 volumes of printed materials already published, plus something on the order of 600,000 being added each year. For nonprint the backlog is smaller, but the rate of publication probably as great, at least in this country.

For a given library, which particular items should be selected? The picture is not quite so staggering as it first appears. We can start eliminating huge sections at once. First, many books published in the past are simply not available to libraries in any real sense. Most libraries can dismiss from consideration millions of old rare books on recondite subjects, as well as works in many of the lesser-known languages (though with the increase of interest in various once-obscure regions of the world, larger libraries have to be more careful than they once were). Yet with well over a hundred thousand titles being published each year in English, the librarian of a school or public or college library has to consider seriously about 30,000 commercial books, 15,000 public documents, and 10,000 periodical subscriptions, plus works in the newer media and a backlog of perhaps a million works. Since any one of these items is a possible choice, the field for consideration is still immense.

In choosing materials for one particular library, we must begin somewhere. How shall we set about? On what information shall we base decisions? First, extensive reading, viewing, and listening are needed on the part of the librarian. Reading, for one, develops judgment and taste — a sense of book values. There is really no fully adequate substitute, and it would be nice, of course, if the selector could read the entire output, then simply order the best. (I have met people who think librarians do that.) Realistically, though, how much can one person read? Good librarians should read eight to ten hours a week on their own time. Some libraries allow time for a certain amount of reading on the job. With practice, it is possible to get the juice of a typical book in a few hours. But if one completes four or five books a week with a reasonable degree of comprehension, that still means only seven or eight thousand books read in a working lifetime — a very small fraction of the total available for potential selection.★ To try to ascertain directly the value of nonprint materials would be even more difficult and time-consuming, since skimming and browsing are less convenient. This means that the librarian has to obtain information about the quality and suitability of materials by methods other than looking at the works themselves, which holds true even if the librarian is responsible for only a part of the entire field of knowledge.

The selector therefore has to build in mind a kind of network of knowledge about potential library materials. Some of this information comes from reviews. Though soon discovering that critiques of this kind are difficult to interpret — and certainly not to be taken at face value — one does learn that some reviewers are more trustworthy than others. Librarians must depend on guides to subject literatures — lists or surveys written by people who may have studied extensively in one area of knowledge. They also make some use of "standard" selection guides, compiled by those who have examined films and read books or reviews (or other guides). So each selector acquires more and more information about books, roughing out what may be thought of as a tentative and perhaps not entirely accurate map of the world of library materials. Its details are never clear. The world of communication is shifting restlessly; parts of it change rapidly. No one is ever certain what the best titles are. This whole enterprise, then, may be quite frustrating, and the librarian often yearns for

★In this connection we all must feel a little like Thomas De Quincey, who confessed among other things that: "In my youthful days, I never entered a great library, suppose of one hundred thousand volumes, but my predominant feeling was one of pain and disturbance of mind. . . . Here, said I, are one hundred thousand books, the worst of them capable of giving me some pleasure and instruction; and before I can have had time to extract the honey from one-twentieth of this hive, in all likelihood I shall be [dead]." (*Collected Writings,* ed. David Masson [London: A. & C. Black, 1896–1897, vol. 10] p. 38.

definite, unqualified, reliable (scientific?) evaluations. Such are very seldom to be had. As a rule, judgments simply have to be made on the basis of the sketchy information available.

A more detailed discussion and evaluation of guides, reviews, and other services will be given later in this book, but before taking up those matters it will be necessary to set up a framework by considering some general topics, such as types of libraries and clienteles, library selection principles, and general standards for judgment.

2. THE LIBRARY
IN ITS ENVIRONMENT

Having observed the magnitude of the flow issuing from the producers of communication materials, we are ready to make a tentative approach to the problem of selection for libraries. This overall view may be thought of as *macroselection;* it involves general principles. At the outset, let it be understood clearly that selection never occurs in a vacuum. It is a service for people. Choices of books and other items are always made in terms of those who use or may use or should use a particular library.

Only the initiated can imagine the wondrous variety of libraries in the world. They differ in their purposes, in the ways they are administered, in the services they offer, in physical facilities, and above all in size and nature of their collections. No two are alike. All supermarkets may resemble each other—not all libraries, except in the most superficial ways.

Roles of individual librarians, moreover, are different with regard to responsibility for selection. In one situation, a part-time person may spend a few hours a week at the task but deal with all types of materials on all subjects—at least not deliberately excluding any. The library's entire annual budget for new resources may total less than a thousand dollars. Great comprehensive libraries, at the other extreme, have staff specialists (bibliographers), each dedicated to one division of knowledge (as, the social sciences), or one format (as, monographs), or one part of the world (as, the Slavic countries). Each specialist may work virtually full time at the selection and acquisition of materials.

Libraries, then, look different, are different. Do the selectors in these widely-divergent institutions share any general principles? Yes; even the librarian who occasionally recommends a single title has something in common with the one who over a period of years uses practically every working hour to select materials, spending millions of dollars. The work of each is based on presuppositions about the library and its users — their needs, and how those needs ought to be met.

Parts III, IV, and V of this book will discuss materials suitable for three major types of libraries (school, public, and college) as well as, to an extent, special and university libraries. It is in order first, however, to emphasize the differences among types, because the beginning student is apt to minimize them and even the experienced practitioner, after spending twenty years in one library, may lose awareness of how other libraries operate.

Most libraries have something to do with formal educational programs. School, academic, most public, and some special libraries serve students (for a definition of special libraries, see below). Looked at in a slightly different way, most libraries are connected to a parent institution to which they have a primary obligation. The university library's main function is to provide for the students and faculty. The special library (that of a medical society, for instance) is set up to serve the needs of the association and its members. Here there is a sharp gap between public and other types of libraries. The "parent" of the public library is ambiguous to say the least — perhaps it is the city government, perhaps the people who make up the jurisdiction.

A brief introduction to these types of libraries from the standpoint of their collections will help set the stage for a discussion of general principles of selection. The order will proceed, roughly speaking, from those libraries serving more specialized clienteles to those with responsibility toward the entire public. It may be theorized that this order also represents a progression from the less troublesome to the more difficult problems in selection.

SPECIAL LIBRARIES

Some collections are gathered and organized for the benefit of particular groups of people. These collections usually cover a limited subject range and perhaps include only a few formats, such as books and periodicals. Such libraries are classified under the vague and nondescriptive term *special* — a word which suggests, if nothing else, that they are more specialized in purpose than public libraries or school libraries. Most special libraries are operated by business firms, organizations, or societies, but they can be found also on university campuses in the form of medical, music, botanical, or other subject libraries.

A few specific examples: A daily newspaper may establish a library to support the work of its staff — reporters, editors, advertising personnel, and other functionaries. Along with reference books, a newspaper's library will contain huge files of clippings and photographs. A similar library at Time, Inc., has over 500,000 file folders and a good collection of other materials, used by its fourteen research librarians as they deal with 100,000 queries a year.[1] The National Trust for Historic Preservation set up a record-keeping service in 1949, and out of it evolved a library of 9,000 books, 13,000 file folders, clippings (many of them converted to microfiche), and periodicals, as well as records of the organization itself.[2] A library for business management may include works on accounting, law, politics, economics, psychology, sociology, marketing, government regulations, and other subjects. The same company may operate a technical library, with materials on, say, biology, chemistry, and art as they relate to the manufacture of paints. Any agency of government may establish its own library of most needed information. A submarine may have a library for its crew; an ocean liner for its passengers. (I once traveled on a Russian ship through the Baltic Sea and found its small library made up chiefly of the writings of Lenin and others true to the cause.)

The special library may provide recreational material along with the serious, businesslike tomes, but because it exists primarily for the needs, often research requirements, of the organization that supports it, the collection is chosen carefully, and its limits are clearly specified. Its materials must serve a definite purpose. Usually the emphasis is on printed works, but special libraries in such fields as art, music, and cinema collect slides, recordings, films, and related forms.

ACADEMIC LIBRARIES

For a large group of libraries, the parent body is a post–secondary educational institution. The college or university library has a more diversified group of users as a rule than does the special library, yet has no direct responsibility for service to the general public. For each library, basic questions regarding the educational philosophy and procedures of its parent institution must be answered before selection can proceed effectively. The curriculum is of prime importance. Recommendations by the teaching staff are encouraged earnestly, though there has been a healthy (and healthful) tendency over the past few years for librarians to take over the final responsibility for building collections.[3] Librarians are in a position to see the academic program as a whole and to make judgments among conflicting interests. Student suggestions are encouraged and valued, especially in the area of so-called recreational reading.

A major, frequently-discussed question in planning for collection development is whether the budget for materials should be apportioned among departments of instruction. Having retained, say, twenty-five or thirty percent for general needs, the library can allocate the rest according to a formula that weighs such factors as departmental enrollment, course offerings, present state of collection, and costs and volume of publication in the field. Some plans also take into account the actual use of library materials by the departmental personnel. McGrath suggests that the two most important considerations are use and cost of materials.[4] Goyal even recommends as a factor the "importance which society attaches to the work of the department."[5]

The principal advantages of allocation are that (1) each department is encouraged to take an interest in library purchases, and (2) funds may be expended according to need and potential use so that no field is overlooked and none developed disproportionately. There are several disadvantages, the main ones being that (1) faculty in a department may assume the money has been given to them for their own use rather than for the benefit of the entire library and the institution, and (2) the librarians' flexibility is reduced in that there is less money for large purchases which serve several programs. Schad, in a perceptive article, argues that no formulas to date are very satisfactory, and that, if used, they should be treated as general guidelines only.[6]

Junior and Community College Libraries

Beginning at the turn of the century in the United States, the two-year college movement has developed rapidly in both size and diversity.[7] Originally, the so-called junior college tended to replicate the first two years of the standard four-year, or "senior," college, but now has increased its functions to serve a wide variety of students and even the entire community. Some students take vocational courses in such fields as agriculture, mechanics, or electronics; others are preparing to enter liberal arts colleges or universities at the third-year level; still others come in for evening classes in practical or theoretical subjects. Not only are there differences among the students, but one college differs from another, depending upon its sponsoring institution and especially upon its location, for most students live in the immediate area of the college. Many of the students are both highly intelligent and already well-educated; some are rejects from other institutions; some are attempting to make up for what the self-flattering establishment calls "cultural disadvantage." Various subjects are taught, and many methods of instruction are used. In art and music, for instance, the approach often is not so technical or so historically oriented as in more traditional schools.[8]

The 1979 ACRL standards for two-year learning resources programs call for the very large institution to have a center housing collection of over 100,000 units, including both print and nonprint.[9] The production of nonprint materials often is under the guidance of this center, and the products are added to the collection. The fact that so many media formats are gathered has led to the use of terms like "learning resources programs" or "media centers," though in 1976 Dale found many centers still describing themselves as "libraries."[10]

Four-Year College Libraries

The "senior" college is somehow traditional in American higher education, though here again change and variety are everywhere. Since World War II, many of these institutions, especially those supported by the public, have become universities, and others have added some graduate work or have broadened their programs beyond the liberal arts to include vocational and professional programs (or vice versa). Nevertheless, many people believe that the privately-supported four-year college offers the really liberating education. Often there is a sense of community at such colleges, and the librarian can know the personal interests of faculty and even of many students.

These students, despite the fact that they come from greater distances, form more homogeneous groups than those found in typical community colleges. They are more alike in ability and even in economic and social background; therefore the library collection is somewhat more unified. It also tends to be deeper and larger, sometimes running into the hundreds of thousands of volumes. In fact, the 1975 ACRL standards for college libraries specify, for example, that, in order to be classed Grade A, the library serving a college with 2,000 students and 200 faculty, with 20 major or minor fields, must have 142,000 volumes of print or microform equivalents.[11] Most of these libraries are made up of print materials only (plus microform copies of them), while nonprint items are purchased and serviced by other agencies on campus, though the Library-College movement has been energetic in making its case for the individual use of all media.[12] Student papers for upper division courses require depth in many subjects. Foreign language sources become a little more important. Students of environmental science, urban affairs, pop culture, and similar contemporary subjects (as well as debaters and other speechmakers, of course) gobble up books, periodicals, pamphlets, and government documents on current social issues, just as they do in other types of libraries.

A hard problem is presented to the college library if the faculty are expected to do research based primarily on source materials in the collection. If they are, thousands of specialized items are needed in such fields as literature and history, and the problem of building a collection that will serve the greatest number of people becomes extremely difficult. Miller and Rockwood warn against the notion that a college library is a university library in miniature.[13] Unless the former has unusual wealth, it must spend most of its materials budget on titles which meet student needs rather than those which support esoteric research.

University Libraries

About the time of the Civil War, Yale became the first American institution to confer the degree of doctor of philosophy. Since that time research and graduate training have been the characteristic function of the university, though teaching has in recent years regained a good part of its lost ground.

Students here range from the bewildered, homesick beginner to the harried middle-ager verifying the footnotes in a six-hundred-page dissertation. As for faculty, some of them teach general introductory survey courses, while others are concerned with highly specialized fields. A professor may, for instance, spend an entire lifetime studying one author, though using data from several disciplines and points-of-view in attempts to reach a fuller understanding of that person.

Traditionally, faculties have had great power over selection for American university libraries. In 1963, Perry Danton published an important work in which he charged that because of such policies, collections had not been developed as well as they should have been. He advocated that that responsibility for selection be placed in the hands of librarians with good subject backgrounds.[14] The extent of Danton's influence is not known, but twenty-five years later Baatz, in a survey of nineteen research libraries, found the bulk of selection being done by librarians.[15] Nevertheless powerful faculty members can be very demanding where their own interests are concerned, and Perdue is about right in stating that in a university, "collection development is, more than anything else, a political task."[16]

It is becoming more common for the large university library to have a collection development officer who reports to the chief executive of the library and who makes the final, effective decisions about what to add, using the advice of faculty, staff, and others in the academic community. There may be a group of bibliographers, each with a clearly-defined area of responsibility. Other librarians, especially those in reference services, may be active in recommending titles.

Sizes of university library collections go from a few hundred thousand to ten million items. In recent years, more attention has been given to gross size as a measure of the collection's worth. A number of formulas have been developed — all of them, of course, subjective estimates at base. In 1969, Robert B. Downs made the judgment that a university offering doctorates in the major areas of knowledge should have a library of 1,500,000 or more volumes, and should spend at least $750,000 a year for books, periodicals, and binding.[17] This rough figure might well be approximated also by extrapolating the 1975 Standards for College Libraries. The 1979 Standards for University Libraries, recognizing the difficulty of applying quantitative standards, merely say that "collections shall be of sufficient size and scope to support the university's total instructional needs and to facilitate the university's research programs"[18] — a statement hard to contradict.

In a university library the proportion of titles in foreign languages is larger, perhaps going over 50 percent. Numerous materials may be of historical interest only or may be in the collection not because they are "good" but because they indicate something about human folly. Chiefly for these reasons, the library has thousands of books which are borrowed only once in ten years or longer, and which don't seem to be used much in the building either. The well-publicized and highly controversial "Pitt Study" confirmed in a general way the findings of many others when it concluded that over a seven-year period, only 51.6 percent of the books in its Hillman Library had actually been checked out even one time. Nearly half the books, it would seem, had not been borrowed at all during the period.[19]

In view of the apparent little use received by many materials and of the increasing costs of adding and keeping each item, there is now a growing stress on limiting collection size. The arguments in favor of this apply most pointedly to university libraries. Some opponents of the hairy behemoths have borrowed the phrase "zero growth"; others speak of "steady-state"; still others prefer the term "self-renewing," as having a more positive sound.[20] The main arguments are the expense of maintaining and servicing large collections, and the difficulties created for the reader by big complex catalogs and twelve-tier bookstacks.[21] The British librarian B. J. Enright entitled a paper "Bibliochlothanasia," from the word *ochlothanasia,* meaning death from overcrowding.[22]

On the other hand, big libraries, other things being equal, have the advantage of being more likely to supply the materials wanted by users. Any item, however obscure, boring, or idiotic, may help some scholar to better understand human nature. Kronick describes "the excitement of receiving from some dusty corner of the building a volume which is still unopened although it may be well over a hundred years old. This is the stuff of scholarship."[23]

Those who advocate zero or near-zero growth generally emphasize careful selection along with weeding, storage, and interlibrary cooperation. Osburn urges the general need for greater selectivity, based on the predicted research needs of the local academic community.[24] The overall policy of the library with regard to size and rate of growth has a strong bearing, therefore, on the work of those who choose materials to be added.

In the last ten to twenty years, a great many studies have been published about university library collections,[25] partly because this type of collection offers so many problems and partly because the people who wish to do research are often associated with universities. These papers deal with such matters as prices of materials, why people don't obtain the works they are looking for in the library, and optimum sizes of collections, as well as criteria and evidence which may be used when selecting and discarding titles. Some of these studies will be cited in Chapter 4, which deals with "scientific" approaches to collection-building.

School Libraries (Media Centers)

The collection for the elementary, middle, or high school (or for grades K–12) must serve a variety of people. In most schools, there are students from various backgrounds, with diversified interests and attitudes toward society (and toward everything else, including library materials). In spite of the fact that most school libraries serve students of a limited age level, it is remarkable what differences in ability and concern can be observed. Then there are the faculty, needing materials both for advanced ideas about the topics they teach and for information about the profession itself.

Often called "instructional materials centers," "teaching materials centers," or "media centers," these libraries are more likely to house and service nonprint as well as print materials. There are two principal reasons for collections to be so broad: (1) Projectable materials are used for many of the same functions as are served by books, pamphlets, and periodicals. The catalog that leads to a book can lead just as efficiently to a film on the same topic; thus a person needing a film on the history of New England or the art of making pies can find it through the appropriate subject heading. (2) Because the collection of both print and nonprint usually is small, as compared with a university library's holdings, there is a greater economy in having all types of materials under one manager. The materials of print, however, are used typically by individuals; nonprint may be used either by individuals or by entire classes.

In size, the high school collection of today may well exceed the college collection available to students two generations ago. Whereas national standards for 1945 assumed that the largest school libraries would "probably not exceed 10,000 titles,"[26] the 1975 guidelines, *Media Programs, District and School,* recommend that the school have at least 20,000 items, including 8,000 to 12,000 printed volumes, with larger schools owning many more. Sixty thousand titles should be available in a large school, though not all need be on campus.[27] In Lowell Martin's opinion, "twenty-five thousand volumes in the school would leave specialized and subject reading interests unserved."[28] These recommendations and judgments are of particular interest in the light of that segment of current opinion which proclaims that large libraries should limit their growth.

While selection of materials usually is regarded by school librarians as one of their major responsibilities, it is an activity which by its nature can be deferred in the face of lesser duties which appear more urgent. Therefore, the librarian should, with a generous hand, allocate time for perusing reviews, for previewing materials, and for talking with faculty. Vandergrift wisely urges librarians not to worry about taking time away from students in order to serve them better in the long run with a good collection.[29]

Obviously the advice of teachers and other interested parties must be sought and taken seriously. Should students be encouraged to make recommendations for purchase? Most emphatically in high school, and Nemhauser reports interesting results with elementary school children.[30] The experience of evaluating books is itself educational, in that the student becomes acquainted with the wide array of materials on the market and is impressed by the difficulty of choosing. Moreover, the student who has participated in building a library is more likely to have respect for it. According to the 1975 guidelines, while selection is "coordinated by the director of the district media program and the head of the school media program respectively," the process should involve "the media staff, curriculum consultants, teachers, students, and community representatives."[31] The primacy of the professional must not be denigrated in this relationship, for it is the librarian who is in the best position to evaluate advice.

The first obligation of the school library is to the student as student. A basic question, then, is: What does the school consider its work to be? Is it concerned mainly with passing on the heritage of the past? If so, the library will consist of relatively few titles, comprising books deemed highly significant. Numerous copies of each will be required. The recommendations of faculty will be given greater weight. If, on the other hand, each student is expected to explore problems related to his or her own particular interests, with large blocks of time for individual study, it will be necessary to provide a wide variety of titles in many forms, with only a few copies of each title. Student recommendations then become more important. Shapiro suggests that "among our youthful patrons there are many young people whose mathematical, scientific, artistic, and literary capabilities are so special that they are left without materials" in the young adult collections of public libraries.[32] It may be asked whether the same is true of school libraries. If the school should adopt the "Back to Basics" approach to education, with its emphasis on fundamental skills, including reading, that would suggest the traditional print-oriented school library as opposed to one collecting other media formats, which the Back to Basics people consider frivolous.[33]

The obvious importance of the school's curriculum as a basis for selection of materials should be noted, but as Miller observes, " 'knowing the curriculum' — often defined as knowing what is taught to whom and when — is not quite adequate for responsible collection development. If the collection is to undergird and help implement the curriculum, the media specialist must analyze teacher intent, selection of content, and strategies."[34]

Next in importance are materials for the faculty, followed closely by those which are needed in connection with extracurricular activities. Debate and theatre activities stimulate library use, as do other activities when accompanied by cooperation between sponsor and librarian.

The problem of censorship is acute in both public and private schools. Parents tend to feel that since they are paying heavily, they ought to have some say about what their own (and others') children see and hear. They may claim that the future of society is at stake. A 1977 survey by the National Council of Teachers of English found that book censorship in secondary schools was on the increase. More objections were being raised by parents, especially. "Bad" grammar and profanity were major targets, along with erotic passages.[35] Although the survey did not find ideological issues to be primary, it is apparent that as time draws the nation farther and farther away from the period when it was united by World Wars, there will be more controversy about ideas taught in the schools. No group—whether organized by race, sex, profession, or anything else — wants its members or ideas disparaged, either directly or indirectly, before the young; in fact, most people yearn for commendation. Yet if all persons, groups, and ideas were presented in an equally favorable light by library books, an overwhelming dullness would result, scarcely relieved by contempt for the falsity of the picture. "Sexism, Racism, and Other 'Isms' in Library Materials: Interpretation of the *Library Bill of Rights*" (1973) is a basic document for consultation.

Selecting for the school library, always interesting, is likely to become more challenging. It is not a responsibility to be dodged or neglected. As Vandergrift puts it: "Those who select materials for school media programs must do so with knowledge, with insight, and with judgment but also with courage, with imagination, and with style."[36]

PUBLIC LIBRARIES

The principal marks of the public library are that it is tax-supported and that its collections are available to all within the jurisdiction. Though its roots have been traced to many different places and times, this sort of library, as we know it, began in both England and America around the middle of the nineteenth century. Its primary purpose was to afford the poorer classes the moral and educational benefits of reading, but because it has had no parent institution, its mission has been less well-defined, and like an orphan who has lived in different foster homes, it has not been quite sure whom it ought to be trying to please. From the first, there have been differing opinions, about the kinds of materials that should be offered,[37] and social developments since then have made the question even more debatable. As the older generation without formal education died off and as the public school extended its scope to include more years of the life of youth, the library's educational mission became less urgent, but still much of its use comes from those in formal or informal school programs. Needs for factual information and for recreation have been given more attention.

There has grown up also a more hard-headed (more business-like? less charitable?) tone. As early as 1930, F.K.W. Drury, Librarian of the Denver Public, was comparing the institution with a business: "In many respects the selector for a library may be compared to the buyer for a department store . . . [seeking] out the sort of goods which he believes will sell."[38] By the 1970s this analogy was not uncommon.[39]

The public library is undergoing change also in basic organization. The big downtown central library is being used less, and there is some feeling that it should be split into two (maybe more) parts — one perhaps for commerce and industry, the other for the so-called cultural subjects, such as the fine arts. Branch libraries differ widely from each other, depending on the economic and ethnic qualities of the neighborhoods in which they are located. There are efforts to serve rural areas through libraries set up on a countywide basis. More and more, also, public libraries are being linked together, and with other types of libraries, in regions and states, so that an item not available in one may be obtained from another.

Because the public library is for all, the range in people served, not only potentially but in actual practice, is wider than that found in any other type of library. A few adults, for instance, want research materials of the highest level, while others need materials which, though related to their mature interests, are written on the level of the third or fourth grade.

Seeing the immensity of their possible audience, librarians are disturbed by the fact that the majority do not avail themselves of the institution's collections or services. In the last decade or two, there has been a renewed interest in doing something for the disadvantaged of society — the aged, the poor, the physically handicapped, the oppressed; those who need facts but don't know how to get them. So far the problem has been that these people, not realizing the value of information, have been difficult to draw into the library. Countless schemes, ingenious and otherwise, have been employed in an effort to attract these and other nonusers. David W. Davies, ridiculing efforts to get people into the building with fiestas, movies, judo demonstrations, and other "attractions," argues that public libraries should concern themselves with serious reading matter.[40] Pauline Wilson believes that the librarian had best recognize the fact that forty percent of the people are not going to use the library anyway, and then do a better job for those who will appreciate the effort.[41] Other cultural institutions that receive some tax support fail to attract anything like a majority of the population, so why should librarians worry themselves sick? Public libraries were founded, it is urged, not by the clamor of vast majorities but by the leadership of a comparatively few effective citizens.

There is, then, some considerable feeling that public libraries should not fail the classes and groups whom they have served so capably thus far, while reaching out gradually to other segments of the population. Needless to say, the policy of the library on these matters will have a significant effect on its plans for collection development.

As suggested before, the use of the public library by students, especially secondary and college, is extensive in most communities. The high school library cannot afford to supply materials on the far-ranging interests of all its students, and the college library often does not have enough copies of works required for large classes. Moreover, older persons returning to college on a part-time basis frequently find the public library more convenient to their normal travel patterns.

In size, public library collections range from a few hundred through the nearly ten million volumes owned by the New York Public Library, but because of heavy duplication of titles both in main libraries and in branches, the number of separate titles per volume count is smaller than in university libraries. The Chicago Public Library in 1979 claimed 6,164,605 volumes, but only about a tenth as many titles: 684,412.[42] In fact, when Lowell Martin surveyed the library in 1968, he found that unless the librarians thought that there was need for three or more copies of a title, they ordered none at all.[43] The public library is also likely to stock nonprint materials, though not on the same scale as the school or junior college library.

Smaller public libraries and even some of fair size are often scenes of pleasant, leisurely association. Librarians know many of the users in a personal way and thus, while perusing information about books for possible purchase, can imagine a real person who will be glad to see a certain title on the new-book shelf. Very large libraries, for obvious reasons, do not have this quality, and sometimes the huge public libraries seem among the most impersonal of all institutions. Surveys of the community are of special importance to public libraries, whatever their size, because unlike school and academic libraries, they have no narrowly-defined purpose toward which their collections are directed. There are a number of books on the techniques of community surveying, and a number of published surveys. A special attempt is needed to get feedback from patrons — representing if possible the full range of community opinion. On the one hand, the public library has no faculty with easy access for making complaints; on the other, it is more likely to hear a great whining sound as small groups grind their axes.

The Public Library Mission Statement, replacing the standards of 1966, emphasizes the importance of gathering materials which deal effectively and fairly with the great needs of modern society.[44]

A rule of thumb is that two thirds of the materials budget be spent on adult materials, one third on those for children up to age thirteen or fourteen.[45]

The head of the library usually has the responsibility for choosing materials, though the ultimate authority rests with the board and duties are delegated to the staff. Many libraries have selection committees who consult bibliographies, publishers' catalogs, and reviews; then recommend titles. The small library may have one committee; the larger may have separate committees for children's and adults' books. If there are branches, their librarians are also involved. Participating in such deliberations can be a most fascinating aspect of public librarianship.

For the selection process then, libraries differ widely in type and size, as well as by individual institution. Nevertheless, a few central issues are faced by all kinds, and there are general principles that apply in some way to every library.

3. FUNDAMENTAL PRINCIPLES OF SELECTION

While each type of library (and indeed, each individual library) faces its own dilemmas in selecting from the tremendous amount of materials available, there are general principles which apply, at least in some measure, to practically all. Again, it is the public library which, largely because of its lack of a parent organization, finds these dilemmas most acute and these principles the most difficult to apply, so this type will be the one most in focus in this chapter.

THE PREEMINENCE OF THE USER

The first rule in selection is that libraries exist for patrons, not for librarians. Though some materials may be gathered for the use of staff, as staff, in their work, these publications are also for the ultimate benefit of the public. A Gutenberg Bible might bring over a million dollars at auction but would be worthless in a library unless at least one person were to become interested in it. Apart from human beings (and maybe bookworms, of course), library materials are of no value.

It is virtually impossible to overestimate the varieties of people who use, or might find it profitable to use, library collections. We think of the various groups who may be enriched, but the library really provides for one individual at a time, and one person may be a member of several statistical groups. Each person has distinct interests, needs, wants; different capacities for reading, learning, enjoyment. Viewed in this light the simple motto "The right book for the right reader" becomes significant. It has been predicted that librarianship will develop in the future a specialty called something like "psychobiblionics," using the discoveries of psychology as a base and stressing the deep analysis of readers' interests and needs. This knowledge, together with what is being learned presently by research on indexing and information retrieval, may serve to carry out realistically the motto just quoted. In the meantime, however, knowledge in this area is partial and inexact. My purpose in this section is merely to make a few general suggestions illustrating the point that selection is for real individual people, not merely for abstractions, and that these people present an amazing array of interests and tastes.

Does anyone doubt the differences among particular readers? Here are a few examples representing people I happen to know about: A professor has a consuming interest in automobiles of several vintages, spouting their specifications like a fountain. A teenage boy with a similar interest searched old periodicals for information about the ill-fated Edsel, pointing with a mixture of contempt and satisfaction when he saw one in the original steel. An elderly woman, a fiend on the subject of antique buttons, constantly seeks new details about their design and manufacture, and lectures on her hobby with authority. A young man becomes an expert on the history of chess; an older one knows what Gabby Hartnett and Stan Hack batted in 1935. An attorney devotes thousands of hours to the study of the Battle of Franklin in the last days of the Civil War. Other patrons are concerned at a very deep level about energy and the environment. Who is to say that any of these interests are somehow not legitimate, or that they impose no obligation on libraries?

How do we learn about a person's interests as they relate to library materials? The process involves some guesses, because people can't be interested in anything until it comes to their attention. Topics, ideas, and individual books which are publicized by television, radio, periodicals, and newspapers attract wide interest. The concerns range over local, national, and international situations.

In measuring interest, durability is to be considered along with intensity. Immediately after the Jonestown deaths in 1978, readers wanted books and periodicals about cults and related topics. This brings up the key problem with materials dealing with "current events." Such works are issued in profusion. Some of them elucidate crucially important problems and satisfy significant inquiries, but in a year or two many may have historical value only. Left over, they do about as much for library shelves as last year's political posters do for telephone poles. Paradoxically, intensity of interest sometimes means short-term interest. A book or film likely to be useful for a long period ordinarily is a better bet for purchase than one interesting for the immediate future only.

Concerns of people may be measured also by the amount of opposition to certain books or ideas. If there is pressure to remove a book from the library, does not this indicate an unusually strong interest? If so, there is a case for ordering more copies, or at least for obtaining in the future books espousing similar ideas. Think of all the books published in any given year, and of the small fraction which are noticed in any way by the general public. Those which stir up excitement are truly exceptional.

There is something (though not much) to be said for getting a book just because patrons will expect to see it on the shelf. I have heard it opined that a library would have to buy the *Encyclopaedia Britannica* and Bartlett's *Familiar Quotations* even if no great use were predicted for them, because every library is supposed to have them on view. While such a principle of selection could result in a horrendous collection if followed regularly, its public relations value recommends its use now and then.

There is no substitute for knowing the people who use the library, and to do the best job, the librarian really ought to be acquainted with them personally — should recognize those materials which mesh with their interests as individuals. This being virtually impossible, at least on any large scale, familiarity with the community may be established on a secondhand basis through surveys, as mentioned in the previous chapter. With some libraries it is feasible to ask each user at the circulation desk whether there are any suggestions for new purchases. People appreciate the personal attention, even if they have no immediate responses. Such a simple procedure helps the library satisfy the needs of its present users, but how can it attract new users? In an unfortunate kind of cycle, the person who does not use the library is the one least likely to come in and explain why. Even surveys uncover such cases in only an abstract way. Migrant laborers, for instance, do not often say to the local librarian that they would like such-and-such titles. People who make a trip in to the library and don't find what they need are likely to conclude that this is an institution irrelevant to their purposes, and that it might as well be avoided. There is a danger that those groups that do use the library will get more and more of what they want on the shelves, to the neglect of the needs of other, potential users. As leaders of society, library users may pass on the benefits of information to other people, but democracy depends on a *large* segment of citizens becoming informed themselves.

Some of the differences among people may have to do with the geographical locations in which they live — in the city, the suburbs, or the country; the Southwest or the Northeast. Other differences may be due to occupation or social class. Ennis and Fryden, studying the circulation patterns of a branch of the Chicago Public Library during a steel strike, found that workers with this sudden abundance of leisure time seemed to favor mysteries and westerns, perennial escape reading;[1] businessmen, according to a survey by *Fortune* magazine some years ago, wanted something "hotter than a mustard plaster" and preferred Mickey Spillane. But it is difficult to generalize about reading habits, since the people who read the most are the ones most likely to defy categorization.

Differences in the reading abilities of users are illustrated clearly by the wide range that can exist among students in one grade in school — abilities varying by as much as ten grades. The increasing number of older people with their distinctive interests suggests that libraries should provide more materials suitable in subject and format to these individuals. Hear a sixty-year-old quadriplegic, bound to a wheelchair: "This rare, precious jewel that I have been blessed with — my mind — I want to keep highly polished and glowing. . . . What can I say but that books are my very life and I can't wait for the day to begin to continue the magic that is reading."[2]

What other minority groups are there in the community served by the public or other type of library? Are there those who would profit from books in their native languages? Perhaps there are racial and ethnic groups that need materials about their own histories, cultures, and problems. Their leaders should be consulted, because mistakes can be made if a librarian does not know a group well.[3] What about the six million Americans who are mentally retarded?[4] Other small sections of the population would read books about particular vocations, social issues, religions, or hobbies. Searching out and serving these members of the community presents a tremendous challenge to the modern librarian. Would that time allowed more of this work to be done.

Needs versus Wants

The sociologist Herbert Gans, in a paper about the urban public library, has noted two conceptions: "The *supplier-oriented,* arguing that the library should achieve the educational and cultural goals of the librarian; and the *user-oriented,* arguing that the library should cater to the needs and demands of its users."[5] Our first fundamental principle (that libraries exist to serve patrons, not librarians) makes the supplier orientation undesirable, but we still have to deal with the two factors of need and demand. While the reader is in focus during process of selection, this does not necessarily mean that the librarian always gives priority to those materials for which there is a huge public clamor. Indeed it sometimes seems that great noise, as infrequent as it is, signals a relatively poor book, which meets few real needs. People can confuse needs and wants. I may *wish* for a book which says that installing a wood-burning stove is a simple thing, well within my limited capabilities; I may *need* one which points out the difficulties and dangers of my project. May it be said also that while I may want a light novel, what I really need may be the emotional breadth of *War and Peace?*

Almost all writers on the subject of needs and wants in library service are willing to make some compromises. Even Drury qualified his department-store approach by adding: "It is the aim of the selector to give the public, not everything it wants, but the best of what it will read or use to advantage,"[6] and again, speaking of periodicals: "The standard should be kept as high as the readers will accept, with the future reference value in mind."[7]

The whole issue is much the same as the traditional one of demand versus value. (People usually want what they demand; also they demand the books they want, provided they know of the existence of such works.) For decades librarians have debated about whether to buy the books that are sure to be requested and used or those that are of true importance and quality, even though requested by only a few. We say that one librarian emphasizes the demand theory; another, the value theory. Each of these librarians is concerned about users and materials, but selection by demand (wants) in its extreme form may overlook vital differences among materials, and extreme emphasis on value (needs) may treat materials as ends in themselves. Both librarians may choose works for future as well as for present use, but the proponent of the value theory tends to emphasize the former; of the demand theory, the latter. Fortunately, a compromise between the two extremes can often be worked out. Lionel McColvin, the great English librarian, was perhaps too pessimistic when he said that for "intellectual and aesthetic" interests, "the volume of demand will often be in inverse ratio to its value" (he did add that in the practical category this rule did not hold).[8]

The needs/wants way of thinking about selection is not peculiar to public libraries, but it is more appropriate to them than to academic, special, or school libraries. In college libraries, at least in those that rely to any great extent on consultation with faculty for the selection of books, it may be assumed that the works gathered and then urged upon students are the "best" (or at least of fair quality), and since these are the very ones students ask for (because if nothing else they are on course reading lists and are necessary for getting by), wants and needs tend to come together more closely. One should never be too sure about this apparent harmony, however. What would students read, given absolutely free choice?

University and other research libraries may assemble special collections that are of little intrinsic value, just to have examples of what some people have written and others may have read. And there is D. J. Urquhart's theory of the "manurial value of pure rubbish." As Maurice Line has explained it, "The really bad article or paper stimulates the production of the adrenalin in the reader or hearer, and hence provokes him to ideas and arguments that would otherwise never have entered his head."[9] To complicate the issue, there are books like Stanley's *How I Found Livingstone,* which Florence Nightingale characterized as "the very worst book on the very best subject."[10]

For high school libraries, the value/demand conflict was pointed up a few years ago by the National Study of High School English Programs. Surveying 158 libraries in forty-five states, the investigators found no clear correlation between magazines ordered by school librarians and the titles actually read by students. *Playboy,* for instance, ranked fifteenth in student popularity but was found in none of the libraries studied at the time. *Saturday Review* was taken by ninety-nine percent of the libraries but ranked twenty-seventh in student preference. The same general conclusions held for book titles.[11] McColvin may not have been so far off.

We must return to the public library, though, for it is here that the conflict between want and need is most difficult to resolve. There are incisive points to be made on either side of the issue, and numerous statements can be found advocating strongly the position that libraries, especially public ones, should appeal to users' wants and demands.

The Case for Emphasizing User Wants

Go back as far as 1894. The librarian of the St. Louis Public Library states his position in simple terms: "In the first place, we try to provide the books people want — not those we think they ought to read."[12] The great Charles Cutter wrote in 1901: "The poor in intellect, the poor in taste, the poor in association are always with us. The strong in intellect, the daring in thought, the flexible in spirit, the exquisite in taste are only sometimes with us. We must manage somehow to provide for them both." [13]

Other proponents of the demand theory ask: Who are librarians, to impose their tastes about what is best on the citizens who support the libraries and pay their salaries? Are librarians omniscient, that they may dictate what the people are to read? Do you want to be labeled an "elitist?" People should be provided with materials they will use, even if those things are loathed by highbrows. Even if the library's primary obligation were to educate the public, does that preclude gathering materials of several ranges of quality? In this connection, note a statement by the great Argentine librarian, author, and professor, Jorge Luis Borges:

> I tell my students that if you begin a book, if at the end of fifteen or twenty pages you feel that the book is a task for you, then lay that book and lay that author aside for a time because it won't do you any good . . . If you don't like De Quincey then let him alone, my task is not to impose my likes or dislikes on you. . . . If you find your way to a few authors or a few authors find their way to you, then that's as it should be. [14]

The case continues: The public foots the bill; it should be able to find the reading matter and other media formats which it wants, educational or not. What sense does it make to buy "quality" books if so few care for them? In the Baltimore County Library System, which is modeled on the popular bookstore, one librarian says simply: "The quality of the item is unimportant relative to its publicity and the number of people who ask for it." [15]

A further rhetorical question: What is all this opposition to "series" books for young people? Haven't we all read and enjoyed them? Such books amuse, they build the reading habit, and may even have a favorable influence on thought and behavior. Note the personal experience of a professor of physical science in a major university: "My interest in science was first stirred by reading the adventures of an extraordinary young man, who combined the ingenuity of an Edison with the moral integrity of a Plato and the get-up-and-go of a Horatio Alger hero. His name was Tom Swift."[16]*

This line of reasoning, which emphasizes demand in its theory of selection, gives weight also to observations by such investigators as G. Robert Carlsen, Professor of English and Education, University of Iowa.[17] After extensive studies, Carlsen has described how an individual may progress from sentimental romances, cheap adventure stories, and lurid shockers through popular contemporary novels to works commonly acknowledged as great. It seems to follow then that in almost any situation, low-quality reading materials can serve a useful purpose and thus do have a certain value. To deny readers such pleasures is like expecting a human being to be born as a 190-pound adult, rather than as an infant who will grow up slowly. And the same arguments may be applied to films and recordings.

The Case for Emphasizing User Needs

From the beginning of the public library movement, there have been claims that the individual and society are made better by reading. In 1849 for instance, the British House of Commons had a Select Committee on Public Libraries which held hearings and elicited testimony from a number of witnesses, one of whom was asked: "Would you say that the habits of the people had improved . . . particularly with respect to temperance?" The reply, of course, was "Yes," and the witness went on to say: ". . . now the bull-baiting has gone altogether, and although the dog-fighting does exist, it is only amongst the more ignorant of the people."[18] Though a part of the theory was that any kind of reading would help keep people out of mischief, there was feeling also that use of libraries should have a positive effect on behavior. If anyone presumes to think that such hope has gone forever, that person should note a statement in *American Libraries*

*According to the Weekly Newsmagazine, the leader of UCLA's student "revolt" in 1968 also had been excited in his early years by reading about Tom Swift ("U.C.L.A. Bruin With a Bite," Time 91 [7 June 1968]: 79).

for January 1977: "When a viewer draws a unique, highly personal revelation from a film, the difficulties for the programmer melt away; success is not measured in circulation figures, but in lives altered by a confrontation with inner reality."[19]

That libraries should meet peoples' needs by supplying materials of high quality has been a judgment often declared. In an article about modern poetry, Bill Katz contended, "I firmly believe that those who build a collection only on the basis of demand are dead wrong, and a trifle muddled in their approach to what libraries are all about."[20] Ralph A. Ulveling, for many years Director of the Detroit Public Library, wrote in 1959, "There are cheap, worthless novels that have no place in a library even if they achieve 'best seller' standing. Likewise there are books of ideas that belong in a comprehensive book collection even though most people consider the ideas impractical or unsound."[21]

Dean Jesse Shera has brought his colorful style to the question: "The public library cannot, and should not, try to pander to every reading taste, or lack of taste, for if it does, it will be like the fabled chameleon, which turned red when put on a red cloth, green when on a green cloth, but died of vexation when placed on a Scotch plaid."[22] In the same volume, political scientist Edward C. Banfield declares, "The public library should leave the light reader to the rental library, the drugstore, and the supermarket."[23] At the risk of over-balancing this side of the controversy, one other opinion will be quoted here, that of the Italian librarian Rinaldo Lunati: "Just as it is not possible to consider that one has too much of what is good and is selected from the best, in the same way one cannot have too little of books that are bad, which are in fact those from which no usefulness or benefit can be expected."[24]

There is loyalty also to the traditional view that the library has a positive obligation as an institution for education. The Public Library Association, in a 1967 official statement, termed this kind of library an "open door to 'the wisdom and experience of mankind.' "[25] The librarian is seen as a force for constructively influencing human thought and behavior, not as a politician with ear flat on the ground, seeking cheap popularity and desperately trying to stay in office.

Others have expressed the value theory by insisting that the library ought to be improving the reading tastes of its patrons, and presenting them with information which they may not otherwise choose to search out; that there is no reason for it to exist in competition with the smoke shops and airport counters which stock the cheapest of paperbacks. Who can justify spending taxpayers' money for trash? Or even worse? Look, it is urged, at the low level of reading done by most people (that is, by those who read at all). Note some of the titles which have made the all-time United States best-seller list: [26]

> *In His Steps,* by Charles M. Sheldon, 1897
> *How to Win Friends and Influence People,* by Dale Carnegie, 1937
> *I, the Jury,* by Mickey Spillane, 1947
> *Peyton Place,* by Grace Metalious, 1956
> *The Carpetbaggers,* by Harold Robbins, 1961
> *Love Story,* by Erich Segal, 1970

Though the best-seller lists do include significant works also, the unmotivated reading tastes of the American people are not inclined very steeply toward the great and the noble. The exiled Spanish historian, Salvador de Madariaga, was cynical about "countries proud of their level of literacy. Books and newspapers are very largely goods belonging to the stimulant or stupefying group, such as alcohol, tobacco, or even opium and cocaine." [27] Surely, the contention goes, libraries should aim higher than this. Eric Moon, while editor of *Library Journal,* once examined informally the collections of a group of public libraries, finding that the least important books of some authors were plentiful, whereas their landmark works sometimes were absent entirely. He therefore urged that many libraries "buy less of the flotsam which is washed up each week or month by promotion-activated demand" and obtain more substantial works. Even if a library selects what readers want, it should consider their long-term interests, not just the immediate. [28]

A good, if rather extreme, description of the value theory in practice was given some years ago by Jerome Cushman, then librarian of the Salina, Kansas Public Library. Referring to the English translations of the nineteenth-century Danish philosopher Søren Kierkegaard, Cushman checked on the circulation of this author's titles several months after they had been acquired and found that of nine volumes, three had been checked out once each. The other six had not circulated. "Pretty damning evidence of wasting the public's money; or is it? If Mr. Kierkegaard, speaking from the nineteenth century, has set some of the best minds of today on fire, why should not the library give him a similar chance in Salina?"[29]

Some Conclusions

Can the conflict be resolved? Undeniably both of these viewpoints, and their variations, make a good deal of sense, and the gap between them cannot be bridged easily. Perhaps we may agree on some assumptions which, even if they do not reconcile the differences, will provide a base from which the selector may work.

It is fundamental that, in a free society, the public library exists to render a service to the people. It takes account, then, of what the citizens themselves want. The people judge. In a closed or totalitarian society libraries may still avow that their major purpose is doing good for the people, but this assertion generally means meeting "needs" in a way beneficial to the leaders. Those in authority decide what is good for the population they rule, as a means of establishing or increasing official power. One of the prime ways of relieving the people of their freedom is to do for them what government "knows" to be best. The rulers judge, ultimately for their own benefit.

Totalitarian societies, then, are well equipped to change people's thinking and culture. If librarians select largely according to what the public wants, will not the people merely remain at their present level and fail to go beyond the limits of their present experience? The reply of the democratic faith is a resounding

"No." The people themselves should be given the opportunity to improve their knowledge and tastes voluntarily. Changes for the better need not be imposed from above. Demand for library material is to be assessed in terms of what the people will prefer if presented with quality works along with the commonplace.

Not all wants for particular titles are immediate and expressed. A person may have an almost uncontrollable desire for a Rolls-Royce after having seen one parked at the curb, or even because of a four-color advertisement, but demands for quality in the library develop more subtly. One who has never read Shakespeare will hardly start a riot to obtain a copy of *Othello*. The work has to be sampled. Appreciation comes slowly. The greatest writers, composers, and artists of the past were not admired generally until the public had a good chance to become acquainted with their work. While it is obvious that people are not tearing down the doors to consume the "best" reading matter, they are not blatantly rejecting it either. Many can and do improve their tastes; they seek some guidance as to what is good.

Charles Frankel, a professor at Columbia University and president of the National Humanities Center, spoke informally of his own father, who "had an eighth-grade education and read a lot in libraries. He believed those books were selected; that it was much better to go to a public library to find a history of the Revolutionary War than going to the corner drugstore which was selling books. There was some librarian who . . . put his or her mind to the task of picking out a group of books that had some validity and some interest."[30]

The public library then is omitting a very useful function if it fails to make available the best for the small number who will appreciate it. Here, in fact, the library has an advantageous flexibility as compared with other public services. The water system can't very well offer plain water to the majority of homes and send pink champagne to a few others, through the same pipes. The library (primarily because of certain characteristics of the publishing industry and of the book trade, which will be discussed later) can serve both the many and the few. The fact that the majority may at the moment prefer the average or the inferior does not mean that minorities have to be denied. The free society and its libraries do not have to stagnate at the lowest common denominator. Quite the contrary; it is the free society, rather than the closed, that offers the stronger possibility of change for the better. Public libraries are one of the prime instruments for facilitating (not forcing) this change. The library, then, becomes a place of adventure — a place that is interesting to explore for the sake of making discoveries, just because it provides new and unfamiliar kinds of materials, of the sort not recognized as valuable until they are seen.

This analysis may seem incomplete or unrealistic to the librarian of the small or medium-sized public library who has become disillusioned by the clamor for junk and the slow pace of improvement in people's reading tastes. Patrons are panting for *Sweet Savage Love,* whereas the beautiful expensive art book, even though of permanent value, will be noticed by only a few and appreciated by even fewer. Such problems are real, but it may be asked whether, in the long run, the library will not receive stronger support if it provides recognizably worthwhile materials. A good deal of the library's backing comes from people who don't use it themselves but who, paradoxically, feel that it ought to have a good influence on others.

Is there not something to be said also for the librarian who, as a professional, "is assumed to know better what is good for the client than the client himself"?[31] In our society, we hesitate to oppose the voice of the expert to that of the people, but the very success of democracy depends on properly appreciating and evaluating experts. Hear Professor Frankel again: "Democracy is being sold down the river if it's interpreted to mean that people with no training have exactly the same amount of ability in these matters as people with training. . . . If I can't tell a good book from a bad one, at least most of the time, there's an awful lot of public money that's been wasted on me."[32]

The librarian does not stand alone in facing this dilemma. Indeed it must be dealt with in one way or another by most professionals and by a good many other people as well. The teacher in school, college, or university constantly faces the question. The author may sacrifice some element of literary quality in order to increase sales. The newspaper editor may stir up violent feelings (and increase circulation) where a more sober, factual approach would be better for the community. And what of television— should the publicly-supported network offer the same selection as commercial stations, or should it offer the opportunity for viewing something more thought-provoking or of better quality? If not the latter, why does the public network exist? It would not be unfair to say that compromises occur in all these activities. The librarian may as well become resigned to living with some tension on this matter of user wants versus user needs (as well as on many others). At times there is a tendency toward the value factor; at others the immediate wants and demands of the majority seem overwhelming. The fact that the librarian feels an inner conflict over the problem does not mean that he or she lacks integrity. Perhaps it means the opposite.

HOLDINGS OF OTHER LIBRARIES

Decisions about buying books, singly or in groups, are influenced at times by facts about other collections in the community. It makes sense to reject an expensive item of predicted little use if it is easy to obtain from a neighboring library.

Recent years have seen the establishment of many systems and networks of libraries. Such plans have been stimulated by federal and state legislation, by state library agencies, and by groups of librarians who have seen the need for cooperation. The members may be publicly-supported libraries in a state, private college libraries in a geographical region, or some other combination. Libraries of all different types, such as school, public, academic, and special, are linked in many state plans, with the hope of providing better service for all. In systems or networks, the participating libraries may contact one another by teletype or by wide-area telephone service (WATS lines) so that requests for books in one library can be communicated quickly to other libraries in the system, and the desired books dispatched. A truck may be used to make regular trips around a circuit. The libraries may offer reciprocal borrowing privileges so that patrons living in one town can take books from the library in the next town, or students of one college use the library of another, without paying a fee. In many systems a headquarters library with a larger collection and more specialized staff answers the more difficult reference questions and loans materials as requested. The National Council on Library and Information Science has proposed an elaborate plan for a wider sharing of resources. One purpose of the Ohio College Library Center and other online computerized data bases of holdings and bibliographic information is to make it possible for each participating library to locate materials in other member-libraries. If one library debates the purchase of a large or expensive set, it may base its decision in part on the estimated cost of obtaining the title from another collection at the time the work is actually needed.

Clearly, the organization of systems and networks in whatever combination means that the local library is relieved of some of the pressures for supplying particular materials, but the cost of interlibrary transactions and (especially) their inconvenience to the patron also are notable factors in the equation. Needless to say, the local library collection is still the most important one. If you go into a store to buy a pair of shoes and are told, "We don't have your size, but we'll be glad to order them for you," your disappointment is hardly assuaged by the clerk's eager smile.

LACUNAE

Each decision to add or to reject a title must take into account also the present state of the collection. Only rarely is a librarian appointed to start building from scratch. (Such a situation is most interesting and challenging, but disconcerting in that there is no predecessor to take the blame for mistakes). With on-going libraries, it is wise to check for gaps. Librarians apparently have not been greatly concerned when a reader leaves the building without the material being sought, but really, an event of this sort is a very serious thing. It is more important to record such a disappointment than it is to chalk up another item in circulation. Fortunately we are getting good studies of why people do not find copies of the titles they want on the shelf. (See, for instance, articles entitled "Causes and Dynamics of User Frustration in an Academic Library"[33] and "User and Library Failures in an Undergraduate Library."[34]) At Cambridge University in England, bundles of pink slips were distributed in the stacks and readers were asked to insert one of the slips in the spot where they failed to find a book being sought.[35] With the use of newer methods of data processing and information handling, it may be more feasible for libraries to keep track of such unsatisfactory occurrences and then rectify them for future users by filling the gaps which have been indicated.

In this same connection, sometimes it is claimed that a library collection should be "balanced." Of course, there is no such thing in the absolute, for if perfect balance ever were achieved, that delicate state would be destroyed with the addition of more books or new readers. The real goal is to build an optimum collection for a given community of users or ought-to-be users. In such a library, it would be the part of common sense to have a few books that appeal to each interest, rather than to fatten up some areas too fast. If, among users, there happen to be about as many dog-lovers as cat-fanciers, and if a number of books about each kind of animal are available, then it would seem good for the library to obtain the best on each subject, rather than forty dog books and one cat book. (This notion need not imply that every time the library orders a cat book it has to get also one of the other kind just to prevent growls of dissatisfaction.)

In order to be fair and to insure the presentation of as much truth as possible, there should be some materials on all (or just about all) sides of controversial issues. An old dictum has it that the librarian should, *qua* librarian, have no politics, no religion, and no morals. Some would add: no level of intelligence. A more positive formulation would be: The librarian should have a humane sympathy for people of many political, religious, and ethical views, as well as for those with different degrees of intelligence. All responsible opinion should be represented, even if in condensed form, but there is no reason to give absolutely equal time to flat-earth advocates in order to balance those of the spherical and pear-shaped persuasions. One or two works on the former position should suffice in the average library.

There is much to be said for strengthening a special, though perhaps little-used, collection housed in its own room. The library, regardless of its type or size, then gains real distinction. It is able to help some few people who cannot be served adequately by other libraries. Even a small public library may collect virtually all of some type of material on a given small topic, such as local history, regardless of quality. The library of a private college may become a repository of materials on the group which established that institution. Some vague belief in "balance," then, should not be allowed to interfere with building special collections of value, use, and interest.

GUARANTEEING FREEDOM TO READ

Related to the demand/value, want/need dilemma is the dichotomy of censorship and intellectual freedom. While this issue has arisen principally with respect to books and periodicals, there have been recent instances involving films and similar formats. Actually the handling of these matters is better thought of as the responsibility of library administration, but since rejection is the counterpoint to selection, the question has some relevance here.

In its worst form, library censorship means the withdrawal of an item (after it has been selected advisedly) because someone (or some group) objects to it. But the charge has been made that librarians themselves practice some degree of censorship simply by neglecting to obtain materials that they fear may excite opposition.

If a book (or film, or recording) is not predicted to be in any demand, then it ought not be selected. Similarly, a book estimated to have little or no value for the collection is also to be dismissed. In neither case has there been censorship. Librarianship is *not* censorship, whatever some people say.[36] If, however, a moderately-priced book is of some use to a group or of great use to even one person, then it should not be rejected merely because the majority may be opposed to it. Such action would violate the fair rights of the community. What is more likely to happen, though, is this: A book *not* objectionable to the majority is turned down because of a minority, usually a noisy one. Such an incident is clearly in violation of the majority's right to read. No one is (or should be) forced to read a book or view a film that is offensive, but no one has the right to forbid another to read it. The person who dislikes the material, or who thinks that it would damage him or her in some way, is free to avoid it.

In this connection there is a problem also in distinguishing between true and artificial demands. For decades there have been groups, usually minorities, who have tried to get their members to insist that librarians provide materials about and favorable to their particular organization. Some of these contending groups have been religious, others political, and still others ethnic. The good librarian examines carefully the expressions of such demand. If there is more than coincidental similarity among letters asking for certain materials, it may well be concluded that the messages have been artificially stimulated, that they may not reflect the real wants or needs of the individuals who signed them.

Assessments of value enter in also, and here the matter becomes more difficult. To say that a book is so false or so poorly written as to be worthless is not to say that people should be protected from it. The issue is complicated by the fact that a book may be judged to be lacking in value for the very same reason that people find it objectionable. A groundless, irrational attack on one group in the population would be a case in point. Another would be a book written mainly to provide a channel for obscenity. In considering a book of both minimal value and great potentiality for trouble, the librarian may go through some uneasiness. Careful introspection is required to determine whether a negative decision will violate some one's right to freedom of information. Analogies on this subject are very tricky, but perhaps it is not irrelevant to observe again that, for some purposes, a heap of well-rotted manure is more valuable than a pile of gold coins.

In a classic, frequently-reprinted essay on this topic, "Not Censorship but Selection," Lester Asheim traces the often thin line between the two. A short, incisive book on this relationship is LeRoy C. Merritt's *Book Selection and Intellectual Freedom* (New York: Wilson, 1970, 100 pp.). Every librarian should be familiar with the *Freedom to Read* statement (adopted in 1953, revised by the American Library Association Council in 1972, and being revised again) and with the *Library Bill of Rights,* adopted in 1948, amended in 1961, 1967, and 1980 by the ALA Council. Several interpretative statements have been produced in connection with this document, the ones of most significance for selection being "Free Access to Libraries for Minors" (1972), "How Librarians Can Resist Censorship" (adopted 1962, revised 1972), "Statement on Labeling" (adopted 1951, amended 1971), and "Sexism, Racism, and Other 'Isms' in Library Materials" (1973; being revised). *The School Library Bill of Rights* was adopted by the American Association of School Librarians Board of Directors in 1969. Ralph E. McCoy has compiled an excellent list of works on the topic: *Freedom of the Press: An Annotated Bibliography* (Carbondale, IL: Southern Illinois University Press, 1968, unpaged) and its ten-year supplement, 1967-1977, *Bibliocyclopedia* (1979, 559 p.). The *Newsletter on Intellectual Freedom,* issued six times a year by the American Library Association, is instructive for its revelations about human nature and as a practical map of trouble spots.

OVERALL CONSIDERATIONS

These principles apply to the practice of selection for libraries in general. The larger goal must always be in the selector's mind as judgments are made from day to day, for the main task is to develop a collection rather than merely decide whether an individual work is a good one. This task is not accomplished smoothly or easily. It is a little like redesigning and enlarging a building that is already being lived in, under next-to-impossible conditions. The analogy goes something like this: The builder (librarian) works according to a plan (philosophy of selection) that is subject to continual refinement; moreover, the specific blueprints will be altered as the needs of the occupants (library patrons) change and as they move in or out of the building. The builder is never sure what materials are going to become available on the market, or what new ones will be invented, and must make a careful judgment on the suitability of each one (though fortunately a few substandard bricks will not cause the structure to topple). Entire walls may be knocked out and rebuilt differently; new stories or extensions may be added to the original structure. Other buildings in the vicinity must be considered, as well as the changing character of the neighborhood. The builder does not know how large the structure may become, but does know that it will never be finished.

WRITTEN POLICY FOR SELECTION

Every library ought to have a carefully-thought-out selection policy — a blueprint. In a small library it may be possible for the policy to be carried in the selectors' heads, with adjustments being made quickly as conditions change. Such an unwritten policy may suffice in a school, special, or academic library where the collection is shaped and modified by the needs of the parent institution. Most libraries, however, and especially public ones, can be developed more efficiently and with greater satisfaction if the policy is spelled out explicitly.

The selection policy (an acquisitions policy is similar) ought to explain the dimensions and limits of the collection being developed, answering such questions as these:

Who has the authority for making decisions about the materials?
What forms of materials are to be obtained? (Films? Recordings? Printed materials only?)
What subject fields are to be emphasized? Which ones are to be covered only in a general sense?

What ages of readers are to be provided for?

What levels of materials are to be considered? (Scholarly and specialized? "Popular"?)

In what languages will the library collect?

The predominant theme of a selection policy should be a positive emphasis on patrons' needs and rights. It need not have a defensive tone, but at times may be used legitimately as a buffer against unjust complaints by disappointed people. If someone has an objection to a book that has been added, or blames the library for refusal to buy something, the librarian can cite the stipulations of official policy. The plaintiff then has the right to attempt to have the policy changed, but the basis of the argument has been shifted from the particular title to a more general question of principle.

Good samples of library selection policies have been collected by Calvin J. Boyer and Nancy L. Eaton in *Book Selection Policies in American Libraries; an Anthology of Policies from College, Public, and School Libraries* (Austin, TX: Armadillo Press, 1971, 222 p.) and by Elizabeth Futas in *Library Acquisition Policies and Procedures* (Phoenix, AZ: Oryx Press, 1977, 406 p.). A committee of the American Library Association Resources and Technical Services Division has prepared "Guidelines for the Formulation of Collection Development Policies," in *Guidelines for Collection Development,* edited by David L. Perkins (Chicago: ALA, 1979), p. 1–8.

4. OBJECTIVE EVIDENCE ON USE OF MATERIALS

One way to estimate what library patrons will need, and especially what they will want, is to determine what kinds of materials they have used in the past. This approach is basically scientific, whereas that discussed in Chapter 3 is more humanistic. Both methods are useful, and in our present state of knowledge about selection, we cannot afford to neglect either. With the tremendous growth in the number of items available for purchase, the objective method is gaining ground, especially in large institutions. Many of these studies are classed under BIBLIOMETRICS — quantitative measurements applied to library materials or to bibliographic references.

STUDIES OF COLLECTION USE

Some libraries keep good records and then analyze them to determine the use of materials by subject, by date of publication, by language, as well as other facts. Detailed circulation statistics yield good-quality information which may be then applied to future selection decisions. Especially significant are facts about the characteristics of the items that patrons ask to be borrowed from other libraries. A record of such transactions will suggest some of the kinds of materials, even if not specific titles, which should be obtained.

There is a growing, but as yet largely unsystematized, body of published research which can also add to the selector's background of information. When reports of investigations made in local libraries are published, they become useful in two ways: they can be taken as models by other libraries, and they offer conclusions which, after proper allowances for local differences (no two libraries are exactly alike), can be used when making decisions.

As an example of the collection-use study in real life: the Engineering-Transportation Library of the University of Michigan found it necessary to cut costs and considered reducing the number of subscriptions to periodicals and other serial publications. Concrete data were gathered in order to help with these decisions. The cost to the library for each serial title was recorded, along with the requests made by users for each title and the time required to fill each request. From these data, certain generalizations were derived: (1) an item already owned by the library could be delivered to the requestor in about five minutes; (2) filling a request for an item *not* held in the university required, on the average, five days or 7,200 minutes; (3) there were 87 titles that received only one use each, and these titles together cost $1,902 per year. The 87 requests had been filled in 435 minutes (five minutes each), while the waiting time would have been 626,400 minutes (7,200 minutes each) or 10,440 hours if the materials had not been available in the library system.

After such conclusions are drawn, there is still the need for a decision. Assuming that next year will be similar to this, is it desirable to increase total delivery time by 626,000 minutes in order to save $1,902? How seriously are patrons inconvenienced by delays of this length? They do not of course spend the time waiting around — they leave and return later; but they like it much better if periodicals are available for immediate use. In the Michigan study, other possible courses of action were presented by the author, based on further conclusions suggested by data.[1]

Some investigators have produced results that appear to be applicable to libraries generally, although especially to those of the same type. At a small university, McGrath and Durand examined the courses offered by the various departments of instruction and assigned to each course a class number, according to the Library of Congress classification system for books.[2] Later, McGrath tabulated the use of materials in both this and another library, asking: Are students and faculty more likely to charge out (or to consult in the library) those materials whose subjects correspond to the LC classifications assigned to their courses? The answer was: Yes, to some extent. It was concluded that since this method allows reasonably accurate predictions about the subject fields in which people will seek materials, bibliographic services which give the subject class number of each book listed (for example, *American Book Publishing Record*) can be used to advantage when deciding what to order.[3]

One of the libraries at Cambridge University in England tabulated for various Library of Congress classes the number of books held and the number used, either inside or outside the building, over a short period of time. For instance, in law, the library had 270 volumes, which were used a total of 120 times, so there were 44 uses per 100 volumes. In anthropology, however, the number of uses was only 1 per 100 volumes held, and in music, only 3 per 100. For many subjects, the surveyors recorded the number of times a person failed to obtain the item looked for. In history, 33 percent of the searches ended in failure; in sociology, 56 percent.[4]

Buckland, observing use of the University of Lancaster Library in England, made explicit what had been intuitively thought about many libraries when he estimated that in only 6 cases out of 10 did the user find on the open shelf the material being sought. The "Satisfaction Level," therefore, was 60 percent.[5] Other investigations have resulted in similar conclusions. While Buckland's solution involved reducing the length of loan periods in order to get books back on the shelves faster, the problem plainly is related to the number of additional copies obtained by the library in the first place.

Other studies have been designed to find the specific reasons why readers cannot find the books they are looking for. These causes include ignorance or carelessness on the part of the user, improper shelving of books, and theft, but many of the failures can be traced to decisions made about ordering books. In one library at Case Western Reserve University, for instance, 220 of the 423 requests were not immediately satisified. Among the reasons for these 220 failures were: book never acquired by the library (52), and all copies of the title either in use or being held for someone (81).[6] Therefore, 133 of these failures had to do with selection of materials. This and related studies tend to reinforce the traditional feeling that academic libraries often do not provide enough copies of titles for which demand is great.

A well-designed study by Metz at the Library of Congress found that monographs were used more than serials (in proportion to the Library's holdings of each) and that foreign-language materials received relatively little use.[7]

CITATION STUDIES

In addition to studies of local use, there are bibliometric analyses which go beyond one library, asking what materials are being used by people in a given subject field or in a certain geographic area.

One of the most widely used bibliometric methods is the analysis of bibliographic citations. Such studies now number well into the hundreds, appearing in monograph form as well as in journals of librarianship, sociology, general science, and other disciplines. They are based on the postulate that when a writer makes a bibliographic footnote, it usually indicates that the author has examined the publication cited and has found it of help, or at least of interest. Thus deSolla Price suggested years ago that articles most frequently cited by other writers be published together as a *U. S.* (or *World*) *Journal of Really Important Papers.*[8] This assumption that frequently-cited publications are important was substantiated by Virgo[9] and is made also by many others, though serious question has been raised about it.[10]

Procedures for citation studies vary according to investigator and purpose, but in the abstract, such a study might look like this: First, a source journal or book or encyclopedia is chosen (the 1980 numbers of the *American Journal of Sociology,* for instance). Then the bibliographic references (citations) made by the writers of the articles are recorded. One citation might be: "Meyers, *Journal of Applied Behavioral Science,* 1975." When the citations (several hundred, or perhaps even thousands) have been noted, they are sorted by, say, date of publication or age (our sample item being listed as "1975" or "5–10 years old"); by language (our citation is in the "English" column); by subject (ours is in the subject category for general social science, LC class HI);

and by form (we have a periodical, as opposed to a monograph or dissertation). We may also chalk up one more citation for Meyers and one for the *Journal of Applied Behavioral Science.*

After all the tabulations have been made, we may conclude (very tentatively, of course) that writers in sociology make most of their references to sources which are very recent, generally are in the English langugage, are in serial form more than in monograph, and are classified for the most part in three major subject areas.

Tabulation of periodical titles which received citations (counting citations to issues published in last two years) may reveal a pattern like this: Journal A, 138; Journal B, 96; Journal C, 81; and Journal D, 72. Perhaps fifty other periodicals were cited, varying from 60 citations received by one title to 1 citation received by each of forty periodicals. The selector might conclude, then, that these four "top" periodicals, those whose recent issues have received the greatest number of citations, are highly important and that they should be ordered by the local library, or if already taken, should not be dropped. Relative expense also enters in, however, and if it costs $80.00 a year to acquire, service, and house periodical A, while the same costs for periodical B total $40.00, then the latter is, so far as the particular study goes, an apparent better buy.

Two Australian psychologists, concluding that citation analyses give a clear, objective picture of a journal's importance, declare that librarians should subscribe to the journals ranked high by this method rather than to those named as important by professors.[11]

The Institute for Scientific Information, which publishes *Science Citation Index, Social Sciences Citation Index,* and *Arts and Humanities Citation Index* (all based on the assumption that bibliographic references have considerable validity) issues in connection with each of these titles an annual volume of statistical data, *Journal Citation Reports.* Each volume lists, in several different rank orders, the journals which have received citations from a great number of source publications. Thus by using the *SSCI Journal Citation Reports,* one can come reasonably close to telling the serials cited most frequently by American writers in social sciences. In one table, the *JCR* begins with the titles receiving most citations and goes down to those receiving the fewest. The 1978 volume indicates that 5,578 references were made to the *Journal of Personality and Social Psychology,* while the *Harvard Law Review* was second with 4,828. Cawkell is right in his remark that "quite a lot of information can be obtained by using *JCR* for an hour or two and taking notes."[12] The reports are particularly significant for special libraries and special subject collections. Of course, a journal may rank low in *SSCI Journal Citation Reports* merely because it receives few citations from social scientists, whereas scientists may cite it frequently; its citations may be recorded in *SCI Journal Citation Reports.*

While periodical titles are the form most often ranked by citation counts, monograph titles may be evaluated in a similar way,[13] though of course the average monograph is cited less frequently than is the average journal.

Applied to collection building, there are certain limitations to the citation counting method: For one thing, many librarians already know that the high-ranked periodicals are good; they need to know whether to subscribe to those that rank low on the list, for instance, those that receive only two or three citations.[14] Here the differentiation made by the citation count is too slim to be taken seriously in most libraries. Another difficulty is that citation studies show what materials writers (usually scholars) refer to, but not much about what materials are used by undergraduates or the general public. In this connection, however, it should be pointed out that very often library users seek certain materials in the library because of footnote citations read in other publications. Since it is evident that, in the aggregate, users are more influenced by bibliographic references than by indexing and abstracting services, it follows that in many libraries, especially academic ones, citations are a reasonably good predictor of user requests.[15]

Another problem in the application of citation counts is that because any journal may be cited by publications in different fields (for instance, writers in psychology make references to articles in sociology journals and vice versa), the entire pattern can become amazingly complex. It is somewhat simplified for the librarian who is selecting for a special subject library (such as botany or geology) and needs to know which publications are being cited by writers in that field alone.

All things considered, data gathered from citation counts are worthy of consideration by selectors in many sorts of library situations, especially for college, university, and research collections.[16] When examined prudently, these studies not only suggest individual serials and monograph titles, but also help establish the overall patterns of literature used by scholars in various disciplines.[17]

Such analyses may reveal the relative ages of materials preferred by writers in certain subjects.[18] Scientists and social scientists tend to use newer works, humanists older ones. There is, however, a little evidence that in American Literature, at least, the secondary works used are recent, though the primary source materials are mostly old.[19]

Citation studies, in agreement with collection use studies, seem to indicate that in the social sciences and now even in the sciences, American writers use relatively few materials in foreign languages. This finding suggests that when considering an expensive German or French work, the selector should hesitate a moment, determining whether there are strong reasons for entering an order.

A citation study may give an indication of the forms or types of materials used in a particular library. One librarian analyzed the references made in the masters' theses written in his university's College of Engineering. One third of the citations were received by journals; two thirds by other forms of publication; yet the library was spending thirteen percent more for serials than for books. As a result of the citation study, the expenditure for subscriptions was reduced—without adverse effects, apparently, for circulation went up.[20]

As more citation studies are completed, as procedures are refined, and as the findings of the individual projects are worked into a more meaningful overall pattern, it seems likely that this method of surveying the use of materials will prove increasingly helpful.

CONCLUSION

This short survey gives only a small sample of "scientific" studies which apply to library collections. On noting these examples, the student may be disappointed at the tiny degree to which knowledge of collection development is advanced by any one investigation. Results must be interpreted cautiously. When an analysis is made in one library, application to another must take into account the differences between the two situations. Furthermore, such studies generally reveal what materials have been used, not what ones should have been used. Since they forecast the future solely on the basis of what has happened in the past, they say nothing about fresh ideas or new philosophies. We still do not know a great deal about use of materials inside the building, though research has discovered that, in a general way, this use parallels recorded circulation.[21]

Only a fool, therefore, would take the results of these studies as Holy Writ and apply them without a large measure of human judgment. Kronick is quite right in warning against the possibilities for misinterpretation and abuse.[22] He falls short, however, in assessing the difficulties found also with traditional selection methods. In the mind of the selector, there should be a great deal of information that has come from studies of use. Furthermore, research of this sort can be done in almost any library, to provide better impressions of what users want. The methods and techniques developed in larger libraries can be used also in smaller ones.

PART II

BACKGROUND TO BOOK SELECTION

Of first importance in practically all general libraries are the materials of print. The traditional concern with this medium is reflected in the origin of the word *library* itself, from the Latin *liber,* book. (Our word *book* comes from the Old English *bōc,* having to do with beechwood.) It is important therefore to know how and by whom books are produced, to explore the standards by which they may be judged, and to consider those channels that have been set up to publish evaluations of individual titles.

5. BOOK PUBLISHERS
AND PUBLISHING

It is time now, before going further into the principles of selection, to make a brief examination of the sources of supply. The group of greatest concern to most libraries are the producers of books, for these publishers are the prime sources from which libraries draw. Some of the organizations that deal in films, recordings, slides, videotapes, and other formats will be given in the chapters on particular types of material.

While books are published chiefly for individuals, schools, offices, and bookstores, some firms are quite conscious of the library market and will plan in terms of what libraries need. In this chapter, then, we shall try to get some idea of the people and organizations responsible for the publications whose great numbers have been discussed previously, and then see what significance this information has for library collections and services.

PUBLISHERS IN GENERAL

Because they differ in so many ways, there is danger of oversimplification in any short description of publishers. They vary in size, in kinds of materials issued, in sophistication, in procedures, in business acumen, in integrity, and in other ways. Is publishing primarily a business or a profession? The answer is: Both. "The true publisher," says John P. Dessauer, "moves with equal comfort in the world of mind and art and in the world of commerce."[1] Herbert S. Bailey, of the Princeton University Press, speaks of the publishing house as an institution which both reflects and influences society, "permeated with the interest and variety and excitement of the books it publishes."[2]

Observed from afar, the publisher seems to be a coordinator of the work of many others, such as the author, editor, designer, typesetter, printer, binder, warehouser, and wholesaler. The publisher combines talents, activities, and machines so that ideas in the mind of an author are "made public" and get to the book-shelves of home, office, or library. This process usually requires some capital outlay, because bills must be paid before the first copy of a book is sold.

It is important to note the difference between publisher and printer, though one firm may be both. In fact, until the early part of the nineteenth century it was common for one person or company to combine the activities of printer, publisher, and bookseller, but as machinery and methods became more compli-cated, specialization set in. Today it is rare for one firm to un-dertake all the separate activities necessary for the final product, though recently some publishers have (again) installed their own equipment for setting type.

The publisher as such, then, usually does not own the huge, expensive complex machinery necessary for efficient book pro-duction. This point is significant in that, though some publishing houses have relatively large investments, it is possible for a per-son to start in the business with only a few thousand dollars, using the same printers and binders that serve the largest firms. A Utah man reported that he set himself up as publisher of his mother's books, spent $5,000 for printing, binding, and advertis-ing; and eventually came out with a profit.[3] Do-it-yourself can be carried even further. I once knew an old fellow who wrote a book; set it up in type by hand, one letter at a time; printed it on a press in the basement of his home; sent the sheets out to be bound by professionals; then stored the copies and sold them himself, one by one. John Bartlett and Carl Sandburg are among those who have printed their own works.

Because activities like this are possible, there are thousands of tiny publishing houses in the United States, including some com-mercial firms, church presses, committees pushing causes (right-eous or wicked), and others. Only a small fraction of American publishers produce as many as a hundred new titles a year. Sev-eral hundred firms each publish as many as five new works a year. Thousands of companies or persons each send out even fewer. These facts should not lead one to underestimate the re-sources and talents of the larger and the better publishers but should indicate the possibilities available to people who are willing to take a chance.

Issuing a huge variety of new titles every year does not give a publisher any great competitive advantage. Books are not commonly bought by brand name. The purchaser of an automobile which turns out to be a lemon may swear off that brand for all time; a reader who gets a poor book may avoid that author in the future but probably won't take the pledge to reject every other book issued by that publisher. The truth is that there are significant differences in quality among publishers, but the general reading public is not ordinarily conscious of them.

While selling a few copies each of a big list of titles is not economically desirable, selling tens of thousands of any one title is profitable in the extreme. The first copy of a book is the one that costs money; each additional copy is then produced for much less. Note some of the outlays which typically accumulate for a sizable commercial publisher *before* the book's first copy leaves the bindery:

1. The manuscript must be found. Perhaps a literary scout is used; perhaps the publisher cooks up an idea and seeks an author to work it into a book. "Some of our most successful books are developed in this manner," said John Farrar, of Farrar, Straus & Giroux.[4] In any event, the discovery costs money, for the publisher must have manuscripts read and evaluated, usually by several people. The vast majority of offerings so treated will then be returned to their originators at the firm's expense — a total loss and worse. Bailey, in 1976, pegged this cost at $1000.00 per title accepted for publication.[5]

2. The manuscript must be edited in the publisher's office. The substance of the author's content is checked, the organization of the work is evaluated, the worst defects in style cleared up. These editors receive far less credit than they deserve because publishers do not wish to distract attention from the author.[6] Some editor later must give attention to thousands of details pertaining to spelling, punctuation, bibliographic notes, etc. An editor is sure to telephone the author several times, usually long distance, to argue about minutiae.

3. The typed and edited manuscript must be transformed into a book. The production department oversees the preparation of the physical product. It determines such matters as the number of pages, the sizes and styles of types, the layout of illustrations, plus the kinds of paper and binding. To achieve distinct character and a good visual effect, an expert designer is needed. Much of this work must be paid for before the material even goes to the printer. In the printing shop, the first step is again the most expensive part of the operation. Compositors must set the material, using either the old-fashioned metal type or the newer photographic processes, and pull proofs, which are read in the shop and sent first to the publisher, thence to the author. Corrected, they go back again along the same route. Once the type and illustrations for each page have been assembled, plates must be made and gotten on the press, where precise adjustments often are necessary to make sure that every part prints well and in the right place. But once this stage has been reached, additional copies whiz through at terrific speed, especially if the printing press is large and modern. About the only added expenses here are paper, ink, and press time. Upon receiving printed copies, the binder must set up jigs and prepare stamps for lettering. Again the big effort is made for the first copy.

Once all this work is done, copies pile up at a very small cost per unit. Curtis G. Benjamin uses a hypothetical example to illustrate this "economy of scale." If the fixed expenses of a certain book total $10,000.00, this figure plus the variable costs may make the first thousand copies come to $11.30 each. For 100,000 copies, however, the total fixed costs remain the same, and the variable costs per copy are reduced, so that each finished copy may cost $.77, about seven percent of the unit cost in the small quantity.[7] The percentage paid the author as a royalty may increase with volume of sales, but other expenses come down. Generally, it is said that the publisher must sell over 7,000 copies of a book during the first two years in order to break even, but for narrowly specialized books, the prices are high and the crucial point may be as low as 300 copies. After the break-even point has been reached, however, profits can roll in. The firm therefore is able to take a chance on a few doubtful titles, with the hope that one of them will be a sensation. Unfortunately (perhaps fortunately for the reading public), it is terribly difficult to predict what kind of book will have a wide appeal. There are hundreds of instances in which the skinny turkey rejected by many publishers became a golden goose for the one who finally accepted it. Cass Canfield, after a long career as head of the firm now known as Harper and Row, observed wistfully:

> Still it comes as a shock to realize, after many years in the business, how very few are the specific guidelines one has found reliable. For instance, as a result of long experience, one should have a reasonably clear idea of what is likely to appeal to the general public. Not so. Like any publisher we keep records of the sales of our books over the years, records of failures and successes. I have pored over them, trying to find the guidelines, and come up with findings . . . vague and murky.[8]

He added, though, that in publishing more specialized works, such as textbooks, experience allows an editor to make better predictions.

Traditionally, up until the first decade of the twentieth century or perhaps the Great Depression of the 1930s, publishing was considered an "occupation for gentlemen" —those not overly concerned about money.* The man of culture might issue a book with a predicted sale of a thousand or two because he liked the content and thought the work should not be allowed to die. Bennett Cerf described the staid publishers of the 1920s as "dignified, conservative members of old, old families. They wore gold watch chains across their fat bellies, and they would sit in their offices and never dream of going out for a book."[9]

Then after World War II, publishing of books became more profitable, and favorable returns on capital were envisioned. The bankers invested. Sheer monetary yields became, for the man-

*Frederic Warburg said that the title of his book *An Occupation for Gentlemen* (Boston: Houghton Mifflin, 1960) was suggested by a question asked him at a cocktail party: "Tell me . . . is publishing an occupation for gentlemen or is it a real business?" (p. 11).

agement of many firms, a stronger consideration. Cerf in another place wrote about the shock of seeing certified checks waved by the tycoons of Wall Street, whereas big business had once "dismissed publishers as pipe-smoking dreamers, lounging against fireplaces in their tweed coats." [10] This change in ownership probably has had some effect on the quality of product offered. A manager of a newer-style publishing firm, seeing the manuscript of a novel submitted by a young unknown, is less likely to contemplate soulfully the possibility that someday the author may win the Nobel prize for literature. Next year's report to the corporation stockholders is far more important. What if the author does win the prize ten years from now? That will be poor consolation to the manager who for nine years will have been out of a job. Perusing the advertisements in *Publishers Weekly,* one may be forgiven for sometimes wondering what the industry is coming to.

Another cause for worry is the number of mergers among publishing houses. Many of the old respected names are now mere appendages. In 1972, the fifty largest American publishing houses accounted for seventy-five percent of the dollar value of books produced. The remaining twenty-five percent was divided among several thousand small companies. Money received for mass market paperbacks goes to a very few separate publishers. [11] Publishers are bought out by gigantic corporations, such as those in communications and electronics. For some years, therefore, there has been the fear that the quality book for the small audience may be on the way out.

While such fears are not unfounded, it seems safe to say that we shall have good books for specialized groups as long as it is possible for the little firm to exist. It is not easy, maybe not possible, for large publishers to drive small ones out of the market. There is even some reason to think that the latter have an advantage. John Fischer, then editor-in-chief of *Harper's Magazine,* said in 1963, "Publishing is a peculiarly personal business. Whenever a firm gets so big that it can no longer give constant, intimate attention to each author — if it begins to turn out books like so many cans of beans — then it probably is on the verge of a decline. Its writers will soon drift away to smaller, nimbler, more imaginative publishers." [12] In any event, many companies do not have publicly-owned stock, and thus are in one sense freer to produce books for small audiences. Furthermore, even large corporately-owned houses publish, on occasion, potentially unprofitable or even unpopular items. McGraw-Hill issued Eldridge Cleaver's *Soul on Ice* at a time when the reception of such a book might well have been hostile. Books of poetry are published with slight hope of commercial success.

MEANING FOR LIBRARIES

The technology of book production and the economic structure of the American publishing industry have significant implications for libraries. The great number of firms (maybe as many as 10,000, even taking into account recent mergers) makes possible a wide variety of reading matter. Compare publishing with such enterprises as network television, which depends on an audience of millions "assembled" at one time. Even newspapers have only limited appeal to readerships with specialized interests, except, of course, in a geographic sense. But the publishing of trade books can, in the words of Jason Epstein, "still be carried on largely within the interstices of modern culture, where eccentric forms continue to flourish in the few remaining pools of life." [13] When Sigmund Freud's book *The Interpretation of Dreams* was first published in England, the author was relatively unknown, and five years passed before six hundred copies of the book could be sold. Imagine a television program which required five years of performances to gain a total of six hundred viewers! Yet Freud's ideas were important, and it was the technology of printing that allowed their distribution to a small number of adventurous readers. [14]

The great number of small houses is insurance that any idea, however offensive to the majority, has a good chance to be distributed. Suppose an author writes thoughtful but unpopular recommendations for society. Most firms may fear these ideas or even abhor them, yet if they have any merit at all, it is a good bet that some publisher will take a chance and give them life. There are thousands of "noncommercial presses whose materials deal with innovative and original subjects in innovative and original ways."[15] Even in the unlikely event that no established house will touch the manuscript, the author still can become a personal publisher and get the thoughts into print. Should the American communications media ever lose their freedom, the last to go under will be the book. It is quite true that publishers act as gatekeepers who can encourage or impede the flow of some kinds of information,[16] but we have thousands of these gatekeepers, and it is also possible to climb the fence.

There are other characteristics of the industry which give publishers greater freedom from the pressures of conformity and censorship. Because they do not depend on advertisers for any significant part of their revenue, they need not fear boycott from this source should they publish distasteful ideas. The fact that a house does not build patronage around a brand name means that a controversial book will not seriously damage its reputation. There are a few notable exceptions to this conclusion. Textbook publishers have been threatened because of political or social ideas unpopular in some localities, and in the 1950s, Macmillan was attacked disgracefully for publishing the ideas of Immanuel Velikovsky, considered unorthodox by practically all scientists. In the main, though, pressures against book people are far less effective than those against other communications entrepreneurs.

Publishers' products fit in especially well with the library's traditional obligation to store and distribute ideas for small groups, or even for one person. The individual, with unique interests, is regarded as important. Reading itself is an individual activity. Libraries provide materials for the few even when these few are in a lonely place at the vanguard (or the rear guard) of society. Dean Shera remarks that "whereas the mass media, the newspaper, radio, television, are declaratory, the library is interrogative. . . . In the library the patron is not told what to think or when to think it, but in his search each must discover for himself the thoughts and opinions of others."[17] Virginia Mathews and Dan Lacy note that "the library, all librarians, are almost alone among the agencies of our society in dealing with the consumer of information as an individual and with the communicators as a collection, rather than the other way around. As such, libraries can be seen as strongholds of individualism and nonconformity." [18] The total image suggests that in a library, the individual investigates; in the mass media, crowds of people are told what to think about and how to think about it.

At the same time, the fact that great numbers of copies can be printed almost as inexpensively as a few means that they can be circulated around the country — around the world, even —without excessive cost. New machines can take blank paper and other materials and produce a bound book in two minutes. Opinions and information printed in one city can be sent to people in any other, to be used when the reader desires. Libraries, obtaining a few books from each of many sources at relatively low prices, can offer different approaches to the same topic.

There is also a negative result of having so many small publishers: a lack of coordination, sometimes becoming chaotic. On some subjects there is wholesale duplication. As soon as it becomes apparent that a topic such as environmental pollution, burglary prevention, or nuclear power has caught the public interest, numerous firms rush into print with look-alike books, promoted by their loudest hucksters. The death of Elvis Presley triggered a flurry of publications. In the case of Idi Amin Dada ("Big Daddy"), death wasn't necessary; his life alone inspired a score of books. One can sympathize, for a change, with the catchy title of an article: "Wading through the Tut Glut, or What's New on the Nile." [19] Most of these vogue works soon go out of style. A cartoon shows books about Watergate being sold at 89¢ a pound. This chaos and waste may be necessary, however, to freedom itself. Better that than the alleged efficiency which comes from overregulation.

BEGINNINGS OF AMERICAN PUBLISHING

On this continent, the first book was published in Mexico, probably in the year 1539, certainly within the first century after

Gutenberg's invention. The first work in the English colonies came from the press in Cambridge, Massachusetts, in 1639, nineteen years after the landing at Plymouth Rock and three years after the founding of Harvard. The sheet was called *The Oath of a Freeman*. The next year appeared *The Whole Booke of Psalmes,* known as the "Bay Psalm Book," which had been issued several times previously in England. Books were published at a miserably slow rate in the early years. Charles Evans, in his *American Bibliography: A Chronological Dictionary of All Books, Pamphlets, and Periodical Publications Printed in the United States of America* . . . (Chicago: Privately Printed for the Author, 1903–1934, 12 vols.) — a fascinating set! — attempted to list publications by year, and though his work is admittedly incomplete, it does afford some idea of the slow growth rate. Evans was able to find only sixty-three titles for the period 1639 through 1660. (Later searchers, of course, have discovered more.) Throughout the colonial period, the rate of publication continued low. Even in 1853 there were, according to an estimate at the time, only 733 new works published in the United States, including 278 reprints of English books and 35 translations.[20] After that, and especially in the twentieth century, production was accelerated, so that we now have over 40,000 titles per year.

The histories of individual firms provide delightful reading. Knowing something of the people who have worked behind the scenes adds to both the enjoyment and the understanding of a book being read. A few of the American companies still doing business can trace roots back to the eighteenth century. The Philadelphia firm now known as J. B. Lippincott Company was established in 1792. After the turn of the century began such well-known publishers as Harper & Brothers (now Harper & Row), John Wiley & Sons, the Houghton Mifflin Company, and Little, Brown & Company. A great many firms have, of course, dissolved or at least merged with others.

A FEW REPRESENTATIVE TRADE* PUBLISHERS

The general reader holding a book may be lamentably unconscious of the firm which issued the work, but this fact does not mean that one publisher is about the same as another. The variations in size of output, in quality, in purpose, and in subject matter are evident, and even after mergers, the original firms maintain a semblance of their old characters. Library selectors soon learn their way around in such tools as *The Publishers' Trade List Annual* and come to know publishers' characteristics from first-hand examination of their products. Unfortunately, there are editors who have splendidly sensitive noses leading them to manuscripts that are needed to fill gaps in human knowledge but who are accursedly careless when it comes to such matters as proofreading. Some publishers also neglect to specify high standards from the book manufacturers who serve them — typesetters, pressmen, binders. Not always is the saving in cost passed along to the consumer. Other publishers produce works which almost invariably reflect competent authorship, careful editing, and quality format.

The catalogs and notices distributed by these firms are a prime source of information about books and in most libraries are used as selection tools. Here are some notes on a sample of better-known United States publishers:

Doubleday & Company, Inc. This firm produces over 600 new books a year on many subjects, from the popular to the scholarly, but is often identified with best-selling authors such as Herman Wouk, Norah Lofts, Daphne du Maurier, Peter Benchley, Allen Drury, Alex Haley, Victoria Holt, and Isaac Asimov. Irving Stone's biographical works are included in its catalog, as are Bennett Cerf's gags and Bruce Catton's fine histories of the Civil War. *Julie Eisenhower's Cookbook for Children* is listed along with such heavy works as Frederick Copleston's long history of philosophy, the huge *Anchor Bible* set of commentaries, and André Malraux's landmark *The Voices of Silence*.

Dodd, Mead & Company. Though well past the century mark

*Trade books are those produced for a general, rather than specialized audience; hence sold through the regular bookselling *trade*.

in age, Dodd is relatively small, publishing 100 to 150 titles a year. It is loved by mystery fans for its Agatha Christies and by theatre-goers for the works of George Bernard Shaw and the *Best Plays of* [the year] series. It also fields a line of juveniles and likes to reissue classics.

McGraw-Hill, Inc. A concern formed in 1916, when McGraw, a book publisher, obtained the Hill journals; it still has *Business Week* and about forty other periodicals. Its many departments, the result in part of the assimilation of other firms, are represented by a wide range of publications, including nonprint. Its "Trade Order List" requires over five hundred pages. At one time McGraw's scientific, technical, and textbook publications had a dull-looking format on slick paper, but they have improved. These are the publications for which the company was best known; however, it also issued Walter B. Pitkin's famous *Life Begins at Forty* and has kept up Richard Armour's poetic meanderings. In the last couple of decades McGraw-Hill has offered luxurious sets such as the *Encyclopedia of World Art,* plus the Boswell papers and some extensive religious writings, for example, the works of Thomas Aquinas and the *New Catholic Encyclopedia.* In addition to books on education, medicine, and law, McGraw-Hill publishes a wide variety of works in science, from the *Encyclopedia of Science and Technology* to *Danny Dunn and the Smallifying Machine.*

Harcourt Brace Jovanovich, Inc. Another house which has developed through mergers a large diversified list was founded as Harcourt, Brace in 1919. Shortly afterward it published one of the notable books of the time, J. M. Keynes's *Economic Consequences of the Peace,* and the next year came up with Sinclair Lewis's *Main Street.* It merged in 1960 with the World Book Company, noted for tests and textbooks; took its present name ten years later; and has become one of the larger American houses, with some 800 titles a year. The huge series, International Library of Psychology, Philosophy and Scientific Method, is but one of its productions. Among the outstanding writers who have been published by Harcourt are Carl Sandburg, James Gould Cozzens, Eudora Welty, T. S. Eliot, William Golding, Virginia Woolf, Mary

McCarthy, Joy Adamson, Günter Grass, Anne Morrow Lindbergh, Jessamyn West, and Lewis Mumford.

Harper & Row, Publishers, Inc. The J. & J. Harper firm started in New York City in 1817, then became Harper & Brothers in 1833. Row, Peterson & Company, mainly known for schoolbooks, began in 1906. In 1962 the two merged. Another of the large houses, issuing over a thousand new titles a year, this organization produces trade books, textbooks, and religious, medical, and juvenile books. Its offerings range from Al Capp to the heavy philosophical works of Martin Heidegger and long sets of historical writings, such as The Documentary History of Western Civilization series. In 1956, the company published a book by a young senator from Massachusetts, *Profiles in Courage.* Eleven years later came William Manchester's *Death of a President.* Harper's list of well-known writers includes Peter Drucker, Laura Ingalls Wilder, John W. Gardner, Gore Vidal, John Gunther, E. B. White, Thornton Wilder, and Richard B. Morris. It has produced such series titles as Everyday Handbook, History of Europe, New American Nation, and Library of Philosophy and Religion.

Random House, Inc. A medium-sized to large firm issuing over 500 new books annually, it originated in 1925 when Donald Klopfer and Bennett Cerf bought the Modern Library Series and then began to publish other books on the side "at random." It has since merged with Alfred A. Knopf and has been sold to the huge conglomerate RCA. Random House rendered a fine service to the cause of intellectual freedom in the 1930s by fighting a court battle for permission to publish James Joyce's *Ulysses* in the United States. Other eminent authors it has published include William Faulkner, Robert Penn Warren, and William Styron, in addition to the anthologies compiled by Cerf, of course. Though responsible for Shirley Temple Black's *Favorite Tales of Long Ago,* it has on the credit side the noteworthy *Random House Dictionary of the English Language* and the *Random House Encyclopedia.*

Viking Press. Organized in 1925, Viking fielded a list of 4 titles that fall, and is now issuing 150 to 200 new ones a year. Among its noted authors have been John Steinbeck, Saul Bellow, Graham Greene, Gerald Durrell, James Joyce, D. H. Lawrence, and Iris Murdoch. The excellent Viking Portable Library series was begun in 1943. The firm also publishes works in history, biography, science, art, and a few other fields, as well as reports by Ralph Nader.

Charles Scribner's Sons. Producing 300 to 400 new titles a year, Scribner's is a venerable, medium-sized house known for its quality books (perhaps with one or two exceptions). It has offered such fine reference sets as the *Album of American History, Dictionary of American History, Dictionary of American Biography,* and *Dictionary of the History of Ideas.* Among its authors have been F. Scott Fitzgerald, Ernest Hemingway, Douglas Southall Freeman, Thomas Wolfe, George Santayana, Reinhold Neibuhr, Jacques Maritain, Allen Nevins, Pamela Hansford Johnson, and C. P. Snow.

SOME SPECIAL TYPES OF PUBLISHERS

Of the approximately 1,400 United States book publishers listed in the *Literary Market Place,* over 400 are classified as *textbook* producers. Some of these firms (for example, Allyn & Bacon, D. C. Heath & Company, Ginn & Company, and Scott, Foresman & Company) are known primarily for this type of book; others are usually identified as trade publishers but also put out a line of textbooks. Such books account for about 30 percent of the sales income of American publishers as a whole.

It must be explained that an old generalization decrees that ordinarily textbooks are not bought by libraries. The typical objections are that textbook style of writing is usually poor, and that the books merely summarize material found in other sources. Paradoxically, if a book has "textbook" in its title, as some books on anatomy and on engineering do, it is likely to be valuable for reference. Also, a good text may well survey a topic clearly and with greater fairness than will a trade book written by an author who has a weak style and strong predispositions. In any case, it is necessary sometimes to buy texts, so this list may be of some use: *El-Hi Textbooks in Print* (New York: Bowker, annually).

The series started in 1956 and has appeared under various titles. Arranged by broad subject headings, it is easy to use, with author, title, and series indexes.

Firms like Phaidon Press, Skira, and Harry N. Abrams, Inc., specialize in quality books on *art and architecture*. Most of these companies publish fewer than 100 titles a year. The books are beautifully printed and are usually expensive. General trade publishers also issue art books from time to time.

Medical books are another speciality. Careful attention to detail is required for their textual matter and for their great numbers of illustrations, often in living (or dead) color. These facts, along with the relatively small market for these books, account for their inordinate expense. Examples of companies seriously concerned with this field are Lea & Febiger, the Williams & Wilkins Company, and the W. B. Saunders Company. The latter became widely known a number of years ago when it issued the dull reports of Dr. Kinsey.

Almost all *religious* organizations operate publishing houses to furnish materials for their own people and perhaps to evangelize others. A few of these concerns have branched out to offer a more general line also. Several of the regular commercial publishers issue religious books—Macmillan, Inc.; Doubleday & Co., Inc.; and Prentice-Hall, Inc., among others—and so do various university presses. Older works, especially reference sets representing conservative views, tend to be reprinted, and to remain available.

Technical book publishers include such well-known firms as the Van Nostrand Reinhold Company (*Van Nostrand's Scientific Encyclopedia*); McGraw-Hill, Inc.; and John Wiley & Sons, Inc. Books on engineering and other technologies demand careful attention to detailed factual information, which is often cast in tabular form. For this reason the publisher's reputation for care and accuracy is of unusual interest to the user. Fortunately, the new printing technologies have simplified this kind of composition.

Vanity presses are those that contract with authors to issue their books on condition that the writer pay costs to be reimbursed with royalties only if the venture results in a profit. "Subsidy presses" would be a more descriptive term, since authors or their representatives subsidize the publisher. Many of these outfits have a bad odor, primarily because of blatant come-on appeals to would-be authors. The products of vanity presses generally are not considered seriously for purchase by small or medium-sized libraries, on the assumption that if a book is good it will be accepted by a standard firm which, far from collecting money from the writer, advances payment against potential royalties. Now and then, however, vanity presses turn out books of value, and there is some feeling that they are less cautious than others when dealing with controversial material.[21] One such publisher does declare that he turned down a manuscript showing how centers of gravity could be shifted to allow automobiles, battleships, and skyscrapers to float on air.[22]

About ten percent of the nonfiction titles published in the United States are from *university* presses, though they enjoy only a small share of the sales market. Most major (and some minor) universities support such departments, which make available works considered unlikely to bring profits to regular trade publishers. These books usually are important for the scholarly minority or for people with regional interests. They may advance altruistic causes. They may bring prestige to the university itself.[23] University press books on the whole are more likely to have permanent value than are most commercial items, hence typically they are kept in print longer. They often have expensive, attractive formats. Naturally there are many exceptions to these generalizations. Though such presses can afford to issue books in smaller quantities because of subsidies, some of their titles do make money, to the delight of their sponsors, and a few even qualify as best sellers. *The Lonely Crowd,* by David Riesman and associates, was brought out by Yale in 1950 and is said to have sold well over a million copies. Rachel Carson's *The Sea Around Us* (Oxford University Press, 1951) passed the 500,000 mark. Other active university presses are those of Cambridge, Columbia, Harvard, Princeton, Chicago, and California. Some academic libraries have standing orders for the entire output of America's university presses. Many of these works are suitable for public libraries also, and a descriptive bibliography, *University Press Books for Public Libraries* is issued every few years by the American University Press Services, Inc., for the American Library Association. There is a similar list directed at secondary school libraries.

Note should be made also of the many *small presses,* which operate on a low overhead, producing books, periodicals, and pamphlets that are, as a rule, unusual enough to have very limited sales. See, for instance "*LJ*'s Small Press Roundup," in its annual December 15 issues.

A private *foundation,* such as the Brookings Institution, may have a publishing arm. Usually its products reflect the specialized field of the organization.

Other specialized publishers are oriented toward such subjects as booktrade and bibliography, law, or sports; or such forms as encyclopedias, Bibles, maps, or children's books.

Only a few publishers have been mentioned by name so far. Along with other information on the industry, good, fairly complete lists of publishers, present and past (about 6,500 active ones in the United States and about 400 in Canada), booksellers and wholesalers can be found in *American Booktrade Directory,* issued biennially by the R. R. Bowker Company since 1915. Bowker also distributes a three-volume set, *The Book Trade of the World,* edited by Sigfred Taubert, and published in Hamburg, Germany, 1972–1979. The American Library Association produces Marjorie K. Joramo's *Dictionary of Ethnic Publishers and Resource Organizations* (2nd., Chicago: 1979, 108 p.), and the Gale Research Company has *Book Publishers Directory, A Guide to New and Established, Private and Special Interest, Avant-Garde and Alternative, Organization and Association, Government and Institution Presses,* 2nd ed., edited by Annie M. Brewer and Elizabeth A. Geiser (Detroit: 1979, 668 p.).

SOME INCLUSIVE, UNSELECTIVE BOOKLISTS

Two basic questions faced by the librarian are: What books are available for acquisition, and from what sources? In the remainder of this chapter, we shall consider a few tools which list the current output of publishers. The terms *in print* and *out of print* (*o.p.*) may need explanation. A book is in print if the publisher still has a stock of it, *or* plans to reprint a supply in the near future. Once the supply is exhausted, the book is considered *out of stock;* if the publisher makes a formal decision not to obtain more copies, the book is then said to be *out of print.*[24] The following bibliographical works show, within limits, what is available from American publishers and give other information useful in ordering. They have considerable value in selection, therefore, and are especially important for identification of the exact spelling of authors' names and the exact wording of titles. Back numbers of these works often form excellent retrospective bibliographies.

For a running account of what books are being published in the United States through the year, there is *Weekly Record,* 1974– (formerly a section of *Publishers Weekly.*) It "conscientiously" lists American books and foreign ones being distributed in this country, with some exceptions. The arrangement by main entry means that the *Weekly Record* cannot be used to determine, say, what was published last week on the subject of racehorses; nevertheless librarians often scan it regularly to spot likely selections. Subject tracings for each entry give an idea of the book's content.

The *American Book Publishing Record,* 1960– is a monthly list of new books. Taking items from the *Weekly Record,* it arranges them according to the Dewey Decimal System, adding author and title indexes. There are annual and larger cumulations, including *American Book Publishing Record Cumulative: 1950–77* (New York: Bowker, 1979), which combines the fruits of twenty-eight years in one sequence, occupying fifteen volumes, and adds a few other entries as well.

Publishers' Trade List Annual (New York: Bowker, 1873– , annually) is a collection of catalogs, representing most (but not all) American publishers. Known as *PTLA,* it intends to list what each company has in print at the time the given edition of the annual is prepared. It cannot be one hundred percent accurate. For one thing, a publisher may have copies of a book returned from retail outlets after the stock has reached bottom. On the other hand, a title may go out of print shortly after the *Annual* is issued. *PTLA* gives the price of each book and sometimes the date of publication, and identifies titles in a particular series. This tool by itself has little practical use, however, unless at the start of a search one knows the publisher of the work being sought.

Books in Print (New York: Bowker, 1948– , annually with one supplement per year) devotes two volumes to listing, alphabetically by author or other main entry, the products of most American publishers (more than those included in *PTLA*), omitting Bibles, free items, those selling for less than a quarter, and a few other categories. There are two volumes also for titles. Thus, *BIP* will go far toward answering such questions as: What books and editions of Thomas Merton or John Steinbeck are presently available from the stocks of publishers in the United States? Each annual now includes over 500,000 titles, representing the output of some 8,000 publishers.

Subject Guide to Books in Print (New York: Bowker, 1957– , annually) deals with most of the items listed in *Books in Print* but arranges them under one or more Library of Congress subject headings. Thus some 450,000 works appear about 600,000 times under some 62,000 headings, with over 53,000 cross references. Some books (for instance, fiction, poetry and drama collections, and texts of the Bible) are not approached advantageously by subject, hence are omitted from this guide.

Forthcoming Books (New York: Bowker, 1966– , six times a year) gives basic information about books planned for publication by United States firms during the five months following each issue. Included are paperbacks, juveniles, reprints, and revised editions. For instance, the November 1979 number lists by author and title books published since Summer 1979, and to be published through March 1980. *Subject Guide to Forthcoming Books* covers the same time span with items arranged under subject headings.

The Bowker Company also publishes specialized lists of in-print works—*Childrens' Books in Print* and its *Subject Guide, Business Books and Serials in Print, Scientific and Technical Books and*

Serials in Print, and others.These compilations in large measure rearrange selected items from the more general guides.

Paperbound Books in Print (New York: Bowker, 1955– , now semiannual) presents an author, title, and subject approach to in-print and forthcoming paperbacks, duplicating a part of *BIP.*

Cumulative Book Index: A World List of Books in the English Language, (New York: Wilson, 1898– , eleven times a year with annual cumulations) is a huge set, supplementing the *United States Catalog,* the fourth and final edition of which was published by Wilson in 1928, in 3,164 pages. A dictionary catalog, with entries by author (personal or corporate), title, subject, and series, it is issued eleven times a year and is now cumulated quarterly and annually, though previously there were larger cumulations. Roughly speaking, *CBI* attempts to include books produced throughout the world in the English language, regardless of country. It deliberately excludes some forms of publication such as government documents, most pamphlets, cheap paperbacks, maps, tests, local directories, and works published in editions of 500 copies or less. The selector should note that items listed in *CBI* may have gone out of print. This tool provides an excellent source for verifying bibliographic information, in that it gives the exact spelling of the author's name, title of the work, publisher, date of publication, and price for each item. It also shows, within its scope, what books have been produced on a given topic. Any one who has had the experience of reading proof will marvel at the accuracy of this set.

With these tools, which give a fairly complete picture of the booktrade in the United States and, to some extent, in other countries, it is possible to determine what books are likely to be available for the library to purchase from jobbers (wholesalers, dealers) or publishers. The array is extensive, but many of these representative tools have their counterparts in other countries, some of which publish on a large scale.

Canadian Books in Print: Author and Title Index (subtitle varies) (Toronto: University of Toronto Press, 1967– , annually), stresses English language titles. There is a separate volume by subject. The monthly *Canadiana: Publications of Canadian Interest*

Received by the National Library is excellent both for its format and for its coverage of many types of materials.

The United Kingdom has weekly and monthly lists with cumulations, published by the Whitaker firm, which also produces *British Books in Print: The Reference Catalog of Current Literature* and *Paperbacks in Print.* Another outstanding tool is *The British National Bibliography, 1950–   ; A Subject Catalogue of New Books Published in the British Isles . . . Provided With a Full Author, Title and Subject Index . . .* (London: Council of the British National Bibliography, Ltd., 1950–   ). Other countries produce similar bibliographic tools.

Also important to the selector on occasion are retrospective bibliographies, which show what has been published in the past, at least so far as the records can be recovered and confirmed. Charles Evans, for instance, in his *American Bibliography . . .* (see p. 72) undertook the task of listing books issued in America from 1639 through 1820. Though he died before the job was complete, later compilers have added to his work. Catalogs of large libraries such as the British Museum (British Library), the Library of Congress, and Bibliothèque Nationale also list, with bibliographic detail, several millions of books each. It should be noted that those libraries which participate in such organizations as the Ohio College Library Center (OCLC) have access by way of computer terminals to many of the bibliographic records listed in the sets discussed in this chapter.

The bibliography collection of a large library is a most interesting place to browse. Here one can get an idea of human thought and publication in its magnificence and its folly. It is a revelation to see what profound subjects and what odd and obscure details the race has considered it worthwhile to write about.

Upon examining these comprehensive bibliographies, one is struck all the harder by the question: Of all this mass, which items are the best? A selector with these tools only would be completely lost in the world of books, except perhaps for a few fields in which he or she happened to be closely acquainted with the literature. For this reason, it is helpful, even necessary at times, to use guides that are selective and/or that include evaluative information about the entries they list. Some of these will be discussed in Chapter 7, after some suggestions about evaluating books, in Chapter 6.

6. HOW TO JUDGE A BOOK

In New York, say, a decision is made to publish a manuscript. The editorial and mechanical processes are set in motion. Some time later (months or years) a box is opened in the receiving room of a California library, and there is a copy of the finished book. It has been chosen from among thousands of available titles. What factors — what information, feelings, ideas — have influenced the person making the final decision? The array of information brought to bear on this one point may, and probably should, be amazingly complex — considerations based on the goals and policies of the local library, on fundamental principles of selection, on what is known about potential use, on the nature and output of producers. All these have been discussed in the first five chapters.

Now it is time to deal with books themselves, judging them in terms of library collections. This process, which may be termed *microselection,* also involves information gained from reviews, bibliographies, and other sources.

During a year, tens of thousands of books may be brought to the attention of a librarian. In the course of a long career, the total may go above a million. For each item encountered, only three choices are possible: to accept, to reject, or to defer judgment until a later time — that is, the book may be a possibility for purchase but not be essential; therefore a decision can be postponed until near the end of the fiscal year. Other evidence about the book may appear, or the budget picture may change. Deferring a decision, though, risks the possibility that the book may no longer be available at that later time.

Many librarians feel that it is a good idea to see an actual copy of the book before making a decision. LeRoy Merritt, the late dean of the University of Oregon Library School, once claimed that a subject expert can in five minutes of direct examination tell more about a book in his or her own field than by reading all the reviews of it ever published. This opinion would seem to hold for a narrow field of knowledge, but most selectors are expected to cover a considerable range of subject matter. Even for the generalist, though, examination of physical copies before purchase can be satisfying and may lead to better judgments. Indeed, to visit the warehouse of a large wholesaler of books is an exciting experience. Dozens of copies of a work are stacked high beside other titles issued by the same publisher. The products of hundreds of companies, brought together under one tremendous roof, give a picture of current publishing activity which, though still partial, is clearer than that offered even by the largest bookstore. The new materials on display at American Library Association conferences and even at state meetings offer a good field for browsing.

Some libraries have worked out plans with vendors, usually wholesalers (jobbers), to receive certain types of new books on approval, with the option of keeping or returning each title. A profile may be prepared jointly by the librarians and the vendor, specifying for each subject the kinds of books to be shipped. For instance, Library A might wish to receive a copy of every new English-language work on sociology *except* freshman-sophomore texts, anthologies, and titles selling for fifty dollars or more. In art history, the same library's profile might call for titles in Italian as well as English, and for books costing up to seventy-five dollars. The art history profile might exclude works about the time before Christ and items in paperback format. The books received by the library are then examined, and if a significant portion are returned to the vendor, the profile must be adjusted, else the expense is too great to make the plan beneficial. Such arrangements are less practical for small libraries with limited budgets.

There is another situation in which selectors choose with books in hand. A library may acquire a huge collection of books from a used book dealer or another library and then have the problem of deciding what items to keep. The Miami (Ohio) University Library, for example, bought about 100,000 volumes from a New York dealer and after six years had reviewed 28,000 titles, keeping sixteen percent of them and disposing of the rest.

Any alert librarian will encounter now and then a book that

ought to be considered for the local collection. Even reviews may be interpreted more realistically if the reviewer is envisioned with the book in hand.

Suppose, then, that whatever the situation, the selector *can* spend some time with books available for acquisition. What points should be looked for?

AT FIRST GLANCE

Does the title of the work make any difference? In some cases, yes. A certain English poet called his verses *Terence*. The change to *A Shropshire Lad* was a "touch of genius: which undoubtedly affected the work's popularity." [2] Graham Greene (*The Power and the Glory*), Tennessee Williams (*Cat on a Hot Tin Roof*), Eugene O'Neill (*Mourning Becomes Electra*), and Alvin Toffler (*Future Shock*) are other writers outstanding for titles that interest. Samuel Eliot Morison bemoaned the fact that the American public wouldn't read history unless it was disguised under catchy titles, [3] and one could wish that some titles were more descriptive and less cute. Even the serious title can be misunderstood, and librarians have favorite howlers. Charles Scribner Jr. has noted that a famous theological work by Paul Tillich, *The Shaking of the Foundations,* was ordered by a construction firm. [4] Incidentally, a work may be published under one title in the United Kingdom and under another in the United States.

The opening line or paragraph may have something to do with a book's popularity in a bookstore or library. British writers seem to outdo Americans on this point, though most detective novelists are good at it. Probably the most famous of all is: "It was the best of times, it was the worst of times."

CONTENT

The most important question to be asked about the prospective book is: What does it say? Is it of use to our patrons? Will it interest them? Will it bring some new, worthwhile information to the collection? Diversity of subject matter and opinion is to be prized in a library. Most cannot afford a great deal of duplication.

In this connection, the acquisition of sets of books often proves an advantage. If a set of, say, fifty volumes on a subject has been carefully planned and edited, it will have far less duplication than fifty separate titles issued by different publishers.

A book may not increase the library's actual store of facts or points-of-view yet present previously collected information in a new arrangement more suitable for some readers. It may summarize or simplify in a skillful manner. For example, consider a library with a few sets of periodicals and research monographs in the field of medicine. Scattered throughout the volumes may be hundreds of facts on the treatment of gout. A new book on gout, while adding no important fact to this store, can be valuable because of its organization and its summary of the data. Travelers' guide manuals repeat information found in books of architecture, geography, economics, history, zoology, and other subjects — A to Z. Books of history distill knowledge from thousands of raw documents. It must be admitted, then, that the larger part of published information is merely a repackaging. The quantity of new research presented in book form is relatively small. An author may make a real contribution by organizing facts in an order pleasing to a certain group of readers, or may juxtapose two ideas in a way that enhances each. Purchase of such rearrangements for the library is fully justified. The pattern of materials bearing information is so extremely complicated that different persons need different approaches. Rather than buy a bolt of cloth, a box of buttons, and a spool of thread, it may be better to get a tailored suit.

The content of a book may be evaluated also in terms of the inspirational value it adds to the library, for people still are moved by ideals. The so-called belletristic writings add significant content to the library without increasing its store of scientific information. All sorts of publications also are worthwhile because of their recreational value.

In larger (and some smaller) libraries, books are obtained for documentary or historical purposes. An old book by Horatio Alger Jr. might be purchased because some users are interested in the literary tastes of a half-century ago — not because the work is adjudged "good," "true," "beautiful," or even interesting for most people now. Again it should be stated that one must not be too narrow in assessing the interests of readers.

Recency

For most works the time of writing is important. The year of the copyright rather than the date on the title page should be used to determine more accurately the effective date of the book's ideas. In terms of its subject matter, then, is the material recent enough? Has this work been superseded by one making use of later research? Publishers like to advertise their latest items, and this, along with the fact that people seem to have a prejudice in favor of the new, creates a demand for the more recent title. Often it is indeed preferable because it builds on previous works about similar subjects.

A persistent question is whether the library should buy a new edition of a work already held. In the case of truly outstanding books, the answer is "yes," especially for books that have gone through as many as eight or ten editions. They surely have something going for them. However, Kathryn Crane in 1970 studied carefully the revisions of books on the subject of Africa and was generally disappointed with the extent of change.[5] An extreme case of a book claiming to be a "second edition, revised and updated" but with practically no changes in text is reported by Scott Bullard.[6] Perusal of reviews in the Reference and Subscription Book section of *Booklist* will sometimes reveal similar judgments. Generalization on the point should be cautious, but this evidence serves as a warning about new editions of run-of-the-mill books, at least. The old edition bearing the honest date of 1970 may be less misleading than one pretending to be a new 1980 update but really containing the same information.

Truth

Most important of all is the question of the book's veracity. Here we face difficult questions indeed. Naturally we look for books that state truth rather than propagate lies. Accuracy, not sloppiness, in verification of data and presentation of fact is paramount. But the answers are not simple. Who is to determine truth? In the area of science, for instance, is it enough to take as true the generally accepted judgments of scientists themselves? Should we reject those books which contradict such findings? If we do, will we run the risk of denying access to ideas which, though not now considered scientific, may some day gain such approval?

As one example of this problem, note books on extrasensory perception. An article by G. R. Price in *Science* said that the evidence for such phenomena was conclusive if one granted the good faith and sanity of the investigators, but suggested that their claims might be fraudulent.[7] R. A. McConnell, in *American Psychologist,* replied, "I can only say that in my opinion, wittily (sic) or unwittingly, Price's article is a hoax about hoaxes."[8]

Speaking practically, we just about have to accept the idea that current opinions of the majority of scientists will give us the best guesses we can make as to what is true in this realm. Such a course insures a greater likelihood that the library will distribute the most reliable information. If we follow the consensus of scientists, the risk of rejecting some important truth, though real, is so slight as to be outweighed in most libraries by the necessity of getting on with the job of selection without undue delay.

If the difficulty is great for books in science, how much more complicated it is for those in the social sciences and the humanities, where agreement among authorities is so much rarer. McConnell went on to say it is safe to believe most of what is said in physics and chemistry books, "but we ought to believe only half of the ideas in the biological sciences — although I am not sure which half. And we should accept as final very little in the social sciences."[9] This statement should give us some pause, though we still come back to the judgment of experts as offering the best bet.

Even after deciding to accept the judgment of authority, how, using only the book itself, are we to ascertain whether it meets the present consensus of expert opinion? The reputation of the author may be estimated (if we have heard of the person at all) and we may have formed some idea of the integrity of the publisher, but what if neither of these factors is known? In any event, abilities of author and publisher are not easy to measure, even after spending considerable time, unless one's background knowledge is exceptional. Reputations are subject to change without notice and do not transfer smoothly from one specialty to another. What are we to make of the advertising for some works: "The real facts behind. . ."? After seeing the virtual hopelessness of making some of these decisions wisely, we are glad to fall back on reviews of books, whether we trust them completely or not.

Not always, though, is a book rejected merely because it is untrue. There are times when false materials serve some purpose. Probably the most interesting headline ever run in the "World's Greatest Newspaper" (the Chicago *Tribune*) appeared on November 3, 1948: "DEWEY DEFEATS TRUMAN." Libraries may deliberately buy some books of questionable authority and unquestionably bad taste just because they are highly controversial and present ideas not easily available elsewhere. For the most part, however, books that add true facts or new ideas to the collection are to be preferred, for obvious reasons.

Freedom From Bias

Discussion of the problem of truth involves consideration of bias. In fact this usually is one of the key questions, since few books are deliberately, completely, and patently false. Treatment of this matter requires attention to the various gradations of bias.

One writer speaks of the scholarly journal *Speculum* as having a "medieval bias,"[10] but what does the critic expect, in view of the fact that *Speculum*'s subtitle is "A Journal of Medieval Studies," and its publisher is the Medieval Academy of America. If this be bias at all, it certainly is not disturbing. On a slightly different level, a work may admit bias, as does the *Encyclopedia of Philosophy*.[11] Such an admission serves to warn the users (if they stop to read the caveat) that the subject is being discussed from a particular point of view, and perhaps lessens the impact of any unfair articles.

Then there is a playful bias, as when Mark Twain said that any library was good if it did not contain the novels of Jane Austen. More serious is the next level — bias in space allotments for particular topics or ideas. *The Oxford Dictionary of the Christian Church* seems clearly to slight the United States; the same thing is true, to an extent, of some editions of *Grove's Dictionary of Music and Musicians*. But in assessing degrees of bias by counting the number of lines given to each topic, some critics go to extremes.

The fifth shade can be called bias by omission. If relevant facts are withheld, the result generally is a distorted picture, and that is the sort of hindrance to truth which should be tolerated only in eulogies on the recently deceased.

Finally, there is plain misstatement of fact, the worst degree of bias. Whatever the motivation, the fruits are evil. At this point, the bias may be said to have become simply falsehood.

REPUTATION OF AUTHOR OR PUBLISHER

As suggested before, the truth of a book may sometimes be guessed from the reputation of its producers. In selection, this information may be used in other ways as well. Patrons sometimes request a book just because a certain well-known person wrote it. Questions sometimes arise, especially with respect to works of literature, about authors like Norman Mailer: If such a famous writer produces a work adjudged inferior, should it be obtained by the library? The answer is "Yes" if the library places emphasis on demand as a criterion; otherwise, probably "No." In some instances a book may be accepted or rejected largely because of its publisher. There are firms that over the years have built up a sound reputation for quality in one or more fields. For other firms the word is not so good. As suggested in Chapter 5, the ability to judge on this point comes only after years of experience.

PRESENTATION

Except for creative literature, the style of writing in a book obviously is less important than the content. Nevertheless, readers often enjoy even a factual book because of its manner of presentation. They may choose it largely because of its readability. Some common ideas are made far more interesting by skillful writers, while the acceptance of good new ideas may be hindered by a miserable, pedestrian style. Unfortunately there is some vague feeling that the author who strives for distinction and interest in a nonfiction book (for example, in a popularization of science) may thereby sacrifice factual accuracy. Scholars sometimes express terrible fears that the innocent general reader may be led astray from the strict truth. While this danger is not to be overlooked entirely, there really is no reason why a book may not be true and have at the same time a pleasing manner of presentation; and anyway, where is the book that cannot be misinterpreted by somebody? The practice of reducing all expressions to the simplest words and all sentences to short declarative statements for the sake of the laziest and most ignorant readers is a trend to be deplored, cursed, and fought.

In organizing the material an author has a choice among several acceptable patterns: chronological, pedagogical, logical, developmental, hierarchical, and even others. Any of these arrangements may be successful, depending on the content and the intended audience. Some books are badly hashed up, but Marshall McLuhan has demonstrated that disarray can be advantageous. Reference books, of course, usually have an arbitrary arrangement (such as alphabetical by small topic) in order to facilitate quick access to specific bits of information.

Content and presentation are considered more fully in Parts III, IV and V below, which deal with types of materials and with particular subject fields.

SPECIAL FEATURES

In some instances a book will be accepted or rejected because of an unusual feature or method of displaying information. For one thing, a detailed, logical, accurate index should be expected in any work except creative literature. Regrettably, publishers sometimes cut corners by supplying no index at all or one of poor quality, for a good index cannot be dashed off easily. It is refreshing to find a review with a stern criticism of a book's index. Daniel J. Boorstin, dealing with the twenty-volume *Annals of America* called it "in one respect . . . 'without peer' . . . probably the worst-indexed work in many a year."[12] Lord Campbell, over a century ago, said that Parliament should pass a bill denying the copyright privilege to any book without an index and should subject the author to a "pecuniary penalty,"[13] and a century later the great Ranganathan said that release of such a book ought to be "an indictable offense."[14]

A book may be chosen over one of its fellows because of its good bibliography or footnotes. While reading any nonfiction book, it is interesting to see whether the author was acquainted with previous leading writers in the field. Many people, a few of them learned, rage against the defenseless (often inconspicuous) footnote, but unless the author is a recognized authority, I, for one, wish to know the evidence on which the statements are based, hence like to see a generous use of bibliographic citations. The historian Perry Miller, writing his famous work *The New England Mind: The Seventeenth Century,* did not use conventional documentation but deposited in the Houghton Library at Harvard a copy with complete bibliographical citations. Readers believed that Miller had consulted practically everything available on his topic. Thirty-five years later, a scholar took the trouble to examine this documented copy and was amazed to find that the historian had really used a very limited array of sources.[15]

Some textbook publishers insist that authors delete references to older materials, probably in an effort to make their products seem somehow "up-to-date." This practice represents bad ethics and horrible pedagogy. Using these works as sources for citation counts would yield strange results, though as indicated in Chapter 4, references (even of this sort) have practical importance, because over and over it has been observed that readers use them to locate other published sources.

Bibliographic notes, then, though perhaps getting in the way of some readers, provide a happy change of pace for others. One reviewer puts the case neatly: The book is "unrelieved by documentation." [16]

Some authors are skillful at manufacturing footnotes made up of facts or ideas which are parenthetical to the main line of thought in the book. The reader then has the choice of perusing or ignoring them. Such "notes" (really some of them run to several pages) can be of more interest than the regular text.

One way of repackaging information is to put it in pictorial form; some people find diagrams, maps, and drawings easier to understand than written text. These features can vary in quality, as well as in size, in degree of detail, and in clarity both of concept and of printing. A poorly conceived diagram, for instance, is frustrating to the reader; a good one takes the place of long explanations in the text.

PAPER, TYPOGRAPHY, AND DESIGN

Needing to make a judgment on a book in hand, the librarian surely will not neglect its physical characteristics. The quality of the paper may present a problem, for many books deteriorate rapidly. In recent years considerable research has been completed on permanence and durability of papers, and one result is that some books now are being printed on paper with an expected life of three hundred years. The American people have been going through a period in which everything is manufactured to be disposed of; perhaps the worm is turning. Durability may become a virtue. Unfortunately, recycled paper has up to now proved generally unsatisfactory for books. So far as appearances are concerned, probably the best paper for books is that which is noticed least. It is less distracting. In some books, though, especially in the field of art, tinted or otherwise unusual paper may be justified as adding interest.

Margins should bear such relation to the type forms that the proportions are harmonious and pleasing. Gutter margins (down the middle of a double-page spread) should be wide enough to allow for rebinding.

Unfortunately some publishers cut costs by failing to provide running heads, which give, say, the chapter title on the left-hand page and the sub-topic on the right.

The type style ought to receive special attention. Is it appropriate? Legible? According to the National Study of High School English Programs, many of the "classics" found in high school libraries should have been replaced with new editions, because "too often, the shopworn look of such books, as well as their old and inferior typesets, make them far less attractive than crisp and inviting new works of far less literary value."[17] The same is true of books in many public and college libraries. Excellent writing is poorly served by execrable typography.

What are the goals that reasonably may be achieved in this area? At its best, typographic design accords with the nature of the book's content. There are styles that remind us of the nineteenth century; others clearly imply, "These ideas are novel, avant-garde." Some types are graceful, and well suited to books in the humanities. Some are starkly clear, and appropriate for scientific writing. For straight narrative, the lines of print should lead the reader at a good pace, with few interruptions. If the material is complicated and difficult to grasp, the page should be set up so the outline is clear and units of thought stand out. Key points may be emphasized by the use of boldface or italics. "The typographer's skill in the manipulation of well-known type display relationships can reduce any complexity to understandable units . . . of the whole subject."[18] Moholy-Nagy declared that typography "must be clear communication in its most vivid form. . . . combining elasticity, variety, and a fresh approach to the materials of printing."[19]

In many books the typical page of type looks dull and uninteresting — a condition that might be corrected by the expense of a little money and imagination on the part of the publisher and printer. A good example of imaginative typesetting is an article on the subject of whiskey, published in *Horizon* (9, Winter 1967, p. 120). The lines are wavy as if seen by a person under the influence. In fairness, it should be admitted that the respected critic of typography Stanley Morison was opposed to such tricks, at least for standard books. In his pamphlet *First Principles of Typography,* he declared, "Even dullness and monotony in the typesetting are far less vicious to a reader than typographical eccentricity or pleasantry." [20] A more balanced view was expressed by the founder of the Doves Press, T. J. Cobden-Sanderson: "The whole duty of typography is to communicate to the imagination, without loss by the way, the thought or image intended to be communicated by the author." [21]

Judgments on typography may be made subjectively, as when we say that a page is "right," is pleasant to look at, invites reading. However, a considerable amount of objective research has been done on the impact of printing types. The quarterly *Visible Language: The Journal for Research in the Visible Media of Language Expression* (successor to *Journal of Typographic Research,* quoted above) shows the advance of this line of thought. To indicate a few facts briefly, height of type is measured in *points*, and there are approximately seventy-two points to the inch. Thus twelve-point type is one-sixth of an inch from the top of a capital to the bottom of the "y". It is thought by many that the most satisfactory size for adult trade books is eleven point, or possibly a little smaller, leaded two points (that is, with two points of space added between the lines). The requirements vary, though, with different styles of type.

For best reading, each line of type should consist of fifty to sixty characters, making it about four inches long. A newspaper column is too narrow; a very wide page does not make for efficient eye movements. In children's books, the type should be larger. Undoubtedly children in the lower grades could read more poetry, fiction, and even books of science if the type and other parts of the format were adapted to their needs. Eighteen-point type is used for adults with defective eyesight, and some publishers offer fourteen-point for those with normal vision. Some public libraries issue separate catalogs of titles in large-print editions.

Authors sometimes have taken great interest in the typography of their books. William Faulkner was concerned about the spacing for *The Sound and the Fury* (being a tale told partly by an idiot, it is not easy to follow) and at one time wished to indicate the different narrators by different colors of ink. He wanted the design of type in Benjy's section to suggest as far as possible the idiot's thought processes.[22] George Bernard Shaw was another who insisted on certain type styles and careful spacing. A (probably apocryphal) story has it that he gave such insistent instructions on equality of space between words from line to line that the compositors were obliged to divide the indefinite article *an,* placing the *a-* at the end of one line and the *n* on the next.[23]

There are many other variations which may be taken into account by the book designer. A very simplified approach is made by Howard Greenfeld in his *Books From Writer to Reader.* Better is Marshall Lee's *Bookmaking: The Illustrated Guide to Designing, Production, Editing,* which has been issued by Bowker in a 1979 edition (485 p.). Specimens of book pages in a number of different types are given in *The Making of Books* by Sean Jennett (5th ed., London: Faber, 1973, 554 p.). The periodicals *Fine Print, Book Production Industry,* and *Publishers Weekly* are also recommended to the librarian interested in typography and good printing, or in the latest methods used by the industry.

PHYSICAL SIZE

Should the size of the volume make any difference to librarians and readers? Ranganathan recommends a front cover height between 15 and 25 centimeters (roughly 6 and 10 inches) with the width about seven/tenths of that and with the thickness of the book not to exceed 5 centimeters (about 2 inches),[24] but that seems too much of a step toward uniformity. An odd size or unusual shape may add to the interest of a book.

BINDING

"You can't tell a book by its cover" but that cover can't be ignored in making an evaluation. It should be examined from the standpoint of expected use. Note that a book is lost on the library shelves if the title is omitted from the spine. If the title is vertical rather than horizontal it is not so easy to read.

Trade books, produced mainly for sale in bookstores, have their bindings hidden by dust jackets, so there may be some tendency to reduce quality. The bindings should be durable, easy to open, and of workmanlike quality. The new, plastic, water-resistant cover materials are an asset for most books, and continuing research and experimentation probably will lead to more improvements.

Traditional methods of binding involve sewing groups of pages together with thread. "Perfect" binding is faster, glue being applied to the spine edges of the leaves just before the cover is fitted about them. (A writing pad, designed so that pages can be torn out easily, is made on the same principle, though the pad pages are not so secure.) Formerly used only for paperbacks, perfect binding now is found in many hard-cover books. The method has been improved so that these bindings are now almost as strong as the ones which are sewn.

Standards for bookbinding have been formulated carefully, but it is not practical for the individual library to make tests. Overall quality of workmanship is especially difficult to judge objectively.

PAPERBACKS

Books with paper covers have a long history, going back to the seventeenth century, and with the start of the Penguin series in the 1930s they have had a big impact on the trade. Benjamin, in 1977, judged that ninety percent of books published would continue to be hardback,[25] but there are strong indications that the 1980s will see far more paperback originals.[26]

There is a sharp difference between the two principal kinds of paperbacks. Those for the mass market usually are smaller in size, printed in huge editions, often with lurid covers, and sold along with magazines on newsstands in air terminals, bus stations, drugstores, and variety stores. The number of titles so issued in the United States runs one to two thousand in the typical year. Over half of these are fiction, and the average price is about $2.00. Trade paperbacks, manufactured in smaller quantities (usually less than 20,000) are sold in the regular book outlets. The total United States output is ten to twelve thousand volumes a year, and the average retail price is about $6.50, with some works selling for twice that amount.

The difference in price between a paperback and its hardbound counterpart is far greater than can be accounted for by the mere binding and paper. Whereas the average mass-market paperback costs about 10 percent as much as the average hardbound, and the trade paperback runs 30 to 50 percent as much, the actual difference in manufacturing costs is perhaps 25 to 30 cents.[27] One factor in the price differential is that paperbacks, especially the mass-market sort, are distributed without great overhead cost. Usually, but not always, the difference in price reflects also the fact that the paperback is a reprint, and that most of the publishing expense has been charged against the original (hardbound) edition. Those who wait for the cheaper reprint are a little like people who refuse to pay the price to see a first-run movie, but watch for it to appear as the late show on the tube. In the case of books, the value of the information is often in its recency—the first year of a book's life is usually its most useful—so the library hardly gains a great bargain by waiting for a cheap reprint. It should be noted that for some works the original editions are in paperback only, and the content of these is likely to be more recent than that in the average hardbound. A few works are issued simultaneously in paper and hard-cover editions.

Under many circumstances the paperback is worth its price for libraries, and there is no reason to despise it (or to cherish it either, so far as that goes). If a certain title is needed in the library, and if the hard-cover edition is out-of-print, an available paperback is a much better buy. To locate a used copy of the hardbound book could take weeks and cost tens of dollars in staff time and even then, a premium price might have to be paid.

Paperbacks are a good buy also for those titles whose circulation is likely to be low. If it can be predicted that a work will be read so seldom that its paper cover will last indefinitely, that it will not wear out before the content becomes obsolete, there is little point in buying the hard-cover edition at greater cost.

For academic libraries, if extra copies of a title are needed for reserve, these might as well be paperbacks, for the next teacher of the course will be honor-bound not to use the same reserve books as the predecessor required, and the library should not be left with unwanted copies of an expensive hardbound. The same principle holds for any situation in which extra copies are needed for a brief time only.

A minor consideration is that some hardbound books are too heavy and bulky to hold comfortably in the hand; hence for these titles paperback editions are better.

Some people prefer paperbacks on principle, perhaps as reverse status symbols, or perhaps because they are more easily carried around in pocket or purse. Libraries, especially public, report greater and greater use of this format. The Metropolitan Library System serving Oklahoma City and County found paperbacks far more cost-effective than hardbounds.[28]

NEED FOR OTHER EVIDENCE

Were it possible to examine each available book before making a decision to purchase or reject, the foregoing are some of the things that one would look for. Even then, it would be frustratingly difficult to make up one's mind on many books. Not only would evaluation of content be nearly impossible for some items, but even problems of format would cause some indecision. Anyway, as things now stand, the librarian has to make choices on many publications sight unseen, so must depend on reviewers, bibliographers, and guide-compilers whose contact with the work is more direct. Aids, lists, guides, and reviews must themselves be evaluated, and such considerations will be taken up next.

7. GENERAL AIDS AND GUIDES

Since no librarian can make much headway in examining directly all items of possible choice, it pays to consider the value of bibliographies, aids to selection, and guides to the "best books." Such lists have varying degrees of authority and practical utility.

Every bibliography is of potential use in selection, because it represents a group of materials brought together by some similarity or common principle. Looked at conversely, it is a device that allows us to ignore for the time being all other items. It narrows the great bulk of material into manageable proportions. Even the trade bibliographies discussed in Chapter 5 are a help in that they leave out most of the world's published matter — that from other countries and/or in other languages. In one sense, a bibliography is analogous to a map — helpful *because* it omits things that are not of interest, allowing us to grasp more clearly the information we need. If it omitted nothing, the map would be as large as the territory described, and be of no practical value. Bibliographies are useful because they select and omit in somewhat the same way.

No bibliography, then, is all-inclusive in the sense of listing every item in existence, but we say that one is "comprehensive" if it includes all the publications within its announced scope, while it is "selective" if it chooses certain items on the basis of quality, usefulness, or a similar criterion. Many comprehensive bibliographies are large, but some of them are quite small—for example, a list of all materials published between 1814 and 1819 in Costa Rica on the subject of wooden nickels. Conversely, a selective bibliography may be large — for instance, the best books in English for the general reader.

Whether comprehensive or selective, bibliographies help to narrow the range of choice. They may list materials on one subject only (as, *Bibliography of Swimming*), or according to level or levels of readership (as, *Gateways to Readable Books*). Or they may include only one of the various forms of publication (as, *Ulrich's International Periodicals Directory*), or restrict themselves to publications of a certain date (*Bibliography of Boxing . . . Books in English Published before 1900; Bibliography of Fossil Vertebrates, 1964–68*). A list may be limited to the publications of a person or persons (*Bibliography of the Writings in Prose and Verse of the Members of the Brontë Family*). Sometimes a bibliography represents choice in two or more dimensions. *Canadian Selection: Books and Periodicals for Libraries*, a large volume, is a "selective guide to significant English language books and periodicals, written for adults, about Canada, published in Canada, or written by Canadians" — preface. Some bibliographies are made with the individual scholar in view, but these also are useful to library selectors. Anyone who doubts the great number of published bibliographies should examine Theodore Besterman's *A World Bibliography of Bibliographies* 4th ed. (Lausanne, Switzerland: Societas Bibliographica, 1965, 5 vols.)

While all sorts of bibliographies offer help, this chapter will be concerned in the main with tools made primarily for the use of librarians in building collections. Guides (of one sort or another) to the "best" reading date back to early times. A large one published in 1893 was the *Catalog of "A.L.A." Library: 5000 Volumes for a Popular Library, Selected by the American Library Association and Shown at the World's Columbian Exposition* (Washington: Government Printing Office, 1893, 592 p.). There were several later editions and many successors.

Upon first looking into some of the current tools, one may receive the impression that they are the dream solution to the problem of selection. They may appear to be better and more valuable than they really are; therefore, the following caveat is given.

LIMITATIONS OF GUIDES

As products of human judgment, these lists are not to be regarded as infallible in any sense. The difference between Book A, included in a standard guide, and Book B, on the same subject but not included, may be negligible. It is by no means inconceivable that, for many libraries, Book B is better. Assuming that library clienteles differ from place to place, a guide will not be equally good for two different locations. The best books for the suburbs north of Chicago will not all be the best for rural California.

What about the actual use of the books recommended? Are those which are listed in the standard aids (or reviewed favorably) more likely to be borrowed from a library than are other books which are not listed or reviewed? Several studies have attempted to supply an answer. A thesis produced at Kent State University dealt with the question of whether books entered in Charles B. Shaw's *List of Books for College Libraries* (Chicago: American Library Association, 1931, 810 p.; supplement, 1931–38 (1940), 284 p.) — a fine tool in its day — were more likely to be charged out of the university library than those not listed. The answer was basically negative.[1] Another student checked the circulation records of the Northern Illinois University Library to determine whether books rated highly according to the reviews listed in *Book Review Digest* were more often used than others in the collection. Again the answer was negative, apparently showing that, if demand is a strong part of selection policy in academic libraries, *Book Review Digest* is not very useful as a guide to choosing titles.[2] In a more detailed study, Herbert Goldhor, while librarian of Evansville Public Library, examined his collection in Dewey Decimal section 612–613.9 (a part of medicine) and found that books which were on certain standard lists, or had been reviewed favorably, circulated a little more, but not much more, than titles not so honored.[3] The general findings of these studies indicate tentatively either that (1) people using a library do not discriminate between good books and poor, or (2) guides and reviews do not adequately separate the two kinds. At least, it would seem that users of libraries do not particularly care whether selection is based on standard lists and/or favorable reviews. Goldhor interpreted his results to mean that patrons themselves do not distinguish the poor from the excellent, hence that librarians ought to give greater emphasis to the value factor in selection.

Another reason for exercising care in the use of lists is that they quickly go out of date. New and significant books are being published every day, and there is the possibility that any title on the recommended list has been, or soon will be, supplanted by a better one.

Guides are criticized also on the grounds that they cause the librarian to slough off responsibility for selection. Jesse Shera, while Dean of the School of Library Science, Case Western Reserve University, objected that standard lists seem to "reduce the essential problem of book selection to a mechanical operation, to confess the librarian's failure to perform adequately one of his most important tasks."[4] (The force of this criticism is modified when one realizes how difficult it is to amass enough knowledge to make adequate judgments about books.) Dean Shera also attacked the quality of selections in the guides: "We think we could make a good case for their emphasis on mediocrity. The very process by which they are compiled guarantees that they will contain no very 'bad' books, but, by the same token, they will probably not list any really 'good' books either."[5] The Italian librarian Rinaldo Lunati is also opposed to the "so-called 'lists of the best books' " except for small collections.[6] A part of professional expertise, however, is knowing when to disregard standard lists and when to employ them, and how to employ them to the best advantage. Like all tools they must be used with discrimination. Effective actions are based on an understanding of the weaknesses and strengths of one's advisors.

USES OF GUIDES

Now that the reader has been forewarned, it is in order to mark the legitimate place of aids and guides in selection. They are helpful, first, for the person who is new in the game and who may be overwhelmed by the number of choices to be made. It is literally impossible to become familiar immediately with all the good books published. Help is needed, and urgently. In somewhat the same vein, guides offer aid and comfort to the librarian who has to select in unfamiliar subject fields. In either situation, badly-needed advice might as well come from standard guides as from whatever individuals might happen to be consulted. The lists will at least provide a minimum collection of reasonable quality. At their worst, they certainly are better than random guesses. Even the knowledgeable expert in a subject field may find that a guide to best books will serve to refresh the memory. Having half forgotten some book which in the past has proved useful, one may be delighted while scanning a list to have the title jump out.

These compilations are welcome also when one faces the unpleasant responsibility of weeding. Many libraries are so full that new books simply cannot be crowded onto the shelves, so some things have to be discarded. "Weeding" is a poor word for this process, because it implies that these books were unwanted in the first place. The British prefer the term "thinning," which suggests removing the less healthy so that the better works can have a chance to stand out and be used. If some books, then, must be discarded, they should be the ones which have received little use in relation to the time they have spent on the library's shelves,* or are in a poor state of repair, or whose contents are no longer relevant. There are always many candidates for removal, but the actual decision can be painful. In some cases a book may be spared if it is listed in a standard guide.

The counterpart of thinning is deciding what titles to keep when quantities of material are donated to the library. The librarian, facing a pile of dusty books straight from a local attic, examining titles never before encountered, and wondering which volumes to keep, welcomes an objective estimate. If other evidence is lacking, one may decide to keep those mentioned in the guides while throwing away the others.†

On balance, then, the library, makes a good investment in buying the best of the current guides that are related to its needs.

---

*Unfortunately, use inside the building is difficult to measure.

†One of these guides had the honor of being mentioned in William F. Buckley's *National Review*. Columnist Russell Kirk spoke of donating several hundred books to a public library; then complained that nearly half of them had not been kept. He listed some of the titles committed to blazes (without saying whether or not they were duplicates to the

Used with judgment and flexibility, the guides really can be a help in selection.

WAYS TO LOOK AT GUIDES TO BOOKS

The character of any guide is determined largely by the people responsible for its compilation, so these should be investigated as thoroughly as possible. All sorts of persons issue lists of "good" books, and give advice on what their fellow citizens ought to read. Take as an extreme example the case of the governor of Indiana, campaigning in the Democratic primary of 1968. Met by a Boy Scout bugle band at Huntington, he "declared emotionally, 'The Boy Scout Handbook — next to the Bible — is the finest book that ever existed.' "[7] The Honorable Richard J. Daley, until the day of his death mayor of Chicago, once claimed that distinction for *Robert's Rules of Order*. Many published lists, prepared with greater sobriety, are more reliable if less interesting and dogmatic.

Some of these lists are compiled by a prestigious institution. A college or university may publish a catalog of its own library, on the assumption that it has been selected by competent scholars. In 1953, for instance, there appeared the *Catalogue of the Lamont Library, Harvard College*. For a particular field, the catalog of a special library may represent a good approximation of the best materials on that subject.

In some instances an individual may take the responsibility for selection of a large list, though that may be rarer in these days of the passed buck. One can admire the audacity of a man like W. S. Sonnenschein, who compiled, with the help of his family, a huge, carefully-chosen list: *The Best Books: A Reader's Guide to the Choice of the Best Available Books (about 100,000) in Every Department of Science, Art and Literature . . .* , the third edition of

library) and went on: "Among the confused excuses put forward by the book-burners was the argument that they are guided in selection by the *Standard Catalog for Public Libraries* [predecessor of *Public Library Catalog*], published by the H. W. Wilson Company. If a book isn't recommended in this holy and infallible work—why, to Gehenna with it!" (Russell Kirk, "From the Academy: Librarians and 'Fahrenheit 451,' " *National Review* 19 (17 October 1967): 1124.)

which was completed in 1935 in six volumes. The set continues to be of some use in thinning.

In addition to learning something about the compilers of a guide, it is also essential to consider its purpose and its intended audience. Until these are known, the tool simply cannot be interpreted satisfactorily. A list may be designed specifically as a library buying guide; it may be aimed primarily at booksellers (and be of some use to libraries if approached with an understanding of its focus); or it may be a reading guide of such character that the library finds its recommendations significant.

The scope of the guide should receive careful attention, because its title may not indicate all its limitations. What forms of material are listed? (Books only?) What subjects and subdivisions are covered? (Does SCIENCE include psychology?) Especially important are the publication dates of the items recommended. (A guide may comprise only those books published, say, between 1900 and 1950.) Some guides include no out-of-print titles. This limitation gives a list a certain element of practicality, in that the library is often spared the trouble of searching for books not easily obtained (although any listed item may drop out of print at any time. In fact some studies show that a remarkable number do so in a very short time). Such a restriction means, however, that many important and valuable books, especially in the humanities, are eliminated arbitrarily, just because they happened to be out of print at the precise time the guide went to press.

Another question: does the publication include most of the important books on a topic, or does it narrow the choice to a few of the "very best"?

Akin to, but different from, degree of selectivity is evaluative information, such as descriptions and ratings, for items entered. Are the titles annotated? Authoritatively? Are books of greater potential use so designated by some symbol? Does the list indicate which of its selections may be considered the best books in a given class or on a given subject? If any such ratings are provided, the list is made more useful for the smaller library, but the questions of authority and reliability of the compilers become even more pertinent.

REPRESENTATIVE GENERAL GUIDES

For small and medium-sized public libraries and for building core collections in larger ones, the best guide is *Public Library Catalog,* 7th ed., 1978 (New York: Wilson, 1979, 1,353 p.) This series began in 1934 (though its roots go back another quarter century) and was known through the first four editions as the *Standard Catalog for Public Libraries.* The current edition lists 8,045 titles for adult readers. The basic hardbound editions, which appear every five years, are supplemented by annual paper volumes. The catalog lists no works of fiction, because of the companion set, *Fiction Catalog* (see p. 389).

Selections are made by consultants from public and academic libraries chosen by the Wilson Company as representative institutions; therefore the guide has relevance for academic as well as public libraries.

The arrangement by Dewey Decimal Classification facilitates comparison of books on each subject. Other strong points are bibliographic information for each entry, together with quotations from reviews and a long index of authors, titles, subjects, and analyticals. Out-of-print books are omitted.

The Public Library Association's *Books for Public Libraries, Nonfiction for Small Collections,* 2nd ed. (New York: Bowker, 1975, 220 p.) is a good, though unannotated, buying list of approximately 5,000 in-print titles for the circulating nonfiction collection. Some paperbacks are included. The Dewey arrangement provides for representation on such subjects as Child care, Interior decoration, Movies, Russian literature, and Logic.

Senior High School Library Catalog, 11th ed., 1977 (New York: Wilson, 1977, 1,416 p.), begun in 1926 and formerly called *Standard Catalog for High School Libraries,* now lists over 5,000 titles. A new edition appears every five years, and there are annual supplements. Titles are selected by a committee of experienced school librarians. Otherwise its policies for inclusion and its method of arrangement and indexing are similar to those of the *Public Library Catalog.* Starting with the 1966 supplement, the catalog is aimed at grades ten through twelve only, because of the inauguration of the *Junior High School Library Catalog* (4th ed., 1980, 939 p.), also published by Wilson.

Books for Secondary School Libraries, 5th ed. (New York: Bowker, 1976, 526 p.), compiled by a Committee of Librarians from member schools of the National Association of Independent Schools, lists about 6,300 titles by Dewey Decimal Classification and gives the complete bibliographic information, including Library of Congress subject headings, but is not annotated.

The Reader's Adviser: A Layman's Guide to Literature, 12th ed. rev. and enl. (New York: Bowker, 1974–77, 3 vols.) first appeared in 1921 as *The Bookman's Manual,* primarily for the use of booksellers. The bibliography still has some of that tone, but is now planned for librarians and general readers also. It lists about 35,000 titles covering many fields of knowledge, but is strongest in the area of creative literature. For the most part, it is confined to books in print. Annotations and survey notes are compact and well-written, and the whole set conveys a humane rather than institutional flavor.

Books for College Libraries: A Core Collection of 40,000 Titles, 2nd ed. (Chicago: American Library Association, 1975, 6 vols.) is aimed at four-year colleges, but is also of use in public and, especially, junior college libraries. The first edition (1967) included titles published up to the date *Choice* began, in 1964. (*Choice* is discussed on p. 130.) The list represents the judgment of many specialists and, according to a long separately-published review, its "quality of selections and coverage vary greatly, ranging from good through excellent to superb."[8] Complete bibliographic information (Library of Congress cataloging) is given, and the arrangement is by LC class. Out-of-print titles are included, but in-print editions of individual works are recommended where available. The list is available in machine-readable tape form. The ALA also issued James W. Pirie's compilation, *Books for Junior College Libraries: A Selected List of Approximately 19,700 Titles,* in 1969.

The American Library Association and its divisions have published other guides, general and special, and have also distributed leaflets and pamphlets recommending books for various ages and purposes. In addition, associations such as the National Council of Teachers of English and the American Association for the Advancement of Science have issued guides which are of help to librarians. For instance, the College English Association has prepared *Good Reading: A Guide for Serious Readers,* edited by J. Sherwood Weber, 21st ed. (New York: Bowker, 1978, 313 p.), issued by various publishers with various editors since the 1930s. Under different auspices there is *Good Reading for Poor Readers,* compiled by George D. Spache, 9th ed. (Champaign, IL: Garrard, 1974, 303 p.).

Another work which serves very well as a guide to "best books," though its basic purpose is quite different, is *Book Review Digest, 1905–* (New York: Wilson, 1905–), which indexes and digests book reviews in about eighty periodicals, some popular, some scholarly, but most of general interest. Altogether about 6,000 books published or distributed in North America are evaluated each year. Issued monthly except February and July, the *Digest* has annual cumulations, with a handy cumulated index to subjects and titles and a long index by author and title, covering 1905 through 1974. The typical entry gives complete bibliographic information, a descriptive note, and digests of critical opinion from several sources; hence it is excellent from the standpoint of the value theory of selection. For an interesting experiment, one might choose a few now–famous titles published in the early part of this century and then check contemporary critical opinion reviews to see how well they match current opinions.

The small group of general guides discussed above is representative of those most widely used in libraries. There are countless others which have various degrees of authority, completeness, selectivity, reliability, and general usefulness. Practically all subject fields have bibliographies, some of them highly specialized (for example, *Select Bibliography of South African Native Life and Problems; Selected Bibliography for Chicano Studies; Guide to the Literature of Mathematics and Physics, Including Related Works on Engineering Science; Bibliography of the Dog; Check-list and Bibliography on the Occurrence of Insects in Birds' Nests*). Though some of these compilations may seem curious, they are important for showing what has been published on different subjects. Each gives a map of the world of books according to a certain specialized interest. Many of these bibliographies are evaluative and/or selective.

There is available in most libraries a tremendous amount of opinion about books. It should be searched out, weighed, and used for particular topics. Such information is a part of that network of knowledge which must be tapped if selection is to be intelligent.

8. BOOK REVIEWS

The working tools discussed so far, including national bibliographies, publishers' catalogs, general library guides, subject bibliographies, are all (with the exception of *Forthcoming Books* and its *Subject Guide . . .*) out of date when they come from the bindery. How then is the selector to obtain information on the suitability of books currently being published — about 160 each working day in the United States? One answer is: Read the reviews. They describe new books and usually give evaluative judgments by persons likely to be knowledgeable in the subjects covered. With experience in judging reviews, the selector is able to make assessments that would be difficult to formulate even upon reading the book itself. A 1975 survey shows the great importance attached to "favorable reviews" by all types of libraries.[1]

Book reviews go back to the nineteenth century, and now are about as plentiful as weeds; they crop up in nearly all periodicals and newspapers. Some journals are devoted entirely to such pieces (*Contemporary Psychology* and *Philosophical Books,* for example). Even small and obscure publications have their book review sections. Peter Berger once wrote, joking probably, that "the sensible person reads the sociological journals mainly for the book reviews and the obituaries."[2]

GENERAL REMARKS ON REVIEWS

In determining the place of book reviews in the building up of library collections, it may be better to look at them first in terms of the reading public, for whom most of them are prepared. Why are these notes and criticisms published so widely? For one thing, they represent news. People are interested, presumably, in books and ideas. One critic is dismayed that television is reviewed so little as compared with books, and points out that *Time,* in one thirteen-week interval, dealt with 102 books and 52 films, but only 5 TV programs.[3]

As an example of the seriousness with which a review may be taken: Norman Podhoretz, editor of *Commentary,* describes in his autobiography the inner conflict he went through while deciding that his review of Saul Bellow's novel, *The Adventures of Augie March,* should be unfavorable. Then, at a party some three years later, a drunken stranger, who turned out to be one of America's leading poets, staggered over to him and threatened, "We'll get you for that review if it takes ten years."[4]

In many periodicals, reviews appear late — sometimes long after the book has been published. Scholarly journals are exasperatingly slow, with lags of a year or two not uncommon. Such reviews still have value for the reader and may even influence selection in a library, but a 1981 review of a 1979 book is remarkably like a plate of cold fried eggs. A few editors make a conscientious effort to keep up to date, a practice which requires good planning and constant attention. In order to insure promptness, some journals send reviewers not the finished book but mere galley proofs, obtained from the publisher. From these long sheets the content of the book may be ascertained, but there is no way to determine whether errors will be corrected. The quality of paper and binding cannot be evaluated; neither can the illustrations, as a rule. It is fortunate, nevertheless, that at least a few periodicals use galley proofs for reviews, because promptness is so important to librarians.

Before a journal publishes a review the editor must decide that it is needed. To select the particular books to be reviewed is itself no easy task. Let us assume that of all the new books available in the English language, the journal has space to treat about one in thirty. Which one will be most appropriate for this journal? Presumably the editor chooses titles which promise most interest for his or her own readers, but may decide that a poor book can provide the starting point for an interesting review.

Another question is: Who should be asked to write the review? To obtain a criticism that shows subject competence, literary skill, and reasonable objectivity requires some knowledge. Shall the book be sent to another specialist in the field covered by the work in question, or would an amateur be better able to interpret the book for the journal's readership? Do readers like to see the same reviewers over and over? Here is the advice of Richard Kluger, former editor of *Book Week,* on "How to Pick a Book Reviewer":

1. Be suspicious.
2. Good writers often make good reviewers.
3. Good young reviewers are better than old bad ones.
4. Experts often know a lot about their subjects.
5. Poets should not review poetry.*
6. Liberals make better reviewers than conservatives.
7. Sometimes the person you'd most like to review a book turns out to be a splendid reviewer of it, even if he's not a writer.[5]

Many years ago Henry Seidel Canby and Amy Loveman established excellent principles to guide in the selection of reviewers for the old *Saturday Review of Literature.* Though these are negative, they reflect a high standard of choice:

1. The reviewer must not have written a book, or be preparing a book, on the same subject as the one now to be reviewed.
2. The reviewer must not be a personal friend or opponent of the author.
3. The reviewer must not have had his own books reviewed by the author of the book being considered.
4. The reviewer must not be known as a strong opponent of the main ideas in the book to be reviewed.[6]

Unfortunately, though these standards have been repeated in essence many times, not all editors follow them, as we shall see presently.

Do reviews influence people to buy books and to borrow them from libraries? It is difficult to say; too many factors have to be

*A professor of English deplores the practice of having novels reviewed by practitioners in the field. The resulting reviews are likely to be "frankly catty," or "overgenerous." (Geoffrey Wagner, "The Decline of Book Reviewing," *The American Scholar* 26 [Winter 1956–1957]: 33.)

accounted for. Some feel that reviews have little to do with the popularity of a book ("Reviews alone don't sell books," the distinguished publisher Alfred A. Knopf once declared). On the other hand, according to the 1975 survey, 96.2 percent of the publishers questioned did feel that favorable reviews sell books and 60 percent were afraid that unfavorable ones are detrimental.[7] A negative review may be better, though, than none at all. It is even possible that length of the review is significant, a short review implying a negligible book and a long one signaling that the book is important.

Though there is little evidence that a patron's choice among older books is influenced by the reviews they received, it is entirely reasonable to suppose that reviews of current books influence the public. In bookstores customers were questioned about the sources of information which had led them to buy. Eleven percent specified book reviews; only four percent advertisements. Twenty-one percent were influenced by friends, relatives or associates, but these persons may, in turn, have seen reviews or ads.[8] (Forty-seven percent mentioned browsing.) One investigator found that most readers of Erich Segal's 1970 novel, *Love Story,* had heard of it through another person. She then checked with the person named and so on back to the start of the chain. The first link, in over half the cases, was *The New York Times* — an ad, review, or note. Apparently this impact was greater even than Barbara Walter's television announcement that the book had made her cry all night.[9] Sometimes even scandalous publicity about a title creates wide interest in it. The library, on the basis of the demand theory, can buy prominently-reviewed books with the assurance that they will be requested by patrons. On this assumption, the popular newspaper and periodical reviewing media, especially, ought to be consulted regularly.

CAUTIONS ON THE USE OF REVIEWS

Having noted the possible place of reviews in assessing demand for books we shall now deal with them as aids to estimating quality, stressing first some of the factors which make them less than adequate; then commenting on the relative seriousness of these complaints.

Lack of Discrimination

A familiar charge has been that book reviews are not critical enough, that they either take no position on a book's value or are entirely too favorable. Louis Bromfield, over fifty years ago, tabulated reviews from fifty newspapers and literary periodicals for a year (thus using, of course, a small portion of the total media available) and found that 137 works in that year alone had been called "the best novel of the year," and he further ascertained that similar praise had been given to 27 biographies.[10]

Some years after that, LeRoy Merritt also noted this tendency, using a different approach. He studied *Book Review Digest* for the year 1948, analyzing the plus and minus signs then used by the *Digest* to designate favorable and unfavorable reviews, and found "a reluctance to condemn, and a strong tendency to say nothing one way or the other."[11] In 1956, according to a new sample, things had not changed much, except that there were more favorable and fewer noncommittal reviews.

In a later analysis, Guy A. Marco measured reviews' favorability on a scale of 0.00 to 3.00 (the former indicating all reviews to be negative, the latter all positive) and found the aggregate index for the reviews listed in *Book Review Digest* for 1957 to be 2.75. To the extent that pluses and minuses in *BRD* were accurate, this score also represented extremely high praise for books listed there.[12] It is no wonder that Elizabeth Hardwick, now on the staff of the *New York Review of Books,* was more than slightly caustic, writing:

> Sweet, bland commendations fall everywhere upon the scene.
> . . . A book is born into a puddle of treacle; the brine of hostile criticism is only a memory. Everyone is found to have "filled a need," and is to be "thanked" for something and to be excused for "minor faults in an otherwise excellent work." "A thoroughly mature artist" appears many times a week and often daily;

many are the bringers of those "messages the Free World will ignore at its peril."[13]

Did the same criticisms apply to the more scholarly journals? Not exactly, but an analysis of three leading sociology periodicals over selected years from 1949 to 1969 found that 68.3 percent of the reviews were positive; 18.2 percent, negative; and 13.5 percent, neutral.[14] The first number of the *Political Science Reviewer* complained (perhaps in part to justify its own existence), "It is no secret that individuals selected to review are sometimes obliged, in order to insure their pecking order in the profession, to render favorable reviews knowing that critical matters were overlooked by the author, his analysis was faulty, or the very purposes of his book were trivial."[15]

All this would indicate that up through the 1960s, a favorable review conferred little distinction on a book. In the 1970s, however, a reaction set in, and even the best books had their small faults blown up for public observation. Critics ridiculed authors with such witticisms as: "But the volume is pleasantly weighty in the hand, and when not otherwise employed would make an excellent door-stopper." With their rhetoric, reviewers became reminiscent, in tone if not in length, of the savage nineteenth-century critics who wrote for the *Edinburgh Review*. Currently there seem to be modifying trends. Praise comes a little more easily from reviewers, though scathing comment is frequent (for example, *"Scoundrel Time* is a tainted sandwich — one slice of inner life between two layers of bad history"[16]). More reviews show balance in their assessments.

Actually there are many reasons why the average book should receive at least a modicum of favorable comment. It has gained some distinction just by being published at all. Even the lowly work of a vanity press has the confidence of its author, who believes it good enough to risk money on. Since commercial publishers claim to accept, on the average, only one manuscript in ten (some say in twenty), a book which barely stumbles off the press has passed several hurdles, and is considered good by a few people, at least. Also, the fact that a book is reviewed means that it has interest for someone beyond the publisher and author. If a "standard" or popular journal runs a review, it is because the editor guesses that the book will have some appeal for thousands of people. A natural inclination to give readers news about "good" books, since that is more pleasant than complaints about poor ones, may out-weigh the editor's tendency to stress the controversial. In fact, one purpose of the reviewing system is to spread the word about worthwhile books. "In the last resort, the function of reviewers is to provoke other people to read good or interesting books," says John Putnam.[17] Furthermore, the review editor often gives priority to works by authors who are well-known and well-thought-of.[18]

All these considerations lead to the conclusion that reviews showing extreme hostility are often unwarranted. From the standpoint of library selection, a distribution of opinion between favorable and unfavorable reviews is far better. Criticisms then can reflect true discrimination, rather than follow the rhetorical style of the particular decade. To the library selector, an unusual book advancing novel themes may be considered a high priority item, even though reviews are almost sure to be mixed. Moreover, pontifications like Dwight MacDonald's denouncements of the *New York Times Book Review* for its mid-cult values need not be taken as gospel.[19] Some of the same people who read the general reviewing media are using the library — especially the public library — and mid-cult or not, they expect to find there the things they see reviewed.

Uneven Coverage

Some books thought by editors to be important or newsworthy receive, from the librarian's standpoint, almost too many reviews — perhaps fifty or sixty. On the other hand, a very good book may get too little notice. The editors of *The American Scholar* once asked a group of knowledgeable persons "to name that book published in the past quarter of a century that they believed to have been most undeservedly neglected."[20] The enthusiasm for a few of the unrecognized titles was considerable.

Fortunately, the review journals designed for library use have wide coverage, but there is no guarantee that all good books are included.

Bias

S. I. Hayakawa, in his well-known *Language in Thought and Action*, spoke of the difference between an author's reporting of facts and expressing personal feelings about a subject. It is significant that Hayakawa chose book reviews as prominent examples. "Some reviewers will be found to say little about the book and a great deal about their own tastes. Others write almost pure news stories, with little expression of their own likes or dislikes."[21]

Again there are several kinds or levels of bias. One may say that a journal is unfair in that it chooses to review books in certain subject fields, of certain length, of certain levels of difficulty, or in certain kinds of covers, but where is the commentator standing while making those accusations? Another kind of bias may be seen in the favor expressed for a particular set of ideas — religious, political, moral, educational, scientific, or whatever. Henry Regnery, a "conservative" publisher, once compared reviews of ten pairs of "similar" books, ranking opinions on the liberal-conservative political scale. He reached the tentative conclusion that *Library Journal* and *Booklist* were not decidedly biased, but added: "I think that rather consistent bias is indicated on the part of the *New York Times*. . . . If a similar examination were made of *Harper's, Atlantic,* the *Washington Post, Book Week,* or the *New York Review of Books,* the results would be about the same."[22]

How shall we look upon such analyses and charges? In Regnery's study, the evidence was meager and the critic still didn't clearly place the bias in the publications rather than in his own head. That reviewers follow the general editorial policies of the magazines which publish them does not necessarily mean that they willfully distort the truth. If a book is published extolling the virtues of evil and a theological journal takes issue with these views, that may be called bias, but such a review surely would not be damned (except by sinners, of course). Even then, some publications will fool the reader by acting out of character at times.

All this discussion must not be taken as an effort to minimize the importance of vigilance in the interpretation of reviews. To point out the fact that ideological prejudices and biases are difficult to spot and to measure is not to deny their existence; it's just that too much depends on the point-of-view of the person who makes the charge. The librarian's intelligence is taxed to the utmost in trying to discover the coverage and positions of the various media, in order to distill valuable information from them.

Related to the question of bias in journals is another objection to book reviews: that they sometimes are warped by personal considerations—that the reviewer may have a stake in the opinion offered. For years there have been suspicions that a literary establishment centered around the *New York Review of Books* and a few other journals not only gives preference to the works of certain publishers but assigns to particular books the reviewers known to be favorably disposed. One critic praises the books, plays, or ideas of other members of the in-group, then is recompensed when his or her own work comes up for evaluation. In a slashing book on this matter (which was published to mixed reviews), Richard Kostelanetz has a chapter entitled "The New York Literary Mob."[23] Somewhat different is a tabulation once made by *Time:* In reviewing books that complain about conditions in the public schools of the United States, each writer helped the reputation of a colleague:

> Holt lauded Kozol's book in the *New York Review of Books.* Kozol praised Holt's book in *Life* and Friedenberg's book in *The Christian Science Monitor.* Coles exalted the Kozol and Friedenberg books in reviews for the *New York Times.* Friedenberg, in turn, gushed over Kozol's writing in the *Saturday Review.* Kohn, who included a short story by Kozol in an anthology called *The Age of Complexity,* is writing a Holt rave for the *New York Review of Books.*[24]

It is no wonder that a critic once suggested that the title of one journal be changed to the *New York Review of Each Other's Books*. A thorough analysis, perhaps achievable by computer, of the links between authors, critics, and reviewers might throw more light on the subject.

Examination of general reviewing media does suggest the possibility that they favor certain publishers and authors. Furthermore, a sociologist suspects that "reviewers are more likely than other persons to have distinct personal biases for or against the authors of the works they review."[25] To get a balanced assortment of criticisms, the librarian needs to work with a variety of journals.

Hasty Composition

Although there is a strong demand for prompt reviews, there is also a tendency to fault them because they have been composed too quickly. Consider the plight of the reviewer, especially one writing in a popular journal for a general audience. The load of new books is staggering. There may be no time for a second reading of the book. The reviewer may be conscious of certain impressions but have little chance to assess their weight or to savor the writing and let it sink in. Will the impressions be the same if the book is re-read next week? By then the deadline will be past. Stanley Edgar Hyman referred to the reviewer's task as "wonderfully challenging and sharpening (one must begin to figure out the book from the first sentence), but it is also nerve-racking and wearying."[26] A writer for *Time* recalled reading eight books a week and reviewing five of them, "always dreading the moment when he had to sit down at the typewriter to turn out his 1,500 to 2,500 words."[27] The great historian of literary criticism, René Wellek, surely committed understatement when he remarked, with particular reference to the field of literature: "Ordinary book reviewing still mediates between the author and the general public by the old methods of impressionistic description and arbitrary pronouncements of taste."[28] Only a few, like Dr. Johnson, can write review after review fast, with little revision, yet produce work of real literary value.

From the standpoint of the author reviewed, a hastily-written article is not so pleasant either. In a posthumous essay, C. S. Lewis declared that the first thing he learned from reading reviews of his own books was "the extreme rarity of conscientiousness in that preliminary work which all criticism should presuppose. I mean, of course, a careful reading of what one criticizes."[29] John Updike called reviews of his books "humiliating. : . . All the little congruences and arabesques you prepared with such delicate anticipatory pleasure are gobbled up as if by pigs at a pastry cart."[30] Edmund Wilson once expressed his irritation:

> For an author, the reading of his reviews, whether favorable or unfavorable, is one of the most disappointing experiences in life. He has been laboring for months or for years to focus some comprehensive vision or to make out some compelling case, and then finds his book discussed by persons who not only have not understood it, but do not even in some instances appear to have read it.[31]

That Wilson's charge was not entirely unfounded was shown by a 1951 study which pretty well proved that most newspaper and even some scholarly reviewers had used mainly a publisher's handout rather than the book itself as a basis for their remarks.[32] There is a general feeling that such miserable practices continue, but it is to be hoped that they are exceptional.

As to the less serious shortcomings of reviewers, their lack of perceptiveness is regrettable but to some extent understandable. We really cannot expect promptness and profound thought both in the same review. George Bernard Shaw refused to produce one of his famous prefaces unless he had several months to write and revise. We can't afford to wait that long to obtain a masterpiece for a review. The important thing is that library book selectors recognize the level of quality likely to be found in reviews, and appreciate the fact that such opinions do contribute valuable information to our store of knowledge about books.

Now that the warning flags have been hoisted, it is safe to conclude with a word of appreciation for the multitudes of excellent, perceptive reviews that do appear. Intelligent, critical evaluations of books are by no means unusual. Many reviews are a delight to read; some are substantive essays in their own right. At its best, a review continues the work of scholarship started in the book itself. A serious treatise usually builds on facts and ideas previously known. It brings in new data or gives a fresh interpretation, thus carrying on an old discussion and at the same time initiating a new one. The good reviewer advances this process another step by pointing out what is significant in the book, what its principal contribution is. This critic may add supplementary matter, may oppose some or all the work's conclusions, but builds on the same structure of ideas as did the author. For the librarian, such pieces are invaluable aids in forming judgments about the particular work's uniqueness and merit.

SOME TYPES OF REVIEWING MEDIA

To make sense out of the overgrown jungle of reviews is a good-sized task. It is a pleasant one, though, and the more one learns, the more interesting it becomes. This is another way in which a librarian becomes a real professional. Gradually impressions are formed as to which journals just tack on reviews, apparently to fill space, and which ones treat reviews as serious business.

Reviewing media should be considered also in terms of audiences for which they are published. The same work will be reviewed differently for one group of people than for another; hence an intelligent interpretation depends on a knowledge of the intended readership. For a given book, a reviewer in one field may see great value, while a periodical in a different area may find it uninteresting or useless. The point is illustrated in a playful way by the review of D. H. Lawrence's famous novel, in *Field & Stream:*

> Although written many years ago, *Lady Chatterley's Lover* has just been reissued by Grove Press, and this fictional account of

the day-by-day life of an English gamekeeper is still of considerable interest to outdoor-minded readers, as it contains many passages on pheasant raising, the apprehending of poachers, ways to control vermin, and other chores and duties of the professional gamekeeper. Unfortunately one is obliged to wade through many pages of extraneous material in order to discover and savor these sidelights on the management of a Midlands shooting estate, and in this reviewer's opinion this book cannot take the place of J. R. Miller's *Practical Gamekeeping*. [33]

From the standpoint of library selection purposes, three groups of reviewing media may be identified: (1) general, (2) subject-centered, and (3) those prepared for the booktrade and for libraries.

General

Reviewing media aimed at the general public carry fewer reviews, as a rule, than those issued for librarians and booksellers. The former naturally are confined to books of wide interest (fiction, biography, history, and current affairs are given considerable attention); hence they are helpful to public librarians in particular and should not be neglected by others.

The New York Times Book Review probably is the best such service issued in connection with any American newspaper, reviewing about 2,500 items each year.[34] According to one study it was very prompt in reviewing a sample of titles on the ALA Notable Books list.[35] It features well-known reviewers and is a favorite advertising medium of the publishers. Added attractions are special departments, such as "Crime" and "Paperbacks: New and Noteworthy." There is a cumulative index to the reviews: *The New York Times Book Review Index, 1896–1970* (New York: The New York Times and Arno, 1973) in five large volumes—approaches by author, title, byline, subject, and category).

Other leading papers also have book review columns and even special sections. They should be read by the librarian in self-defense, if for no other reason, because patrons will peruse them and want to read some of the books reviewed.

The New York Review of Books, which began in 1963 during a newspaper strike in the city, is a most interesting journal, with its long reviews (about four hundred a year) sometimes covering several books each, and its great ugly caricatures of notable personages. Its political position has been described as "cocktail-party revolutionary." It has excited fierce controversy, but its defenders have been staunch ("the most respected intellectual journal in the English language," said one).[36] The same author summed up its strengths and weaknesses as a book review medium: "Neither as good nor as necessary as it once was, but still the repository of selected magnificent reviews."[37] The *Review*'s early position that any book is to be considered guilty until proved innocent has been tempered a bit. It does give favorable reviews when it takes a notion—sometimes on unlikely occasions. The reviews often take the form of long, rather opinionated essays which wander out into general discussions, having used the book merely as a jumping-off place. (One of its lengthy reviews was reprinted later as a short book). This practice may be disconcerting to the busy librarian who prefers quick recommendations, but it provides good reading for those who have the time.

The wonderful *Times Literary Supplement* (London) resumed publication in the fall of 1979 after a lapse caused by a strike. Its many reviews, almost all knowledgeable, witty, and urbane, cover the most interesting books currently produced in Britain, plus a few from other countries.

The *Saturday Review* began in 1924, and had *of Literature* as an added part of its title until 1952. It carries semipopular discussions of recordings, films, theatre, and other forms of communication. Its criticisms of books are usually perceptive and sometimes long, but as a review medium it is not what it once was, despite recent attempts to improve its quality.

Books & Arts, a fortnightly (once a supplement to the *Chronicle of Higher Education*), deals with books on many subjects, plus fiction, as well as films, television, and records. Reviews are knowledgeable and often lengthy. They sometimes include lists of other titles by the reviewed author and excerpts from forth-coming books.

A number of monthly magazines are known for good reviews. *Harper's* has a few long and a few short ones in each issue. *Atlantic* usually publishes one long, several short, and a group of very short reviews; the latter, by Phoebe-Lou Adams under the heading "PLA," being remarkable examples of conciseness. *Commentary* has several good-sized reviews each month.

The weekly *New Republic* has long been known for its high standards of reviewing. In 1971 it initiated an interesting series: "reconsiderations" of classics, beginning with a long "review" of *The Varieties of Religious Experience,* written by William James in 1902, and continuing with such works as Graham Greene's *The End of the Affair.* Sometimes a person, rather than a book, is reconsidered. The general newsweeklies *Time* and *Newsweek* with their signed reviews are useful for fairly substantive information and also serve as good indicators of the public's interests.

Of the quarterlies which cover several fields, *The Yale Review* gives special attention to reviews. Its "Reader's Guide" section is found at the beginning of each issue, and longer criticisms are given in the part "New Books in Review."

Subject-centered Periodicals

Typically the "scholarly" or specialized journals publish competently-written reviews, but these do not differ from reviews in the better general media as much as might be expected (though one in *Art Bulletin.* [61, June 1979] does have 131 footnotes). Some years ago, Victoria Hargrave made a close comparison of the two types, finding that scholarly periodicals were a little more likely to be evaluative and that their judgments usually were less favorable to the works being reviewed, but concluding that in many respects the two types were alike.[38] That generalization probably would still hold for most fields of study, but the wide differences among journals and among individual reviewers must not be overlooked. Perhaps it should be repeated here that one trouble with the typical scholarly journal is its tardiness.

Some of these periodicals publish 150 to 200 pages of book reviews each issue. To chose titles almost at random there are: *American Historical Review, American Political Science Review, American Journal of Sociology, Modern Language Review, Philosophical Review, Speculum.* Hundreds of others carry large book review sections.

Recent years have seen the growth of a special kind of medium, the journal devoted entirely or almost so to reviews of books in a single discipline. For instance, the American Psychological Association decided some years ago to start *Contemporary Psychology* and to omit reviews from its other journals. Though the author of a psychology book may feel that too much depends on a single review in this journal, the assurance of a capable reviewer may be a consolation (or a cause for regret, depending on the evaluation of the book). Other journals in psychology—those not published by APA—may, of course, review the work also. There are dozens of similar publications, including *Reviews in American History* (and others for history), *Reviews in Anthropology, Classical Review, Philosophical Books,* and *Political Science Reviewer* (an annual).

Booktrade and Library

Those journals aimed directly at booksellers and/or publishers have information which may be useful also to the library. Among these, *Publishers Weekly* is perusable for its section "Forecasts" about books to come. Here some 4,400 adult and 600 juvenile books are previewed briefly (and usually a bit over-enthusiastically) each year. The advertisements of new books are most interesting. Sometimes a title by an important author may be selected and ordered merely on the basis of such an ad. The articles about book production and selling also are good background for librarians.

Another medium, which began as a service for booksellers but which is now prepared for librarians too, is *Kirkus Reviews*. It comes out twice a month, giving short, sometimes witty, reviews of books to be published within the following six weeks or so, based on galley proofs. Publication date and other order information are given. Its cumulated indexes are a convenience. This publication is better than its low-cost format might suggest. It is often used by public libraries and would be of help also in school libraries. Furthermore, a sampling indicates that about a third of the books it reviews are relevant to college libraries. In a typical year it will deal with about 4,000 books.

British Book News must be classed somewhere in here. A monthly with some added numbers, it gives short reviews of current British books, under ten subject headings.

Another group of journals is published especially for librarians, and many of these have good general reviews of books. The best example is *Library Journal,* which comes out twice a month, except for July and August, with numerous reviews (over 6,000 a year, counting all types) arranged by large topic, such as Reference, Arts, Biography, Education, Music, etc. Many of the reviews are written by librarians with special interests in the subject covered by the book, but professors and other authorities also contribute. They are economical of words, and often indicate clearly whether the item is recommended. Without taking anything from the excellence of *LJ,* a caveat needs to be inserted here: to the beginner, these reviews may appear to be the answer to a prayer, but their brevity can lead to oversimplification. Since 1968, an annual volume, *Library Journal Book Reviews,* has reprinted all reviews of adult books from *LJ.* The companion periodical, *School Library Journal,* carries reviews of books and other materials for children and young adults. It cumulates the book information yearly in a bound volume, *School Library Journal Book Reviews.*

Booklist, published by the American Library Association, is made up of two distinct parts (until 1969 it was entitled *Booklist and Subscription Books Bulletin*). In the first part, *Booklist* proper, general books, all of which are recommended in some measure or other, are given short reviews (or long annotations). Written by members of the journal's own editorial staff, they are more consistent than are those in *Library Journal*. (Both media are a kind of antithesis of the *New York Review of Books*.) *Booklist*, like *LJ*, is well indexed and usually is quite prompt with these reviews, covering about 6,700 titles a year. It includes audio-visual works and has a special editor for these nonprint materials.

The second part of this periodical gives long, detailed analyses of new reference books. Each review is prepared by a member of the ALA Reference and Subscription Books Review Committee or by a guest author, and is sanctioned by the other fifty members of the committee before going to press. A detailed manual advises reviewers on what is expected. The size of the Committee and the complexity of the procedures tend to delay publication, but the finished reviews are authoritative. Factual information about each title is given, along with a clear indication of whether the committee recommends purchase or not. This cold, impersonal objectivity is rare and valuable, though reviews in other journals are more lively and witty.

Library Review, published in Scotland, has a special "Review Feature" in each issue, covering materials on one theme—science, the arts, or whatever.

On a more specialized plane, *Choice: Books for College Libraries*, published by the Association of College and Research Libraries, is designed for undergraduate collections but also is useful in the high school and public library. It has short reviews (about 6,500 of them each year), written chiefly by college faculty members. Authors of particular reviews are not indicated, since their contributions are rewritten in the editorial office. The reviews are available also on cards. Most of the titles dealt with are automatically recommended, though in some instances the reviewer will point out the existence of a previous, better book on the same subject. Special introductory sections deal with such topics as outstanding reference books, government publications, erotica, Communism, atlases, "sleuthography," and so on. Reviews generally are of good quality, but are slow to appear. Reviews for the period 1964–1974 are published together in *Choice: A Classified Cumulation*, edited by Richard K. Gardner and Phyllis

Grumm with the assistance of Julia Johnson (Totowa, NJ: Rowman & Littlefield, 1976–77, 9 vols.).

As a means of locating previously published reviews in various sources there are several excellent indexes. *Book Review Digest,* though somewhat limited in coverage, has the advantage of offering excerpts from the reviews. A cumulated author-title index, dealing with the years 1905–1974, was published in 1976, in four volumes. Covering the same years with a somewhat broader scope is *The National Library Service Cumulative Book Review Index, 1905–1974* (Princeton, NJ: National Library Service Co., 1975, 6 vols.).

Book Review Index lists reviews from a much larger group of periodicals than does *BRD,* and is more prompt, but does not give excerpts. *Current Book Review Citations,* begun in 1976, covers reviews published in over 1,200 periodicals, by author and title of book.

Canadian Book Review Digest and *Canadian Book Review Annual* are valuable for use both in that country and in the United States.

Several more specialized, expensive indexes to reviews have been published during the last few years, but when in the small library it seems important to find an elusive review, there may be some profit in going directly to annual indexes of periodicals in the relevant subject field. Usually, more concise evaluations of older works can be found in encyclopedias, handbooks, and annotated bibliographies.

PART III

SELECTION OF PARTICULAR TYPES
OF PRINTED MATERIALS

This part of the book will consider some of the kinds of printed materials, other than "common" books, that are collected by most libraries. Each of the five types discussed in this section — free and inexpensive publications (Chapter 9), government documents (Chapter 10), periodicals (Chapter 11), reference works (Chapter 12), and out-of-print books (Chapter 13) — has its particular values and presents its own problems in selection. Each type also has its appropriate guides and other selection tools that are useful to the librarian.

The approach in Part III will be general so far as subject matter is concerned. A wide range of topics can be found in each of these kinds of publication. In Part V, reference will be made to some of these special forms of material in connection with the subject fields discussed there.

9. FREE AND INEXPENSIVE MATERIALS

Because the main object in selection is to obtain, within the budget, the best material for the library's patrons, it pays to survey the wide range of useful material offered at low cost. A surprising number of such items are available, and by a sensible use of selection tools, the librarian can stretch dollars. False economy, however, must be resisted. No material is really added to the library without cost; even the smallest item involves some expense. If the great Charles Cutter was right when he said, "A librarian ordinarily collects pamphlets as unhesitatingly as a little dog runs out and barks at the passing buggy," [1] let us hope that things have changed.

For a publication which is advertised as "free," what are the costs involved in making it part of the library?

1. The decision to request the item takes time — expensive human time; yet it is poor economy to ask for materials without thinking. What a wretched mess of stuff would be accumulated if donors — personal, commercial, institutional — were asked to pour in anything they thought the small library could possibly want. Even if a pile of books is delivered to the door by a generous attic-cleaner, time is required to sort out any volumes that should be kept and to dispose of the remainder.

2. Any procedure for ordering costs a little (though every library should have a form on postal cards for requesting quickly and efficiently "free" books, pamphlets, films, and other items that are offered). When the material arrives, unpacking boxes and sorting the mail adds to the cost.

3. To process and prepare material for readers' use takes supplies such as ink, labels, and cards, but the big cost here is staff time — salaries and overhead. The unitiated are astounded at the total. It is true that pamphlets may be housed in vertical files and given subject listing only, thus reducing the expense, but good cataloging and classification for a "free" book costs as much as

for an expensive one. It can go well above ten dollars per title.

4. After a book has been put in place on the shelves, the costs continue. Money is needed just to keep it there year after year, even if the poor thing be touched only by the hand of the duster. A conservative estimate of this annual expense for an average-sized book would be forty cents.

5. Ironically, it even costs money to rid the library of material. After a decision is made to discard an item, and it is stamped and signed, changing records in the catalog and/or other files may easily require a couple of dollar's worth of time — more in the average library.

For these reasons, most of the general selection criteria will hold, in modified form, for inexpensive or free items. All material ought to be chosen with care. A book is not to be obtained just because of its low cost. One gets the impression that there are a few librarians who have not learned this lesson: one high-priced (say, fifty-dollar) book may be worth more to a library than twenty cheap (three-dollar) ones. Furthermore, though processing costs could run over ten dollars for the fine book, they might well approach two hundred dollars for the twenty cheap ones. All this is said not to minimize the importance of lower-priced materials, but to emphasize this most important consideration: how much does an item cost fully processed, and how much is it really worth to the readers? The latter figure is hard to estimate. It may be many times the size of the former.

EPHEMERA

Certain printed items are made to be used briefly and then thrown away. Some of them, such as greeting cards and wedding invitations, usually are printed well; others, such as tickets and memos, don't look very good. For some libraries, materials of this kind are appropriate and worthwhile. A collection of matchbook covers may provide raw materials for research in social history. A group of posters may be of interest to artists and designers. (Here cataloging costs can be held to the minimum.)

PAMPHLETS AND SIMILAR FORMS

Definitions of the word "pamphlet" have varied considerably over the years;[2] even now there is not complete agreement. The most commonly accepted upper size limit is forty-eight pages. Frequently a printer will arrange type forms so that eight pages go through the press on each run. Since the finished publication is then made up of these gatherings (or signatures), printed on both sides to make sixteen pages each, it is logical for the line between pamphlet and book to be drawn at some multiple of this number.

This kind of publication often presents discussion of a topic in a length suitable to the needs of some readers at a particular stage of growth or interest. The heavy volume on the one hand seems forbidding; the periodical article on the other may be incomplete, or may be bound in with a load of other matter which is not of concern to the particular reader.

The manner in which pamphlets and periodicals relate to, and supplement, one another is worthy of further note. Lester Condit spoke of pamphlets as used in the early seventeenth century to distribute information in science, and referred to the Royal Society of London's *Philosophical Transactions,* perhaps the earliest English-language periodical, as being really a collection of pamphlets.[3] Frank Luther Mott, in his monumental work *A History of American Magazines, 1741–1850,* termed the magazine "a bound pamphlet."[4] The two forms of publication are in many ways similar. In our time, however, to publish a periodical in good format is quite a financial undertaking, generally requiring heavy capital outlay and a big organization. For this reason, it may be said that, theoretically at least, pamphlets are the more likely to present unusual ideas. They often advance points of view not easily found in periodicals of the type considered "standard" for smaller libraries. They represent the ideas of people with strong opinions. This is the very reason why a good number of pamphlets, posters, and similar materials are free or inexpensive. They are subsidized by people who believe in their messages (or who expect to benefit by their advertising value).

The pamphlet then is one of the best vehicles for bringing divergent opinion into the library.

The fact that so many pamphlets are instruments of propaganda has led to a general suspicion or even fear of them. In the United States just prior to World War II, this feeling was especially strong, and warnings were issued against the danger that such materials might bring about an imbalance in favor of some odious point of view. Worries were voiced about pamphlets written for purposes of deceit — to warp the minds of the unsuspecting. Depending on the breadth of the definition assigned to the word *propaganda,* it may be asked whether heeding these strange warnings would leave much of anything in the file. Such cautions ill become a free society. Some pamphlets which advocate unpopular ideas may in the long run prove to be the most valuable publications for people to read. It little profits a person to read over and over the things that agree with established prejudices. In any event, if dangerous ideas are being promulgated by way of pamphlets, responsible citizens ought to know about them firsthand.

Those pamphlets which are viewed as ephemeral are taken lightly in many libraries. Neglect of such items may make good sense up to a point; permanent works plainly are more important. But how many times have librarians overlooked materials while they are readily available, only to buy them later at inflated prices? A description found in Saul Bellow's novel *The Adventures of Augie March* may be instructive. Augie once worked for a man named Einhorn, on the Chicago south side. Einhorn was something of an operator.

> He sent away for everything that was free: samples of food, soaps, medicine, the literature of all causes, reports of the Bureau of American Ethnology and publications of the Smithsonian Institute, the Bishop Museum in Hawaii, the *Congressional Record,* laws, pamphlets, prospectuses, college catalogs, quack hygiene books, advice on bust-development, on getting rid of pimples, on longevity and Couéism, pamphlets on Fletcherism, Yoga, spirit-rapping, anti-vivisection; he was on the mailing list of the

Henry George Institute and the Rudolf Steiner Foundation in London, the local bar association, the American Legion. . . . And all this material he kept; the overflow went down to the basement. . . . some of it, when it went out of print, he sold to bookstores or libraries.[5]

Though pamphlets are the form of inexpensive material most often collected by libraries, other forms (including nonprint) should not be overlooked. Posters and charts often are available at very low cost. Study prints (pictures of various sizes) illustrate ideas and facts in many fields of interest. A file of clippings on matters of local concern is well worth the trouble. If a staff member ever has any time to spare, it may be spent profitably in such efforts.

REPRESENTATIVE GUIDES

George Peabody College for Teachers. *Free and Inexpensive Learning Materials.* (Nashville, TN: The College, 1941– , biennially)

This periodic list has been valuable over the years, but its future is not known. It encompasses pamphlets as well as such other materials as pictures, posters, maps, and charts, using general headings of interest to the classroom teacher. The topics (not the same in every edition) include Africa, Philosophy and religion, Sewing, Alcohol and drugs, Diseases, and about a hundred more. Altogether some 3,000 to 4,000 items are noted in a typical edition of the guide.

Vertical File Index: A Subject and Title Index to Selected Pamphlet Material. (New York: Wilson, 1932– , monthly except August)

The name of this index is derived from the type of filing cabinet used for these materials, in which the folders are placed in vertical (straight up) position, rather than lying flat or horizontally.

Arranged by subject heading, the list includes a wide assortment of topics from Hobbies to Taxes. Price or ordering instructions are given for each item.

Public Affairs Information Service Bulletin. (New York: PAIS, 1915– , twice a month with quarterly and annual cumulations)

This venerable publication includes printed works (many of them low-priced) in all the usual formats. Its scope is "information likely to be most useful and interesting to legislators, administrators, the business and financial community, policy researchers and students."[6]

Priscilla Gotsick, et al. *Information for Everyday Survival: What You Need and Where to Get it.* (Chicago: American Library Association, 1976, 403 p.)

Made up for the most part of free and inexpensive easy-to-read materials on vital problems, this list can be used for selection in most public libraries and many others besides.

Sources: A Guide to Print and Nonprint Materials Available from Organizations, Industry, Government Agencies, and Specialized Publishers. (New York: Gaylord Professional Publications in association with Neal-Schuman Publishers, Inc., 1977, three times a year)

This compilation is arranged alphabetically by name of issuing agency, and its principal value lies in this list of suppliers. Access to individual publications, however, is facilitated by title and subject indexes.

The Educators Progress Service, Randolph, Wisconsin regularly issues several lists, such as: *Educators Guide to Free Science Materials; Educators Guide to Free Health, Physical Education and Recreation Materials;* and *Educators Guide to Free Social Studies Materials.* While known primarily for nonprint materials, the series also include printed ones.

Two discerning articles by Ned Kehde in *American Libraries* point out the significance of political and social pamphlets in our time and give sources from which they come: "The New Left and a New Age of Pamphlets," (Vol. 1, October 1970, p. 873–877) and "The American Right and Pamphleteering" (Vol. 1, November 1970, p. 965–967). Mr. Kehde has also edited and compiled a 515-page catalog of United States and Canadian pamphlets: *The American Left, 1955–1970* (Westport, CT: Greenwood Press, 1976). A regular feature of the journal *Collection Building* is the list "Free and Inexpensive Materials" by Kathleen Weibel.

Shirley Miller points out something of the amazing variety of materials which a librarian may obtain simply by touring the city and seeking items from such places as the chamber of commerce, travel agencies, stores, banks, the sheriff's office, and political party headquarters.[7]

GIFTS AND EXCHANGES

Materials come to the library from many sources — some of them other libraries. Gift and exchange lists are sent out by one library in the hope that other institutions can use the discards. Though the process is costly, it does save many books from destruction. The materials usually are offered free except for transportation. While perusing such lists the librarian fights hard in order not to be discouraged by the quality of the materials offered. In a more systematic way, Universal Serials and Book Exchange (formerly U.S. Book Exchange), a nonprofit organization in Washington, DC, offers books, periodicals, and pamphlets from a stock of millions of items. Costs of operating are covered by membership fees and handling charges. From the standpoint of both compiler and scanner, exchange lists work better for periodicals because dozens of separate issues can be brought together under one title, whereas, for monographs and pamphlets, a separate title must be used for each item.

Individuals and families — usually well-meaning friends of the library — bestow gifts, and it is one of the delights of librarianship to find in a box of dusty books some long-sought item. It does happen. An unfortunate aspect, though, is that now and then some person will overvalue a donation. This may be a natural tendency to prize highly what has been collected over the years, or it may be an attempt to gain an unfair tax advantage. Letters of acknowledgement, therefore, should, while having a courteous tone, be carefully worded. A librarian who places a definite value on a gift may be called upon by the Internal Revenue Service to defend that opinion. Usually it is better for the librarian to advise the donor that a professional appraiser may be of service.

An old rule has it that a library should accept all gifts, provided no strings are attached. That is to say, the library should be extremely slow to make any agreement, oral or written, as to separate housing, classification, or care for the materials so received. Special treatment for any collection is an incalculable expense, and furthermore may be considered unfair by other donors whose treasures cannot be thus honored. The library should have an understanding with the donor that it is free to dispose of any item as it sees fit. Clarity on this point is most important, because a person who has painstakingly built up a collection regards it as an extension of personality — and is right. The sad fact is that usually it represents no one else. That terms relating to donations can be misunderstood is suggested by Randolph G. Adams, who in a famous article told this story: Mr. Edmund Lester Pearson said that he intended to leave his books to a public library, with no strings attached, but "of course, Mr. Pearson hastened to add, he would require the books to be kept in a separate room which was to be equipped with pink silk-damask chairs, silver lamps, and a curator who at all times wore a cutaway coat. Moreover, the catalog cards were to have gilt edges, and each book was to be forever sealed in a cellophane wrapper."[8] To the donor these strings were not stringent.

A different problem is created when religious, political, and other organizations offer gifts of materials, possibly with the intention of using the library as a free center for the distribution of propaganda. Whether to process and keep them or refuse them is a dilemma. On the one hand, to reject materials that set minority groups in a favorable light smacks of censorship. On the other hand, if such gifts are accepted, other groups will see their chance and there will be no end to future donations. The objection is logical and the fear real. Therefore the library might be wise to announce that, at its own discretion, it will charge a processing fee of five dollars or so for each book added to the collection. As a result of this compromise, those believing strongly in their positions could be represented, and the library would be protected against spending its scarce processing money on acquisitions of relatively little interest. Such a plan would not, of course, do away with charges of unfairness, but it might reduce them considerably. Another compromise is to place such "unwanted" materials in a collection off to themselves, without benefit of processing.

No one should conclude from these remarks that gifts are mainly a nuisance to libraries. Once the library makes clear its policies and procedures with regard to retention and disposition, gifts can be highly important in building collections, especially in times of economic difficulty. What better inexpensive memorial to a deceased person is there than a book given to a library? Important and expensive reference sets have been donated by groups which have sponsored their publication. Every library should compile and have available a list of materials it wants but cannot afford. Many potential donors simply do not know that gifts are appreciated. Stories about aggressiveness and the use of strategy to obtain valuable donations are an interesting part of the lore of librarianship.

10. PUBLIC DOCUMENTS

Following the discussion of inexpensive materials, it is now appropriate to turn to government publications, because many of them are low-priced pamphlets (though some long sets cost hundreds of dollars). That governments — local, state, and national — as well as international organizations should publish on such a large scale is a remarkable development, reflecting, at least in free societies, faith in the people's ability to use information. It is significant that a study of Russian scientists some years ago found that they used practically no government-sponsored reports in their research.[1] Do government publications present a fair and unbiased picture? According to I. F. Stone, they "don't like to lie, because a lie can be discovered. What they do is leave out part of the truth."[2] Yet there is no good evidence that in this respect they are much worse than other publications.

For the librarian, document territory is a strange but interesting and important part of the world of books. These publications include some of the dullest, most routine matter ever lodged between covers; but also some of the most fascinating — colorful and well-written. Even the dull material is sometimes important. As for the economic aspects, the United States federal government in particular often provides good value for the dollar, in spite of the sharp price increases of recent years. For many subjects, even those not related to government operations or problems, a document will present approaches and coverage not found in encyclopedias, periodicals, or commercially-produced books.

In spite of these facts, there is ample evidence that these materials do not receive use commensurate with their value, and Fry is undoubtedly correct in the opinion that "government publications are recognized as probably the most neglected and under-utilized information resource available to the public."[3] Even at the university level, a survey indicated that faculty use "is not keeping pace with the increasing emphasis given them [documents] by librarians and commercial publishers," though social scientists did make substantial use of them.[4] Fortunately public documents are beginning to receive more attention. The many indexes now being published make their use easier and more practical.

A good continuing service for the general library is the regular feature of the journal *Government Publications Review*: "Selection Guide to High Interest Government Publications," which lists federal, state, and international works, plus some from foreign governments, and now and then those issued by American cities.

There are several ways to consider the millions of government publications that have been issued and are still coming. Probably the most obvious approach is by level of "authorship," or jurisdiction.

INTERNATIONAL

What happens in any part of the world can affect the lives of people in the smallest American town. The books, pamphlets, and periodicals issued by the United Nations and its agencies, such as UNESCO or the Food and Agriculture Organization (FAO), and by other international organizations, such as the World Bank, are highly significant for students and for other citizens. An excellent overview is given in Peter I. Hajnal's *Guide to United Nations Organization, Documentation & Publishing, for Students, Researchers, Librarians* (Dobbs Ferry, NY: Oceana Publications, 1978, 450 p.) After a description of UN structure and publication patterns, the author gives "a practical guide to the use, acquisition, and organization of United Nations publications," and "a select annotated bibliography of primary and secondary material" (p. xxviii).

The majority of these international publications are listed in *UNDOC: Current Index* (New York: United Nations, 1979–), which succeeds a series of indexes which began in 1950. This comprehensive checklist, published ten times a year with an annual cumulation, offers access by subject, author, and title. The annual *United Nations Publications in Print* (New York: UN Sales Section, 1977–) is a buying guide useful to medium-sized and larger libraries. Publications of other international organizations are listed in *International Bibliography, Information, Documentation* (New York: Unipub, 1973–   ).

U.S. FEDERAL

At the next level are the independent nations, the most important for our purposes being the United States federal government, which issues each year over 30,000 items which might be termed "of general interest." Most of these documents are available in microform — microfilm, microcards, or microfiche — produced either by the Government Printing Office or by private firms. If an item is expected to receive relatively little use in the library, a microform is a particularly good buy, but many of the documents are of such great interest as to justify the acquisition of regular paper editions. Federal documents are commonly considered under three heads, corresponding to the branches of government: legislative, executive, and judicial.

Legislative

When a bill is introduced in Congress, it is printed for distribution. Congressional committees hold hearings on pending bills, and these proceedings also are recorded and printed — hundreds of thousands of pages a year. Obviously some of the topics are of general interest. Many of the speakers testifying at these hearings have a personal stake in the proposed legislation, but very often the documents also contain expert information presented by authorities on their subjects (for example, see the National Arts and Humanities Foundation, Joint Hearings. . .).

If the bill is passed it is printed as law; these laws are later grouped together as the *Statutes at Large* and are in turn organized in a more understandable form as *The United States Code*. All are crucial to the American citizen because they represent actions of Congress and tell a person things which can be done (legally), things which can't, and things which *must* be done. *The Congressional Record,* which was read, along with other strange documents, by H. L. Mencken (because, he said, it represented attempts at expression by human beings), is an eye-opener in showing what goes on (and on) in the United States House and Senate (for instance, over 2,000 words commending Dave McNally for pitching the Baltimore Orioles to a 9–3 victory over Cincinnati in the 1970 World Series — a matter of considerably higher interest than are tributes to fellow politicians).

Executive

Moving on to the White House and the executive departments of the federal government, we may think of their publications as being of three types: (1) Some documents are official-sounding and have to do with the operation of the government itself. Such works, though important, usually are dry and tedious, as, *The Interstate Commerce Commission Reports* and *Budget of the United States Government.* The *Federal Register,* which publicizes executive orders and proclamations of the President, along with minute rules and regulations of the various departments of the executive branch, is fearsome to contemplate but is relieved by such trivia as holiday proclamations. The regulations are organized systematically in the *Code of Federal Regulations.* (2) Some documents are devoted to the distinctive characteristics or problems of the United States or a part of it, as, *Surface Water Supply of the United States,* the Department of Commerce's *Climatological Data,* and treatises devoted to protection of the environment. (3) There are publications designed mainly to help the individual citizen or family, explaining how to select tires, how to build a catfish pond, or how to choose clothing. The Department of Health, Education, and Welfare had a kit called *The Power of Positive Parenting.* Data and constructive ideas on education, public health, social security, and similar concerns are distributed by the new DHHS. Short pamphlets give helpful hints from the Department of Agriculture to both rural and urban dwellers. (These few samples simply are not adequate to show the scope and variety of the offerings.)

Many federal government publications have more than one

use. The huge volumes issued by the Bureau of the Census (Department of Commerce), representing information gathered at a cost of over a billion dollars, are consulted by people in many different endeavors. The *Statistical Abstract of the United States,* published each year by the same department, gives millions of bits of information for a few dollars. Facts about the budget, customs duties, and income tax are promulgated by the Treasury Department. (I know a man who saved some four hundred dollars in personal income taxes one year because he took a few minutes to consult *Your Federal Income Tax,* published by the Internal Revenue Service and then selling for fifty cents.) A character in Arthur Hailey's novel *The Moneychangers* refers to the U.S. Treasury's popular pamphlet *Know Your Money* as 'the forger's handbook" because it helps counterfeiters avoid the more obvious mistakes, which people can spot.[5]

Some of the publications issued by the executive branch are elaborate, representing millions of dollars spent in research and on fine printing. For instance, the U.S. Navy's *The Marine Climatic Atlas of the World* (in six volumes) is a marvel of fact-gathering and of the presentation of millions of small data in graphic form. The reports of the National Aeronautics and Space Agency showing planets and moons also represent excellence in text and picture. For a colorful set on an unpleasant subject, there is the three-volume *Poisonous and Venomous Marine Animals of the World,* sponsored by agencies of the Army, Navy, and Air Force. The many publications on fishes, birds, and national parks show the nation's wealth of resources.

Judicial

From the judicial branch of the federal government, the most important items distributed are the decisions of the United States Supreme Court, called *U.S. Reports: Cases Adjudged in the Supreme Court.* (Each case is also published separately.) During a typical term, the court reviews about one hundred and fifty of the thousands of cases presented for its attention, and these decisions are of central importance in American life. Paradoxically — and maybe tragically, when the future of the republic is contemplated — this highly provocative, widely-quoted, and oft-cursed journal of opinion is seldom read comprehensively. Librarians could increase the significance of their service by making it more accessible, for the opinions of the justices might be better understood if more citizens read them directly, instead of depending on the hastily-produced analyses in the newspapers or on the television.

Lists of Federal Documents

The most thorough (though not complete) listing of current federal items is:

U.S. Superintendent of Documents, *Monthly Catalog of United States Government Publications,* 1895– (Washington: Government Printing Office, 1895–)

The catalog began when the Office of the Superintendent of Documents was established, under the jurisdiction of the Public Printer. With its subject, author, title, and series indexes in each monthly number, plus semi-annual, annual, and comprehensive indexes, the set as a whole is a reasonably complete bibliography of all the branches. Its predecessors (large index sets) are good for reference work, but not for selection. The arrangement of the *Monthly Catalog* by issuing agency (as, Agriculture Department, Labor Statistics Bureau, Energy Department, Copyright Office), gives a further subject approach. Periodicals are listed once a year in a supplement. Though a bit frustrating to use either for selection or for reference work, the catalog can be mastered comfortably with a little practice and more patience. True, its usefulness for selection is limited because it does not evaluate items, but its complete entries do show what is (or has been) published.

U.S. Superintendent of Documents. *Selected United States Government Publications,* 1928– (Washington: Government Printing Office, 1928– , now eleven times a year)

This catalog is free to those who request it (and practically every library should). It announces new materials likely to be of interest to the public, hence is indispensable for school and public libraries, and of considerable value in college libraries.

Several compilers have prepared guides and lists for government publications. Among the best for the smaller library is:

W. Philip Leidy. *A Popular Guide to Government Publications*. 4th ed. (New York: Columbia University Press, 1976, 440 p.)
Leidy sorts out about two percent of the items listed in the *Monthly Catalog* over the past few years and arranges them under such topics as Astronomy, Carpentry, Civil rights, Travel, Watergate investigation, and Weeds.

Walter L. Newsome. *New Guide to Popular Government Publications, For Libraries and Home Reference* (Littleton, CO: Libraries Unlimited, 1978, 370 p.)
This is a well-indexed list of recent (mostly) titles, selected with discernment.

A less selective aid in this area is John L. Andriot's *Guide to U.S. Government Serials & Periodicals* (McLean, VA, Documents Index, 1959– , title varies, now four volumes every two years). Two guides to more specialized types of United States federal documents are *Government Reference Books . . . A Biennial Guide to U.S. Government Publication* (Littleton, CO: Libraries Unlimited, 1970–), an annotated work intended for all types of libraries, and Nancy Patton Van Zant's *Selected U.S. Government Series: A Guide for Public and Academic Libraries* (Chicago: American Library Association, 1978, 172 p.), which is addressed to small and medium-sized academic and public libraries.

Important documents of several kinds, but chiefly of the United States federal government, are listed in *Vertical File Index*, *Public Affairs Information Service Bulletin*, and in such periodicals as *Library Journal* and *Booklist*. *RQ*, published quarterly by the

Reference Services Division of the American Library Association, is especially good for its reviews of documents on specific subjects. A regular feature of *Documents to the People* is an article on "Documents in the News," which indirectly provides hints to selectors.

Documents of foreign governments are of interest to larger American libraries. In the United Kingdom, Her Majesty's Stationery Office issues noteworthy maps and beautiful materials of use in history and art, for example, the publications sponsored by the Royal Commission on Historical Monuments. Also offered is a general line of official reports.* Some other governments publish in their own languages and in English as well. Materials containing statistical data and information about a country's people are of special interest.

STATE AND LOCAL

Documents representing the various state governments are, on the whole, less interesting than federal publications; nevertheless, they include many individual items that are worthwhile. Those produced by the government of the library's home state are of particular interest. A good many documents issued by the states of the union are listed in:

U.S. Library of Congress, Exchange and Gift Division, Processing Dept., *Monthly Checklist of State Publications* (Washington: Government Printing Office, 1910–)

The *Checklist* also includes some publications of state-supported societies and institutions. Periodicals are listed in the June and December issues. In these and other issues appear such disparate works as directories, bibliographies, arrest warrant forms, and even a pamphlet called "Naughty Names."

---

*But not all publications of the British government come from Her Majesty's Stationery Office. See Eve Johansson, *Current British Government Publishing* (London: Association of Assistant Librarians, 1978), 64 p., or Frank Rodgers, *A Guide to British Government Publications* (New York: Wilson, 1980), 750 p.

David W. Parish, in his *State Government Reference Publications: An Annotated Bibliography* (Littleton, CO: Libraries Unlimited, 1974, 237 p.), declaring that "more than 20,000 official state publications are released each year . . ." (p. 5), lists those which are most important and most representative.

County and municipal governments publish books, pamphlets, and other materials, many of great practical value to citizens. People need to know laws and ordinances, what their city is doing about various problems, even facts about streets and their names. The general library will collect some of the publications of (other) major cities. A core collection by category and type of material is suggested in *Organizing a Local Government Documents Collection,* compiled by Yuri Nakata, Susan J. Smith, and William B. Ernst Jr. (Chicago: American Library Association, 1979, p. 4–6). The bibliographic control of such pieces has been greatly improved by:

Index to Current Urban Documents (Westport, CT: Greenwood Press, 1972– quarterly).
   Arranged alphabetically by city (or county) and by subject, it lists documents of the "largest cities and counties in the United States and Canada." Included are guide books, maps, environmental impact statements, and many other items. Reports of special interest are singled out in each issue.

For medium-sized and large libraries, a tool of extremely high value is the selected, annotated list:

Municipal Government Reference Sources: Publications and Collections, ed. for American Library Association, Government Documents Round Table, by Peter Hernon, John V. Richardson, Nancy P. Sanders, and Marjorie Shepley (New York: Bowker, 1978, 341 p.)
   The work is ordered, in the main, by state and then by city, with a subject index.

11. PERIODICALS

There is still some truth to the old dictum that the eighteenth was the century of the pamphlet (especially the political tract); the nineteenth, the century of the book; and the twentieth, that of the periodical. The growth of this form in our century was once facilitated by favorable postage rates, by fast production methods, and by the absence of other forms of communication that could be received in the home on a regular basis.

Periodicals began their rise in the last third of the seventeenth century, primarily to disseminate ideas in science. Only a small amount of new information was discovered at one time, and it could be announced quickly in a short article (a kind of extension of a personal letter) without the necessity of waiting for a total book to mature. By the nineteenth century, magazines were used for creative literature, though such writing was considered pretty low.

As indicated in Chapter 9, a journal really is something like a group of pamphlets, a fact hinted at by the word *magazine,* which suggests a storehouse or collection. Now the term is used almost interchangeably with *periodical* and *journal,* at least in the United States.

The ideas published with relative speed may later be digested, condensed, reworked, and woven systematically with other information to form a monograph (treatise on one subject). Encyclopedias contain many facts and ideas which appeared first in journal articles.

The periodical's natural advantage over the book is thrown away when editors build huge backlogs of papers awaiting publication. Each is then delayed like a jet plane circling an airport, waiting for a chance to land. (Incidentally, books on occasion can be published quickly, sometimes in a few days.) The editor of a journal may suffer embarrassment, however, by trying to cram in too much material before a certain deadline. Near the end of the Second World War, the old *Collier's* (now defunct) was working on a timely topic — an article by Quentin Reynolds, painting an authoritative picture of how difficult the invasion of Japan was going to be. The article was printed two days after the Japanese surrender. The *U.S. News* of November 5, 1948, ran an article, "Formula for Victory Used by Mr. Dewey's Campaign Managers . . ." referring to the futile race against Harry S. Truman.[1]

In the area of science, the periodical is now challenged by the research report, a separate publication giving results, or perhaps an account of the progress, of one project. Distribution of these reports can be made to persons who are interested in the specific information contained. One need not pay for a whole volume of a journal, it is urged, in order to get the very few articles that are wanted. This type of publication obviously has several characteristics in common with the pamphlet, though it is distributed to a pre-established list of subscribers. To identify the particular reports required by one person is a relatively expensive process, and for a library, these reports are more difficult to catalog and to house than are books or bound volumes of periodicals.

SOME TYPES OF PERIODICALS

Why is a paper of a certain length published as a periodical article rather than as a pamphlet or other "separate?" What principles do editors use in deciding on the particular group of articles to be published? A magazine gathers writings together according to some characteristic or, as is true of most, set of characteristics.

Probably the most common denominator is subject matter, examples being *Quarterly Review of Biology, American Political Science Review, Art Bulletin, Money, Country Music Review,* and *Gambling Illustrated. Journal of the . . . Society* is a typical form of title.

Periodicals specialize further by level of difficulty (any article in *Popular Science* requires less expert background than any substantive article in *Physical Review*). On this scale, *Scientific American* is somewhere between the other two. Another denominator is the age of readers, ranging from *Jack and Jill* to *Aging Success-*

fully. (Somewhere between these two is *Modern Bride. Bridegroom* folded.) Locality may be the common characteristic of journals, as in *Arizona Highways* and *Pennsylvania Magazine of History and Biography*. Numerous other titles identify the content with a state or other locality, for example, *Utah Cattleman*. This title suggests also that occupations of readers may distinguish magazines from each other. *Inland Printer, Prairie Farmer,* and *Broiler Business* exemplify this difference. Magazines that cover many subjects, or even just one, may be characterized by their editorial points of view. In this respect, isn't *Reader's Digest* rather different from *The Village Voice? Hustler* from *The Journal of Sex Research?* Periodicals may be used to represent organizations, as *Columbia University Forum* and *Ford Times,* or even *Bell System Technical Journal*. Churches account for thousands of periodicals at one level or another. The "house organ" is for the employees of (usually) a large corporation, but may have general interest as well.

Academic people make a sharp distinction between those periodicals which are "refereed" and those which are not. To be published in the former, an article must be examined by several experts in the subject, who decide whether the paper meets certain standards of quality.[2] These referees may not know who wrote the paper and so ought to be free of certain kinds of prejudice. Presumably this process screens out the poorer submissions and encourages publication of the better.

It can be seen from the foregoing that most individual periodicals have several distinguishing characteristics. There seems to be a clear trend toward magazines aimed at smaller audiences with special interests. The big mass-circulation journals have not prospered in recent years. One after another they have folded, owing to various causes. This fact reinforces the general library's responsibility for meeting the needs of individuals.

USES OF PERIODICALS

In Chapter 9, the point was made that periodicals by nature are less likely to present the unusual idea than are pamphlets, partly because journal publishing by nature demands a sizable organization or at least access to capital.

If a new journal is to be launched successfully and attract subscribers and advertisers in a competitive market, the promoters must find and pay skillful editors and talented writers. For well-printed, colorfully-illustrated periodicals the required investment may run easily into millions of dollars. It is true that underground dissent (and some other) magazines are printed via offset at very little expense and without the help of the Establishment, but even these publications represent groups with some degree of organization. For the individual, the mimeographed single sheet may have to serve as the vehicle.

In spite of these reservations, Dean Peterson, of the University of Illinois School of Journalism, did not overstate his case when he declared, "The magazine by nature was admirably suited for a highly important role in a democratic society, that of introducing new ideas, putting them up for critical examination, and if they had merit, feeding them into the mainstream of thought."[3] Frank Luther Mott in his classic history speaks of "a certain fascination about old magazines. It springs, I think, from their personal quality. The distinctively human element is never long absent from their pages. . . . The magazines have always echoed popular ideologies, presented personal but representative emotional responses, interpreted the men and women of their own days."[4] Such notable writers as Loren Eiseley, James Baldwin, Norman Mailer, and Edmund Wilson have used magazine articles as effective means of presenting what they had to say to the public. Writers of fiction like John Updike, and poets such as Ezra Pound have reached audiences via periodicals. Presidents of the United States, along with would-be- and ex-presidents, have made appeals in them. Popular journals, with their reasonably up-to-date facts in articles of a length preferred by many readers, have been a recognizable force for education. Note this confession: "I was brought up to believe that reading magazines was a sin, or at least a waste of time. In spite of that I managed to read a lot of magazines . . . My education (and certainly my general knowledge) probably owes more to magazines than to books."[5]

It is only fair to observe, however, that in a circulating library as contrasted with a reference library, the value of periodicals is somewhat less than that of books and pamphlets. It is not very convenient to lug home a big volume with two hundred articles in order to study just one of them.

As for the scholarly and professional journals, there is evidence that they are not widely read. A study of periodicals in psychology, conducted under the auspices of the American Psychological Association, concluded that very few persons were reading current numbers. "About one-half of the articles, mainly research reports, were read by less than 1 percent of the respondents questioned on them."[6] Therefore the small or medium-sized public library need not feel too badly about inability to afford them. Indeed a study in England found that "academic" periodicals were not greatly used in public libraries.[7] For the few people who are interested in high-level research, periodicals do provide important sources of information. Scholarly journals are necessary in university, large public, and specialized libraries, where they are used far more frequently than are monographs.

SELECTION PROBLEMS

Choosing current periodicals for a library is quite a different matter from the selection of books. In some ways, it is easier; in others, more difficult.

The relative size of the total population from which titles can be chosen is indicated by comparison of the 9,500 currently-published United States journals of some general interest with the 40,000 new books issued each year. Even so, it is not feasible to examine copies of more than a small fraction of the journals available, though a sample does provide a good picture of the whole. Periodicals remain fairly stable in subject matter, in point of view, and even in quality, over a period of years, partly because they represent groups, commercial firms, societies, or "establishments." Most popular journals, at least, are edited to formula. "The formula, not the editor, gave a magazine its character and continuity. . . . Editors could come and go, but the essential personality of the magazine could remain virtually unchanged."[8] The old *American Magazine* is one example: From 1915 until the Great Depression its editorial policy was based on the proposition that the individual ought to achieve victory over adverse conditions such as lack of education, health, opportunity, or money. There are glaring exceptions to this rule of magazine stability. Some periodicals do change. Edmund Wilson, while noting their continuity, compared them with people:

> Magazines, like other living organisms, develop according to certain laws and pass through regular life-cycles. . . . They have a youth, a maturity and an old age. In its earliest years, a magazine may seem spontaneous, novel and daring; but by the time it has reached its maturity it has, as the French say, "taken its fold," and it succumbs to the force of inertia against which the youngest and freshest editor is as powerless as the oldest and stalest. Thereafter, it grows old, declines and dies.[9]

Or, some say, commits suicide. This analogy between periodical and person is a favorite one. James Thurber in an interview once expressed concern about the "matronly girth" of *The New Yorker*.[10] Another writer described "an almost inexorable life-cycle of American magazines that follows the pattern of humans: a clamorous youth eager to be noticed; vigorous, productive, middle-age marked by an easy-to-define editorial line; and a long slow decline."[11] *The Saturday Evening Post* has shifted direction several times in its efforts to escape the hand of death, even resorting to "dyed hair and false eyelashes."[12] The *American Mercury* has certainly had a checkered career, in terms of both format and editorial policy. In another sharp reversal, *The North American Review* and *The Living Age,* once periodicals of the highest type, particularly the former, were bought out just prior to World War II, taken over for purposes of Japanese propaganda.

But in spite of exceptions and scandals, the general rule still holds up: periodicals are relatively stable from year to year,* and

---

*In a characterization of *Music Review* over its first quarter-century, Guy Marco personified the magazine as "youthful, British, and musical . . . his ear is uncommonly good, and he stands ready to defend its judgments against all challengers. The music he one of the best ways to evaluate titles is to examine back issues located in an existing collection, or obtained from the publisher as sample copies. To predict what a given journal will be like in 1983, look at the issues for 1981. For books there is no similar way of judging (except in the case of new editions, where quality may sometimes be predicted on the basis of previous editions). The relative constancy of each periodical means that lists of recommended titles are effective for a longer period of time than are guides to the best books.

Offsetting this advantage in periodical selection is the fact that in choosing a given title, the librarian is or seems to be making a commitment for several years ahead. If a subscription is stopped after a year or two, the resulting stub set is more likely to be lost on the shelves. It may be a vocational failing on the part of librarians, but there is a kind of discontent with incompleteness. In the 1970s the need to prune subscription lists has been painful for this reason and because each discontinued title represents a confession of failure of sorts. Adding to the difficulty is the surprising number of magazines, even those highly advertised, that die in their first years. If the library has bought the first issues on the strength of ballyhoo, the lonesome copies are left. On the other hand, if the first numbers are refused at the time they are published, they may be difficult to obtain later, because journal issues are not kept in print as books are. The problem is further complicated by the high birth and mortality rates. In a given year, several hundred United States periodicals may go out of business to be replaced by as many new ones.

CRITERIA FOR SELECTION

In general, the librarian's overall principles for selection will be applied to periodicals. Needless to say, the characteristics of the community and particularly those of the library clientele are im-

likes most is of the nineteenth and twentieth centuries . . . opera is his preferred medium. . . . He reads one or two new books each week. . . . Never without charm and finesse." (" 'And Radiate Its Own Vitality;' *The Music Review* Over Twenty-five Years." *Music Review* 26 (August 1965): 246.) This is still a fairly accurate description.

portant background factors when decisions are made on periodicals, as on books. Rural interests differ from urban. The elderly like some magazines; the young like others. Many readers have their own favorite subjects. However, Katz's criterion — "the overriding single purpose of meeting an individual need is quite enough"[13] — applies more to monographs than to magazines. Preferred will be those titles which several patrons find useful, which bring diversified information into the library, and which give reliable information. There are a few tests that may be used specifically and fairly easily for selecting periodicals.

Lists of Indexed Journals

To what extent, if any, should standard indexes (such as *Readers' Guide to Periodical Literature, Social Sciences Index,* and *Art Index*) be used as selection guides? Imagine two journals equal in every respect except that one is indexed in a standard service owned by the library and the other is not: The indexed journal is sure to have more use than the unindexed one. There are also practical matters such as this: If a student is writing a paper and sees listed in *Readers' Guide* (say) an article which looks relevant, that person feels terribly frustrated when the library cannot supply it. Actually the article may have little value — titles often are misleading; but it sounds so good that the student considers the library woefully inadequate if the coveted text cannot be furnished. Such situations argue for subscribing to magazines which are indexed. Add to all this the fact that in general, the quality of indexed journals is at least reasonably high, and there is a good case for the library's use of these indexes as lists for subscriptions. Thus Andrew D. Osborn states the orthodox case: "The periodicals which are of greatest potential value in a library are those that are covered in abstracting and indexing services."[14] The English writer Donald Davinson is in general agreement,[15] but Katz demurs.[16]

When a librarian subscribes to periodicals just because they are included in the standard indexes, a vicious circle may be created. Titles are chosen because they are indexed; then when it is time to vote on titles to be indexed in the future, which ones get support? More than likely, the very ones already subscribed to. Librarians need to think carefully before voting. It is difficult for new periodicals, even of high quality, to break into the select, privileged company of indexed publications. As already suggested, periodicals usually represent organized groups of some sort. If they are selected for the library on the basis of indexing, the collection will have even more of a built-in conservative cast. Many ideas found in new periodicals will thus be excluded from the library. Furthermore, if it is true that the future content of a magazine will be shaped in terms of its present subscribers, as seems likely, the vicious circle will be projected into the future.

Other Standards

Another consideration in selecting periodicals is that in many libraries, readers are more likely to use bibliographic citations than indexes when they decide what articles to look for.[17]

As discussed in Chapter 4, larger libraries (and possibly some smaller ones) may well profit from the results of citation analyses in deciding which periodical titles to buy, to retain, and to bind. Perhaps the best question to be asked is: How many heavily cited articles are we likely to get for our dollar if we take periodical A? How many if periodical B? While the results of citation analysis are rather difficult to apply to specific monographs, they are somewhat easier to handle with respect to periodical titles, but again there should be a warning about oversimplification.

A good deal of evidence about journal use in individual libraries is being amassed by local surveys. To an extent, these results can be applied in other libraries. Sociologists and librarians also are interested in the journals in various disciplines. What are their rejection rates? A journal that is choosey about what it accepts for publication is probably better than a journal that accepts almost everything sent in.[18] (Periodicals that commission articles instead of relying upon submissions are another matter.) There is interest also in the way that journals are ranked by contributors. In any given field, which periodical is the first choice of scholars who have papers ready to submit for publication? If the paper is rejected by that first choice, what journal is second choice? Third? As more and more studies are made of periodicals, their editors, their contributors, and their readers, librarians can glean information useful in selection.

The selection of periodicals, then, presents yet another area of tension between practical demand and the library's responsibility for promoting variation and value. It needs the bulk of the titles indexed in the standard services to which it subscribes, but surely ought to save some funds for a few periodicals that are unusual in format, subject matter, and viewpoint.

BIBLIOGRAPHY OF CURRENT PERIODICALS

The number of magazine titles is so great, and their changes in status so frequent, that obtaining basic facts about them is almost as difficult as for monographs. One outstanding aid is *Ulrich's International Periodicals Directory: A Classified Guide to Current Periodicals, Foreign and Domestic* (New York: R. R. Bowker, annually). The main volume deals with about 75,000 titles from all parts of the world, and is kept up to date by *Ulrich's Quarterly*. While its degree of comprehensiveness and its lack of evaluative information preclude its use as a selection guide in most libraries, its subject arrangement does offer help to those choosing periodicals in the very large or highly-specialized library. As an acquisitions tool it is excellent.

Standard Periodical Directory, 1981–82, 7th ed. (New York: Oxbridge Communications, Inc., 1980, 1,709 p.) is also arranged by subject. The latest edition includes over 66,000 titles, but some of them have such infrequent publication schedules that they ordinarily would not be called periodicals. The descriptive annotations are a help, and the list is good for identifying obscure magazines.

Ayer Directory of Publications (Philadelphia: Ayer Press, annually) notes titles published in each city of the United States, Canada, and assorted territories and has a classified arrangement by type and subject. The information given for each entry is that of primary interest to advertisers. A similar tool covering the United Kingdom, Ireland, and other countries is *Willing's Press Guide,* an annual published in London since 1874.

The Working Press of the Nation vol. 2, *Magazine and Editorial Directory* (Burlington, IA: National Research Bureau, Inc., annually) gives an annotation for each of about 4,800 United States and Canadian titles. The subject arrangement (Bookkeeping, Plastics, Meats) is of help to the selector.

A much more specialized compilation whose information helps one to spot the publications of national groups in this country is Lubomyr R. and Anna T. Wynar's *Encyclopedic Directory of Ethnic Newspapers and Periodicals in the United States,* 2nd ed. (Littleton, CO: Libraries Unlimited, 1976, 248 p.). Arranged in the main by nationality (Czech press, Turkish press), this work includes brief annotations.

Specialization in a different sense is found in *From Radical Left to Extreme Right: A Bibliography of Current Periodicals of Protest, Advisory, or Dissent . . .* vol. 3, 2nd ed., ed. Theodore J. Spahn, Janet P. Spahn (Metuchen, NJ: Scarecrow Press, 1976, 550 p.). The titles and long annotations in this guide make an interesting commentary on the thoughts of our fellow human beings.

SELECTION GUIDES

Lists of the "best" journals are not so abundant as those of "good" books, but there are two which can be called outstanding. Here is the librarian's premier guide for this format:

Bill Katz and Berry G. Richards. *Magazines for Libraries: For the General Reader and School, Junior College, College, University, and Public Libraries,* 3rd ed. (New York: Bowker, 1978, 937 p.)

This large volume gives an indication of the audience or type of library for which each title is deemed suitable. The descriptive and evaluative annotations include a good deal of subjective opinion, but generally are sound. About 6,500 titles, "which the editors and contributors believe to be the best" are arranged by subject, with cross references and a title index.

Selma K. Richardson, *Periodicals for School Media Programs* (Chicago: American Library Association, 1978, 397 p.)
Another top-notch selection tool, this guide is useful in public as well as school libraries. The long annotations are descriptive and evaluative. The range in reading level is wide — from the automobile magazines and *TV Guide* through *Musical Quarterly* and *Harvard Business Review*.

A good guide to related materials (NOPSES — non-periodical serials) is provided by Joan K. Marshall in her *Serials for Libraries: An Annotated Guide to Continuations, Annuals, Yearbooks, Almanacs, Transactions, Proceedings, Directories, Services* (New York: Neal/ Schuman Publishers, 1979, 494 p.) which describes about 2,000 selected titles arranged by subject. Various types of journals and other serials are evaluated by the quarterly *Serials Review,* which also contains articles with interesting background information.

NEWSPAPERS

Dating back to the sixteenth century in England, the news-type publication hit a peak about the middle of the twentieth century with the huge metropolitan dailies. Mergers and deaths have taken a toll, and, as with magazines, the publications appealing to a specialized audience (suburbia, for instance) seem to be winning out.

Newspapers, are, unfortunately, considered a nuisance in some libraries, because they are difficult to house, get so badly mauled, and are pored over by people who, it may seem, have nothing else to do. Even at their worst, though, newspapers record bits of human behavior that otherwise would be forgotten, and at their best they describe important events and present editorial comments that are significant in society's decisions.

Newspapers are among those materials chosen by the small general library because of local interest. Any school library should maintain a file of the school paper, and with the public library should save three or four papers from the nearest metropolitan area (including some minority opinion) and at least one of national stature, preferably the *New York Times* or perhaps *The Christian Science Monitor*. Larger libraries, of course, will subscribe to more and will preserve files, usually on microfilm. The superiority of the latter form was indicated years ago when the library of *Newsweek* magazine in New York, having obtained files of the *New York Times* on microfilm, tried unsuccessfully to sell its full-sized paper files of the newspaper; then failed in attempts to give them away; finally offered to pay the city refuse collectors to cart them off and again was turned down.[19]

In addition to the newspaper listings found in the guides noted above, there is *The Working Press of the Nation:* Vol. 1, *Newspaper and Allied Services Directory* (Burlington, IA: National Research Bureau, Inc., annually), which is divided into eleven sections, each representing a certain type of paper. *Serials Review* has a regular feature, "Newspapers in Review."

12. REFERENCE WORKS

One of the major purposes of the typical modern library is to supply information as patrons ask for it. Accurate data are needed in business, in government, in the professions, in the home. The more one operates according to facts, the more likely the success of the venture. A well-chosen group of informational works, therefore, is one of the most valuable parts of the library. Pauline Wilson, discussing use of the public library by social activists, concludes that they are best served by a good reference collection, along with current books on social problems.[1]

That person is incomplete who has not experienced the satisfaction of finding in a book the answer to a question. Who is there who can resist the pleasure of browsing over columns of unrelated trivial facts? In a slightly more earnest vein, the American historian, Allan Nevins, speaking of reference books as valuable sources of information for scholars of the future, adds that "even the craggiest, most stonily factual reference book, when a little mellowed by time, becomes a quarry from which some perceptive scholar can extract handsome building materials, as John Stuart Mill did from the venerable *Annual Register,* and James Ford Rhodes from the *Tribune Almanac.*"[2]

WHAT IS A REFERENCE BOOK?

As to the nature of a reference work, it is best described simply as a book or set used for reference; one consulted for specific information; any work that answers a question. As Patrick Wilson puts it, books used in information service constitute "already prepared answers to questions."[3]

A book may be utilized for reference even though written and edited with the idea that most users will read it straight through. On the other hand, one designed for reference use may be read continuously (it is said that some readers so treat the unabridged dictionaries and general encyclopedias). Any book with a good index has some reference value, as does one which is so ordered that a given piece of information can be found quickly. Examples of the latter are: histories (usually arranged in some kind of chronological order) and textbooks, which often have a systematic order (as those in anatomy, physiology, and engineering do) giving them a logical, easily-followed plan. Most reference books, though, are arranged in some arbitrary fashion — alphabetically more often than not. Or they may be arranged by time (as, a dictionary of dates); by geographical area (as, maps in an atlas); in tabular form (as, books of statistics); or according to some other special plan (as, a bibliography classified according to the Dewey Decimal system).

BUILDING A REFERENCE COLLECTION

In gathering a good collection of reference works, the primary concern is the library clientele and the questions they may be expected to ask. While many of those questions are similar in all communities, it is important that the local library keep a record of unusual questions that cannot be answered, and attempt to fill the gaps in its collection. The information requirements of the hitherto unserved should be considered also. Even if the library has joined with others to form a system with central reference services, there is satisfaction to both librarian and patron if the information can be supplied on the spot.

As to facts likely to be asked for: questions about people are frequent in most libraries. Interest in world affairs or in foreign travel raises the need for information about places. Public libraries have questions about practical household matters (how to remove spots) and, in many areas, about gardening (how to remove dandelions). Clubwomen and businessmen (also clubmen and businesswomen) have their needs for specific information. Consumers need better data as economic conditions get tougher. Facts on schools, jobs, recreation, and health are of constant interest, as are those on ethnic minorities and on women. Since public libraries are used so heavily by students, there must be information about books and authors, as well as data in the natural and social sciences. Librarians delight in odd questions like

"Can you give power-of-attorney to a dog?" and "Who wrote 'Odious Wrecks'?", but there are the important and significant questions as well. Again it must be said that types of libraries and needs of clientele vary greatly.

The main goal in the building of a reference collection is to be able to supply as many trustworthy, likely-to-be-asked-for facts as possible, with a minimum of duplication and overlapping. When a person comes to the reference desk asking, "What is the freezing point of alcohol?" one reliable source is sufficient. If the same fact is available on thirty different pages in the reference collection, twenty-seven or twenty-eight are superfluous;* in fact, they may get in the way. A good reference department will of course obtain information wherever it may be found, perhaps telephoning an authoritative person, consulting an on-line data base, or referring the client to another agency. It need not be confined to printed sources. But the problem under discussion here is the selection of books and similar repositories.

Developing a solid, compact, efficient reference collection free from unnecessary duplication is no simple thing. The problem of overlapping tools is created by the nature of the reference book publishing industry in the United States. Here are some historical roots which have led to this situation: During the early years when the country was being settled, reference and similar books were marketed by traveling salesmen, a practice which continued well after the Civil War.[4] With their heavy samples, these peddlers walked the cities and towns, even calling on farmhouses. It was in the publishers' interests to produce the kinds of books that would sell to these families. Even today, most reference sets are not designed primarily for libraries. In order to assure a profitable volume of sales, publishers aim their compilations at homes, offices, or the public ar large. Perhaps there will come a time when librarians get together and produce one huge reference set, planned rationally for their own needs, and provided with an apparatus for keeping it up-to-date. In the meantime,

---

*It is some advantage to have reference tools that are arranged in different ways, say classified and alphabetical, even if the data are similar. Also, librarians have to allow for the fact that some books will be stolen or mutilated.

libraries must continue to buy new and expensive volumes in order to obtain a few facts not hitherto represented in the collection; but the goal is to bring in as many of these new facts as possible.

MAKING A REFERENCE TOOL

Because of the simple, painful truth that many books repeat the same facts, the remark made in Chapter 6 that most represent a repackaging of information goes doubly for works of reference. It is extremely difficult to obtain new, significant data. There is no great problem in finding a new, previously unpublished fact (e.g., the number of hairs on the hide of the neighborhood tomcat) but this fact can hardly be called *significant* (at least to non-cats). To publish loads of significant facts is no great task either, but they usually have been published somewhere before; they are not *new*. To get data both new and important is quite a problem, as any writer of a doctoral dissertation will agree. Somewhere there is related the sad story of the advanced graduate student who (in the Ivy League, no doubt) wrote his dissertation on the subject, "The Left Hind Leg of the Grasshopper." Required to defend the scope of his research, the candidate apologized for being unable satisfactorily to do so. "I came to this university to study the *middle joint* of the left hind leg of the grasshopper, but because the professor of that specialty was on a leave of absence, I was forced to enlarge the scope of my study to these unmanageable proportions." The student probably produced some new facts, but it is too much to ask that any one book contain very much information which is both new and important.

The laboriousness of finding and organizing facts for a reference work is shown by the case of the *Columbia-Lippincott Gazetteer,* published in 1952. Two kinds of people were necessary: research specialists in the subject matter, to produce the raw data, and highly trained workers in the reference and library field, to distill, check, shuffle, and process the material. Original data were obtained from one research man on the staff who described an obscure railroad in Burma. As a prisoner of the Japanese during World War II, he had been forced to help build it; thus knew every painful inch.[5] The filing of the entries required such intense concentration that a person was exhausted after working at it for four hours a day. One hundred and fifty people, knowing among them fifty-five languages, worked for five years to produce the 5,500,000 words.[6] Each person, therefore, produced an average of twenty-five typewritten pages a year.

A first-hand account of the care necessary in checking facts for a reference book is given by Nicolas Slonimsky in his preface to the fifth edition of *Baker's Biographical Dictionary of Musicians*. For example, there are many accounts which place the number of people attending Beethoven's funeral at twenty thousand. Slonimsky, after some sensible calculations, reduced this figure to "hundreds." He confirmed the idea that Beethoven had died during a violent thunderstorm by consulting the report of the Vienna Bureau of Meteorology for 4 p.m., March 26, 1827. The editor obtained hundreds of birth certificates from all over the world, since musicians traditionally seem to have claimed lower ages than the facts would support. There was the case of Sigismond Thalberg, who

> . . . openly asserted that he was the natural son of Count Moritz Dietrichstein and Baroness von Wetzlar. Yet the birth certificate states unambiguously that his parents were Joseph Thalberg and Fortunée Stein, both of Frankfurt. The certificate also indicates that both parents were married, but it does not state clearly whether they were married to each other. At this point, my investigation had to stop.[7]

In spite of such care, the preface to the Supplement, published seven years later, acknowledged errors that had slipped by and later were discovered.

For a reference work of great size, the sifting and processing of information is a tremendously costly job. *Webster's Third New International Dictionary* (published as one big volume in 1961) cost over $3,500,000, according to its preface. The *Oxford English Dictionary* is another matter: work started in 1879, and the letter T was being completed when the editor died in 1908. Over twenty years later, 1929, the main set was completed, marked by a modest celebration during which the original editors and printers "stirred unquietly in their graves."[8] Then it was time to start work on supplements. (Nevertheless, the *OED* proceeded far faster than similar dictionaries produced on the European continent.) *The New Encyclopaedia Britannica* (15th ed) is the work of 4,000 contributors from 131 countries. A thousand other persons were involved in planning and editing the set. Altogether it required some twelve years and thirty-two million dollars, in addition to printing costs.[9]

JUDGING THE REFERENCE WORK

What standards for evaluation are valid and at the same time feasible to apply? A good outline for this purpose was prepared many years ago by Isadore Gilbert Mudge, and is included in the ninth edition of *Guide to Reference Books,* compiled by Eugene P. Sheehy (Chicago: American Library Association, 1976, p. xiii–xv). The actual assessment of a specific work is quite difficult — more so, if anything, than for a general "stack" book.

Of supreme importance is the authority of the editors and contributors, but judging their qualifications and scrupulousness can be a tricky thing. Even when the editors are known as leading researchers in the field, is it certain that they took direct, personal interest in the book? Is it possible that they lent their names and prestige to the venture for advertising purposes? The list of contributors should tell something, but the question is, how much of the final work was written by each? Encyclopedias with great numbers of university presidents on their contributor lists may be saying that each wrote a paragraph about his or her own institution (admittedly the president is competent on *that* subject). Judging authority, then, requires more than glancing over a long list of names and degrees.

The main product of authority is accuracy, and good editors will strive to make their books reliable. That the task is not always completed satisfactorily is admitted by frank editors such as Edward Tripp, who at the time was in charge of reference books for the Crowell company: "A book like our *Readers' Encyclopedia of American Literature* contains perhaps 100,000 separate facts. As every reference publisher knows, it is not humanly possible to get every one of them right. . . . It may take hours to track down one tiny fact." [10] Since reference works do vary in accuracy, and since this characteristic is so important, it would be useful for the selector to make a complete check. Such a close examination being utterly impossible, a spot check of information has to suffice, and unless the sampling is very well done, it is likely to be inconclusive. The fact that a book agrees with the previous works may mean merely that one copied from another instead of trying to establish its accuracy independently.

Freedom from bias is a criterion of particular significance in reference works. By their nature, they suggest authority and finality. People tend to think "The *Encyclopaedia Britannica* says this, so it must be true;" whereas for a general book, written by a plain human being, there is more suspicion of fallibility. The *International Encyclopedia of the Social Sciences* gives warning however, that, in its subject area, "the data of reference volumes are collected by editors with social predilections and published under auspices, whether commercial or governmental, with political preferences." For this reason, they contain "errors of fact and slanting interpretations that are seldom signaled." [11]

Again, judgments are difficult for the individual librarian to make, and on all these points, knowledgeable reviews and analyses are the best guides.

Elegant writing is not crucial in a reference work, but clarity in style is essential, and is less difficult to judge.

The scope of the book or set is highly important to the individual library and can be determined by most selectors if they have access to the work in question. Sometimes the coverage can be ascertained from the title. Note such descriptive and delimiting titles as: *Short-Title Catalogue of Books Printed in Spain and of Spanish Books Printed Elsewhere in Europe Before 1601 Now in the British Museum,* or the simpler *Handbook of American Indians North of Mexico,* or even *A Bibliography of French Plays on Microcards* (a real list, 689 pages long). In other instances, the title may be far less definite and yet be more descriptive than those commonly used for regular trade books these days. Some titles, though, simply are not precise. Does "psychology" include materials on psychiatry? Is the subject of geography given space in a reference work on science? Does "literature" mean merely English literature, or does it include other languages? Is the term confined to creative works or is it perhaps used in a wider sense to indicate sermons, philosophy, and political tracts, or even writing itself, as in *A Guide to the Literature of Chemistry*?

In a reference work, the physical format of the book is of unusual interest. The binding must be sturdy; the paper of good, permanent quality. The type may be small (assuming that not much is to be read at any one time), but clarity and legibility are vital. Illustrations, graphs, and charts should be of such character that the information can be extracted from them quickly and without confusion.

Special features such as bibliographies and maps may be factors in deciding whether to choose or reject a work. (Unfortunately, these features may duplicate information contained by other works in the reference collection. For instance, a short list of persons added to a general dictionary is superfluous if the library has good biographical sets.) A well-organized, detailed index or cross-reference system is of inestimable value.

SOME SELECTION AIDS

For reference materials in general, the best bibliography so far as American libraries are concerned is the well-known *Guide to Reference Books,* 9th ed. compiled by Eugene P. Sheehy (Chicago: American Library Association, 1976, 1,015 p. plus supplement). Though not exhaustive, this work considers about 10,000 titles; hence it is not very selective either. Furthermore, the lag between date of items listed and date of publication of the guide is a disadvantage in selection. There is what the compiler calls a "disappointingly small number of imprints as late as 1974." The annotations, which usually accompany the more important entries, are of help in choosing works for medium-sized and larger collections. Sheehy is a standard work and no library can very well do without it.

Many American libraries will also want its English counterpart: Walford, Arthur John, ed. *Guide to Reference Material*, 3rd ed. (London: Library Association, 1973–77, 3 vols.). Naturally this work includes a great many more British publications. The arrangement is interesting and useful — by Universal Decimal Classification. Almost all the entries have good descriptive annotations.

A topical, unselected list of reference books produced in the United States in the previous year is offered by *American Reference Books Annual,* ed. Bohdan S. Wynar (Littleton, CO: Libraries Unlimited, 1970– annually). The entries include short reviews. Of the 12,339 titles covered in a seven-year period, 818 are selected for *Best Reference Books, Titles of Lasting Value Selected from American Reference Books Annual 1970–1976,* ed. Bohdan S. Wynar (Littleton, CO: Libraries Unlimited, 1976, 448 p.).

This title gets us to those bibliographies which are more selective, hence of greater use in smaller libraries. William A. Katz's *Introduction to Reference Work,* vol. I, *Basic Information Sources,* 3rd ed. (New York: McGraw-Hill, 1978, 367 p.) is an excellent guide to titles and to classes (e.g., Encyclopedias). More specialized by type of library is a work produced by the American Library Association, Reference and Adult Services Division: *Reference Books for Small and Medium-sized Public Libraries,* 3rd ed. (Chicago: The Association, 1979, 214 p.). Planned for the use of libraries serving 10,000 to 75,000 people, with some applications in college libraries, this book has over 600 entries, annotated and arranged in seventeen broad subject categories, roughly corresponding to Dewey classes.

The Enoch Pratt Free Library, Baltimore, has for many years produced a superb little book explaining important reference titles to library users: *Reference Books: A Brief Guide,* compiled by Marion V. Bell and Eleanor A. Swidan (8th ed., 1978, 179 p.). It is also an excellent guide for the selector.

For libraries in Canada, and also of interest to many in the

United States, there is Dorothy E. Ryder's *Canadian Reference Sources, A Selective Guide* (Ottawa: Canadian Library Association, 1973, 185 p.), supplemented by a 121-page volume in 1975 and by annual listings in the August number of *Canadian Library Journal*.

Two annotated guides which are of practical use in school libraries are: *Guide to Reference Books for School Media Centers,* by Christine L. Wynar (Littleton, CO: Libraries Unlimited, 1973, 473 p., 1974–75 supplement, 1976, 131 p.) designed mainly for students, teachers and librarians in elementary through high school; and Carolyn Sue Peterson's *Reference Books for Elementary and Junior High School Libraries,* 2nd ed. (Metuchen, NJ: Scarecrow Press, 1975, 314 p.).

REVIEWS

The reviewing of reference books is a continuing problem.[12] Promptness is, if anything, even more desirable here than for other works, but the research necessary to produce an evaluative review takes an inordinate amount of time. There are several avenues (in addition to *American Reference Book Annual*) for keeping up with the current output. They have different virtues: none are both thorough and prompt.

For in-depth analyses of individual titles, the reference and subscription books section of *Booklist* is best. Some of the longer reviews represent as much research as a scholarly article. The "Notes" are less complete but more prompt. These reviews and notes are reprinted annually in book form. Of equal importance, but for different reasons, is the *Reference Services Review,* which has two regular features of interest here: State-of-the-art surveys by field or topic (such as political science, chemistry, classical music, law), and Linda Mark's "Reference Sources," identifying new titles and indicating where they are reviewed. The latter section has a subject index and is cumulated annually in a separate volume. Charles A. Bunge, with the help of the staff of the Madison (Wisconsin) Public Library, compiles "Current Reference Books" in *Wilson Library Bulletin.* Aimed at the small and medium-sized general library, its reviews are brief and prompt, but coverage does not extend to large sets. *RQ*'s short reviews of reference materials are well-written and reasonably prompt. A list of outstanding reference books published in the previous year, as compiled by the Reference and Adult Services Division of ALA, is given each year in *Library Journal*'s April 15 number. *LJ* also deals regularly with reference books, as do *Choice* and other reviewing media.

13. OUT-OF-PRINT MATERIALS AND SUBSTITUTES

Though many libraries are concerned mainly or entirely with currently produced books, others collect those published in previous years. Selection of out-of-print material presents two peculiar problems: (1) An individual item may become available at a certain price for a short time only. The price is determined basically by supply, demand, and condition. A book currently selling in a given range may go higher, or may drop — especially if the title is reprinted. There are also variations in price from dealer to dealer, even if the condition of each copy is similar. (2) Often a vendor has a single copy for sale, and if that one is passed by, the librarian may not be able to locate another easily. Let us say, then, that a copy of a desirable book is offered for twelve dollars. It perhaps should be snapped up immediately. If priced at thirty dollars, the same title may be rejected. A quick decision is required because the work may never again be obtainable at the price quoted. For new books, there is at least a standard list price, and that figure remains constant for several months, allowing the library a little leeway.

OUT-OF-PRINT MATERIALS

The relative importance of out-of-print books will vary in different kinds of libraries. To sketch in some general considerations, such works may be highly desirable for the small, specialized collection, depending on the people who use it and on the particular subject emphasis. A library providing materials for scholars on such a subject as Kentucky folklore or the history of architecture probably would be quite interested in obtaining old materials. Some specialized research librarians consider their chief duty that of building collections with items which, in the main, are no longer available from the original publishers. On the other hand, a library serving a commercial or manufacturing firm may require only the most recent facts and have very little interest in books that are not current.

For elementary school libraries, out-of-print items are seldom considered for purchase; in high schools, they have relatively little importance; but for college libraries, they often are esteemed significant — more often in the humanities and social sciences than in the physical or biological sciences. University libraries find out-of-print books essential, especially in those times when their collections are rapidly expanding. The large popular library often buys older materials, generally as replacements for things which have been lost, but these institutions are interested mainly in current publications.

So a general rule may be formulated: The relative importance of out-of-print materials tends to increase with the library's size, degree of scholarliness or specialization, interest in historical research, and rapidity of expansion.

Another rule is that, other factors being equal, the newer, current, in-print book is to be preferred to the older, out-of-print item, particularly in the general library. There are two reasons for this generalization. For one thing, the new book ought to be better in content; it should be built upon information contained in previous books on the subject and should add facts or interpretations of its own. Obviously this happy result does not always occur, but there is some reason to believe that scholarship tends in the general direction of advancement. Furthermore, a really good older work stands a fair chance of being brought back into print when copies become scarce.

There is another reason for obtaining the title which is still in print: it is less expensive to acquire. Picture, if you can, two books of exactly the same value to the library. Say that one is in print, listing at twenty dollars; the other is out-of-print, appearing now and then in the catalogs of used book dealers at prices ranging from eight to twelve dollars. Which item is the better buy? The new one. It may be ordered along with a number of other books (all on one purchase order, with one check paying for several books) and it will be billed at a discount. With the other, older work, some time may be spent locating a copy fo sale. As Felix Reichmann says in an authoritative paper, using dealers' catalogs to "locate a specific title is at present the most expensive and least effective means of acquisition."[1] If a listing is spotted, a special order, perhaps a telegram, will be required. After this procedure, the dealer may merely write back stating that the book has been sold to some one else. Even if the transaction is completed, a special payment must be processed, and the total cost to the library may well exceed twenty-five dollars.

The Challenge of Locating Out-of-Print Works

These exceptions and problems still leave some instances in which the out-of-print item is clearly better than anything on the new book market, and any librarian worthy of the name will take up the challenge of finding it, or a satisfactory substitute. Many libraries send lists of "desiderata" to used book dealers, who in turn do the searching and quote prices on the copies discovered. Whereas it is costly and frustrating to try desperately to locate a used copy of a given individual title, the purchase of older works to build collections as a whole often is advantageous. Searching for good used books is one of the most interesting parts of selection and acquisition. Old book stores, dusty as they are, with books piled waist-deep on the floors and stretching maybe fifteen feet high on shelves, are fascinating places for the person who can spare a little time for exploring. That these institutions are vanishing from the United States is a source of real regret. To discover a book long desired gives a genuine satisfaction — the kind of feeling that comes from fitting a part into a jigsaw puzzle, or from finding a specific article, corresponding to a footnote citation, in a long run of bound periodicals.

Even scanning the lists and catalogs issued by used book dealers has its interest. Reichmann has expressed it well: "Selecting and ordering from dealers' catalogs or similar lists is the most painless, efficient, and at times the most thrilling method of buying o.p. books in their original editions."[2] To spot a likely title; to debate inwardly about its condition and value as against its price; to place an order; then open the box from the dealer, see what the copy really looks like, and envision its being used by this or that reader — all add to the richness of librarianship.

After the great 1871 Chicago fire, which destroyed the Chicago Public Library, William Frederick Poole, librarian in the period following, faced the tremendous task of rebuilding the collection. He made a practice of "reading" some 1,000 to 1,500 pages of dealers' catalogs each week, often during the evenings, in an attempt to find suitable books.[3] To him the job apparently was not a burden.

Lawrence Clark Powell, who was for some years director of libraries at the University of California at Los Angeles, used to claim that he had had a "biblio–geiger counter" implanted in his little finger so that he could detect book bargains. And consider the bargains he found! Once in the 1950s, going into the basement of a London bookstore, Powell saw on the floor a mound of pamphlets and was told that they were merely the dregs left from a fine collection, the best of the lot having been sorted out

> I reached for a handful of the pamphlets, and jerked back my hand.
>
> "What's the matter?" the dealer asked. "Did you see a spider?"
>
> "Maybe it was," I said, reaching again and leafing through the pamphlets on the top of the mound.
>
> What had happened was that my counter had jumped to maximum register and my heartbeat had matched it. I quickly turned off the counter and looked at something else.

Having received permission to take the lot to his living quarter in order to examine it more closely, Powell worked into the night, and toward morning found the cause of the disturbance in his geiger counter: a seventeenth century pamphlet published anonymously by William Penn, in an edition so rare that only one other copy was known. He bought this one (then worth probably a thousand dollars) for his library, paying two dollars (less the twenty percent library discount).[4]

Treasure hunts are always fun, but perhaps it is partly the bar gaining element that makes the purchase of old books so interesting — the chance to match wits with a learned opponent. Again, the competitive element spurs interest. University librarians get unholy pleasure from obtaining the fine private collections of professors who spent their careers at rival institutions.

Some Aids

To get back to the smaller purchases, and to some of the more useful of the many sources of information on the values of older books:

American Book-Prices Current 1894/95– (New York: Bancroft-Parkman, Inc., 1895– annually, subtitle and publishers vary) gives the amounts paid for books and serials, plus other items which, when sold at auction in one of the specified places, have brought twenty dollars or more. (The figure is lower for previous years.) Note that the listing includes many items which have been published or sold outside the United States; the word *American* is a misnomer. Each book so auctioned is well identified by author, title, edition, place and date of publication, size, condition (for example, "marginally wormed"), date of sale, and the price it brought. Among the literary works listed, there will appear occasionally a catalog of a used book dealer, considered so valuable that it has been put up for auction. With its five-year indexes, this set may be used in checking prices of used books offered for sale in present catalogs and other places. Conclusions should be drawn cautiously, however. *ABPR* says merely that one purchaser, on one occasion, was willing to pay the stated price. If the auction happened to occur on the day of an ice storm, during a strike by city transit workers, the prices bid may be unrealistically low. A British counterpart to *ABPR* is *Book Auction Records,* (Folkestone, Eng.: William Dawson & Sons, Ltd., 1903– annually, publisher varies).

Bookman's Price Index: A Guide to the Values of Rare and Other Out-of-Print Books, compiled by Daniel F. McGrath (Detroit: Gale Research Co., 1964– annually. Subtitle varies) is a kind of composite index to a collection of dealers' catalogs, mostly

American and English. After each entry, there are names of vendors who have offered copies for sale, and the prices they have asked. Therefore, if a desired book is found on a dealer's list with a price of thirty dollars, a check of McGrath may be called for. If three stores have listed the book in question previously at seventeen, nineteen and fourteen dollars respectively, it probably isn't a good buy at thirty of today's dollars unless deemed essential to the library.

A similar work is compiled by Mildred S. Mandeville: *The Used Book Price Guide: An Aid in Ascertaining Current Prices* (Kenmore, WA: Price Guide Publishers, irregularly). *The Book Collector's Handbook of Values,* by Van Allen Bradley, 3rd ed., 1978–1979 (New York: G. P. Putnam's Sons, 1978, 590 p.) is also based on dealers' catalogs as well as auction records.

For determining what bookstores specialize in what fields of interest, a good guide is *Book Dealers in North America: A Directory of Dealers in Secondhand and Antiquarian Books in Canada and the United States of America 1980–82,* 8th ed. (London: Sheppard Press, 1980, 395 p.). It includes geographical and alphabetical sections, but most important is the part devoted to subject specialties. Here can be found a list of dealers who specialize in books about Sports and pastimes, Crafts and useful arts, Biography, and other subjects.

An interesting periodical in this field is *AB Bookman's Weekly,* which lists items wanted by dealers for their customers. It publishes an annual, the *AB Bookman's Yearbook,* which includes a large section, "The O. P. Market: A Reference Directory of Specialist and Antiquarian Booksellers."

Though the procurement of out-of-print titles is really a job for the top-level specialist, it offers also a challenge to the beginner who is willing to learn. These basic tools give a start in a complex area.

REMAINDERS

There is a category of books representing a sort of intermediate state between in-print and out-of-print. A publisher unable to sell the complete stock of a title through the usual channels may turn over the unsold copies to a remainder-publisher at a greatly reduced price. The reduction is then passed on, in some measure, to the ultimate buyer. Thus a work with an original list price of $35.00 may be offered at $12.95. In 1978, Pierian Press of Ann Arbor, Michigan, began publication of *Best Buys in Print,* a quarterly guide that makes it easier to locate particular works for sale by remainder companies.[5]

SUBSTITUTES FOR HARD-TO-FIND WORKS

Suppose an out-of-print book or periodical that is urgently needed by a library cannot be located at anything like a fair price. What other possibilities are there?

Reprints

It could be that a needed title has been reprinted in full-size paper format. There are several hundred firms whose activity goes like this: They discern that a certain book or periodical set is in demand and, obtaining a copy of the original, they photograph the pages of text, then make offset printing plates, and produce up to seven hundred (maybe more) copies. Most of these books, the reprinter hopes, will be bought by libraries. This sort of business grew rapidly after World War II because of the huge expansion of many library collections, the drying up of the supply of original copies, and newer printing techniques. The reprint usually is expensive, but in most cases has a longer life expectancy than the older original. The *Guide to Reprints* (Kent, CT: Guide to Reprints, Inc., 1967– annually with supplement, publisher varies) is a cumulative list of available, bound, full-sized, reprinted items (chiefly those produced by the photo-offset process) issued in editions of two hundred or more copies. This annual now lists about 80,000 titles in several languages. The *Guide* is so planned as not to duplicate items in *Paperbound Books in Print,* but it does overlap *Books in Print.* The same titles can be approached through the *Subject Guide to Reprints.*

Another possibility which may be classed as a kind of reprint is the electrostatic copy made from a microfilm of the original. *Books on Demand* (Ann Arbor, MI: University Microfilms, 1977) is a three-volume set, listing by author, title, and publisher the works offered by this means. Other titles are provided to order. These books are produced on good-quality paper, but they have their disadvantages: they are (have to be) expensive; bindings are unattractive; print is not always clear; half-tone illustrations are terrible. In many cases, though, electrostatic copies are preferable to obtaining the material on interlibrary loan. Depending on the urgency of the need, therefore, it may be better to continue the search for a used copy, and if the need is not strong, to wait hopefully for a regular reprint edition.

Microforms

It is not quite right to consider microforms as mere substitutes for hard copy, because many titles are available in this format only. In other cases, the library has the choice of buying either microform or full-sized material. For little-used matter, microforms are generally the better buy, primarily because of the saving in space. Another advantage is that up to this time they have been less subject to theft and mutilation. In small and medium-sized public libraries, the first choice is likely to be hard copy, because microforms are objectionable to some patrons, and because mechanical readers are not available in homes.

Microfilm usually is 35mm wide and wound on a reel. Some people dislike to thread and crank the film through a reading machine; cartridges relieve the awkwardness. The typical reel fits into a box about 3⅞ by 3⅞ by 1⅝ inches. A full reel of film, photographed at a reduction ratio of something like twenty to one, can contain seven to ten days of *The New York Times* (the equivalent of several books). Each newspaper page is thus reduced in size to about 1¼ by ¾ inches.

Microfiche is photographic film also, but is flat and rather rigid. Sheets come in such sizes as 5 by 3, 6 by 4, and 8 by 5 inches. Images vary from the size indicated for typical microfilm to much smaller. One 5 by 3 fiche may carry a thousand book pages of text. On ultramicrofiche the images are so small that the entire text of the Bible, about 1,250 pages, can be placed on one clip about 1½ inches square. Some publishers offer interesting combinations of text in book form with illustrations on microfiche.

Microprint and microcards are about alike, the former being usually 6 by 9 inches; the latter, 5 by 3. Both are opaque, so that light is reflected from the surface of the image into the eyes of the reader. They can be produced in editions, and the unit cost is lowered if large numbers are made.

The catalogs of microform publishers from many countries can be consulted via *Micropublishers' Trade List Annual* (Weston, CT: Microform Review, Inc., 1975–) whose format, appropriately, is a set of microfiche. The same firm issues *Guide to Microforms in Print* (authors and titles), along with its *Subject Guide.* . . . Larger libraries may have need of the *National Register of Microform Masters* (Washington: U.S. Library of Congress, 1976– annually, with cumulations), which gives information on masters "retained solely for the purpose of making other copies."

For reviews of new microforms, the best one source is *Microform Review,* which deals not only with the content but is systematic also in its information about technical matters, such as the kind of film and the reduction ratio. *Cumulative Microform Reviews 1972–1976* (Westport, CT: Microform Review, Inc., 1978, 619 p.) is an arrangement by subject.

PART IV

NONPRINT MATERIALS

Media of communication come in many shapes and forms. Having sampled the supply of books, periodicals, pamphlets, and other printed formats, we now must turn to an even more diverse group best described by the unfortunately negative term *nonprint*. Here are found some of the most stimulating of all the graphic materials that express emotions, values, and ideas. We have before us a far-flung area, changing fast, and full of tangled forms. Probably the best way to make sense out of it is to go from general to particular after a chapter of orientation.

Part IV emphasizes the materials which are more general in subject matter. Reference to these media as they apply to specific subject fields will be held for Part V.

14. NATURE AND USE

During the long history of "libraries," many different kinds of materials have been collected, housed, and serviced. The ancient Babylonians, Assyrians, and others used clay tablets bearing cuneiform symbols for their records. In Egypt, the papyrus scroll was the typical medium. The Greeks also found this form useful, but when their supply of papyrus was restricted, they were adaptable enough to use animal skins (parchments), which were best handled in codex (book-like) form. Medieval libraries housed manuscripts written and copied with painful slowness. After the advent of printing from movable type (perhaps the first example of mass production) in mid–fifteenth-century Europe, libraries began to specialize in books and pamphlets along with (later) periodicals, maps, and the like, printed on a Chinese invention — paper.

In the last hundred years, other media of communication have been developed and have received wide use in education, in entertainment, as art forms, and as repositories of fact and idea. Susan Sontag, referring to the nineteenth-century French poet Mallarmé's statement that all things exist in order to end in a book, adds, "Today everything exists to end in a photograph."[1]

Because these media serve many of the same functions as print, they are a logical extension of the resources traditionally collected by libraries. In the 1920s, sound recordings came into American public libraries, and most librarians since then have felt some obligation to enlarge their collections beyond mere books. There is a tendency, even, to extend the referents of the term "books" to include all the various media, and some of the firms that once produced traditional books only now publish nonprint works also, and vice versa. In spite of the fact that nonprint media are sometimes less convenient to use, they are of unquestioned value for supplying information, inspiration, and enjoyment.

There is no clear line to separate print from nonprint media. Indeed, a copy of a film is called a "print", and also may include written material. On the other hand, some books are embellished with acetate overlays to illustrate such information as the members of the human body, the parts of the automobile engine, or the characteristics of geographic territories. Both print and nonprint formats include pictures, of course. Accompanied usually by words, illustrations are reproduced on paper as well as on film, and may make up ninety percent of a book. We even have books and magazines with pictures arranged so that a reader can flip the pages to produce the effect of motion. In most cases, however, nonprint formats involve a much higher proportion of pictorial matter. That is why they were once designated "visual" materials. (Note how useless *that* term is, for distinguishing print from nonprint!)

In the library the use of one medium often shades into and leads toward the use of another. A patron interested in books about architecture is naturally attracted to films, filmstrips, and other forms which present the subject vividly. The reader of poetry would be uncharacteristically lacking in imagination if not interested in hearing the poet's own voice on recordings. The impossibility of drawing lines to separate one media format★ from another is clearly evident when we start to classify materials for the sake of discussion. We could begin by dividing the silent materials from those that include sound — music or talk — but to some persons the significant question is whether or not the format shows motion. Following this line, motion pictures would be placed on one hand and "still" media on the other. The fact that nonprint materials usually have to be projected or played by machine is an important aspect; some of them, however, (such as models and mock-ups) can be viewed directly, while print substitutes such as microfilm require a mechanical reader of some sort. In fact, there is a close parallel between a microfilm of a book and a slide or filmstrip. One is to the printed page what the other is to, say, a painting. Microforms that are linked with synchronized sound carry the parallel further. In a pinch, slides and filmstrips can be viewed with reasonable satis-

---

★I shall use the expression *media format* to refer to a particular type of material, such as motion pictures or filmstrips or slides or sound recordings.

faction on some microfilm readers. Also, like microfilm these formats (along with motion pictures) compensate for their inconvenience in use by storing a great deal of information in a very small space. Since in this area, then, several classifications are reasonable, and none adequate, it is somewhat arbitrarily that I have, for the sake of discussion, divided nonprint into three categories: motion photography, still photography, and audio recording.

In spite of the differences among these media (to be delineated more fully in Chapter 16), there are some generalizations that can be made about nonprint as a whole before approaching the particular formats.

VALUE AND USE OF NONPRINT MATERIALS

In a classic work on the theory of signs and "meaning," the philosopher Charles Morris pointed out that the visual sign has never been supplanted by its traditional rival, language. One reason for the effectiveness of the former is that it often is iconic (that is, similar in some respects to that which it denotes) and that an iconic sign gives something of the same satisfactions as the thing denoted would give, were it experienced directly.[2] A picture of a dog is "like" a dog. Where a word is symbolic (is a sign of; stands for) something else — some referent — a picture is at the same time both symbolic and "real." A photograph is an abstraction (is symbolic) of an object or of an occurrence, and though it may portray the object more directly than does its linguistic counterpart, it usually is subject to many different interpretations; it means different things. A picture of a city slum may be an abstract way of saying "poverty," or "apathy," or "misery," or "ugliness," or "social neglect," or "bad government," or possibly even something pleasant. At the same time the picture is a clear and definite representation of one real scene.

While it is virtually impossible to measure accurately the relative stimulus values of pictures and words (the old problem of comparing apples and oranges — or more likely, apples and baked Alaska), still there is experimental evidence to show that some facts are remembered better from pictorial than from verbal presentations. Also, pictures, especially those in "motion," carry information rapidly. One instant can show as many bits of concrete information as several pages of print. Motion pictures can also create an illusion of actuality — a point marked by Marshall McLuhan with his comment on the "birth of the movies, the moment that translated us beyond mechanism into the world of growth and organic interrelation."[3]

Common sense suggests that for carrying some kinds of messages, the film, sound recording, and similar media are better vehicles than are the printed symbols of typography. A battle of the Civil War may be described vividly by the words of Bruce Catton, but a motion picture can virtually recreate the scene. Television depictions of gruesome events in Vietnam undoubtedly conveyed more of the essential horror of that war than did accounts in the evening newspaper.

In sound recordings, the iconic element is also clear and important. To take one example: bird songs are well described by such writers as A. C. Bent in his detailed *Life Histories of North American* [birds] series, wherein the call of a cuckoo "consists of four notes, two rapid, then a pause, and then two more, all of the same cadence, sounding like *hoo-hoo hoo-hoo.*" How much better this sound can be communicated by a good recording!

When several media are assembled, well coordinated, and presented to an audience in one program, the impact can be enormous. The alternation of film sound recording, live persons, and so forth allows the most effective use of each mode. A huge screen may be divided into areas to receive separate projected images. Slide projectors, sound motion picture projectors, loudspeakers, live actors and other "devices" may contribute to the total effect.

Another advantage of the newer media — both of the great majority which display pictorial illustrations and of all others which are iconic — is that such presentations can be understood and enjoyed by a wide range of ages and levels of intelligence. Texts (words), not being iconic, do not reach audiences of such breadth. While it requires considerable background and experience to understand the writing in a medical textbook, printed pictures and film slides on the subject are more accessible. A time-lapse motion picture* of a spider spinning its web or of a flower completing the cycle from seed to bloom is a fascinating sight to almost every age. In this respect a book, especially one without illustrations, is hard-pressed to compete. It is true that children often read "grown-up" books, and that for some subjects adults can profit by the simplification in children's books, but a good pictorial presentation is far broader in its appeal.

It would be a serious mistake, however, to forget the efficiency of plain words. Because of their almost unlimited levels of abstraction, they are in many situations more economical than photographs or drawings, even when they are not the only possible medium of expression. Such picture magazines as *Life* and *Look* soon learned that words could say what it took too many photos to portray. In the early days of television sportscasting, it was thought that the picture would be sufficient without comment by an announcer. Such proved not to be the case. The upshot was that we got more commentators per game than we ever had with radio. Even with bird calls, some data are better expressed by printed text. For example, Bent says that of 30 instances of the bird's sound, 20 slur upward, 6 slur downward, and 4 are single notes. Undeniably this fact is quicker read than heard. A videotape is excellent for analyzing the action of a football game, but when we need statistical summaries of games played in the nation during a season or a decade, we hasten to use the page of printed tables.

With print, moreover, it is somewhat easier to ignore what is not wanted — a real advantage in today's glut of communication. In one experiment, a newspaper printed two facing pages, one about men's interests, the other about women's. Ninety percent of the men said they saw "their" page, but forty percent said they never saw the "women's" page, though they must have, since it was at the same opening.[4]

---

*Made up of single frames photographed at regular intervals — hour, day, week — of the same scene, and then projected at the speed of a regular motion picture. The extreme opposite, slow motion, is equally interesting in its way.

Ron Powers, a newspaper critic of television, has described his reactions to various versions of a William F. Buckley Jr. *Firing Line* program. Watching the live event, he received the impression of hostility. The version coming from the TV set was pure debate. The audiotape without picture "came across . . . as *two disinterested voices joining in a quest for truth.*" The fourth version, the printed transcript, enabled Powers "to articulate to myself the essential threads of discussion on the topic."[5]

The obvious conclusion to be drawn from all this is that many kinds of media — words, pictures, combinations — are effective in communication. Both print and nonprint are flourishing, as attested by the billions of dollars spent on them each year. That so many varieties of format are available presents a challenge to the librarian. Problems of selection are magnified, for, as Asheim says, "the librarian has a role to play in identifying the most effective means for the dissemination of different kinds of messages to serve different purposes for different audiences."[6]

PLACE OF NONPRINT MATERIALS IN THE LIBRARY

Both aural and visual media (especially 16mm films, sound filmstrips, tapes, and videorecords) are expanding their coverage into practically all fields of interest. Among the several uses of these media, there are three which make them especially important for library collections.

Instruction

Films, recordings, and the like are valuable, first, as instruments of teaching and learning. They portray facts, stimulate emotions, raise questions for discussion. In this role they are an accepted part of the libraries or instructional media centers of school and junior college libraries. More attention has been devoted to the educational aspect than to any other, so that these media are sometimes considered mere "aids" to classroom teaching. In this connection the Dean of the Graduate School of Education, University of California at Los Angeles, had some strong words:

> The cant in audiovisual education is that the audiovisual presentation must be built into or made an extension of whatever the conventional teaching procedures may be. It is rarely assumed that youngsters are free to use such materials on their own initiative: to record tapes, to make records, to prepare films, or to use any of these which are available. Invariably the teacher intervenes in some way between student and the learning device. Herein, I think, lies the heart of the problem.[7]

Libraries, both school and other types, are places of free choice, allowing students and others to select for themselves among a wide range of materials. Here nonprint materials become even more significant as true sources of learning. Gathered for the individual, they express a recognition of each person's importance. David Riesman's comment about the neighborhood librarian who is a help to children because she does not appear in the direct line of authority — does not force one or another title on the child[8] — applies also to nonprint media, and probably not to the young only, but to adults as well. A medium which appeals to one may be ignored by another, and rightly so.

Entertainment

Looking at foreign countries as examined by the camera of a discriminating traveller; enjoying music in a sound recording; following the development of a complex plot in a well-directed movie; living the career of an admired personality through an accurate documentary film — these are a few of the entertaining experiences offered by nonprint media. In fact, one objection (a rather weak one) to the use of such media in the classroom has been that they entertain rather than discipline the student mind. It has long been recognized (in spite of certain opposition to the novel) that libraries ought to provide books for amusement, and with a probable increase in leisure time brought about by shortened hours of work, one of the most important functions of the library will be to supply a wide variety of materials which entertain in a civilized way.

Preservation of Facts and Ideas

Many ideas and raw data are captured in their original state on films and recordings. Jussim emphasizes the need for great quantities of records pertaining to a single subject (for example, "all the stereographs of Niagara Falls ever produced") in order to "permit the verification of hypotheses about the nature of various phenomena."[9]

Libraries also have a responsibility for preserving the more significant local materials. Just as the alert public library staff saves the most useful printed archival records of local interest, it also feels a need to collect for historical purposes those records which appear in other forms. Videotapes or sound recordings of local personalities and of visiting dignitaries, motion pictures of interesting occasions, and photographs of city streets are a few examples of the infinite number of possibilities. Special libraries save materials relating to their own narrow interests. University libraries and archives collect on a wider basis.

It was suggested many years ago that a library might record local history by selecting several vantage points in the city; then each month snapping a photograph from each point, always positioning the camera in the same way. By this method of sampling the passing scene, there would be gathered over the years a unique visual record of the changes in buildings, automobiles, costumes, and people. Even the bulldozers of urban "renewal" would not destroy such scenes. Many residents of a city are acutely conscious (some even proud) of their own history. The library serves them well by keeping such records.

The Library's Overall Responsibility

In view of the public interest in nonprint materials, and because of the importance of such means of communication, it is plain that many larger libraries should and do invest heavily in them. After a national survey of nonprint in public libraries, James W. Brown concluded that, "the action is considerable."[10]

The Chairman of the Commission on Instructional Technology warned of

> . . . two kinds of schoolmen who are likely to shortchange their schools in the future; those ultraconservatives who refuse to believe that the new developments in educational technology have something genuinely important to bring to the improvement of instruction, and those ultras at the other extreme who plunge too hastily into expensive investments without reliable knowledge of their value and without adequate competence to employ the equipment effectively.[11]

The advice has relevance also for libraries. The Audiovisual Committee of the Public Library Association recommends that for small and medium-sized libraries, fifteen percent of the materials budget go for audiovisual resources,[12] for large public libraries, ten to fifteen percent.[13] While such figures are arrived at arbitrarily, they do suggest a sensible reference point from which a given library can begin deviating.

The smaller library must proceed a bit more carefully, as it does in collecting books. The addition of a nonprint media format may call for purchase (and along with it, maintenance) of equipment for viewing or listening. Furthermore, to do justice to the handling of these media and to advise patrons on use, it is necessary to have staff members with special qualifications. Personnel are almost sure to fail with nonprint materials unless they have professional training or equivalent experience in this specialty. Like marriage, therefore, the decision to incorporate nonprint media should be made "not unadvisedly or lightly." For the individual library, the question is: If we are to give the best service possible with our funds and staff, how thin shall we spread our funds and talents? In deciding how best to allot its budgetary resources to provide most for its actual and potential users, the librarian, using the best advice available, must make decisions among broad areas of material.

One dimension of the problem is the amount of nonprint material on the market. The number of new educational titles runs into the tens of thousands each year, the total of "in-print" items running into the hundreds of thousands. When to these groups are added the whole of non-educational production, it becomes clear from the grand total what the dimensions of the problem of selection are.

If the library has a written selection policy, that document should define clearly the scope of nonprint media to be gathered by purchase and gift, and give, as well, some of the criteria used for selection of specific formats and materials. The policy should state also under what circumstances the library will buy or rent items. Rental of a motion picture film, for instance, is indicated if the use is predicted to be only two or three showings a year. (The cost of processing rental papers should not be overlooked.) If the library is a member of a system, or is on a film circuit (which circulates motion picture prints to each participating institution), then purchase is far less urgent.

When a library decides to add a new media format, whether slides, sound recordings, motion picture films, or any other, it should be prepared to invest a substantial sum for the materials, for personnel to service them, and perhaps for equipment. In the case of a public library, for instance, it is important for people to know about the new format and to pass along the word —"You can get filmstrips at the library." Winning public acceptance requires more than a few dozen items in the format chosen.

This chapter has dealt with general considerations that must be borne in mind when planning for nonprint resources and formulating policies with regard to collecting them. The next two chapters will attempt a more specific presentation of the relative values of various kinds of media formats, and of particular types of materials.

15. GENERAL PRINCIPLES AND GUIDES

Each medium of communication, whether visual, aural, tactile, or a combination, has its distinctive properties and conveys different kinds of information to different people with various degrees of effectiveness. The question is not whether one type is inherently better than another. Each is good and efficient in terms of some persons, messages, and purposes. The present chapter will elaborate on this generalization.

CHOICE OF MEDIA FORMATS

While school libraries may wish to add nonprint media one subject area at a time,[1] the public library may find it more desirable to proceed by format. This means that before deciding to make the first investment in a medium new to the collection, the small library must evaluate the qualities of that type of material and what it can contribute to library patrons. Some of these factors will be illustrated with examples of media formats, but more specific notes on them will be held for Chapter 16. One can note from the following outline that there is overlapping among the elements to be evaluated. They should be considered as a group rather than individually. It is the overall worth of each medium that is to be judged.

Effectiveness of Communication

Which media are best for portraying what topics or kinds of information? Unfortunately, it is extremely difficult to measure these important qualities. A good deal of research has sought answers to the question, but has been, on the whole, inconclusive; variations among content and among persons are too great. Some media convey their messages through two sensory channels (as, eye *and* ear). Are they more effective than those accessible through one channel only? Recent studies say, "Not necessarily," but the complete answer is an extremely complicated one. It probably cannot be obtained until we have more fundamental knowledge of the human nervous system and how it encodes stimuli coming in by ear, eye, and other sense organs. We need a better understanding of how rapidly a person can assimilate bits of information. Too, we need carefully controlled experiments with media and different kinds of people.

Another crucial question for selection: Is color more effective than black and white? For conveying some kinds of information, No. The simple black and white may be less confusing. Yet color, where skillfully used, almost always brings more pleasure to the viewer and for some presentations is an aid in making facts stand out, or in providing verisimilitude. Even where color does little to distinguish a particular message, it seems to be preferred, perhaps because more and more people are being conditioned by color television.[2]

Pictures in motion obviously hold attention, for the eye is attracted by movement. They are excellent for presenting concepts in science and technology—all the way from the operation of planetary (revolving) gears in small machines to spacecraft orbiting the sun. Motion pictures can also capture the authentic flavor of historical events and are an excellent means of preserving theatrical performances for study and enjoyment. But for other purposes, the motion may be wasted or may even be a hindrance to quick understanding.

Is realistic detail a characteristic to be demanded? Not always, for there is some evidence that it can interfere with the transmission of the basic information intended.[3]

Questions of a more general nature are suggested. How is the behavior of a group of people affected by their viewing of a film on political chicanery? What if the film is a recording of a secret meeting of schemers? The number of such questions is infinite. Librarians will be particularly interested in future research on the relationship of the various media to different types of learning and to the characteristics of individual users. We would like to know a great deal more even about the influence of reading.

Purposes and Uses

If it is assumed that a library collection is primarily for use by individuals (as is often the case with the public library), those media used best by one person or perhaps by a small group are given preference. Recordings, slides, filmstrips, videorecords, and film loops typify this quality. Sixteen-millimeter motion pictures are another story, but it is becoming more and more common for individuals to view them, and this is entirely feasible with the use of compact rear projection equipment. Filmstrips may be viewed on relatively simple projectors by one person or a small group. If the materials are to be presented to larger audiences, or are to be handled by operators with some know-how, the field is open to more types of resources.

Convenience of Use

For the typical library patron, a format that is quick and simple to utilize is, other things being equal, preferable to one that is slow and cumbersome, or that requires special skill. Slides, transparencies, and filmstrips have the advantage of being relatively easy to use. Film and tape require no fuss if in the form of cartridges or cassettes (the latter do not need to be rewound at all). So far there is not a satisfactory cartridge for 16mm films. Should one be marketed widely, that would improve the relative position of this format. Even portability should be taken into account. The old 78 rpm disc recordings were unsatisfactory in this respect; after being lugged home they played for such a short time. Far better are the long-playing discs or tapes. Videorecords may prove very convenient in this respect.

Equipment Required

Related to convenience of use is the matter of equipment needed in connection with any given format. The cost of a 16mm motion-picture sound projector may present no obstacle to the showing of films in schools and colleges; hence the format may be given high priority. For a public library the question of the projector looms larger. The library itself may have film showings, but circulation for home use will be limited. Equipment for 8mm loops, though costing less, is likewise extremely rare in the home. A projector for two-by-two-inch slides or for filmstrips, on the other hand, costs as little as sixty dollars, with hand viewers selling for much less. Moreover many homes, particularly in reasonably affluent areas, have slide projectors and small portable screens. Videorecordings playable on home television sets are a natural for public libraries, and will probably become very popular if perfected and standardized. Phonograph record players being common, the library renders a valuable service in offering discs to be played.

The library may loan equipment for use at home, and if so, it is doubly important that such machines be easy to operate, so as to reduce damage and save maintenance time.

The library may have to make an additional investment in special cabinets or shelving, necessary if films, filmstrips, transparencies, and so forth are to be housed compactly. The trend toward arranging together on the shelves all kinds of materials, print and nonprint, which pertain to a given subject means deeper, slightly more expensive shelves and more floor space.

Durability

Formats that give longer service and that are less subject to damage or deterioration ordinarily offer a wiser investment of library funds. Disc recordings may be ruined by scratching but are much less subject to breakage than they were a couple of decades ago. Tapes and motion picture films can be mangled. For any filmed material, preservation is a little more of a problem than it is for books, the main factors being temperature, relative humidity, and air purity. It should be noted, though, that damage to nonprint materials generally is inadvertent (at least so far), whereas books and periodicals often are mutilated deliberately. Fortunately dogs are not fond of chewing film.

Price

Of the individual items typically collected by libraries, the most costly is the sound motion picture. A 16mm color sound film may well cost over four hundred dollars. A 1978 study of a selection of films from eleven companies found that the average cost per minute was $14.10.[4] A library usually prefers to rent rather than buy a film unless its predicted use is great, because the rate for rental usually runs about ten percent of the purchase price. Super-8mm films are about seventy-five percent the price of 16mm. Slides cost in the neighborhood of two dollars each, though there is a great variation from this price for individual items. Filmstrips are around thirty dollars; recordings up to fifteen dollars a disc; sound tapes somewhat higher. Is a sound motion picture worth as much to the library's users as forty or fifty more recordings or an assortment of other lower-priced items? Considerations of this sort are hard to evaluate; yet they are involved in the decisions which a librarian must make day by day.

The British writer C. J. Duncan has prepared a chart of selected media, showing that items which are simpler and cheaper tend to be more specific in subject range. If a film, for instance, is produced at great cost, it is likely to be less specific; that is, the argument will be "diluted or blunted to make the material and vehicle more suitable for a wider audience and thus allow the high costs to be recovered with more certainty."[5] This being true, libraries which intend to serve the individual would do well to consider carefully those less costly items which appeal to narrow interests. Fortunately there are thousands of films available on very specific topics.

Expense in terms of library staff time also varies with different media. Slides and other small items require processing time out of proportion to their sizes, and are troublesome to circulate. Usually it is necessary to inspect film prints and recordings when they are returned to the library by borrowers. Phonograph discs can be examined visually in a minute but rewinding films and filmstrips takes time. If the circulation of such prints is above fifty per day, the task of inspection becomes so great that electronic equipment is recommended; however, such machines cost several thousand dollars each.[6] If repairs have to be made on the films, even more staff time is consumed.

CHOICE OF SPECIFIC MATERIALS

Once a library has decided on the media format it will collect for the time being, and has made plans as to the order in which it will add other formats, there still are decisions on whether to order or reject individual items. For each of the thousands of pieces of material that come up for consideration in the course of a year, certain questions must be asked. Some of the criteria parallel those which are used to judge books, but are, if anything, even more difficult to apply. In general, the questions concern:

1. Basic criteria for acquisitions. Does this piece of material represent a real addition to the library? Does it display ideas or facts that have not been, up to now, accessible in the collection? Is their addition desired? This criterion is really very hard to apply, because some people apparently "do not like novelty . . . they actively retreat from it."[7] For them, materials must be regular and organized. Other people prefer surprises and new ideas.

Is the work accurate, up to date, truthful? As noted in the discussion of books (Chapter 6), these questions are fundamental, and not nearly so easy to answer as may first appear. Films made for propaganda (using the term in its worst sense) are certainly less valuable than those which give a fair and objective account. However, propaganda cannot be detected "scientifically," and the library has the obligation here, as in other media, to offer a wide range of opinion. Even to label a film as "true," "false," or "questionable" would be an infringement on the patrons' rights to make their own judgments.

The reputation of the sponsor may be such that one can have confidence in the material's content, but with institutions once highly respected (such as churches and charitable organizations) being ravaged by scandal or challenged by dissent, librarians can't use this criterion in anything like an absolute way. Reputations here are more fleeting even than those of book publishers.

Free material typically represents an expenditure on the part of some organization for the purpose of promoting its own cause. A filmstrip distributed by the government of the USSR (or of any other country) hardly springs out of pure generosity, nor does a motion picture offered by an automobile manufacturer. However, if it is clear who the sponsoring group is, then no great harm is likely to come about.

Notwithstanding these considerations, general standards of novelty, truth, recency, and accuracy can be applied to nonprint media, and should be.

2. The arrangement of the material. Is it felicitious? Is there a progression from known to unknown, or is the development logical? Or is the sequence worked out satisfactorily according to some other plan? Even a mixed-media hodge-podge may be acceptable on occasion. Are outlines and summaries handled well? In reading a book, we may skip about and, to some extent, make our own arrangement. Since this kind of scanning is more difficult with the typical audiovisual format, the question of its basic arrangement is crucial.

3. The content. Is it such that the particular medium is needed to present it well, or is this the kind of subject that would be better understood or appreciated through some other vehicle? This standard will become more applicable as research uncovers more about the effectiveness of various media formats in relation to subjects and purposes.

4. The technical quality. Is it satisfactory? Is the workmanship of sufficiently high quality? Are detail and color reproduced with fidelity? Those who have been brought up on high-quality materials are quick to criticize products that are noticeably below standard in these respects. Sound recordings that are not clear and faithful seem terrible. Photographs that are a little out of focus or badly composed are no longer acceptable.

5. "Commercials." Are distracting elements eliminated or at least kept under control? In free materials, is commercial huckstering held to a level that users can tolerate? Some films loaned free by profit-making organizations are unobjectionable in that they do not press a point too far. In this class, for instance, are

many films of travel agencies and other groups whose main purpose is to make a geographical area seem interesting, rather than to demand, "Buy your ticket at _____." With items that advertise a certain product or promote a doubtful cause, the problem is a little more serious. Not that there should be an absolute rule against advertising—after all, periodicals advertise all sorts of things; yet the problem is different, too, because in nonprint materials, the worthless or offensive matter cannot be skipped so easily. Such messages get in the way of the user's enjoyment or instruction; hence do not allow the best use of viewing or listening time.

6. Dated information. How long-lasting is the message conveyed? In some areas information goes out of date rapidly; in others it changes slowly. To take a common example, methods and machinery used in some manufacturing processes (a favorite topic for films) are in an almost constant state of change (printing machinery is a case in point). Political situations are often quite unstable, as are sociological conditions. Automobile designs, especially in the United States, are perhaps the best example of all. The principle of the piston engine may be the same in 1981 as it was in 1928, but an illustration of this principle using a Model-A Ford is likely to be more distracting than helpful.

In another aspect of this problem, the information itself may change while the object being investigated remains the same. From year to year, we learn new facts or promote new theories about the world. The atom of gold is presumably the same everywhere and has been so for millennia upon millennia. Yet a film which assumed the correctness of J. J. Thomson's conception of atomic structure (advanced at the turn of the century) would seem ridiculous today. For expensive items like motion pictures, this question is crucial. A film in a fast-changing field should be rented rather than purchased, even if its immediate interest is considerable. Works on literature and history are better bets for the long haul than materials on science. Unfortunately, both with print and nonprint media, many items which seem the most interesting at the present time will have the least appeal in ten years.

7. Service. Are there users or potential users of the library who particularly need the approach taken in this title? This is the ultimate test, for service to the patron is the library's reason for being.

As brought out in the discussion of book selection it would be desirable to examine each item before a decision is made to accept or reject it. This same rule applies to nonprint materials, particularly to expensive ones such as sound motion pictures. Schools therefore need pleasant facilities for both library staff and classroom teachers to preview new productions. Such facilities are of hardly less importance in the public library. Previewing is not done for the sake of selection alone. A by-product of such evaluation sessions is wide, first-hand knowledge of materials. When a patron seeks advice on the best formats and materials for personal or group use, the library staff is able to respond with a greater degree of assurance.

GENERAL GUIDES TO SELECTION

Because frequently it is not feasible to examine an item personally, a librarian must depend on critical opinion in the form of guides and reviews. Even if the librarian does inspect a piece of material before purchase, the informed judgment of an expert will add fullness and accuracy to the evaluation. In this connection, lowly advertisements should not be disdained. The improvement in bibliographic apparatus for nonprint materials in the last fifteen years has been remarkable, though there is still a way to go before services equal those available for printed resources.

For an overview of nonprint materials, there are several bibliographies or "mediagraphies."* One of the best is Margaret I. Rufsvold's *Guides to Educational Media: Films, Filmstrips, Multimedia Kits, Programmed Instruction Materials, Recordings on Discs and Tapes, Slides, Transparencies, Videotapes,* 4th ed. (Chicago: Amer-

---

*We shall have to accept this offensive term, along with "filmographies" and "discographies"—all are being used too widely to ignore.

ican Library Association, 1977, 159 p.). This small book describes lists, catalogs, and review sources, rather than particular films, slides or videotapes. It is alphabetical by title.

A similar guide, but arranged by subject, is Allan Mirwis's *Guides to Educational Media Software* (New York: Educational Media Information Service, Inc., 1977, 150 p.). *Educational Media Yearbook* edited by James W. Brown (New York: R. R. Bowker, 1973– annually) includes "Mediagraphy: Print and Nonprint Resources." Also of general interest is the annual Bowker publication *Audiovisual Market Place: A Multimedia Guide.*

Other tools list specific titles of nonprint materials, and so are useful in a more direct way. The large and colorful catalogs (for example, *Time-Life Films*) issued by the producers and distributors of nonprint materials often are useful in selection and ordering (even more so than are publishers' catalogs for books), hence should be filed for reference. Many selection tools give lists of producers and distributors; they may be contacted for their catalogs and other advertising.

The National Information Center for Educational Media (NICEM) at the University of Southern California publishes a number of comprehensive lists of particular media formats, using a huge data base which is updated constantly. For each format there are approaches by subject and title. The Center has also issued separate volumes, each covering several media on a subject. Their plan is to revise each index every two and a half years. Taken as a set, these indexes form the most important tool for this area.

The Educators Progress Service, Randolph, Wisconsin, publishes a worthwhile series listing "free" items. Unfortunately, titles in these guides are not always available promptly; they often are out on loan to other agencies. The series takes in such annual publication as *Educators Guide to Free Films, Educators Guide to Free Filmstrips* (including slides and transparencies also), *Educators Guide to Free Audio and Video Materials,* and *Educators Guide to Free Social Studies Materials.* Since the titles listed in this series typically represent the work of organizations distributing propaganda or advertising, they should be judged with special attention to points 1 and 5 under "Choice of Specific Materials" above. Some nonprofit (and even profit-making) groups are concerned with the people's benefit; of others one cannot be so sure. The user may be reminded of these facts before a film or other item listed in one of the guides to free materials is requested for loan.

Lucy Gregor Brown has compiled two selective lists, both published by Bowker: *Core Media Collection for Elementary Schools* (1978, 224 p.), and *Core Media Collection for Secondary Schools* (1975, 221 p.). Marion Koenig's *Bowker AV Guide: A Subject Guide to Audio-Visual Educational Material* (New York: Bowker, 1975, 611 p.) is a list of resources, fictional and non-fictional, produced by European countries.

The lists noted above are general in scope. Most others are specialized in terms of subject, format, or audience. For instance, there are guides to media for children, for "disadvantaged" persons, and for other groups. Media on specific subjects will be mentioned in Part V of this book; those with particular formats, in the next chapter.

Government organizations, which publish thousands of documents, also produce a variety of nonprint materials for one purpose or another. Many of these titles are made available to libraries and to private citizens. The National Archives and Records Service, a part of the General Services Administration of the United States Federal Government, has in Washington a National Audiovisual Center to serve educational institutions, industry, government, and the general public. It sells materials produced by such agencies as the Atomic Energy Commission; the Departments of Health and Education; the National Aeronautics and Space Administration; the National Science Foundation; the Department of State; and a number of others. The Center issues *A Reference List of Audiovisual Materials Produced by the United States Government,* together with a *Quarterly Update,* showing items for sale or rental. Other titles are available on loan from the government, and some of them are noted in the various announcements of the Center.

Finding current evaluative opinion on nonprint media items is, if anything, a greater problem than obtaining reviews of books. Though such services are growing in number, they still tend to be a bit unsystematic. It must be noted, though, that both coverage and quality of criticism are improving. The journals aimed at educators are useful to librarians, both for general articles and for notes about resources.

Media Review Digest (Ann Arbor, MI: Pierian Press, 1973–), the successor to *Multi-Media Reviews Index,* lists reviews of individual titles in periodicals, and includes a rating of the favorability of each review.

The excellent journal *Previews,* started by Bowker in 1972 has been discontinued, with the promise of greater coverage of nonprint media in *Library Journal* and *School Library Journal.* The *Audiovisual Librarian* has good notes for selections. In *Learning Today: An Educational Magazine of Library College Thought,* the regular feature "New Learning Resources" is fine for keeping up with new catalogs and lists which become available. *Booklist* reviews 16mm films, filmstrips, recordings, multimedia kits, and some other formats along with books. *American Libraries'* regular column "Mediatmosphere" includes notes about materials.

16. SELECTION

In this chapter, the various media formats will be discussed in more detail, exemplifying the principles of selection mentioned previously, with notes on some of the more specific tools that provide help in making decisions.

MOTION PICTURES

Moving pictures have had a phenomenal growth since Thomas A. Edison's Kinetoscope, introduced in 1893. Thirty-three years later, Melvil Dewey was urging their use in libraries: "If you can carry information or inspiration or recreation to human beings better or quicker or cheaper, the librarian is bound to use that means."[1] Film has been standardized over most of the world in widths of 8mm, 16mm, 35mm, and 70mm. Since there are 25.4 millimeters to the inch, 8mm film is about ⅓ of an inch wide. While the color film with sound is typical of the breed, black and white and even silent films can be effective.

Motion pictures are used to present concrete data; to depict theatrical performances; to portray strange lands; to illustrate concepts that vary as widely as those in religion and science. A class known as documentaries is used to present real-life situations and occurrences. "Personal films," usually short, are designed to let individual viewers perceive and understand according to their own personalities and backgrounds.

There are motion pictures that represent direct photography of things as they are; others are based on dramatized reenactments. Such subjects as energy, ecology, drug abuse, death and dying, the plight of the American Indian, and Black history and culture are currently in the forefront. Complete courses in fields such as physics and language can be taught by film series.

Educational and General Use Films

Until the 1960s the 16mm sound film was the most widely-used type in education; it is still important there and also in the public library. This size is used to depict a wide variety of phenomena, especially in documentaries, travelogues, and training films. Length of running time varies from three to thirty minutes — sometimes more. Because of their relatively high price, 16mm films often are rented, if required for a very few showings, rather than purchased outright, so loan services offer them in great quantities.

Eight-millimeter film came into prominence in the 1960s, and was followed by Super 8mm with a slightly larger frame size. Though the image on these films is only ¼ to ⅓ the size of that on 16mm, improvements in photographic technique and in the physical quality of film itself have made it satisfactory for viewing by small groups. In addition to open reels like those commonly employed for 16mm, the 8mm films often are placed in easily-used cartridges. Eight-millimeter film is also used for continuous loops in which each cycle takes three to five minutes (some are longer), and which can be repeated as long as the user wishes. Thus, 8mm film is employed for "single-concept" and "how-to-do-it" demonstrations, explaining such things as techniques in physical education or even how to operate a film projector. In spite of its advantages, however, 8mm is not gaining great popularity.

In comparison with most other nonprint media, motion picture films receive good bibliographic coverage. One source is *Library of Congress Catalogs: Audiovisual Materials* (Washington: Library of Congress, 1952– , quarterly, with annual and five-year cumulations). Once known as *Motion Pictures and Filmstrips,* this catalog now includes transparencies, slide sets, and videorecordings. Except for the last format, the Library tries to list all items of instructional value issued in the United States and Canada. Each entry has LC cataloging data plus a summary of content. In similar but more limited vein, *The British National Film Catalogue,* 1963– , quarterly with an annual cumulation, lists and annotates British and other films available in Great Britain. It includes a subject section arranged by the Universal Decimal Classification.

Educational Film Locater (New York: Bowker, 1978, 2,178 p.)

is a selected union list of about 37,000 films from fifty separate catalogs of university film centers.

The National Information Center for Educational Media has a four-volume *Index to 16mm Educational Films,* which now has about 100,000 entries, and a one-volume *Index to 8mm Motion Cartridges.*

EFLA Evaluations (New York: Educational Film Library Association, 1946–) is a service formerly issued on cards but now about ten times a year in loose-leaf form. Reviews are critical.

There are numerous guides to films on particular topics, for certain groups of users, or produced by given agencies. The Serina Press in Alexandria, Virginia, publishes several annotated lists of this type, such as: *Guide to Films About Famous People; Guide to Foreign-Government Loan Film; Guide to Films (16mm) About Negroes; Guide to Films (16mm) About Ecology, Adaptation and Pollution;* and *Guide to State-Loan Film (16mm).*

So far as reviews of film are concerned, there are several periodicals of special interest. The *Film Library Quarterly* carries pertinent articles and has excellent evaluations of films from the library point-of-view. Among *Sightlines'* features are "Filmlist" (annotated by distributors) and "Video Playback." *Landers Film Reviews,* published six times a year, evaluates 16mm educational motion pictures and multi-media materials. Judith Trojan's column "Front Row Center" in the *Wilson Library Bulletin* deals in each issue with films on a particular topic or by one director.

Feature Films

The growing interest among librarians in feature (commercial, entertainment) motion pictures was accelerated in the 1970s as more and more titles became available for nonprofit showing. The medium has attracted directors with serious purposes, and films are being recognized as a complex art form worthy of, and receiving, scholarly criticism. Film courses have been conducted at university level for some years, and are coming into the curricula of secondary and even elementary schools. Feature films protected by copyright obviously are not available for general library circulation until years after they have been released, and Limbacher warns that some of those offered for sale may still be protected.[2] Many of the older titles, however, including classics, already have been freed from restrictions of copyright, and the surprising thing is the number of newer releases that are available.

Limbacher limits feature films to those having more than one reel or a running time of at least 48 minutes (with a few exceptions).[3] Most feature films are photographed originally in 35mm or 70mm widths, but there are firms that specialize in reducing them to 8mm and 16mm. The 8mm are satisfactory for individuals or small groups; 16mm can be shown in auditoriums of moderate size. A 16mm feature film costs anywhere from $200 to $1,500, depending on recency, demand, and other factors; an 8mm runs much less. Rental of recent productions (those not available for purchase) is also a possibility.

The past few years have seen the publication of numerous books about feature films—not only the coffee-table type, laden with portraits of the stars, but many smaller books analyzing the work of one director or discussing a particular genre (the western, the gangster movie, etc.). Among the larger reference sets, *The New York Times Film Reviews, 1913–68* (New York: The Times, 1970, 6 vols., with supplements for later years) is a reproduction of critical reviews originally appearing over many years. The R. R. Bowker Company has in process of publication *The American Film Institute Catalog of Motion Pictures*. It proposes to describe "objectively and definitively" all the feature films, short films, and newsreels ever produced in the United States. Plot summaries and elaborate indexes are to be included. Progress so far has not been rapid.

A reference guide of fundamental importance to librarians in this area has been compiled and edited by James L. Limbacher: *Feature Films on 8mm, 16mm and Videotape*, 6th ed. (New York: Bowker, 1979, 447 p.). This work, frequently updated, is subtitled "A Directory of Feature Films Available for Rental, Sale, and Lease in the United States and Canada." About 20,000 titles are noted, and the list is supplemented quarterly in the journal *Sightlines*.

Video

Videorecords, made from television programs and from films, offer interesting possibilities either for viewing in libraries or for circulation and use on home equipment. The editor of *Film Library Quarterly* thinks they may come to supplement film in library collections as the latter has supplemented print.[4] Library experiences, favorable and other, with this medium have been surveyed by Goldstein.[5] The principal formats so far have been tapes and cassettes, in widths of ¼ inch to 2 inches, but the disc type may win out eventually.

Videorecords have several advantages: they can be duplicated fast, are relatively easy to use, play for a long time (tapes up to four hours), and are durable, even with repeated playing (some discs are not affected at all, though they can be damaged in other ways). Should a sizeable percentage of homes purchase the machines for playback, and should programs become available on a wide array of topics, this format could become extremely important for libraries, especially public.

Because videorecords carry a great amount of data in a small package,* they have, like books, the advantage of portability. They may be used for text but are better for pictorial matter. As with most other nonprint (and even print) media, many libraries produce or reproduce materials for their own collections; with this format, however, the question of copyright can be especially tricky. Nevertheless, the preservation of entertainment and news programs is a valuable service.

NICEM publishes an *Index to Educational Video Tapes*. Another guide, *The Videologs* (Edison, NJ: Esselte Video, Inc.), lists (in separate volumes) thousands of programs for health sciences, business, and entertainment. Videorecords are reviewed in *Booklist* and other journals.

*For instance, the twelve-inch disc with the equivalent of three hundred books, each over 360 pages in length.

STILL PHOTOGRAPHY

This topic encompasses media formats less exciting than those that involve the illusion of motion, but their usefulness for library purposes should not be underestimated. It has been shown that for some subjects their effectiveness rivals that of the more expensive motion pictures, and in general they offer a greater degree of flexibility. They are available for a tremendous variety of subjects, and for most levels of audience understanding.

Filmstrips

Usually made of 35mm film packaged in cylindrical containers 1½ inches high and 1½ inches in diameter, filmstrips are literally strips of film, each made up of 20 to 100 (maybe more) individual frames. They may be in color or black and white; some are silent; some have a sound track; others are accompanied by sound recording on tapes or discs. The latter combinations create a few cataloging and shelving problems in libraries.

This format, which was developed about 1920, is good for presenting straight facts as well as for teaching viewers how to do things. Filmstrips are more flexible than motion pictures in that the viewer or lecturer may linger on one frame and pass quickly over another. Though used frequently in the classroom (probably more often than any other projected format), they are, if anything, more natural for individual study and enjoyment, since the equipment is easy to operate.

NICEM's *Index to 35mm Educational Filmstrips* (now issued in 3 vols.) notes twenty-one configurations of accompanying materials. This format is noticed also with brief reviews in other journals devoted to nonprint matters, and in *Booklist*.

Slides

The slide is about the smallest unit of material handled by the library. The bother of ordering, housing, and circulation is partially compensated for by its great flexibility in use. Slides may be shown or viewed in any quantity and sequence desired, and one may be studied carefully while the next one is passed by quickly. Typically they are made up of 35mm film chips in cardboard, plastic, or metal frames measuring 2 by 2 inches. Old-fashioned lantern slides measuring 3¼ by 4 inches are still produced in very limited subject fields. The clearer image made possible by the larger size is for some subjects worth the cost, but the bulkier projectors are becoming rare. Many slides are sold in sets which treat specific topics. They are available also with sound accompaniment by various means, but special projection/playing equipment is required. Slides are a natural for such subjects as architecture, painting, and the other fine arts. Slides made from images as seen through a microscope are valuable in such fields as botany, zoology, and bacteriology. One procedure for choosing slides is perusal of the producers' and distributors' catalogs. The best inclusive guide is NICEM's *Index to Educational Slides*.

Since photographs of this kind are made by so many people with their own cameras, many scenes of interest to the community are captured, and patrons often are happy to present the library with duplicates.

Transparencies

Although they can be viewed by individuals, transparencies generally are used with overhead projectors for groups. Many different sizes are available, the most typical dimensions of the image being a 10-by-10–inch frame, though many are 7-by-7. Even more than other nonprint materials, they are likely to be produced locally by teachers or lecturers for specific presentations, but they are issued also by commercial firms in a wide range of subjects, and in numerous series. Books of paper-like masters can be used to print individual transparencies as needed. For presenting charts, graphs, and similar information step by step, transparencies are highly efficient. They are useful also for explaining mathematical concepts, as in geometry. Again, NICEM has the best listing: *Index to Overhead Transparencies*.

SOUND RECORDINGS

Coincidentally, Thomas A. Edison, a chief inventor of the motion picture machine, was also one of the principal devisers of the sound recording, in the year 1877. (It was over thirty-five years later that he hooked the phonograph and camera together to make "talking pictures.") In the near-century since the first recording, the machine has caught some strange and interesting phenomena. Among the sounds of history that have been preserved, however imperfectly, are William Jennings Bryan's "Cross of Gold" speech in 1896, Big Ben tolling in the twentieth century, and assorted noises of the Spanish-American War.

Though the ear takes in information very slowly as compared with the eye, it picks up some nuances that are missed in reading print. Sound recordings therefore have a vital place in the transmission of ideas in addition to their main use: entertainment and aesthetic pleasure.

The two formats now most often used are discs and tapes. The former come in several sizes and speeds, with 33⅓rpm LPs (Long Plays) being dominant. Familiar for years, discs are still sold in huge quantities and produce a high-quality tone, though they develop ticks and crackling sounds and lose their high frequencies through repeated playing. Discs are at the present time preferable for library collections. They are often borrowed for home use because so many people have players.

Tape recordings have been used since the 1940s, and probably will improve in the next few years. They come in three formats: open reels, cartridges, and cassettes. The latter two are easier to play; the former gives the highest fidelity. Distracting noise produced by tapes has been reduced in recent years, and as a wider selection becomes available, their position in the library collection is sure to improve.

Considerations with respect to both disc and tape will be altered if digital recording becomes the common practice. As with videorecords, incompatibility among the products of competing firms will be troublesome.

Sound recordings are classified also into two categories — musical and nonmusical. Their popularity in the former area is well known, and will be discussed more fully under the subject of Music in Part V. Nonmusical recordings preserve many peculiar and fabulous sounds of nature, human and otherwise. They afford the imaginative reenactments of historical events, such as the signing of the Magna Carta and the burning of Joan of Arc. They are excellent for current events; they preserve interpretations of poetry and drama by various readers; they record the interviews of oral history; they indicate the quality of delivery by actors and public speakers; they document sounds for science. Libraries render an especially important service to the blind by supplying recorded materials such as "talking books."

The *U.S. Library of Congress Catalogs: Music, Books on Music, and Sound Recordings* (Washington: Library of Congress, 1953– , semiannually with annual and five-year cumulations) includes musical, educational, literary, and political recordings. Antoinette Maleady has compiled an annual *Index to Record and Tape Reviews, 1972–* (Metuchen, NJ: Scarecrow Press, 1973– [publisher and title vary]), which includes both musical and spoken records. There are several annual reviews.

Other Formats

Multi-media kits are composed of several different formats, including as a rule both print and nonprint (such as, study prints, sound recordings, filmstrips, booklets, artifacts), all directed toward a given learning objective. One of the kits is said to contain slides, a guide for bartenders, and samples of liquors to be mixed and tested. More conventional topics, such as how to drive a car, are the rule. These kits are found in the school library more than in any other type. The same is true of "realia," a group which includes specimens, models, and educational mock-ups (such as replicas of the parts of the human body, or of mechanical equipment) that can be taken apart and reassembled.

PART V

SELECTION BY SUBJECT FIELD

There are many ways to slice the mass of published materials for the purpose of closer observation: old versus new, theoretical versus practical, light versus heavy, English versus foreign language, and so on. All things considered, the most convenient approach seems to be by subject. Frequently the reader who comes to the collection is interested in a specific topic that is a division of a larger field.

The pitfalls and inconsistencies of subject classification are well known. To divide up learning in any absolute fashion is preposterous, for like a river it is fluid, changing. If it could be cut into divisions, the parts would flow back together. Attempts to classify knowledge and to establish subject disciplines are artificial. The processes by which these fields are formed are long, and would seem to be largely matters of chance. Once a field has been defined and has gained loyal adherents, it tends to harden in its mold (though all the while changing its terminology and making a pretense of being adaptable and expansive). Reorganizations occur, but the tendencies toward crystallization will not be denied.

Nonetheless, subject classification does provide a reasonably intelligible map of the world of materials, so the following part of this book is set up largely according to these commonly recognized areas of knowledge: the social sciences, the humanities, and the sciences. Creative literature will be considered as a subject within the humanities, though it is often (and maybe more accurately) thought of as a field apart. Three subjects — biography, history, and geography — hardly fit the major areas at all and therefore are taken up separately.

Rather arbitrarily, I shall use the word *area* for the large sections such as humanities. The words *field, discipline,* and *subject* will apply to subdivisions at the level of philosophy, economics, and chemistry. Smaller units will be referred to as *topics*.

17. BIOGRAPHY

Most books are about people, real or fictitious — their behavior; their ideas and philosophies; their religious beliefs; their social relationships; their biological peculiarities; their tastes and talents in art and music. Of all subjects, people are the most interesting. Books describe scientists, crusaders, philosophers, historians, statesmen, artists, criminals, librarians, producers of literature; even writers of biography. Some works are devoted exclusively to the lives of particular individuals, though, and for these we reserve the term for life writing: *biography* — an English word which came into use in the seventeenth century.

In biography, "that most Anglo-Saxon of literary forms,"[1] several persons may be sketched in a single book; one individual may require several volumes; or it may be simply one person, one book.

PURPOSES AND USES OF BIOGRAPHY

Because of the inherent fascination which human beings hold for each other, one of the major purposes of biographical writing is simply to produce interesting books. This alone would be sufficient justification for the genre. A biography makes for pleasant reading because all the ideas are focused on one person. Background facts are important, but each is presented in terms of its connection with the central figure, who serves as a sort of lodestone, or as the Earth in a Ptolemaic cosmology — all the rest of the universe revolving around and taking its importance from its relationship to the one planet. R.W.B. Lewis applies the term *epochal biography* to the work that concentrates on one person but that includes full-scale portraits of others, like Philip McFarland's *Sojourners* (New York: Atheneum, 1979, 587 p.), where the central person is Washington Irving, and Aaron Burr, Walter Scott, John Jacob Astor, and Mary Shelley are also depicted. This epochal method produces "a certain kind of historical and psychological reality."[2]

Moreover, books of biography are interesting because people like to read about certain types of persons — perhaps identifying with them — even as they may collect souvenirs of the great. If at one time a lock of hair from a hero was considered valuable, why not an account of an entire life? *

It is natural to be curious about people, even about the trivial details of their lives. Did Stonewall Jackson get his nickname because of his steadfastness, or because he was stolid and slow-moving? What happened to the pearl earrings worn to the scaffold by Charles I? It has been said that four hundred thousand volumes have been devoted to the life of Napoleon Bonaparte. Pilgrims have retraced his journeys step by step. *"Des rats de bibliothèque"* have discovered who his mistresses were for each quarter-hour.[3]

Human beings are interesting. There is no denying it. Biography, then, offers one of the more satisfying fields in which to select books and other resources for the library.

Interest in biography goes along with concern for the individual, and though each person is unique, all have a good deal in common with other human beings. It may not be out of place, then, to suggest that good biography serves a teaching function. In the words of the great Dr. Johnson:

> No species of writing . . . can more . . . widely diffuse instruction to every diversity of condition. . . . Every man has, in the mighty mass of the world, great numbers in the same condition with himself, to whom his mistakes and miscarriages, escapes and expedients, would be of immediate and apparent use.[4]

Richard Altick comments on the fact that until well past the middle of the nineteenth century, biography was justified on the basis of its "didactic usefulness," adding, "It is ironic, then, that one should again be led in the 1960s to mention the instructive, inspirational function of literary biography; yet it does exist, and

* With reference to Lord Byron, two ladies sought a bit of hair from one of his dogs — preferably from a part which the poet himself had patted (Richard D. Altick, *Lives and Letters* [New York: Knopf, 1965], p. 122).

it is valuable.''[5] A biography written solely for didactic purposes is likely to be insipid, if not downright silly, but a good biography instructs — conveys information — in many ways. It shows what human beings are like and what they can do; how stupid and cruel they can be; how generous and magnificent. Problems and conditions of marriage and family may be studied through biographical data. Political history is dull without reference to influential persons. In such fields as art, literature, and especially philosophy, biographers examine the minds of creative human beings. To many (though by no means all) critics, the artist or the thinker is inseparable from his or her creation. A painting is not the same after we become convinced that it is the work of a counterfeiter. In short, without biography we would be able to discern far less about the human world around us. We would have many more unanswered questions about people and why they behave as they do. Biography is a basic ingredient in other disciplines.

RELATIONSHIPS OF BIOGRAPHY

Though connected with all other subjects, biographical writing has special kinship with three: literature, history, and psychology. Two of these relationships are suggested by *The Oxford English Dictionary,* which defines biography as "the history of the lives of individual men, as a branch of literature."

This assumption that biography is a part of literature is one of long standing. The writer must deal with hard facts, but must be an artist to structure them, and must use imagination to create a picture. A few biographies have become literary classics — Boswell's life of Johnson being the prime example. The connection between biography and fiction is particularly close. Richard Ellmann, in his work *James Joyce,* wrote "a novel at the same time, and on the same pages, that he wrote his biography. Any attentive reader may find this novel in the interstices of the book's archival reportage," according to Edward Mendelson.[6]

There are degrees of fictionalized biography, and we need a word for biographized fiction. Such a term might be applied to the work of Daniel Defoe, who began his writing career with biographies, and in the course of inventing stories and details, gradually worked his way along to a novel, *The Life and Adventures of Robinson Crusoe* (various titles), in 1719. Later in the eighteenth century, Samuel Richardson completed *Pamela; or, Virtue Rewarded* (1741, 2 vols.) in the form of "letters from a beautiful young damsel." Think of the novels that have been built around one main character or have a personal name in the title: names such as Joseph Andrews, David Copperfield, Tom Sawyer, Myra Breckenridge, Ivan Denisovich, Jane Eyre, Silas Marner, Herzog — the list could go on and on. Then there are books like W. Somerset Maugham's *Cakes and Ale; or, The Skeleton in the Cupboard* (Garden City, NY: Doubleday, 1930, 308 p.), a "novel" about a writer commonly thought to be Thomas Hardy.

Some biographies contain so much imaginary matter that they come very close to historical fiction. Irving Stone's books, such as *The Agony and the Ecstasy: A Novel of Michelangelo* (Garden City, NY: Doubleday, 1961, 664 p.); *Lust for Life: A Novel of Vincent van Gogh* (London: Longmans Green, 1934, 489 p.) and *The Passions of the Mind: A Novel of Sigmund Freud* (Garden City, NY: Doubleday, 1971, 808 p.) could be placed in this group. André Maurois took great liberties in *Ariel: The Life of Shelley,* translated by Ella D'Arcy (New York: D. Appleton, 1924, 335 p.), but later said that he did not approve of that method.[7] Truman Capote's *In Cold Blood: A True Account of a Multiple Murder and Its Consequences* (New York: Random House, 1965, 343 p.), is a fascinating narrative about two killers, but maddening in that the reader can't tell what part of it is true and what part supplied from imagination. *Murder in Coweta County,* by Margaret Anne Barnes (New York: Reader's Digest Press, 1976, 387 p.), is based on a real case. The author interviewed participants and included photographs. The Library of Congress gives it a fiction number in the Dewey Decimal system and a number for (nonfiction) criminology in its own classification. Television shows and published works that assign fictitious names to characters who seem to be identifiable, real persons, then flesh out the characterization with imaginary dialogue and actions, are the extreme of this form.

A great distance from this approach, but using creative imagination, are writers such as Catherine Drinker Bowen, who in her *John Adams and the American Revolution* (Boston: Little, Brown, 1950, 699 p.) made up private conversations. She explained, "The sense of them, the emotional or critical content, I took from Adams's Diary or letters, then paraphrased into dialogue."[8]

Other writers describe scenes of which there is no direct, complete record, but use intelligent, solid deduction, as do, for instance, Benjamin Thomas in his *Abraham Lincoln, a Biography* (New York: Knopf, 1952, 548 p.) and Walter Jackson Bate in *Samuel Johnson* (New York: Harcourt Brace Jovanovich, 1977, 646 p.).

The latter examples point up the fact that, though the tie between biography and creative literature is one of the strongest, there is a natural relationship also with the field of history. Since history is mainly about human life, it deals with individual lives and their influences on one another. Bernard DeVoto, in a salty article, declared flatly that "literary people should not be permitted to write biography."[9] — going on to growl that the accuracy necessary for biographical writing is too much for the literary mind. This requirement of exactness in statement together with the need for thoroughness in research makes biography a part of the discipline of history. It is the combination of hard truth and fine art that makes good biographical writing so difficult, yet so rewarding to the reader. Virginia Woolf (the daughter, incidentally, of Sir Leslie Stephen, one of the main editors of the *Dictionary of National Biography*) put the problem like this:

> And if we think of truth as something of granite-like solidity and of personality as something of rainbow-like intangibility and reflect that the aim of biography is to weld these two into one seamless whole, we shall admit that the problem is a stiff one. . . .
>
> For the truth . . . which biography demands, is truth in its hardest, most obdurate form; it is truth as truth is to be found in

the British Museum; it is truth out of which all vapour of false-hood has been pressed by the weight of research.[10]

On the assumption that persons influence the course of events, things are as they are today largely because of people. Biography, then, helps explain how things came to be. In its own right, biography may well be considered the history of individuals as opposed to histories of groups, countries, movements, ideas, or institutions.

Turning next to biography's connections with psychology and related disciplines, we see a two-way street. Those who write about individual lives have been helped by principles discovered in the social and life sciences. Biography provides, in return, rich resources for psychologists to study. John A. Garraty began preparation for his book *The Nature of Biography* with the realization of "how much of a biographer's success depends upon his understanding of human motivation and of such processes as rationalization, sublimation, and repression. It seemed to me that a biographer might profit particularly from an understanding of how psychologists study human personality."[11] Indeed it would seem impossible to write any kind of biography without some presuppositions as to the nature of human behavior. Even the most idle gossip about people is filled with assumptions about their motivations.

Serious applications of psychology have not been easy, however. The most controversial episode in this relationship was the outbreak of psychoanalytical interpretations in the 1920s (really begun by Freud's *Leonardo da Vinci,* first issued in 1910, but stimulated by *A General Introduction of Psycho-analysis,* published in English translation in 1920). Later writers could not resist the opportunity to theorize about hidden motives and complexes of subjects, to explain quirks of their behavior as symptoms of inner drives. Though it is generally agreed that Freudian psychology contributed a great deal to authors' understanding of their subjects, the misuse of the method has left a bad taste. According to Altick, "The result was a biographical literature which today is of interest only as a bizarre memorial to the spell psychoanalysis in its infant years cast over a whole generation."[12] DeVoto's condemnation in 1933 was scathing: "Psycho-analysis has no value whatever as a method of arriving at facts in biography. No psycho-analytical biography yet written can be taken seriously — as fact. The assertion holds for the work of the master himself, whose study of Leonardo is absolute bilge uncontaminated by the slightest perceptible filtrate of reality."[13] DeVoto's death in 1955 spared him the anguish of seeing the 1966 publication of a book on the life of Woodrow Wilson, written in the 1930s by former Ambassador Bullitt with the collaboration of Freud himself.[14] The blatant misrepresentations were widely criticized in such "rave" notices as "fascinating but distorted book;" "a bad book;" "a mischievous and preposterous joke . . . or else an awful and unrelenting slander." Arthur S. Link, Wilson's most learned present-day biographer, wrote a slashing review, accusing Freud and Bullitt of ". . . bold and uninhibited invention of evidence when necessary to support their psychological analysis."[15]

A name often associated with the use of psychological data in the writing of biography is Lytton Strachey, whose brilliant works, such as *Eminent Victorians* (1918, 310 p.) and *Queen Victoria* (1921, 314 p.), both published in London by Chatto & Windus, set a new style.* Strachey, influenced by Dostoevsky as well as by Freud, was charged with writing books more like clinical case histories than biographies, but his works were highly interesting and widely imitated, and his ironic treatment of Victorian society became extremely fashionable. During the decade of the 1920s he was undoubtedly the most influential biographer in the Western world, but his reputation has suffered since discoveries of his frequent misuse of facts. A recent critic accuses him of having repressed evidence that didn't make a scandalous story.[16] A two-volume biography of Strachey himself[17] reveals enough intimate detail to serve him right.

---

* Bertrand Russell spoke of reading the former work while in prison during World War I, and laughing so heartily that an officer felt it necessary to remind him that prison was supposed to be a place of punishment (*Autobiography* [Boston: Little, Brown, 1968], vol. 2, p. 30).

Meanwhile, the use of psychoanalysis in biography reached another high point in 1957 with the completion of a three-volume work on the life of Freud by a psychoanalyst who knew him, Dr. Ernest Jones. Jones's first volume was almost as much concerned with the amount of money in Freud's pocket as with his ego, superego, and id, and the set has been criticized also for assuming too much about Freud's psyche from inadequate objective evidence.

The controversy goes on. John Mack's work on T. E. Lawrence (*A Prince of Our Disorder* [Boston: Little, Brown, 1976, 561 p.]) and Doris Kearns's *Lyndon Johnson and the American Dream* (New York: Harper & Row, 1976, 432 p.) have drawn acclaim from many critics, as have Erik Erikson's studies of Luther and Gandhi; while Kenneth Lynn referred to "reckless psychologizing" in history and in biography as "comic," "a cancer," and "garbage." [18]

In spite of abuses and objections, the principles and theories promulgated by psychologists, psychiatrists, and psychoanalysts are extremely helpful to biographers, and Lewis Mumford probably was wise in his contention made nearly a half-century ago: "It is better to make mistakes in interpreting the inner life than to make the infinitely greater mistake of ignoring its existence and its import." [19]

PRINCIPLES OF SELECTION

There are challenges in selecting biographies for libraries, but usually the problems are not crucial, so this field is one of the more enjoyable in which to collect.

In the choice of any library materials, the subject is of great (perhaps overriding) importance, and in a modified sense, this principle holds for biography. It seems safe to say that the general reader does not, as a rule, choose a biography because it happens to have been written by Carl Sandburg, Leon Edel, or Margaret Leech, but is more likely to want a life of Abraham Lincoln, Henry James, or maybe even William McKinley. (Ms. Leech actually did make McKinley an interesting subject.) It is also true that numerous critics and historians of biography have emphasized the value of books on unimportant persons. A favorite example is Thomas Carlyle's *John Sterling,* which concludes:

> He sleeps now, in the little burying-ground of Bonchurch. . . . All that remains, in palpable shape of John Sterling's activities in this world, are those Two poor Volumes. . . . A life which cannot challenge the world's attention; yet which does modestly solicit it, and perhaps on clear study will be found to reward it.[20]

In Dr. Johnson's view, that person was very rare about whom a well-written biography would be useless. Geoffrey Wolff devoted a book to minor writer Harry Crosby because "things that are interesting interest me."[21] Though such works about obscure persons have a place in most libraries, practicality insists that priority be given books which depict subjects likely to be of greater concern to patrons. Here the demand theory of selection can be followed without appreciable sacrifice of value.

What kinds of persons are likely to be the subjects of interesting and instructive biographies? For one, there are prominent literary figures. Altick may have been a little prejudiced in favor of his own discipline but was largely correct in claiming:

> Until Boswell's time, most biographies, in the English tongue at least, had been written about saints, divines, monarchs, statesmen, soldiers, retired courtesans, and highwaymen. But ever since, steadily edging out the pious, the powerful and the perverse, one class has claimed the center of the biographical stage: the men and women who have created our literature. . . . For reasons that lie deep in social and cultural history, as well as in homely human preference, people have liked, and continue to like, to read the lives of authors.[22]

Having been impressed deeply by a piece of literature it is natural for the reader to wonder next about the person who wrote it.

Also essential are biographies of statesmen and others outstanding in history and politics. That such an obvious point needs emphasis is shown by the discouraging results of an analysis of Indiana high school libraries made several years ago by three university professors. They discovered that holdings in biography were shamefully weak. Most of the libraries did not even have good lives of such eminent figures as Washington, Jefferson, Jackson, Lincoln, and Wilson.[23]

Again, in view of public interest in subjects like art, music, and science, biographies of persons who have made contributions in these fields are popular and significant.

The relative importance of biographical subjects will vary from one community to another. The Moose Jaw Public Library will need all books (regardless of quality) written about any Moose Jawians, past or present. These stalwarts may be ignored completely by libraries in other parts of the continent. They have their own local-interest people who need to be represented. Even small segments of the community's population are likely to have their heroes about whom they want to read, and about whom others would profit from reading.

A second standard of judgment has to do with how much the writer knew, or learned about the biographee — the quality of the research. Many great biographies have been written by those who were personally acquainted with their subjects, as Boswell was with Johnson. A lesser example is William H. Herndon, who wrote about his law partner, Abraham Lincoln. A biography by a member of the subject's family is by no means a rarity. George Otto Trevelyan wrote of his uncle, *The Life and Letters of Lord Macaulay* (London: Longmans Green, 1876, 2 vols.). A daughter (Margaret Truman) may write the life of her father; a widow (Nadezhda Mandelstam) of her departed. Books of this type frequently go to one extreme or the other: they are likely to be very, very good, or horrid. A writer with inside information has an asset which cannot be obtained elsewhere, but the chances of being fair and objective are sharply reduced. A person writing an autobiography knows facts that no one else can get, but are they all presented fairly in such a work? A good combination of the inside and outside points-of-view is Margaret Lane's book,

The Brontë Story (London: William Heinemann Ltd., 1953, 284 p.), based largely on the 1857 biography by Charlotte Brontë's friend Mrs. Gaskell, with the incorporation of more recent discoveries.

If not an intimate of the person described, the writer has the task of finding evidence from other sources. In unearthing manuscripts, diaries, vital records, and published sources, modern biographers as a whole are miles ahead of their predecessors —so far that a common criticism now is that these better methods of discovery have produced too many trivial facts, obscuring the real personalities. It was a great advance, though, when Izaak Walton used letters, wills, and other papers for his seventeenth-century biographies.

There have always been objections to the use of intimate details. The manuscript of William Manchester's *Death of a President* (New York: Harper, 1967, 710 p.) included material gathered in a ten-hour interview with the President's widow, but some of this was deleted before publication, when she and the President's brothers objected. Arthur Schlesinger Jr., who in his book *A Thousand Days* (Boston: Houghton Mifflin, 1965, 1,087 p.) had revealed President Kennedy's intention of ousting Secretary of State Dean Rusk, tried to justify publishing this information and at the same time defend the Kennedy family's restrictions on Manchester. Schlesinger contended that his own revelations were made in the public interest, while those of Manchester, being of a more personal and private nature, were not.[24] The knife was not quite sharp enough, however, to cut so thin. Personal details about famous people are of interest to the public, and the fact may as well be faced. (Witness the mass of tasteless matter published about Jacqueline Onassis, and even about Amy Carter.) Who is to condemn the patient researcher who used infra-red light to expose the hundreds of intimate passages that Sophie Hawthorne so laboriously inked out in the notebooks of her late husband, Nathaniel? (See, for instance, *The American Notebooks*, edited by Claude M. Simpson [Columbus: Ohio State University Press, 1972, 835 p.])

Not only is it considered legitimate now to reveal practically any fact about a subject, especially if it helps explain behavior, but the writer is aided in keeping track of these data by modern products such as microforms, xerographs, photostats, and tape recorders. With these advantages, the current writer may feel guilty unless every line of evidence is examined carefully, every possible source persistently hunted down.

Francis Russell, a historian working on a biography of Warren G. Harding, was able to use a collection of letters found in a cardboard shoebox (a favorite housing place for such things) — letters written by Harding to his mistress in Marion, Ohio. Included also was some of the late president's poetry, of such banality that not even a biographer should have to read it. But all such discoveries help bring about a truer interpretation of the man. Preparing to write his three-volume life of Garibaldi, George M. Trevelyan, "with long, gaunt, raking steps . . . walked, often in the heat of the south Italian sun, over every yard of Italian soil that Garibaldi and his armies had covered."[25] Samuel Eliot Morison, doing research on the life of Christopher Columbus, took voyages as nearly as possible like those the discoverer himself had made. Others just as patiently explore new fields of thought in order to approximate the intellectual experiences of the persons they describe.

Closely related to the question of thoroughness of research is that of honesty on the writer's part. Most failures on this point are in the direction of glorifying the subject to excess. Abraham Lincoln was so annoyed with a life of Edmund Burke — one which gave its admittedly great subject too much credit while overlooking his faults — that he told Herndon,

> Billy, I've wondered why book-publishers and merchants don't have blank biographies on their shelves, always ready for an emergency; so that, if a man happens to die, his heirs or his friends can purchase one already written, but with blanks. The blanks they can at their pleasure fill up with rosy sentences full of high-sounding praise. In most instances they commemorate a lie, and cheat posterity out of the truth.[26]

The extreme form of such writing is the campaign biography, written typically to minimize the vices and advertise any virtues of a candidate for president of the United States. Guess who is being described here:

> He has stuck with remarkable steadfastness to a forthright course of conduct. He has been unimpressed alike by the portentous warnings of the powerful or the fearful squeaks of the timorous. Respectful of tradition, he has never allowed tradition to cow him. . . . No one shows a more spontaneous delight at meeting new people. . . . And yet the gentleman is not a backslapper.[27]

Or here (but with the improvement created by restraint):

> He is the product of plain, sturdy, devout, pioneering . . . stock. . . . He is an intense, serious, earnest, industrious, ambitious, able man. . . .[28]

A classic example of bad faith and worse taste is "Parson" Weems's story of hatchet-happy young George Washington and the unfortunate cherry tree. Read it and weep that it has enjoyed eighty printings. Weems-ish biographies are about gone now, but some stretching of truth is still not uncommon. Writers have transposed events; have stated as fact what was only probable; and have filled gaps with little patches of imagination. But we have come round again to the point that biography is akin to fiction, and perhaps the most sensible opinion is that of Leon Edel in the first number of the journal *Biography: An Interdisciplinary Quarterly:* "The biographer is allowed to be as imaginative as he pleases, so long as he does not imagine his facts. Saturated with fact, he may allow himself all the adventures of literary artifice, all the gratifications of storytelling — save those of make-believe."[29]

Strict truth is difficult for the biographer to attain; absolute impartiality is impossible, because of the writer's tendency to like (or dislike) the subject. It would seem probable that a truer picture is painted by a biographer who is sympathetic rather than hostile. Catherine Drinker Bowen expressed dramatically her feelings in regard to Sir Edward Coke, the sixteenth/seventeenth-century English jurist about whom she wrote: "My workbook argued the point. 'Coke was brutal beyond any excuse. Must I love him, must I even *like* him?' 'No!' I wrote. 'But I must be engaged with him, married to him, at one with him yet independent, rearing back to look at him.' "[30]

A discussion of honesty leads also to the debunking biographies, of which Strachey's were, in a sense, forerunners. Such authors as Paxton Hibben (who in the 1920s wrote about Henry Ward Beecher and William Jennings Bryan) blasted heroes off their pedestals, then split the pedestals to kindling. Not content with the quantities of unfavorable information available (both subjects were vulnerable), Hibben used the trick of planting false ideas in the reader's mind by saying of a subject that there was no *evidence* that he had done this or that. Though adoring biographies are abhorrent, those written with real malevolence are equally rejectable.

While thoroughness of research, intelligence of interpretation, and honesty of purpose are fundamental to good biography, criteria that can be judged more practically are style and structure. For one example, Douglas Southall Freeman, in what a fellow historian called the "best biography ever written by or about an American,"[31] lets the reader see situations from the same vantage point as Robert E. Lee saw them. Reading an account of the eve of battle, one has much the same knowledge Lee had at the time. In another familiar device, Amy Lowell started a book with an overview of London's West End "while leaves were turning brown," coming to dwell on St. George's Church where two young persons were being married. "To us, they appear uniquely as the future father and mother of John Keats."[32] Such presentations are a long way from the dreary "William Shakespeare, the great English writer, was born in 1564 . . ." and from the amorphous biographies published "by the simple procedure of sorting . . . files of notes into chronological sequence and hurling them at the printer," as Frederick A. Pottle described it.[33]

Another rule in selection for a library: there is some advantage in obtaining for a given person those biographies which balance and supplement each other. After a poet's life of a poet, or a painter's of a painter, the reader may wish a different viewpoint. A Christian Scientist's judgment of Mary Baker Eddy should be modified by some one from outside the faith. A book by a member of the family calls for one by a stranger. A study representing the highest level of research is essential but also useful is one with an interesting, perhaps even anecdotal, presentation. A good autobiography may be supplemented by an objective view. There seems to be a general law that as soon as an important person is glorifed by favorable biographies, hostile ones begin to appear, and vice versa. Usually both kinds are appropriate.

Variety in length is also valuable. Barbara Tuchman criticizes those who "produce a warehouse instead of a portrait,"[34] but the "behemoth," crammed with details, is good for reference work, and some patrons really want that much information. For other readers and purposes, the briefer work with selected information is better. Short sketches, for example, the "psychographs" written by Gamaliel Bradford in the first part of this century, can be intensely interesting, as are the oddments written in the seventeenth century by John Aubrey in his *Brief Lives* (many editions), though some of these are *too* brief — taking only one line.

The human being is intricate, changeable, hard to fathom. Impressions of any person usually are contradictory. No one approach can tell the complete story, and so, as David S. Muzzey has declared, "the story of illustrious men cannot be too often retold. Like . . . mountain-peaks, these men invite description but elude definition; they provoke examination but defy exhaustion. . . . As there are infinite gradations of comprehension, so there are infinite varieties of portrayal."[35]

A NOTE ON AIDS

Selection tools are seldom set up in terms of biography, but most of the general guides do have recommendations for this genre. The *Public Library Catalog,* for instance, in its sections 92 and 920, lists numerous collective and individual biographies. *The Reader's Adviser* has a section called "Literary Biography and Autobiography" in Volume I (p. 716–739) and another in Volume III, "General Biography and Autobiography" (p. 25–85), as well as other references to lives of people in connection with particular subject fields.

Bibliographies in the field of history are often helpful. *The Harvard Guide to American History,* revised edition (Cambridge, MA: Belknap Press of Harvard University Press, 1974, 2 vols.) includes a selective but annotated list of biographies of Americans (Vol. 1, p. 154–274). The American Historical Association's *Guide to Historical Literature* (New York: Macmillan, 1961, 962 p.) lists biographies at appropriate places and still has some use for retrospective selection.

The lives and accomplishments of people can be presented well on film. The NICEM indexes have a heading "Biography" that encompasses materials about individuals.

Biographies are of course reviewed in media such as *New York Times Book Review, Saturday Review, Kirkus Reviews,* and *New York Review of Books.*[36] *Library Journal* devotes a separate section to this field. Moreover, critics of such works find it easy to compare the volume in hand with previous studies of the same person; thus their comments can be unusually helpful.

18. HISTORY

In a famous book first published in 1929, José Ortega y Gasset, the philosopher, a founder of the Spanish Republic, wrote a depressing picture of the "mass man": he is everywhere; he makes no demands upon himself; he is emptied of his own history; he has a "radical ingratitude towards all that has made possible the ease of his existence."[1] In this willful ignorance of history, the mass man doesn't care how things came to be; he merely demands his rights, without regard to the processes that have caused these rights to be defined and recognized. In contrast to Ortega's mass man, the responsible person knows the necessity of trying to understand the past. Unless history (our own and that of others) is read and digested, we are isolated and without roots.

History is also an interesting field for its own sake. Especially popular are those works which focus on the state, with its leaders and their activities. Narrative accounts of politics, wars, and personalities are fascinating stuff. On the other hand, analytical approaches to, say, changes in society, require heavy concentration. Such themes are more difficult to write and read about. To appreciate and really understand history, therefore, character and intelligence are required. The library's responsibility is to provide its public with the best histories it will read. As the Public Library Association's *Mission Statement* expresses it, the insights and values of the past are in danger of being obliterated before they can be assimilated, unless the record of human experience is preserved by some agency.[2]

GENERAL REMARKS

First, some definitions: our word *history* comes from the Greek *historia*, which meant learning; thus Aristotle, for one, studied "natural history," learning about nature. Nowadays, *history* may be defined in its broadest sense to include all that has ever happened, or the term may be limited (and it usually is) to the *record* of that which has occurred. Even more narrowly, history may be described as "critical thinking about the past."[3] J. H. Plumb, of Cambridge University, puts it thus: "The business of the historian is to make sense of the past."[4] As in many other disciplines, emphasis is placed on change rather than on static conditions; perhaps the distinctive characteristic of history is that it appears to flow.

The source records used by historians are fragmentary, and many have been badly mangled. Most of the past has not been remembered at all, and remembered facts usually have not been recorded. Even of the records that have been made, many have been lost or destroyed — sometimes deliberately, in order to fool succeeding generations. Yet, so extensive are those source materials which remain, particularly for recent events, that no one person has the time or ability to digest them satisfactorily. Henry Steele Commager has well observed, "No individual historian, not even the largest committee of historians, can read all those miles of documents, all the newspapers, all the personal records of the combatants of all the countries involved in the Second World War."[5] To place Commager's remark in perspective: this episode covered less than one-tenth of one percent of historical time (the time since humans began to keep records).

Starting like the earthworm in the soil, the historian plows through the materials (documents, newspapers, letters, pamphlets, diaries, inscriptions, and any other evidences to be found); then chooses those considered significant for the particular study; organizes them by hand, mind, or computer; interprets their meaning; asks and seeks answers to pertinent questions; and thus tries to understand what really happened, and perhaps why. Then as historiographer (writer of history), the worker structures material and presents it in a style as clear and agreeable as possible.

The works produced by historians constitute one of the largest and most important fields for the library. Each year United States publishers bring out approximately two thousand new books (counting new editions) falling into the Dewey classification 900–909 and 930–999. In spite of its size, the structure of this literature is relatively clear, compared with that of other disciplines, and disagreement on the value of a given work (provided that work is old enough) usually is not severe. Perusal of lists issued by used book dealers will show that history is a favorite subject with them.

Commager opines that history is more self-conscious than other disciplines.[6] Though this conclusion is doubtful (compare psychology, for example), it is true that historians have been concerned about their own history, as witnessed by titles such as Harry Elmer Barnes's *History of Historical Writing* (Norman: University of Oklahoma Press, 1937, 436 p.); Michael Kraus's *History of American History* (New York: Farrar & Rinehart, 1937, 607 p.); *History and Historians of the Nineteenth Century* by G. P. Gooch, 2nd ed. (London: Longmans Green, 1952, 547 p.); a series of discussions edited by John A. Garraty: *Interpreting American History: Conversations With Historians* (New York: Macmillan, 1970, 701 p.); and numerous biographies of historians. Such works as these help provide background for selection in larger and more scholarly libraries.

TYPES OF HISTORY

There are many ways of looking at the body of historical literature, but for library purposes it may be best to think in terms of four dimensions: space, time, subject, and viewpoint.

Every history is somehow concerned with the dimension of space. Even intellectual and cultural histories involve a country, a continent, or some other geographical limitation. Likewise, any history, of whatever subject, is meaningless without reference to a period or periods in time. Not that lines drawn in space and time are very definite: such limitations are unnatural in a sense, for history is like a huge painting — a canvas that stretches farther than the eye can see. When the historian focuses on one detail or examines one brush stroke with a magnifying glass, there is danger of missing the vital relationship of that part to the whole. But the writer of history must set arbitrary limits, and they must be considered in judging the suitability of a work.

Furthermore, there being no such thing as history *in vacuuo,* each must have a subject — abstract or concrete. Some years ago, it was proposed that a major university discontinue its department of history as such, and that each discipline study the history pertinent to its own subject matter (the department of political science, for instance, would be responsible for the history of politics). The contention made clear, at least, that there is no "history" *per se;* it must be *of something.*

Fourth, every historian must have some sort of viewpoint (philosophy), both on the meaning of happenings themselves and on how history should be studied and presented. Here divergencies within the field have been increasing.

These dimensions will be exemplified below by some representative (not necessarily the "best") titles.

Time and Space (principally)

A set which covers most of the dimension of time and a great deal of space also (and has a definite theoretical and philosophical viewpoint) is Arnold Toynbee's famous *Study of History* (London: Oxford University Press, 1934–1961, 12 vols.). This work discusses the genesis, growth, breakdown, and disintegration of each of twenty-one great civilizations (such as the Egyptaic, Sumerian, Mayan, and Hellenic). Toynbee adduced the challenges which caused each to grow and the reasons for its demise. His general emphasis was on the mystical, with rather little attention given to science or technology. This work has become one of the most controversial histories of all time, and Toynbee's many opponents have called him inaccurate in detail, incomplete in selection of evidence, and idiosyncratic in interpretation. In the last volume of the set, *Reconsiderations* (1961), he replied to his critics and in some instances agreed with them. A shorter approach is his *Mankind and Mother Earth, A Narrative History of the World* (New York: Oxford University Press, 1976, 641 p.).

Another example of a wide-ranging history is the great set that comprises *Cambridge Ancient History,* 3rd. ed. (Cambridge: At the University Press, 1970–   ); *Cambridge Medieval History,* 2nd ed.

(Cambridge: At the University Press, 1966–   ); and *New Cambridge Modern History* (Cambridge: At the University Press, 1957–1970, 13 vols. plus atlas). This set covers all eras and is worldwide in scope, with emphasis on the West. Planned around the turn of the century, it reflects the need (recognized about that time with the rise of academic historians) to have history written by specialists, but coordinated into a manageable whole. Each chapter in each volume is written by an authority — thus reducing the likelihood of mistakes in detail, but precluding a really unified approach or single philosophy.

Quite different, but also covering a long time and wide territory, is the Durants' *Story of Civilization* (New York: Simon and Schuster, 1935–1975, 11 vols.). Starting with *Our Oriental Heritage,* the work has come to a close with the volume *The Age of Napoleon,* carrying the story in Europe to the year 1815. Though criticized frequently by scholars for being anecdotal, naive, and secondhand, the work is wonderfully readable and interesting (to the laity at least), even if some of the later volumes do seem to indicate a bit of fatigue on the part of the authors.

Works may be much narrower in geographic scope than the so-called world histories, yet deal in a more or less complete way with several nations. For instance, there is in progress a long *Cambridge History of Africa* (Cambridge: Cambridge University Press, 1975–   ), and there already exists a one-volume work *The Arab World: A Comprehensive History,* by Peter Mansfield (New York: Crowell, 1976, 572 p.). Barbara Tuchman, in *A Distant Mirror: The Calamitous 14th Century* (New York: Knopf, 1978, 677 p.) deals with several countries, mainly European, weaving in such themes as literature, society, politics, and war. Sir Winston Churchill had a multi-national plan for *A History of the English Speaking Peoples* (New York: Dodd, Mead, 1956–58, 4 vols.). Fernand Braudel chose a title that succinctly defined the space and time boundaries of his work — *The Mediterranean, and the Mediterranean World in the Age of Philip II* (translated from the French by Siân Reynolds; New York: Harper & Row, 1973, 2 vols.).

Another geographical scope for the writing of history is the individual country. In fact, the national state is still one of the favorite areas to cover, as witnessed by several volumes in the *Oxford History of Modern Europe* series. A classic example of the one-nation approach is the *History of England,* by George M. Trevelyan (London: Longmans, Green, 1926, 723 p.). The son of historian George Otto Trevelyan (who wrote about the American Revolution, among other things) and great-nephew of Lord Macaulay, Trevelyan produced many other books, all of them highly readable. He was of the school which believed that good history should be literature (more on this later). Also written in good style with points of wit gleaming here and there is Samuel Eliot Morison's *Oxford History of the American People* (New York: Oxford University Press, 1965, 1,150 p.).

To illustrate further the geographical dimension of historical writing, let us stay with the nation as a unit but shorten the dimension of time. James Anthony Froude's *History of England From the Fall of Wolsey to the Death of Elizabeth* (London: J. W. Parker and Son, 1856–1870, 12 vols.) covers a single country for something over a half-century. Though Froude was one of the more controversial historians (called "Fraud"; his mistakes "Froudacities"), the brilliance of his writing is now generally recognized, and he himself is the subject of a two-volume study by Waldo H. Dunn: *James Anthony Froude: A Biography* (Oxford: Clarendon Press, 1961–63), which concludes that he was a great man and a fine thinker in spite of his tendency to infuriate some people. Of similar dimensions is the *History of England in the Eighteenth Century,* by W.E.H. Lecky (London: Longmans, Green, 1878–1890, 8 vols.), long noted for its delightful style and excellent biographical portraits, as well as for its treatment of political, economic, and social movements. In American history, a comparatively brief time is covered by a long work: George Bancroft's *History of the United States From the Discovery of the American Continent. . . . .* (Boston: Little, Brown, 1834–1875, 10 vols., varying imprints). Bancroft's "drum and trumpet" history went through twenty editions; people liked it because it read like a Fourth of July oration.

Another use of space and time dimensions is exemplified by

the writings of Francis Parkman, who in spite of poor health explored and researched widely to produce such works as *The Oregon Trail* (first published by Putnam in 1849 under the title: *The California and Oregon Trail*), and *Montcalm and Wolfe* (London: Macmillan, 1884). He represents excellence of literary style, and though rebuked for not being scientific enough, he was really a master also of the facts. During the Korean War, General Douglas MacArthur made the successful surprise attack at Inchon Gulf, having derived the idea from reading Parkman's account of how Wolfe captured Quebec. J. Donald Adams in *The New York Times Book Review* once ranked Parkman along with Franklin, Emerson, Washington, Lincoln, and others as one of the ten greatest Americans of all time.

Histories can cover a very short span of time — as little as a year, or, for that matter, a single day. So far as space is concerned, they may concentrate on a region, a state, a county, a city, a university campus, or a building. By the time we arrive at scopes of this size, we are ready to consider historical writings in terms of their content.

Subject

Any type of activity may be the subject of a history. Science, for instance, has been well covered. There are histories of individual disciplines such as biology, chemistry, and physics. Mathematics has several long histories. In the area of applied science are found such works as *History of Technology,* edited by Charles I. Singer and others (Oxford: Clarendon Press, 1954–1958, 5 vols.).

A. T. Mahan wrote a forceful book on *The Influence of Sea Power Upon History 1660–1783* (Boston: Little, Brown, 1890, 557 p.). Translated into German, Japanese, French, Italian, and Russian, it provided those nations with reasons for naval expansion.[7] Strangely, it probably influenced the activities of both Japan and the United States in connection with Pearl Harbor.

Henry C. Lea, a Philadelphia publisher, had masses of materials copied in Europe as sources for his histories of the Inquisition, a work which Lord Acton proclaimed the most important contribution of the New World to the Old.

Histories have been written about education: as a whole, in given countries, by level of school, by subject taught, and in combination. Douglas C. McMurtrie wrote on the history of books and printing in *The Book: The Story of Printing & Bookmaking,* 3rd ed. (London: Oxford University Press, 1943, 676 p.). There is a work called *Moonshine: Its History and Folklore,* and one called *The History of Grasshopper Abundance Surveys. . . .*

But this discussion could go on and on. Practically every theme has been dealt with to some extent. There are histories of politics, of religion, of ideas, of poetry, of art, of medicine, of publishing, of libraries, of prostitution, of speeches, of movies, and (naturally) of history. The specialty of one professor is "The History of Consciousness."

Philosophies, Viewpoints

To emphasize more now the fourth of our dimensions, histories may be distinguished from each other on the bases of their differing views of happenings, or of how history should be written. Here we face more difficult considerations, for the structure of this aspect of the field is more elusive. As Mace declared: "There are two sorts of 'philosophy of history.' One is the philosophy that there *is* a philosophy of history . . . the other . . . is that there is no philosophy of history."[8]

Herodotus, the fifth century (B.C.) Greek long known as the "Father of History," wondered why certain things happened, and interpreted many events as the operation of a sort of fate or destiny. The medieval historians, and many later ones, were inclined toward something of the same view, but not with the same force. To them (and to a few present-day authors), it was God who was working out a pattern and end result. This idea of teleological influences is reversed, in a sense, by most modern historians, who are interested in finding the prior causes for the effects observed. In a variation of this philosophy, Oscar Handlin wrote a book (*Chance or Destiny: Turning Points in American His-*

tory [Boston: Little, Brown, 1955, 220 p.]) showing how the "fate" of individuals and of the entire nation has been determined by factors that seem accidental or capricious.

Another difference in point-of-view may be illustrated by a couple of British historians of the nineteenth century. Thomas Carlyle's famous "great men" theory was elaborated most thoroughly in his 1840 lectures, *On Heroes, Hero-Worship, and the Heroic in History*. "The History of the World, I said already, was the Biography of Great Men."[9] By contrast, H. T. Buckle, writing *History of Civilization in England* (London: J. W. Parker and Sons, 1857–1861, 2 vols.), was interested in how societies and nations are influenced by nature, soil, and the food supply. From him the individual received little attention. This view was echoed in America by Ellsworth Huntington's studies of the effects of climate. For those who like to think that personalities do make a difference, it is a little saddening to approach the end of Braudel's account of the Mediterranean world in the sixteenth century, and to see his final estimate of the effects of Philip II's life and death: "The long agony which ended in September, 1598, was not a great event in Mediterranean history."[10]

For another contrast: Frederick Jackson Turner's famous little work was primarily concerned with the frontier as a force in the development of this country (*The Significance of the Frontier in American History* [Madison, WI: State Historical Society of Wisconsin, 1894, 37 p.]) while recent historians have been more concerned with the city.

In the nineteenth century, as history became an academic discipline rather than a branch of literature written by amateurs with leisure, there was an insistence on so-called scientific history, possibly because of a fascination at that time with the "real."[11] The movement led by Leopold von Ranke at the University of Berlin stressed the importance of objectivity and accuracy in historical research. Some of his followers may have overstated his case; anyway, Trevelyan, Charles A. Beard, Carl Becker, and others down to the present day have attacked the idea, emphasizing that objectivity is impossible and the truth extremely difficult to establish. For a time there was a great gulf between scientific and literary historians, though Henry Adams (famous for his *Education* . . . as well as for long works such as *History of the United States* . . . [New York: Scribner, 1889–1891], nine volumes devoted to the period 1801–1817) managed to combine science in historical method with an excellent literary style.

To many historians, their field is one of the social sciences, in that it seeks causes and laws and sometimes, in a cautious way, offers predictions. Recent studies of groups, such as ethnic minorities, reflect a sociological interest, as do the cliometricians, who make statistical analyses of minute bits of raw data. (One of the most widely-reviewed and hotly-debated of all recent books is *Time on the Cross* [Boston: Little, Brown, 1974, 2 vols.] for which the authors, Robert Fogel and Stanley Engerman, used great quantities of numerical data as a basis for the reinterpretation of slave life in America.) To other historians the discipline is one of the humanities, and involves discussing, explaining, and evaluating important events and unique personalities. The two approaches are not diametrically opposed, for both seek true facts and clear interpretation. In general, the tide seems to be running in favor of the social science orientation.[12]

These examples, chosen sparingly from the thousands of interesting works and people in the historical enterprise, illustrate only a few of the approaches to history. To some scholars, economic causes are uppermost; to others it is ideas that have grave consequences. Some have viewed history as a struggle onward and upward; others, especially since the 1930s, have been more pessimistic. Many famous historians have theorized that there are long-term cycles or spirals to be discerned; others have seen only a linear arrangement. Daniel J. Boorstin had stinging remarks about those who try to make history the study of a series of "Excedrin Headaches;"[13] James Cornell came out with *The Great International Disaster Book* (New York: Scribner, 1976, 382 p.).

There is no end to the games people play with philosophies of history. If the following assessment be true, it is disappointing: "Connections between theory and practice in historical work are usually circuitous and indistinct. The fluid, unsystematic character of the historian's enterprise rarely permits him to go directly from a general theory to a particular proof." [14]

FORMS OF PRESENTATION

The facts discovered by historians, and the conclusions based on such research, are made available to the user in various ways. (Garraty, in his *Interpreting American History,* gives an overview through recorded question-and-answer sessions with twenty-nine leading contemporary historians.)

For recent history, photographs are an excellent means of presentation, and there are a number of interesting pictorial compilations, such as *The Album of American History,* originally planned and edited by James Truslow Adams (New York: Scribner, 1944–1961, 6 vols.) and *The Bettmann Archive Picture History of the World* (New York: Random House, 1978, 223 p.). Looking at more specialized topics, here are the subjects of some recent picture histories: Olympic games, Australia, musical instruments, golf, boxing, Blacks, buildings, movies, carnivals, universities, railroads, canals, automobiles, airplanes.

Reference works, while perhaps less important in this field than in the sciences, are needed in general and in most special libraries. Historical atlases are especially useful. Some of these works are general in scope, while others are limited by time, space, or subject, for instance the superb *Atlas of Early American History* . . . , Lester J. Cappon, ed.-in-chief (Princeton, N J : published for the Newberry Library and the Institute of Early American History and Culture by Princeton University Press, 1976, 157 p.). Other types of reference aids are represented by: *Dictionary of American History,* Rev. ed. (New York: Scribner, 1976–1978, 8 vols.); William L. Langer's *An Encyclopedia of World History: Ancient, Medieval and Modern,* 5th ed. (Boston: Houghton Mifflin, 1972, 1,569 p.); Helen Rex Keller's *The Dictionary of Dates* (New York: Macmillan, 1934, 2 vols.); and the U.S. Bureau of the Census publication, *Historical Statistics of the United States, Colonial Times to 1970* (Washington: Government Printing Office, 1975, 2 vols.).

This latter title illustrates the fact that governments frequently are interested in the histories of their own jurisdictions, and so publish widely in the field. For the United States, the series *Public Papers of the Presidents,* issued by the General Services Administration, is a prime example. For the United Kingdom, some of the historical and archaeological works issued by Her Majesty's Stationery Office are beautiful examples of scholarly detail.

Sound recordings, films, and videotapes are good for preserving contemporary history, especially important public events. Oral history collections have been started in many libraries. Both the recordings themselves and the stenographic transcriptions will be valuable source material in the future. The American Association for State and Local History has published *Local History Collections: A Manual for Librarians,* by Enid T. Thompson (Nashville: 1978, 99 p.).

A Note on Genealogy

Speaking of local collections, mention of genealogists is in order. In the past, they have been frowned upon, in general libraries at least, because some of them became nuisances, perhaps because of over-eagerness. Lately, and fortunately, their demands have been recognized as legitimate, and librarians have responded to their needs. Building a collection requires time and money, and it is good that we are getting aids like Mary Kaufman's "Developing a Genealogy Collection: Some Initial Considerations" (*Collection Building* 1 [No. 3, 1979]:98–101).

SELECTION PRINCIPLES

For evaluating an individual work in the field of history, the general principles of selection require some extension.* Of particular importance are the following:

1. The factual details in the book (or film) should be estab-

*I depend here mainly on suggestions for "consideration by serious book reviewers and readers in general" made by Louis Gottschalk in his *Understanding History: A Primer of Historical Method* (New York: Knopf, 1950), p. 24.

lished by a strict application of the historical method. For this field (as well as for biography and the humanities in general) truth is somewhat more difficult to judge than for the sciences. The rhetoric of historical writing perhaps allows for more ambiguity, less precision;[15] yet with the improvement in methods and techniques for the discipline of history, and with scholars now using statistics, sociology, psychology, and other sciences, there should be improvement in standards of accuracy, truth, and possibly fairness.

The question of whom to trust as an authority is rather less difficult in this field than in some others. Frequently the reliability of a historian can be established or denied by the judgments of colleagues. Regrettably this does not always hold for contemporaries. One reference will exemplify: The controversial nature of James Anthony Froude has been mentioned previously. According to a recent critic, Froude was the victim of "the splenetic attacks of Edward Augustus Freeman." Freeman, one of the most famous nineteenth-century British historians, represented a highly-organized opposition on the part of the clergy. "We know now that Freeman was almost completely wrong in his charges, and that he was motivated by a childish yet ugly malice."[16] In spite of this and other examples, it must be said in fairness that agreement among historians in assessing their colleagues is relatively high.

In any event, the philosophy or frame of reference of any book under consideration ought to be made apparent, and should be acceptable if the book is to be chosen for the library. In this regard, one almost could wish that publishers would revert to titles which clearly reveal, even if in child-like fashion, the authors' prejudices, as in that famous work, *The History of the Rebellion and Civil Wars in England . . . And the Happy End, and Conclusion Thereof by the King's Blessed Restoration, and Return Upon the 29th of May in the Year 1660,* by Edward Hyde Clarendon (many editions). At least we know which side the great Clarendon was on.

2. The work being evaluated should not represent mere hackwork, but ought to present new data or new interpretations. Scholars working in United States history are revising estimates

as to the contributions made, for instance, by Franklin D. Roosevelt and the effects of the New Deal. Their reassessments add a valuable dimension, even when based on the same store of raw material used by "traditional" historians. Most libraries cannot afford the repetition so rampant in this field, but new evaluations are essential.

3. The work's style should be helpful rather than impeding. The belaboring of this point has been frequent, as in this sentence by Morison: "Long, involved sentences that one has to read two or three times in order to grasp their meaning; poverty in vocabulary, ineptness of expression, weakness in paragraph structure, frequent misuse of words, and, of late, the introduction of pseudo-scientific and psychological jargon."[17] In no other field except literature itself is excellence of style so crucial. George M. Trevelyan in a famous essay, "Clio, a Muse," published in 1913, declared, "It is in narrative that modern historical writing is weakest, and to my thinking it is a very serious weakness — spinal, in fact. Some writers would seem never to have studied the art of telling a story. There is no 'flow' in their events, which stand like ponds instead of running like streams."[18]

Allan Nevins, in 1938, advocated the establishment of a popular historical magazine, to be written for the multitude, but Gottschalk was afraid the proposal confused popular writing with good writing: "It does not help the flow of a dried-up stream to widen its outlet."[19] Nevertheless, the profusely illustrated *American Heritage* was begun in 1949, and has proved popular with the laity if not with all critical scholars.

4. Gottschalk's question should be applied: "No matter how limited its subject may be, does the author seem aware of the questions that men at all times and in all places persist in asking?" The latter two points (3 and 4) may be discussed in terms of the rather narrow readership gained by much historical writing. A general complaint is that in our time too many history publications, especially learned monographs and periodical articles, are so lacking in generalization that they interest only the very few. To some historians, "the more generally significant conclusions

are, the less secure they seem," and vice versa. History has tended to become "a study for professionals by professionals"[21] (an affliction which has reached other disciplines as well). Denys Hay, of the University of Edinburgh, asserted, "Articles are of interest to those who write them and to those who read them. I think sometimes that they are almost the same people, so technical are the subjects discussed, so rebarbative the style, so absent the general inferences."[22] Something in all this may help explain why the volumes of Macaulay's *History of England* sold tens of thousands of copies within a few years, whereas now the sales of many authoritative works are numbered in the thousands at best.

For selection in history, then, the problem is to obtain materials on the topics that are most interesting and important, materials which treat these topics at a length appropriate to the reading audience in a manner which these readers find useful and appealing. And at the same time, the librarian must try to be sure that the publications are fair, accurate, significant, and otherwise of high quality. We are again brought up against the demand vs. value controversy. The history that ought to be read may not be the most seductive. The study by Baxter, Ferrell, and Wiltz, quoted in the chapter on biography, also had some harsh things to say about high school libraries and their provision for history. Materials were found to be insufficient in quantity, but that was not the worst of it —

> the fundamental trouble lies in the quality. . . . There is an oversupply of superficial, popular writings hardly deserving the label of history — fictional accounts written down to a reading level below that of the students using the library. Or there are dusty, ponderous tomes bound to kill whatever incipient interest the young people may have.

A further defect, even in moderately stocked libraries, is a lack of balance in the collections. Political and military narratives are dominant at the expense of social, economic, and intellectual studies.[23]

AIDS TO SELECTION

Of bibliographies and guides to writings in history, many are not of value in selecting for the general library, but one which may in spite of its age serve as a starting place is the American Historical Association's *Guide to Historical Literature* (New York: Macmillan, 1961, 962 p.). It represents an attempt to list the best for each subject and country, including reference works, documents, sources, and books for general reading. Its annotations, some of them evaluative, are helpful for the librarian, but are not nearly so decisive as those in its predecessor: *Guide to Historical Literature* (New York: Macmillan, 1931, 1,222 p.) — commonly known as "Dutcher" after the name of its editor, George M. Dutcher.

Highly selective, with long annotations, is W. Warren Wagar's *Books in World History: A Guide for Teachers and Students* (Bloomington: Indiana University Press, 1973, 182 p.). A big dot ("bullet") indicates a title recommended especially for high school students. "History Books for Schools" is a regular bibliographic essay, by different authors, appearing in the British journal *History*. Representative of the more specialized approach is the annotated work by Gwyn M. Bayliss, *Bibliographic Guide to Two World Wars* (New York: Bowker, 1977, 578 p.).

On a national level, *The Harvard Guide to American History* (Cambridge, MA: Harvard University Press, 1974, 2 vols.) is too comprehensive for small libraries to use in selection but is good for larger ones. The same may be said of *Bibliographia Canadiana*, compiled by Claude Thibault (Don Mills, Ontario: Longmans Canada, 1973, 795 p.).

Most of the periodicals in history are laden with reviews, and there are journals devoted entirely, or almost so, to reviews. *History* has short ones; longer ones are found in *Reviews in American History* and in *Reviews in European History*.

The popularity of history is shown by the fact that reviews of such books are a staple of general periodicals, such as *Saturday Review* and *New York Times Book Review*. Items of state or local interest are almost sure to be reviewed in appropriate newspapers and magazines.

19. GEOGRAPHY, MAPS, TRAVEL

As in one sense everything that has happened is a part of history, so, in another, everything that exists is a part of geography. Even fiction, whether in print or on film, has to suggest place. The far-flung interests of this field are suggested by Kenneth Boulding: "Of all the disciplines, geography is the one that has caught the vision of the earth as a total system, and it has strong claims to be the queen of the human sciences."[1]

For library purposes, it is convenient to treat together these two topics (geography and travel) with a distinctive form of publication (maps) for they have a basic relationship. At the same time, there is justification for Broek's complaint that libraries fail to recognize the character of the field when they make "Geography and Travel" into a single subject heading. "One looks in vain for analogous sections in other fields, such as 'Chemistry and Cooking.' "[2]

Geography's close association with history goes back a long way. In ancient times, the extensive travels of Herodotus, as he pursued his researches, gave his works on history a strong geographical content.

Immanuel Kant (1724–1804), who taught philosophy and various sciences for nearly forty years at the University of Koenigsberg, distinguished between the two in this way: History is a study of things that follow one another in time; geography is a study of things that are beside one another in space. Jules Michelet, in his great *History of France,* declared, "At first history is altogether geography."[3]

The fact that geography is concerned with causal relationships gives it a further kinship with history. Both seek to learn how things came to be what they are. Another similarity has been pointed out by Wright: "The 'regional concept' in geography has an analogue in the 'period concept' in history, with an implication of relatively uniform and homogeneous periods . . . and geographers and historians alike argue over the reality and utility of such regions and periods."[4]

THE NATURE OF THE FIELD

Can we say that there is an essence of geography? Perhaps one can be discerned in the phenomena which are studied. The geographer is interested in such things as:

> The number of people in various places.
> What those people and places are like.
> Animal and plant populations and their distribution.
> Weather and climate around the earth.
> Soils and how they differ from place to place.
> Mountains, oceans, rivers, plains, and other physical characteristics of the earth.
> Locations of cities.
> Political boundaries for all levels of jurisdictions.

From these broad topics the discipline can focus on very small matters, for example, the sites of business lunches in New York City (giving The Four Seasons restaurant as the locus of conversations about publishing).[5] All topics in geography have characteristics in common — really not subject matter so much as method or point-of-view.

> Man has always felt himself to be associated with a particular place on the face of the earth. He has identified his tribe or his nation not only with the traditions and customs of his culture, but also with the hills and valleys and rivers and the distinctive plants and animals that together make up his homeland. . . . Man has always been concerned also with what lies beyond the horizon. He wants to know how the unknown resembles his home or how it differs. . . . Long before the dawn of written history there were individuals who were ready to explore unfamiliar places and to describe what they found there. But it was not until the second century before Christ that Erathosthenes first applied the word "geography" to this field of learning.[6]

Primarily a study of places on the surface of the globe and of the atmosphere above it, this discipline takes its name from the

Greek *ge*, meaning the earth. It deals with the interrelationships of places to each other and to human beings. Clearly the field also has much in common with geology, oceanography, and the other "earth sciences." In the United States particularly, geography as a field has evolved from geological science.

THE IMPORTANCE OF THESE STUDIES

Because this is a field of great theoretical interest and practical value, people from earliest times have had a natural interest in it. C. R. Beazley was able to write three large volumes on the *Dawn of Modern Geography* (London: J. Murray; Oxford: Clarendon Press, 1897–1906) covering the years 300–1420 in the Western world. The United States now produces each year four to five hundred new books classified in Dewey Decimal 910–919. Yet so vast is the enterprise of geography that much primary exploration remains to be done in the various parts of the world, and as late as 1967 it was declared that "for much of the world geographical information consists of half-truths which conceal as much as they reveal."[7]

The practical value of geography is seen in the answers it can provide to such questions as: Where shall a given manufacturer locate a new plant? What is the best route from Philadelphia to Horse Shoe Bottom? At what point should a dam be built on X River? (Or should it be built at all?) Particularly important are questions about ecology. What are the dangers that threaten the environment? While many lines of research attack this problem, geographers are especially well situated to contribute vital information.

Geography has a psychological value as well. It helps us understand the earth as home, and gives a sense of belonging to a region. In times such as ours, when traditions and standards seem to be deteriorating badly, people gain strength by feeling an attachment to things that are elemental. We need roots. We would like to know where we are, on a map at least. The British writer Alan Sillitoe, speaking of his sense of place, goes on to say: "My obsession with geographical maps comes from my love and concern with the rest of the world. It has always been quite plain to me that the two must go together. I have always felt that real love begins with one's feeling for the earth, and that if you do not have this love then you cannot really begin to love people."[8]

IMPLICATIONS FOR PUBLISHED MATERIALS

The phenomena described by geography are unusual in the sense that some tend to remain about the same year after year, while others change rapidly. In many of its physical characteristics, the earth is about the same as it was in Aristotle's time. A few new islands have been created by volcanoes, rivers have altered their courses, and mountains have eroded, but these changes seem minor when one considers the great mass of the surface whose general contours have remained virtually the same for centuries. Descriptions of these physical features tend to be enduring, like books in ancient history. True, there is an increase in knowledge *about* the earth, as there is about ancient history, so that concepts (sometimes fundamental ones) are revised, and descriptions must be brought up to date, but the things studied (in this section of geography) are relatively stable.

On the other hand, look at the relationships of human beings to the earth. Here the changes have been far too rapid for books to keep up with. Cities increase or decrease in population. Canals and roads are built or abandoned. Industries move. Political jurisdictions are shifting constantly. New nations come into existence; old ones change names and/or boundaries; territories are disputed. There is a good deal of truth to the statement, "No publications arouse international ire as much as atlases."[9]

These considerations lead to the conclusion that books and periodicals depicting the physical earth go out of date slowly; older publications are still valuable. Citation studies in the closely related field of geology reflect this fact. They show that library materials used for research by scientists in this discipline are considerably older than those used by chemists and physicists.[10] When it comes to political geography and related topics, however, old books and maps may be valuable for historical purposes, but recent ones are all-important. In fact, it is impossible for the library to obtain new materials fast enough to keep up with actual changes and knowledge about them. Geography books of this kind go out of date in the same short time as do bibliographies (and books about the selection of library materials).

The fact that geography (along with geology) is concerned with place — studying phenomena which are distinctive, peculiar to a given part of the earth — is also significant for libraries. The elements studied by chemists and physicists are about the same in Illinois, in Germany, and in New Zealand. The same matter is investigated by scientists in each part of the world. A look at the physical features of these three places, however, shows that they are quite different. These differences help explain another aspect of geographical publications: Among the most important sources are governmental organizations. Most governments feel a responsibility for studying their own territories, since jurisdiction, like geography, is based upon place. It is not surprising, therefore, that in the United States there are many agencies of government collecting data about the country. These include the Geological Survey, the Coast and Geodetic Survey, the Department of Agriculture, the Bureau of Mines, the Department of Commerce, and many others. For the magnificent *National Atlas of the United States of America* (Washington: U.S. Geological Survey, 1970, 417 p.), eighty federal agencies furnished data and advice. Even state and local jurisdictions publish geographical materials. Governments are interested also, it must be granted, in the geographies of rival nations, often for military purposes. These are some of the reasons why it has been said that in the United States over eighty-five percent of all maps are published by government agencies at some level — federal, state, county, or municipal.[11]

An introduction to library research in the field, with several sections useful to selectors in general libraries, is J. Gordon Brewer's *Literature of Geography: A Guide to Its Organization and Use* (Hamden, CT: Shoe String Press, 1973, 208 p.).

MAPS AND ATLASES

One of the principal means of communicating geographical information is the map. The whole earth may be "pictured" on one page, or the map of one city may cover an entire wall. The Argentine author and librarian, Jorge Luis Borges, once imagined a map made in such detail that it had to be the same size as the territory it was supposed to represent.

A good map presents spatial relationships in a simplified, graphic way that makes them clear and intelligible. There is a danger, however, that striving for clarity will produce oversimplification. In writing textual material about the natural beauties of an area, an author can qualify statements, express doubts, "ifs," and probabilities (unless commissioned to exaggerate for the sake of tourist trade). Changes from season to season in forest and desert can be described vividly. In drawing a map, one may crowd in a great deal of information, but there is little leeway to qualify statements. The thought and craftsmanship required for making a really good map are beyond the ability of most people to appreciate. Since the middle of the century cartographers have given ever more serious study to the map as a medium of communication, and to the psychology of the map reader.[12]

The importance of maps in history (and of historical maps) is illustrated by the Webster–Ashburton treaty of 1842. The United States held a map supporting English claims to lands along the disputed border between Maine and Canada. The British happened to have a map which supported American claims. Therefore, Webster was able to justify his final agreement to the United States government and even to imply that he had by diplomatic skill obtained more territory than a less persuasive man might have found possible. Ashburton had the same good luck with the British government.

In the school atlases used in the old German empire before World War I, maps of the United States and of Germany each occupied a single page. The scales were different by a factor of something like five to one, yet the countries seemed to be about the same size. It has been suggested that German children thus were taught to underestimate the relative size and power of the United States, and that this misinformation affected their thinking in regard to their chances of winning the war.[13]

In the last half of the twentieth century, use of new technology such as more accurate surveying and photographic equipment together with computers has resulted in better quality data for maps. "It is quite reasonable to conclude that some form of photomap will become the standard general map of the future."[14]

The number of maps from which the library can choose is relatively large. No reliable statistics on the world's cartographic production are available, but in 1967 estimates ranged from sixty thousand to one hundred thousand sheets per year, counting new and revised editions.[15] Some of these show the physical characteristics of the earth; others show political entities such as cities, states, and nations. Still others emphasize special features: highways, production of cattle, deposits of coal, or other subjects. For good examples of the kinds of information that may be carried, see the excellent *Atlas of Britain and Northern Ireland* (Oxford: Clarendon Press, 1963, 200 p.). Maps are used also to show such things as geographic differences in word pronunciations (linguistic atlases), and the distribution of human physical disorders (the project of the Harvard Graduate School of Design to map by computer the incidence of cancer[16]).

Fortunately, maps are more or less independent of language. An Italian atlas is easily used by an English–speaking person because the conventions of cartography are international. The Italian spelling of city names (*Roma, Napoli, Milano*) and other places is only a slight difficulty. (The use of *Moskva* in Cyrillic characters on Russian maps is a little more of a problem.)

In terms of building up a library, it is fortunate also that atlases tend to emphasize the country in which they are published. (Some call it bias, but it helps to reduce duplication.) There is some overlap among atlases produced in Great Britain, Germany, and the United States, in that each will have material on such territories as France and Bolivia, but each is different in giving details about its home country. Thus a good collection can be assembled if the leading atlas for each major nation is obtained.

Larsgaard suggests that, for the university library, highest priority in map acquisition be given the local county, then the state, region, nation, neighboring countries, Europe, world, and finally other continents.[17] The same order makes sense generally for school and public libraries.

In addition to the regular selection tools, *General World Atlases in Print, 1972–73, A Comparative Analysis,* compiled by S. Padraig Walsh (New York: Bowker, 1973, 211 p.) suggests criteria for evaluation; then lists titles in order of estimated quality, of cost, of page size, and of number of index entries.

One of the best sources for current information about this form of publication is the *Bulletin,* put out by the Geography and Map Division, Special Libraries Association. The regular notes about new maps and atlases, including those of Canada, are of interest in general as well as in more specialized libraries. Of particular help are surveys such as "Maps and Atlases: Basic Reference Bibliography," by Mai Treude (*Bulletin* No. 111, March 1978, p. 32–37).

There are two good tools listing materials which are available: *GeoKatalog International* (Stuttgart: Internationales Landkarten, 1972–   ) includes an annual volume (Band I) that lists maps, atlases, globes, and tourist guides, giving basic bibliographic information and instructions for ordering. Band II, started in 1976, is a looseleaf service, updated regularly, of geographic-thematic maps and atlases, with indexes of map series. The other good source, like *GeoKatalog* in offering worldwide coverage, more or less, is *International Maps and Atlases in Print,* edited by K. L. Winch, 2d ed. (London & New York: Bowker, 1976, 866 p.), a "carto-bibliography" with short descriptive annotations; entries are arranged by territories according to the Universal Decimal Classification. Larsgaard's *Map Librarianship* (Littleton, CO: Libraries Unlimited, 1978, 330 p.) includes excellent notes on lists and sources of maps and atlases.

TRAVEL

Like the Germans, Americans are enthusiastic travelers. In depression days they hop a box car, in affluent times a jet. Each year travel books are issued in profusion. As a class, these books occupy more space in bookstores than in libraries, simply because people like to take them along on the trip rather than borrow them for a short time. Nevertheless they have many uses in libraries.

Some travel guides cover a wide area (Europe, in one volume); others are confined to a single country (France or Italy); still others are devoted to a part of a country (Northern Italy or the South of France). Some guides are more detailed yet, dealing with a single city (Paris) or district (Montmartre), or even a single aspect of a city (Impressionist Paris). Then there are unusual treatments, with titles like: *Turn Right at the Fountain, Turn Left at the Pub,* and *Walk Straight Through the Square* (these outline walking tours in various cities).

Tourist guides may deal with points of interest or with food and lodging, or with all three. There is even a guide for fast-food outlets. Many guide series now emphasize economies of travel. While the famous Arthur Frommer publications (*Europe on $5 a Day*) have raised their limits to $10, $15, and $20 a day, the interest in pricing is still apparent. Regrettably, most of the books issued by the Karl Baedeker firm are now badly out of date, but in their time they were wonders for interest and accuracy,* so that "Baedeker" was for a guide book what "Frigidaire" was for an electric refrigerator. The firm's long and honorable history is being perpetuated by the present owners.[18]

For the United States, the *American Guide Series,* compiled by the Federal Writers' Project during the depression of the 1930s, and published by various houses, is still of value; especially so are those titles which have been revised. Each state has a volume, and there are a few for regions and for cities.

*For an interesting use of an aged Baedeker, see James E. Holroyd, "Baedeker and Baker Street," *The Cornhill Magazine* 173 (Winter 1962/63): 139–145. It is based on Baedeker's *London and Its Environs* for 1881 — the time Sherlock Holmes is supposed to have stalked around the streets and railroad stations.

Many colorful books of geographic description are issued for the gift trade, presumably, but some of these are worthy of library purchase. They usually are interesting to travelers. Often equipped with color plates (sometimes garishly loud), they depict cities, gardens, medieval castles, or other sights.

Traditionally, travel has been a favorite subject for the film formats. "Geography," which includes travel, is a heading with many entries in the NICEM indexes for slides, filmstrips, and films. *Guide to Free-Loan Films About Foreign Lands* (Alexandria, VA: Serina Press, 1975, 283 p.) gives many titles distributed by agencies of governments seeking the tourist trade or good will.

20. SOCIAL SCIENCES—GENERAL

In its broadest sense, the province of social science includes all things which are or could be known about all human beings (and possibly every animal) — their interrelationships; their kinship and family ties; friendships and hostile actions; exchanges of money, goods, and services; communications with each other. These studies deal with organizations and associations of people in religion, business, government, neighborhood, school, and club. In 1930, the famous *Encyclopaedia of the Social Sciences* defined this area as "those mental or cultural sciences which deal with the activities of the individual as a member of a group."[1] Nothing human, however, is really far outside this area. Even thought and creativity are included. The social sciences take in the artist at the easel, the novelist at the desk, the natural scientist in the laboratory, as well as the museum-visitor, the novel-reader, and the insecticide-purchaser.

Obviously no investigator can make any headway by indiscriminate or random plunges into this mass, so social scientists have to plan their efforts in a more systematic way. Usually the individual disciplines are thought of as studying particular kinds of human relationships. The more modern *International Encyclopedia of the Social Sciences,* a successor to (but not mere revision of) the earlier work, carries forward the previous definition and lists the fields within its scope as: anthropology, economics, geography (except physical), history, law, political science, psychiatry, psychology, sociology, statistics.[2]

Others would add linguistics and perhaps communication generally, while questioning the inclusion of statistics, at least in its theoretical aspects. Still others would say that if legal theory is a social science, then theories of education, business, management, and other activities (even library science) should be included also.

Broadly as the social science tent is spread, it is scarcely big enough to cover some of these fields. Perhaps because this group encompasses so many kinds of phenomena and such a variety of approaches, another term, *behavioral sciences,* came into use in the

United States during the 1950s. It represents an area generally narrower, more unified, and more manageable than *social sciences* but does pick up other, related studies: "sociology; anthropology (minus archaeology, technical lingustics, and most of physical anthropology); psychology (minus physiological psychology); and behavioral aspects of biology, economics, geography, law, psychiatry, and political science."[3]

It would appear that problems of unification, subdivision, and territorial priority are more severe for the social sciences than for the physical and biological sciences, where the lines seem somehow more natural, or for the humanities, where less attention is paid such matters.

The conflict between unity and division is discussed in a weighty essay by Salomon Bochner, who terms the half-century 1776–1825 the age of "eclosion" — the period in which "most of our present-day knowledge evolved into its main organizational divisions." The twentieth century, on the other hand, he represents as the age of synthesis.[4] There have been movements, for instance, to ally political science more closely with such other disciplines as sociology, anthropology, and psychology. Even the topic of international relations can use the findings of these fields, as well as those of demography, history, law, economics, and others. Max Lerner some years ago made a significant comment on the basic unity of the area: "All the social sciences deal with the same body of material and data — human behavior in society. . . . Each chooses to emphasize a different phase of that behavior, or, if you wish, to throw a different searchlight upon it."[5] The result is suggested by Thomas S. Kuhn's comment that textbooks encountered in the natural sciences "display different subject matters," whereas in many of the social sciences they exemplify "different approaches to a single problem field."[6]

THE NATURE OF THE SOCIAL SCIENCES

If we think of physical sciences on one side and "literary" or humanistic culture on the other, social science may be considered a third way of looking at things. This way is scientific in that it tries to show how human affairs by necessity are interlocked with the natural and material world; humanistic in the sense that it shows how social affairs are influenced by purposes and philosophies. Sir Charles Snow, famous for his short essay *The Two Cultures,* feels that there is something in sociology that "speaks the language of science, and something in it which is available to persons in the literary culture. It is no better than a very frail and often a very dubious bridge, but I would have thought it could be taught here with advantage to our entire intellectual world."[7]

The British librarian Maurice Line, chief architect of the extensive *Investigation Into Information Requirements of the Social Sciences,* pictures the relations of social science to the other two major areas of knowledge not in terms of Snow's frail and dubious bridge, but of a mass being stretched out in two directions.

> Within our broad definition of social sciences, the differences are enormous. The economic historian has little in common with the econometrician, either in the nature of his subject or his methods of work. Nor has the political philosopher necessarily much in common with the psephologist. In these two examples, as in many other examples of differences, the two extremes tend respectively to the humanities and the sciences.[8]

These two analogies are consistent with evidence from bibliography, which also suggests that the social sciences are between the physical and biological sciences on the one hand and the humanities on the other; citation studies in the various literatures tend to confirm this. First, there are the forms of writings used as sources of information. In their relative dependence on books (as opposed to periodicals) the three areas line up like this: books are used most by scholars in humanities, next by social scientists, and least by scientists. In point of age, the literature cited by humanists is older (partly because so many original source documents are used); social scientists deal with more recent works; and scientists, somewhat more recent yet. In relative use of foreign-language materials for research, however, there is an exception: the social scientists (in the English-speaking countries) cite foreign language sources far less frequently than do natural scientists or humanists.[9]

The social sciences are sometimes thought of as daughters, or perhaps now sisters, of history. Family quarrels are not unknown, but the historians' one-time preoccupation with politics has been tempered by a concern for the significance of economics and sociology. The "fairly distinguished historian" who once considered sociology "an obscene word" is now retired.[10] Social scientists have been perhaps a bit slow in recognizing the crucial importance of the historical dimension, but recent theorists such as Robert K. Merton and Irving L. Horowitz have urged that the oversight be corrected.

A HISTORICAL NOTE

Human behavior has always been interesting to observe, but social scientists have been faced with the question: Do we want to study ourselves objectively? Or even, *can* we really study ourselves scientifically, in any meaningful sense of that word? A look at history shows the rough chronology of the endeavor to understand. The earliest concerns were the heavens (astronomy) and theology; then the earth, especially in its physical aspects; finally the "proper study of mankind" (in Alexander Pope's phrase) — human beings. Berelson and Steiner, noting that the behavioral sciences have come of age in the twentieth century, add, "It would appear that the more intimate (to man) the subject matter, the younger the science. Astronomy before geography, physical science before biology, medicine before psychology —even though in each case the availability of data was in the reverse order."[11]

The progression has not been so neat as that, of course. Human beings over the centuries have shown a propensity for keeping records of self-observation and self-expression. Such records eventually form the basis on which the society comes to regulate the operations of individuals and groups. Even genealogies and chronologies have helped establish social controls. Some of the earliest thinkers whose ideas have been preserved looked within themselves and observed also the behavior of others, asked why people did this or that, and formulated theories attempting to provide answers. Aristotle, in the fourth century before Christ, was intensely interested in politics and wrote in considerable detail also about ethics and about human psychology. But there has been a curious ambivalence in the matter of collecting and analyzing minute personal data. Such research has come rather late. "All the social sciences may be said to possess a long heritage and a short history."[12]

Things began to change in the eighteenth and nineteenth centuries as the industrial revolution, the rise of capitalism, and the rush of the people to urban centers brought great social upheavals of the kind that fairly demand study. These changes, along with the intellectual movement away from rational speculation toward empirical research, produced conditions which were right for the growth of social science. Such crises as economic depressions have been tremendous stimulants to research. The two world wars, especially the second, brought so many problems of maintaining morale, distributing goods, regulating prices, and instructing and propagandizing the people that social scientists were called upon to contribute their knowledge.

Consider the unusual and difficult social situations that have been encountered in the United States. We have tried to assimilate several races and numerous nationalities, and the problems involved in this process have challenged the best in social philosophy and research. What are the reasons for conflicts between people? What more can be learned about such troubles, and how can this information be disseminated so as to reduce the great amount of injustice and unhappiness created by these troubles? Again, if we could learn more about crime and the criminal personality, we could take steps to alleviate a terrifying problem. "There would be no social sciences," said Robert Lynd, "if there were not perplexities in living in culture that call for solution."[13] Part of the interest in this area, then, is due to the fact that people and situations are challenging to analyze by theoretical and scientific means; part is due to the hope of discovering workable solutions to practical problems. Studies of women and Blacks are likely to be supplemented in the 1980s by works about other groups.

Though the behavioral sciences have come to a degree of maturity in the present century, it is only fair to say that the advances in social research have been far less spectacular than those in pure sciences. Simey puts it well:

> The member of the Royal Society of the eighteenth — even the late nineteenth — century would be utterly at a loss to understand the concepts now relied on in the investigation of the material universe, but in matters of government, education, crime, and the literary culture generally, ways of thinking are nothing like so different. The pioneers of the eighteenth century, Rousseau, Howard, Montesquieu, and the French *philosophes* generally, would not feel themselves in an entirely foreign society today. But our natural science, its achievements and potentialities, would both mystify and terrify them, and be incomprehensible to their colleagues who were learned in natural philosophy. How can the social sciences, therefore, be brought up to date? [14]

THE PROBLEMS OF RESEARCH IN SOCIAL SCIENCE

While natural scientists have only in comparatively recent times debated the values and implications of their researches, the social scientists have been conscious of various dilemmas for much longer. These dilemmas are of concern to the librarian also, because they bear on the question of how much and what kind of social science materials should be obtained for the individual collection. The selector forms some general idea of the place and value of books in each major area of knowledge. While this idea may be vague and only in the background when one chooses or rejects a given title — or decides to buy four copies instead of three — it still is present and real. What values are found, then, in books, periodicals, and other social science materials as a whole? What does the library public think of them? Why the mixture of respect, fear, and contempt that seems so common when people view the social sciences? It may be explained by certain facts, opinions, and contentions.

Difficulty of Research

Human beings, observed as phenomena, are about as intricate as anything that can be studied. There are so many variables influencing their behavior at any one time that satisfactory analysis is extremely difficult. To discover the causes of human behavior and their relative strengths is almost beyond our capacity. Even the proposition that behavior is "caused" raises serious philosophical and practical objections. For instance, a Harvard sociologist declares that "to constantly explain away one's failure as a product of one's environment, or worse, of another race's or class's doing . . . is to reduce oneself to the level of an object and further prolong one's dependency on that other group or environment." [15]

Not only are "causes" difficult to find and evaluate, but tests and experiments are much more limited in the social sciences than in the natural. While experiments with rats and other animals do provide some conclusions about human beings, the application of the evidence is subject to considerable uncertainty — more so than most scientists find comfortable. As for testing and observing people's behavior — though it is fairly easy to examine and survey university students, other (noncaptive) groups are less generous in their cooperation. Recent laws and customs respecting the right to privacy have imposed further restrictions.

The areas of research are limited, moreover, by the amounts and sources of funding. A problem is more likely to receive attention if some one or some group — government, business, association, or other — is willing to support the study with money. Those who want the information do not necessarily have at heart the best interests of the people studied, or of the population at large. Even the research method may be influenced by money. For instance, "we suspect that the increasing use of statistical measures in sociological research is related to problems that sociologists encounter when seeking funding for their research."[16]

Despite the innate difficulty of the task, the limited opportunities for experiment, the reluctance of people to be studied, and the restrictions imposed by distributors of funds, the picture should not be painted too dark. The 1964 book by Berelson and Steiner, *Human Behavior,* summarized the facts which had been established with reasonable certainty in this area of knowledge. An analysis by three other authorities, two American and one German, has identified sixty-two major achievements or breakthroughs in social science between 1900 and 1965. Some of the accomplishments came from political groups, some from associations, but most from universities and institutes.[17] An impressive body of information has been gained about human beings and their institutions.

Uncertainty About Social Scientists' Roles

Should the social scientist be strictly objective, remaining aloof from the human scene with its joys and miseries, or should that research person become involved emotionally, impelled perhaps by a desire to make things better? One who takes the latter course may (unintentionally, or even designedly) warp data or interpretation because of a wish for the results to indicate a certain course of action. Does the investigator have some stake in the outcome, such as a preference for one class, group, or religion, or perhaps a dislike of another? Is there a long-standing prejudice for or against, say, the idea of individual responsibility for crime? If so, the conclusions drawn and especially the application recommended may be badly warped.

Even a natural scientist is not likely to do research unless emotionally concerned to a certain minimal degree, but the problem of distortion is far greater with the social scientist. The medical researcher may have strong feelings, wholesome or not, about finding a cure for cholera, and may also prefer the one cure which he or she has hypothesized. However, the chances for testing this remedy are surer, quicker, and more economical than they are for testing a proposed cure for poverty. Even a page on how to make an electric motor from a few bits of metal can be tested in the home. Directions for ridding a society of its crime are another thing. That is why, though "statements of truth can be made about physical events, they are extremely difficult — perhaps impossible — to make about pure social behavior."[18]

There is also a long-standing impression that if social scientists are not coldly objective in their studies, they run into the danger of being used by power groups, bigots, and propagandists. Knowledge can be a force for controlling people, and public reaction to social science research may be influenced unfavorably by such fears. For instance, one article declares, "Many American radicals and some liberals are deeply suspicious of social science, even in its present rudimentary state. They see it as a tool of the Establishment for manipulating public opinion at home, suppressing national liberation movements abroad, and generally keeping a lid on social ferment all around the globe"[19] Others oppose the direct application of social science for virtually opposite reasons. In a University of Michigan study of government officials, it was concluded that "the more sophisticated and methodologically sound the research, the less likely it is to be used by policy-makers."[20] Even Professor Boulding is not optimistic: "There are those, of course, who see salvation in the development of the social and behavioral sciences. I cannot, I regret, share this optimism. These sciences can all too easily play into the hands of manipulators."[21] He adds that information in anthropology is least subject to such abuse.[22]

In answer, many have been swift to point out that knowledge should not always be confused with power; understanding of social behavior need not abridge personal freedom. It is contended that the social scientists simply do not have the ability to manipulate an individual unless that person consents. The defense is not entirely satisfactory, but clearly the danger on this front is far greater from physical and biological scientists, who can produce weapons from germs to bombs, or from pharmacologists, who write books that may be used to select poisons for mothers-and fathers-in-law.

But if the social scientist is to become involved directly, what problems are worthy of attention? Does some research lead to uses that are less than desirable socially? A few years ago, a Nevada gambler faced a problem so pressing that he had the Stanford Research Institute* do a special study for him. The question was how to get more people to gamble in his casinos. Applying motivational research, the institute told him, among other things, to move from Las Vegas and Reno to a more wholesome-appearing place, Lake Tahoe, with its pure blue waters; to replace lizard-faced dealers with smiling folksy gentlemen; to mask the clatter of slot machines with organ music suggestive of rousing hymns; then to give people an excuse for going to this lovely place of deceit — make it seem like a gracious, life-promoting health resort.[23]

Are such studies really proper? Having been bought and presumably paid for, they take precedence over projects of greater social value. There is by no means universal accord on what kinds of problems the social scientist should tackle. In fact, Kuhn "was struck by the number and extent of the overt disagreements between social scientists about the nature of legitimate scientific problems and methods" as compared with a relative freedom from such disagreements among natural scientists.[24] In part, the difficulty goes back to the newness of the disciplines and to the close personal connection between the researcher and the things studied.

A contention made more and more frequently is that social scientists should be able to generalize from their research, rather than merely state findings. Thus an article in *The American Sociologist* claims that "personal caution, cloaked in the name of scientific precision, saps the vitality of the sociological discipline at its core."[25] Furthermore, Nathan Glazer and others see evidence that social scientists are getting more excited about exerting an influence on government and other institutions.[26]

It must be admitted that the body of social science literature suffers in value and use because of these dilemmas. Those studies

*The University later divested itself of the Institute.

which are starkly scientific and objective often lack a certain practical application. Those which address themselves directly to human problems risk the danger of being biased, or at least of losing effectiveness because readers interpret them as prejudiced. In a general way, librarians have to take into account such factors as these in deciding how much to spend on books in social sciences as compared with the other major subject areas. Considerations about demand for and value of materials should be somewhere in the selector's mind as the judgment is made to reject or purchase an individual title.

GENERAL NATURE OF THE LITERATURE

Let us now see what conclusions can be drawn about the nature and use of library materials produced by social scientists. The fact that these sciences are relatively young, while at the same time immensely important to so many people, probably accounts for one characteristic of literature in this area: the variety of sources responsible for publication. "The outstanding organizational characteristic of social science research in the United States is its decentralization. It pervades all major sections of the economy and the society." To Alpert, this aspect has certain advantages: "The multiplicity of organizations which support and conduct research insures healthy growth by sustaining diversified channels for exploration of new areas and untried methods."[27] It serves to indicate also that there are many and various users of library materials in this area of knowledge. Social science information of some sorts and on some levels is needed by administrators, professionals, parents, citizens — almost everyone who wishes to act intelligently. Such a pattern of diversified producers and users, unsystematic as it is, has the disadvantage of scattering effort and producing trivial studies. The result has been described as a "pile-up in a chaos of unrelated monographs and articles."[28]

The fact that materials in social science are produced by so many different kinds of agencies means difficulty for the general library in selection (as well as in acquisition and preservation). The relative authority of writers is harder to assess. Even the reputations of scholars are likely to be more fleeting than in the sciences. Fugitive materials, often printed poorly, prove to have practical use. A mimeographed brochure can be a repository of important ideas, either by reflecting the point of view of some organization or by describing the method used in some otherwise insignificant study. The catalogs of Sears, Roebuck and other mail order houses are full of social history, as are all sorts of old magazines and newspapers.

Then there are the materials of local interest. They can be voluminous, but even the smallest public library has an obligation to preserve them. The author of *Plainville, U.S.A.*, whose pseudonym is James West, was looking for a town to study; then while his automobile was being repaired in "Plainville," a town of fewer than a thousand people, he chose that as the place to be examined. Besides interviewing many of the residents, he ransacked the county courthouse records and the files of the weekly newspaper; read the county's history and many other materials, finally declaring, "For even an isolated community like Plainville, there exists so vast a body of relevant printed and other documentary material that no one could read it all in a lifetime." [29]

There is the further problem of obsolescence in social science publications. In the chapter on geography, a distinction was made between the literature of things which change and of things which are constant. Most of the subject matter of social science is in continual change. Human behavior is the opposite of static; the temporal nature of such processes is a basic consideration in social thought (though the history of social philosophy or of political theory deals with principles that, of course, are stable). Economic conditions are in flux. Even social institutions metamorphose, if slowly. Thus the literature of social science as a whole is similar to that of the human aspects of geography, in that it is difficult for publications to keep up-to-date. On this score, then, there is a contrast with humanistic publications, for they deal with things that are less mutable. As Line puts it, the social sciences "are concerned often with matter which is not merely current but constantly shifting: no other area of knowledge deals with such unstable material."[30] Citation studies suggest that over half of the sources used in research in this area are less than ten years old, and, as Wilson points out, "An enormous amount of work in sociology, political science, anthropology, and economics is simply descriptive and interpretative of present conditions."[31] Yet, to complicate the situation, almost any of the materials may have historical value and need to be retained by appropriate libraries. One of the leading contemporary sociologists, Robert K. Merton, makes the point that "the physical and life sciences have generally been more successful than the social sciences in retrieving relevant cumulative knowledge of the past and incorporating it in subsequent formulations. This process of obliteration by incorporation is still rare in sociology. As a result, previously unretrieved information is still there to be usefully employed as new points of departure."[32] For this reason the library has the problem of collecting new materials while attempting to judge which older ones will remain useful.

So far as languages are concerned, the preponderant evidence is that roughly ninety percent of materials used in research by American and British social scientists are in English, though there are variations from field to field. American writers in education use about ninety-nine percent English-language sources.[33] This pattern of language is due largely to the fact that studies in the social sciences tend to be centered on particular places — the places studied correspond to those in which the studies are carried out; thus Brown and Gilmartin, speaking of sociology, say that "three-fourths of today's research [by Americans] has its setting in the United States."[34] British political scientists, in the main, are interested in British politics. American economists are concerned principally with conditions in the United States. Both groups therefore tend to use published sources in the English language. Humanists, on the other hand, are interested in art, architecture, music, and philosophy produced in many countries other than their own. The pure sciences usually are independent of national boundaries. There are exceptions to these generalizations (for example, Americans' interest in Ancient Greek political thought, and anthropologists' studies of "foreign" cultures), but taken as a whole, social sciences are centered on geographic locality and tend to draw on materials in the language of the place studied. Some authorities have criticized these self-imposed limitations, and it may be that changes will occur.

In social sciences, books and periodicals are of roughly equal importance. Both need to be well represented in the general library. It has been shown that, for sociology at least, books of readings (compiled from periodicals and other books) are used frequently as sources, even by those writing scholarly articles.[35] Government publications are highly significant, traditionally for the fields of economics and political science, and now also in sociology. This fact again may reflect, as it does in geography, the place-centeredness of social science.

POPULARIZATIONS

Though most libraries, even smaller ones, need to give some attention to source materials and to authoritative basic research, they recognize also the need for books and periodicals that are readable by the general public. Some people want to learn about social theory and problems. These concepts and analyses are hard to grasp, however, and popularization is relatively difficult. For comparison, let us again take books in history as a reference point. Most of them are fairly easy for the uninitiated to understand, at least on some level. They may not be interesting for one reason or another, but if the author has reasonable facility with language, they are not hard to read. In the social sciences, however, many of the typical books have statistical tables or deal with hard-to-describe phenomena; hence, though important to specialists, they are not appreciated by the laity. The difficulty here is not so great, of course, as it is in the natural sciences, but there is reason to believe that "public ambivalence toward the social sciences may also be attributable to growing difficulty in understanding the language of sociology and anthropology; a difficulty that sometimes leads to a suspicion that the conclusions of months of research, couched in obscure terminology, merely explicate the obvious."[36]

The game is hard to win, though, because popularizations are likely to be suspect also. Vance Packard, for instance, produced some highly readable books, such as *The Hidden Persuaders* (New York: D. McKay Company, 1957, 275 p.) and *The Status Seekers* (New York: D. McKay Company, 1959, 376 p.), but these works generally were not acceptable to professionals. Robert Ardrey's books, such as *The Territorial Imperative* (Atheneum, 1966, 390 p.) and *The Hunting Hypothesis* (Atheneum, 1976, 242 p.), have been better received, especially his later ones. A famous professor of zoology says that "Ardrey has learned to walk carefully around his academic critics. And yet, when he gets onto a clear stretch of road and pulls out all the stops, he is the only popular science writer who can send chills down this reviewer's spine."[37]

To note some other fields: psychologists have strong resentment against easy explanations for the laity. In economics, there is the opposition to supposed oversimplification, and fear of propaganda in its worst sense. But books which discuss practical problems in intelligent ways are to be prized. Horowitz rightly suggests that "instead of sniping at the sociological 'popularizers' and 'journalists,' we might well start appreciating them."[38]

The recency of materials used by scholarly writers in these disciplines has been emphasized, and there is, of course, a need for up-to-date works for the general public. There is a good deal of truth, however, in Pownall's observation:

> In a number of Social Science disciplines, surprisingly enough, older, more traditional works may better serve the undergraduate student, since such works tend to be more comprehensive, less specialized, sometimes better researched and better written. As a general rule (with many exceptions) this holds true for the fields of anthropology, sociology, and political science.[39]

Magazines are valuable also for popularizing this general area. *Human Behavior, the Newsmagazine of the Social Sciences* is good for the non-expert, though it does waste space trying to dramatize what is already interesting. *Society* is more sophisticated, and

The Public Interest (generally termed "conservative") makes serious applications to current issues and problems.

Again, the importance of social science, when mixed with a certain hostility toward it, produces attempts to suppress various books in the area. Censorship cases seem to involve books of theory and policy more than those reporting scientific research, and historical approaches seem more often under attack than analyses of current problems, possibly because the latter are easier to understand, but more probably because their implications are unsuspected.

SOURCES OF INFORMATION ON MATERIALS

For general background and for lists of selected works, an excellent source is *Sources of Information in the Social Sciences: A Guide to the Literature* by Carl M. White and associates, 2nd ed. (Chicago: American Library Association, 1973, 702 p.). This work has surveys by experts in the individual disciplines. Still of considerable use is Bert Hoselitz's *Reader's Guide to the Social Sciences,* rev. ed. (New York: Free Press, 1970, 425 p.). *Alternatives in Print: An International Catalog of Books, Pamphlets, Periodicals and Audiovisual Materials,* 6th ed., compiled by a Task Force of the Social Responsibilities Round Table, American Library Association (New York: Neal-Schuman Publishers, Inc., 1980, 668 p.) now lists some 23,000 items.

A book review section of unusual value is found in the *Annals of the American Academy of Political and Social Science.* The reviews, written by scholars, are short and generally to the point; they are arranged by topic.

Nonprint materials are used widely in the social sciences. Transparencies present abstract material such as graphs and statistical tables. Motion picture films are especially good for demonstrating concrete situations — showing the actions of people. Social problems such as the plight of the city (or of the farm) are made real by documentaries. Controversial issues may be presented in order to stimulate discussion and send viewers in search of further information. These media impress the responsibilities of citizenship and demonstrate the operations of government. Business and industry are represented by motion pictures showing manufacturing processes and such phenomena as the workings of the stock market. This medium has proved valuable also for the preservation of data used in anthropology.

Films in the Behavioral Sciences: An Annotated Catalogue, by John M. Schneider, Barnett Addis, and Marsha Addis, 2nd ed. (Oklahoma City: University of Oklahoma Medical Center, 1970, 225 p.) still has value for the general library. Harry A. Johnson has edited, compiled, and annotated *Ethnic American Minorities: A Guide to Media and Materials* (New York: Bowker, 1976, 304 p.). *Science Books and Films* includes the social/behavioral sciences.

21. SOCIAL SCIENCES—
PARTICULAR FIELDS

On the surface at least there is a higher degree of unity among the disciplines of social science than in the other major divisions of knowledge. The fields tend to overlap each other, and the province and essence of each is the subject of a good deal of discussion. We may think of social science as a pie which has been cut into six pieces (psychology, sociology, anthropology, economics, political science, and history),[1] but only if we recognize that the divisions are not so sharp as pie-slices, and that no one was around to plan the cutting.

Nevertheless, the separate disciplines do have distinctions which bear on library selection. Keeping abreast of current developments in these fields is made difficult by the fact that analysts emphasize different trends and cite documentation to support their variant perceptions. A few remarks about some of the more important of these individual fields will help bring out more of their characteristics.

SOCIOLOGY

In 1839, the French Positivist, Auguste Comte (1798–1857), coined the term "sociology," using one word from the Latin and another from Greek. This "horrible hybrid," as Robert K. Merton calls it, "has ever since designated the science of society."[2] There has always been some question as to whether sociology is a general and inclusive discipline or just one of several equally important fields. Does it overarch and interrelate the other social sciences, or is it the study of things that are left over after others have staked out their claims? It may be thought of both ways. Merrill speaks of the other social sciences as dealing "with specific aspects of human relationships; the field of sociology is human relationships as such."[3] Talcott Parsons, who has written a great deal at different times about this problem, thinks of the field as one special social science; the theory of the social system being parallel to the theories of personality and of culture.[4] Sociology has a good deal in common with cultural anthropology and with psychology.

In addition to Comte, the most important early theorists were Herbert Spencer (1820–1903) in England, Émile Durkheim (1858–1917) in France, and Max Weber (1864–1920) in Germany. The writings of the latter two are regularly cited today in American books and periodical articles. The works of Karl Marx also have had great influence, particularly in Europe. It is apparent, then, that the roots of this discipline are in the social theories of Europeans, but as a field of scientific investigation, sociology has developed most rapidly in the United States. The first college sociology course in this country was offered by William Graham Sumner at Yale, in 1876, and the American Sociological Society (now Association) was founded in 1906 by a group breaking away from the Economic Association.

The systems investigated by sociology include the millions of single social acts that take place between individuals, plus all sorts of relationships, organizations, and institutions, and finally communities and societies. Some of the institutions and organizations that concern sociology are those having to do with industry, education, religion, medicine, science, and even, in recent years, sports. Not all these specialties have received equal attention so far. Some typical questions dealt with are: Does bad housing tend to produce criminals? What factors account for the divorce rate? What are the attitudes of black people toward war with Russia? Does television have anything to do with violent behavior? Do youthful dissidents become adult dissidents? Are women paid more than men in the Soviet Union?

The conclusions of sociologists are not easy to evaluate. For instance, one of the experiments cited most often in the literature was conducted in 1924–1933 at Western Electric's Hawthorne plant, and the term *Hawthorne Effect* has for a half-century been used to mean that people change their behavior while they are being studied. A 1978 reevaluation of the data, however, concludes that this "paradigmatic foundation of the social science of work" is largely false.[5]

Like its sister disciplines, sociology has a great deal to do with libraries and printed materials. W. I. Thomas, who with Florian Znaniecki produced the landmark study *The Polish Peasant in Europe and America* (Chicago: University of Chicago Press, 1918–1920, 5 vols.; many other editions) was among the first to emphasize the use of documents.[6] Ideas are drawn from government reports, records of organizations, books of theory, and even diaries and autobiographies. Sociology uses a greater variety, if not a greater quantity, of materials than do the other social sciences. In turn, these facts are reworked with new, original data and themes to produce writings which help explain social occurrences or perhaps to recommend action.

The American Journal of Sociology was started by Albion W. Small in 1895, though the founder was questioned as to whether there would be enough writings to fill out a periodical. In less than a century numerous other journals have been established, several of them dealing with specialties within the field. The growth in number of books has been steady and the total American output for sociology, statistics, economics, and political science and related topics is now 6,500 to 7,000 books a year. (The British writer Julius Gould rather chides the American sociologists on their large volume of publications. Referring to a new technical term introduced by Morris Ginsberg, Gould goes on, "Had Ginsberg been an American there would have been, by now, a whole corpus of literature devoted to this concept and its use in empirical research. . . .")[7]

There is reason to believe that books in sociology have been significant influences in the United States. Gunnar Myrdal's *An American Dilemma: The Negro Problem and Modern Democracy* (New York: Harper, 1944, 2 vols.) probably had something to do with the decision made ten years later by the U. S. Supreme Court declaring racial segregation of public schools to be unconstitutional. Frank Tannenbaum's little book, *Slave and Citizen: The Negro in the Americas,* (New York: Knopf, 1947, 128 p.) is said to have helped persuade Branch Rickey to hire Jackie Robinson to play first base for the old Brooklyn Dodgers.[8] The concern of government with the problems studied by sociologists is exemplified by such government documents as the *Report* of the U. S. Commission on Obscenity and Pornography (Washington: Government Printing Office, 1970, 646 p.). There is some feeling, however, that government, being itself near the core of many problems in society, is less able to identify and address the issues that are really critical.

In 1970, professors and associate professors in departments of sociology scored periodicals according to the importance of their contributions to the field. The twenty top-ranking journals proved to be (in descending order):

American Sociological Review
American Journal of Sociology
Social Forces
Sociometry
British Journal of Sociology
American Anthropologist
Social Problems
American Political Science Review
Demography
Annals of the American Academy of Political and Social Science
Public Opinion Quarterly
American Economic Review
Journal of Personality and Social Psychology
European Journal of Sociology
Behavioral Science
Rural Sociology
Human Organization
Journal of Social Psychology
Administrative Science Quarterly
Milbank Memorial Fund Quarterly
International Journal of Comparative Sociology [9]

Established in 1972, *Contemporary Sociology: A Journal of Reviews* is devoted almost entirely to new books in the field, and to articles about the review process, a topic of great interest to sociologists.

POLITICS

In its most fundamental aspect, this field is a study of power, but not in the sense of the householder's exercising power over roaches; it is the study of authority — of authorized power, which in turn involves order and some measure of consent on the part of those who are controlled. The subject of politics, then, has to do with the question of "how particular groups of people have tried to solve the many problems which arise from the interplay of the facts of power, the need for order and the value of freedom."[10] The field takes its name from the Greek *polis* — city-state.

Each society, according to its own basic philosophy, distributes goods and other valuables to persons and groups, and makes decisions (in the form of laws, for example) which regulate certain areas of conduct. The political system is "that behavior or set of interactions through which authoritative allocations (or binding decisions) are made and implemented for a society."[11]

Philosophy plays a larger part in this discipline than in most other social sciences, raising such questions as: What is just? What should be the ultimate aims of government? What form of government best achieves the highest goals?

Reflections on politics go back a long way, possibly to the time an individual was first threatened by someone with power. For one example, among the Hebrews, the prophet Samuel, about the eleventh century B.C., warned against a centralized monarchical form of government. The results of enthroning a king, he said, would include war and high taxes.[12] Against his urging, the people insisted on a king and received the ill-starred Saul. Over a millennium and a third later came landmark works by Aristotle (*Politics*) and Plato (*The Republic*). The question of the individual's relationship to the state is still much with us, and to many writers the wisdom of the ancients still has relevance: "Wherever I go, I meet Plato coming back." Among other "classic" works are Niccolò Machiavelli's *The Prince* (first published in 1532); Thomas Hobbes's *Leviathan* (1651); *Two Treatises on Government,* by John Locke (1690); and *The Federalist Papers* of Hamilton, Madison, and Jay (1788). The latter two works have been especially important to Americans.

The rudiments of political science were taught at Harvard in the 1640s, and something over two centuries later (1858) a chair in the discipline was established at Columbia, with Francis Lieber as the first incumbent. By 1900 courses in politics were common, but until World War II this field was secondary to history in departments of "History and Political Science." In the meantime, the founding of the American Political Association in 1903, with its journal *The American Political Science Review* three years later, was advancing the cause.*

At this time, all the social sciences are struggling to define their own areas of investigation, but political scientists seem to be having the roughest time of it. Thus David Easton's article, "Political Science," in the *International Encyclopedia of the Social Sciences* began with the discouraging note, "Political science in mid-twentieth century is a discipline in search of its identity." [13] Freeman, with reference to these and other issues, makes the doleful comment, "As if especially caused by the gods, political science seems destined to reconsider these same disputes for all ages to come." [14]

Traditionalists in the field favor a theoretical and historical approach, and behavioralists seek to study the political actions of people by scientific observation. The growth of interest in the latter is indicated by a content analysis of *The American Political Science Review* for 1930–1966. It shows a steady increase in proportion of articles with "quantitative empirical content." In the 1930s, the percentage of such articles was 15; in the 1960s it had gone up to 38. [15]

Not only is this field concerned, then, with political theory, it

---

*The importance of this journal is indicated by the fact that Stewart found it to be the most frequently cited in the field by both British and American sources (June L. Stewart, "The Literature of Politics: A Citation Analysis," *International Library Review* 2 [July 1970]: 345–346).

deals also with public law, comparative governments, public administration, and international relations. It describes political behavior at all levels, and seeks explanations for such behavior. For instance: Do voters favor their religions over their pocketbooks? What kinds of scandal hurt or help a candidate's chances for election? How does political corruption in America compare with that in European countries? What dirty tricks are used by political campaigners? Which political parties do American Indians favor? How much do the news media affect the outcome of elections?

Research in political science, while often involving direct observation and interviewing of people, demands also an extensive use of library materials. Books are the vehicle for conveying political theory and philosophy; for empirical studies, original reports and documents are necessary. This is a subject in which governments naturally are highly interested. As noted in the chapter on documents, a sizable fraction of these publications have to do with the operation of government itself, and these are good grist for the political scientists' mill. Especially important are such materials as records of legislative debates (for example, *The Congressional Record*), laws, tabulations of votes, papers of presidents, governors, etc. Frank Sorauf's statement ("Certainly no other discipline can so profit from a mastery of obscure labyrinths of the U. S. Government document file"[16]) is borne out by citation studies. Sarouf also specified the *New York Times,* with its index, and *Public Affairs Information Service* as especially important for investigators in this field.

Politics is a field in which a flow of fresh materials is crucially important for the library. New political issues arise and crowd out the older ones. Different personalities are touted as likely candidates for public office. Each election furnishes millions of bits of data, which may occasion the revision of some books or even the modification of political behavior theory.

Assuming that the effective operation of democracy depends on an informed electorate, the public library in particular has an obligation to present materials that help bring about more intelligent voting. In the case of local referenda, for instance, the better materials on each side ought to be available. It should be understood that political scientists differ sharply about the wisdom of urging people to vote, and Berelson's conclusion should not be forgotten: "Lack of interest by some people is not without its benefits. . . . Extreme interest goes with extreme partisanship and might culminate in rigid fanaticism that could destroy democratic processes if generalized throughout the community."[17] Still, if the library offers, to the best of its ability, arguments on all sides, this should help cool things and lead to better decisions in the long run, despite the discouraging fact that most voters tend to choose publications which reinforce their own prejudices.

For small to medium-sized public libraries, and also school and junior college libraries, Robert B. Harmon has compiled and annotated a list: *Developing the Library Collection in Political Science* (Metuchen, NJ: Scarecrow Press, 1976, 198 p.). Also of use is *The Information Sources of Political Science,* by Frederick L. Holler, 2nd ed. (Santa Barbara, Calif.: ABC-Clio, 1975, 5 vols.), which was prepared originally for junior college students. Its coverage is more general than indicated by the title, less comprehensive than suggested by five volumes.

For politics, important book reviews are published in such periodicals as *Time, Newsweek, New York Times, New Republic,* and *New York Review of Books.* On a scholarly level, *American Political Science Review* includes 150–200 pages of book reviews each quarter. *Political Science Reviewer: An Annual Review of Books* deals at length with non-current works and offers bibliographic essays. *Perspective: Monthly Review of New Books on Government/Politics/International Affairs* carries shorter reviews arranged by topic. A popular illustrated journal, *Politics Today,* which started in 1974, includes notes on recommended books.

LAW

Over two hundred years ago, Edmund Burke, in his speech *On Reconciliation with the Colonies,* declared, "In no country, perhaps, in the world is the law so general a study." For the last decade, Americans have become even more litigous, partly because ever more complicated laws and regulations have been passed, and partly because people have become more keenly aware of their rights and privileges. Many libraries have been caught short of satisfactory legal works. In fact, the need for law materials in general libraries has seldom received due emphasis. Ordinarily it is thought that laws, codified or not, are so complicated and technical that only the specialist, if anybody, can make sense of them. The truth is that after a few technical terms are mastered, such sets as the general statutes of a state are easier to understand than are advanced works in sciences and social sciences. It is the application to particular cases that causes difficulty.

In any event, conditions are changing, for, as Kelly puts it, "Today, in the wake of activism, consumerism and sunshine laws, the public at large has demanded and received legal reference books hitherto unheard of in the public libraries and general academic collections." [18]

While libraries do not give legal advice, even the smallest can provide materials for use on the less difficult questions. Owners of businesses need a place to check various laws. (Large corporations have their own law libraries.) Minorities must have publications to familiarize themselves with their rights. The ordinary citizen may wish to know something about the responsibilities of home-owners or about the ordinances pertaining to dogs or to taxes. Students often have assignments that involve consultation of law sources.

The total volume of publication in law is huge, with extensive annotated sets on many jurisdictions. Jones was not far wrong in saying that the periodicals devoted to law and legal institutions are "equal in volume to the total annual output of scholarly literature in all the social sciences combined." [19] These sets of books and periodicals are prohibitively expensive for small general libraries, but most can afford plain sets of their own state statutes and those of the local jurisdiction. Though the law seems somehow stable, actually it changes rather fast, so that legal information services have to be updated with supplements.

Fortunately, there are good books which the layman can use, such as Samuel G. Kling's *Complete Guide to Everyday Law,* 2nd ed. (Chicago: Follett Publishing Co., 1970, 623 p.), and *Handbook of Everyday Law,* by Martin J. Ross in collaboration with Jeffrey S. Ross, 3rd ed., rev. and enl. (New York: Harper & Row, 1975, 361 p.). More informal is *What Everyone Needs to Know About Law* (Washington: U. S. News & World Report, 1973, 255 p.).

For small libraries, selective lists of legal materials are helpful; for example, "Basic Law Collection," by Frederic D. Donnelly Jr., *American Libraries* 4 (June 1973): 360–363; and Anita K. Head's "Law Books for Social Science Libraries," *Special Libraries* 70 (January 1979): 1–11. Librarians with larger collections may wish to consult *Law Books in Review: A Quarterly Journal of Reviews of Current Publications in Law and Related Fields,* which has a topical arrangement of short reviews.

ECONOMICS

This field relates to and partly overlaps political science, in that it has to do with who gets what, and how. Why are some countries and persons materially "rich"? How can it be made possible for more people to obtain the things they need? Human wants are varied and virtually insatiable. Available materials are scarce. That is why we must "economize" and why we study economics. Included are such special topics as money, banking, business finance, international trade, labor markets, public utilities, and transportation.

The allocation of resources is largely a matter of politics (as noted before) and in the nineteenth century the expression "political economy" was common. To paraphrase an ancient saying, "The government taketh away, and the government giveth (some) back."

The Greeks were interested in the economics of the household (their word *oikos* meant "house;" indeed, this was the primary sense of the term *economics* until the eighteenth century), but the ancients also studied the distribution of wealth generally. Plato and Aristotle saw the close relationship between political and economic affairs. The Bible has a surprising amount to say about this worldly subject. It suggests economic systems, deals with ethical behavior in economic situations, and advances such unorthodox ideas as, "I have learned, in whatsoever state I am, therewith to be content." [20]

It may be said that economics became established as a field in its own right when in the year 1776 a professor of moral philosophy at the University of Edinburgh, Adam Smith (1723–1790), published *An Inquiry into the Wealth of Nations.* Thomas Malthus (1776–1834), whose *Essay on the Principle of Population . . .* appeared first in 1798, was probably the first academic economist (in a "college" founded by the East India Company), as well as the first English economist to work on the problem of depressions. Following him the term "dismal science" was attached to the field. Karl Marx (1818–1883), one of the most powerful and influential social thinkers of all time, published his huge *Das Kapital* in 1867 (in German). He and Friedrich Engels (1820–1895) had issued the pamphlet *A Communist Manifesto* nineteen years previously. Another whose ideas have been used (and abused) widely is John Maynard Keynes, who was born the year of Marx's death and who lived until 1946. His most widely-quoted book, *General Theory of Employment, Interest, and Money,* 403 p., came out in 1936, published in this country by Harcourt Brace, New York.

Down through the nineteenth century, when few concrete facts were available for economists to work with, it was assumed that a few relatively simple principles would explain economic activity and define the ideal economic system. However, the American Economic Association was founded in 1885, and began publication of its *American Economic Review* in 1911. The National Bureau of Economic Research was established in 1920 by Wesley C. Mitchell (1874–1948; known for theories of business cycles), with a number of economists in various colleges and universities cooperating. One result was the development of gross national product figures. As we "progressed" through the twentieth century and the depression of the 1930s, it came to be recognized that economics is a study both of fundamental importance and of tremendous complexity.

In 1946, the Full Employment Act provided for a Council of Economic Advisers to the President of the United States and the Joint Economic Committee of Congress. "This represented, as it were, the legitimation of economics as a profession and the establishment of economists as 'lords spiritual' in the precincts of both the White House and Congress."[21] Leading economists are now among the most important and most highly publicized of the advisors to presidents of the United States.

Economists work with great quantities of minutiae — perhaps, as Johnson claims, more objective data than are used by any other of the social sciences.[22] The field depends largely on printed sources of information. Hoselitz, who was in a position to judge such matters in relation to all the social sciences, said in 1959 and repeated in 1970, "In few other fields of social science are the varied modern uses of print so fully exemplified as that of economic analysis and practical economic activity."[23] Government studies and compilations are highly useful here, as in political science. Citation studies suggest that about a third of the sources used by scholarly writers in the field are government documents. Since the 1930s the United States federal government has gathered more and more economic data, and has made them available through its network of publications. In fact, for many departments of both state and federal governments, the collection of economic information is a major function.

Almost every one is interested in economics on some level, partly because of practical necessity and partly because of an introduction to the field through newspapers, magazines, and television. Inflation, recession, and stock market quotations are constantly demanding attention. Many people are anxious about property values, interest rates, and the amount of unemployment.

Unfortunately, however, scientific writing in this discipline is becoming more technical, opening a gap between the scholarly literature and the laity. Thus a large audience for popularizations has been created, but the problem of providing reliable yet simplified materials is more serious in this field than in social sciences generally. The fact that leading economists differ among themselves in recommending policy (what would be the effect, say, of a reduction in income taxes, or of a discovery of vast new oil reserves?) makes it difficult for the layman to profit from publications in the field, even if self-interest is the only concern. Actually the differences among the truly learned economists are not so much over the meaning of data themselves, as over philosophical and political considerations, but their recommendations are nonetheless confusing. If there is a haunting suspicion that some writers place the grinding of the axe above competent analysis and fair presentation, the fault must lie also with those readers who, ever anxious to find "clear and simple" arguments for a particular economic policy, are all too eager to seize upon such works.

On the credit side are the many scholarly works which are comprehensible to the general reader — even such loosely reasoned treatises as John Kenneth Galbraith's *The New Industrial State,* 3rd ed. (Boston: Houghton Mifflin, 1978, 438 p.). Books and periodicals on consumer economics (such as *Consumer Reports*) are widely used and are certainly worthwhile to the buyer who lacks expert knowledge.

As a general guide to works in the field, the bibliographic essays in John Fletcher's *The Use of Economics Literature* in the Information Sources for Research and Development Series (Hamden, CN: Archon Books, 1971, 310 p.) are still useful. The *Journal of Economic Literature,* published by the American Economic Association, reviews or annotates in each quarterly issue those books considered significant for the field. It also carries bibliographic essays on narrow topics. For the medium-sized and larger library, this periodical is an excellent selection tool.

Many public libraries are able to render a fine service to people in business enterprises. The fact that large firms invest considerable funds to provide their own libraries is testimony to the importance of this kind of information. The public library can supplement such materials and can make an especially good contribution to those companies that are too small to support their own libraries.

Since the 1880s the United States government has distributed information of help in business, including facts and statistics collected by several agencies. The Small Business Administration issues the Small Business Management Series and Starting and Management Series, with such titles as *Starting and Managing a Small Drive-In Restaurant* (1972, 65 p.). A good general aid to selection is *Business Reference Sources: An Annotated Guide for Harvard Business School Students* edited by Lorna Daniells (Boston: Harvard Graduate School of Business Administration, Baker Library, 1979, 133 p.). Joseph C. Schabacker's *Small Business Information Sources: An Annotated Bibliography* (Milwaukee: National Council for Small Business Management Development Systems, 1976, 318 p.) is a classified list with contents and notes and satisfactory annotations, though most of them begin with the word "This." Charles J. Popovich has prepared "A Bibliographic Guide to Small and Minority Business Management" for *RQ* (18, Summer 1979): 369–375.

More specialized are two small books compiled by James B. Woy and published by Bowker: *Investment Methods: A Bibliographical Guide* (1973, 220 p.) and *Commodity Futures Trading: A Bibliographical Guide* (1976), 206 p.)

For the interests of a wider public, there is the *Reference Guide for Consumers,* by Nina David (New York: Bowker, 1975, 237 p.). This lists both print and nonprint resources that help buyers get the best values in the marketplace.

Library Journal's annual article, "Business Books of [the previous year]," published in March, annotates about fifty titles.

ANTHROPOLOGY

By a strict derivation of the term, anthropology would be the study (or knowledge) of man (from Greek *anthropos*) but in its broadest extension it includes also the things that people have done. In a general way the field involves "the full geographical and chronological sweep of human societies."[24] Labeled by Boulding as the "aristocrat of the social sciences,"[25] it is a unifier of more specific approaches to human beings, including the biological sciences. The Dewey Decimal Classification gives more than a hint of this fact by placing anthropology in 572 and 573 under the general heading: 570 — Anthropological and biological sciences. Traditionally (in North America, at least) the field is divided into two parts: physical anthropology (having to do with the biology of human groups), and cultural anthropology (dealing with the behavior and beliefs that people develop and share). Because language is so characteristic of human beings, the study of linguistics is a significant part of cultural anthropology, as is archaeology, sometimes called "the anthroplogy of extinct peoples."[26] This subject, more than other social sciences, ties in closely with the humanities (because of its interest in art, music, religion, language) and with the physical sciences (particularly biology). It "seems to live in a halfway pasture between the storied edifices of science and the misty meadows of the humanities, with fingers clutching in both directions."[27] One suggestion is that it make use of a word now "lying fallow" in the dictionary, and be called "The Science of Humanics."[28]

Since this discipline analyzes the similarities and differences among peoples, its researchers are not confined to their own particular countries in the way that sociologists, political scientists, and economists tend to be. "It . . . seems strange to anthropologists that there have been so many studies made and books written about human nature, religion, law, art, and other aspects of man using information from one small subgroup of humans—namely Americans and Europeans."[29] Traditionally, anthropology has been concerned more with direct observation and interview than with statistical analysis of large amounts of data, but now that information has been gathered from hundreds of different societies, more stress is being placed on historical and scientific generalizations.

No one knows when curiosity first arose about those questions which eventuated in modern anthropology. The roots go back to a remote past. Herodotus gathered anthropological data of a sort, and the Spanish in Mexico during the 1500s were much interested in these matters. A start toward the scientific approach was made by Johann Blumenbach (1752–1840) when he attempted a classification of human races. Landmarks in the history of the field, so far as the United States is concerned, are the establishment of the Bureau of American Ethnology in 1879, largely through the work of the explorer Major John Wesley Powell; the beginning of the scholarly journal *American Anthropologist* in 1888; the appointment of Franz Boaz, trained in Germany, as the first full-time professor of anthropology, Columbia University, 1896; and the founding of the American Anthropological Society in 1902.

The recording and especially the film are essential forms for preserving information in anthropology. The customs of peoples are best examined and compared by the use of a medium that affords realism and detail—the motion picture. "Once lost, these cultures will be gone irretrievably, lost to their descendents, and lost to the rest of the world. Neither print nor tape can ever capture the essence of a culture; only film can do this."[30] Fortunately, almost all peoples of the world have been filmed, some of them over and over.[31] *American Anthropologist* carries a regular section reviewing audiovisual materials.

Because of its stress on gathering information first hand, anthropology, up to now at least, has depended less on printed materials than have its neighboring disciplines. Bibliographies and reviews of literature are a bit scarce. As more observations are completed, analyzed, and assimilated, however, books and related forms will become more and more necessary, as witnessed by the large amount of space that *American Anthropologist* now devotes to book reviews and notes. The great Claude Lévi-Strauss is quoted as saying, "Everything I know about anthropology I learned by reading day after day at the New York Public Library."[32]

Many writings of anthropologists find a popular audience, especially if they describe strange peoples and unusual customs in a non-technical way. *National Geographic Magazine* does this (at least in many of its articles) and some of the books written by

Margaret Mead and Ruth Benedict do also. A classic instance of the popular, readable work in anthropology is Sir James G. Frazer's twelve-volume set, *The Golden Bough: A Study in Magic and Religion,* 3rd ed. (London: MacMillan, 1911–1915) which has been issued in several reprints, though first published in 1894 in two volumes. Frazer (1854–1941), a Scotsman, described vividly the religious beliefs and rituals found in many parts of the world. Though superseded by more precise, accurate monographs, his account is still fascinating to read, showing an active mind working out an idea.

The contemporary works of Oscar Lewis, such as *A Death in the Sanchez Family* (New York: Random House, 1969, 119 p.) should receive special note, as should the books of Lévi-Strauss, many of which have been translated from the French. In a significant essay Susan Sontag says that Lévi-Strauss "has invented the profession of the anthropologist as a total occupation, one involving a spiritual commitment like that of the creative artist or the adventurer or the psychoanalyst." [33]

A good selection of the field (unfortunately now out-of-date) has been compiled by Rexford S. Beckman (with the assistance of Marie P. Beckman), "A Basic List of Books and Periodicals for College Libraries," in Mandelbaum, David G., et al., *Resources for the Teaching of Anthropology* (Berkeley and Los Angeles: University of California Press, 1963, p. 77–316).

Reviews in Anthropology is a quarterly with some survey articles and with long discussions of individual books.

PSYCHOLOGY

The present subdivisions of psychology are not, for the most part, the fruit of any agreed and deliberate analysis. They are historical flotsam. . . . We have inherited a haphazard collection of 'topics,' too often reminiscent of the untutored common sense of an antique faculty theory, and now brashly inflated by a hand-to-mouth empiricism into one great blooming buzzing confusion. [34]

So said a British writer, and Boulding characterized the field as "such a heterogeneous discipline — one might almost describe it as a loose federation of virtually unrelated enterprises. . . ."[35] Psychology may be considered also a pivotal study, hence one of great utility and significance. This view is suggested, even, by the fact that J. Robert Oppenheimer, in 1959, predicted that within fifty years there would be no subject called "psychology" as such, because "I think that different ways of studying man will lead to disciplines which for convenience will have different names, be in different buildings, and will have different professors. But I believe that we are on the threshold of an enormous enrichment in what we know about men."[36] Jean Piaget, the great French psychologist, speaks of the field's key position: "If the sciences of nature explain the human species, humans in turn explain the sciences of nature, and it is up to psychology to show us how."[37]

Even to classify psychology with the social sciences will meet with objections from many. In a number of ways this discipline is a biological or life science, but at the opposite pole, in that it studies man, it partakes of the humanities; thus the Association for Humanistic Psychology stresses an interest in unique human beings, instead of the averages for groups. The dialogue goes on.[38] Beloff gives an inclusive (or perhaps compromise) definition of the field: "The study of that special kind of behaviour which is the outward, observable expression of our inner mental life."[39]

Considered as the science of behavior, psychology naturally is related to many other fields. It depends on physiology and biology for explanations of the human body, as well as for data on other animals. It relates to sociology and the other social sciences in its concern with the behavior of the individual as part of the group. It has connections with business, industry, and the professions for descriptions of human beings at work. In common with medicine and psychiatry it deals with abnormal behavior. Its investigations into learning processes allow it to contribute to the study of education.

The unusual nature and scope of the field demand some discussion of its past. Furthermore, that history is interesting because it is built around persons; or more accurately, psychology retained its focus on individual theorists longer than did other social sciences. What other field has set a parallel to *History of Psychology in Autobiography?* (Worcester, MA: Clark University Press, 1930–1952, 4 vols; Vol. 5, New York: Appleton-Century-Crofts, 1967. Various editors). Historically, the ties of psychology with philosophy have been especially strong. The ancients were concerned about such problems as the relation of mind to body (thus the name, from *psyche* — mind, soul), and how and why people differ from one another. In early modern times, Descartes (1596–1650), in his wide-ranging interests, tried to analyze the human being and came up with the rudiments of a mechanistic view — the nervous system as a series of tubes conducting vaporous animal spirits through the body. Thomas Hobbes (1588–1679), John Locke (1632–1700), George Berkeley (1685–1753), and Immanuel Kant (1724–1804) theorized about how sensations are received and organized.

After some struggle to free itself from "the mother of unborn sciences," psychology found its birth a bit traumatic. In an article about the *Encyclopedia of Philosophy,* the complaint is made that of over 150 persons on the editorial board, "there is no psychologist on the list; is psychology's separation from its alleged forebears so complete? Is there no psychologist who can advise philosophers how to talk to one another and about things and people that are common to philosophy and psychology?"[40] Actually, though some psychologists are not fond of admitting the fact, the field's relation to philosophy is rather close.

In any event, psychology became a science in its own right during the nineteenth century with the work of Hermann Ebbinghaus (1850–1909), who did experiments on human memory, publishing his classic work in 1885, and of Wilhelm Wundt (1832–1920), a psysiologist and philosopher, who set up the world's first psychological laboratory, Leipzig, 1879. Wundt is said to have published 54,000 pages on psychology. Among his American students was G. Stanley Hall, who established the first psychological laboratory in the United States, at Johns Hopkins University, in 1882 (though six years before, William James, in a little room under a Harvard staircase, had set up some equipment including a metronome and a device for whirling frogs around and around).

At about this time began the American domination of the field (psychoanalysis being the exception), and it is said that about two-thirds of the world's psychologists today live in this country. Its 71,000 American practitioners make it the largest of the social sciences.[41]

Contemporary psychology may be thought of in terms of three main groups or schools:

1. Conditioning, Behaviorism, and Purposivism. I. P. Pavlov, a Russian pharmacologist and physiologist (1849–1936), whose *Conditioned Reflexes* was first published in 1921, studied the conditioning of dogs when they were presented with food and the sound of a bell. He had numerous fascinating variations of the experiment — perhaps a forerunner of modern brainwashing techniques.

John B. Watson (1878–1958), an American who went into advertising psychology after having been dismissed from the Johns Hopkins University faculty, had several books with "Behaviorist" or "Behaviorism" in their titles. Watson insisted that psychology should dispense with all references to consciousness and mind; should study observable behavior only. For this reason, A. A. Roback, in his *History of American Psychology* entitles a chapter on behaviorism, "Psychology Out of Its Mind."[42] A present-day psychologist in the behaviorist persuasion is B. F. Skinner, famous for his stress on rewards as a reinforcement of learning, and for his belief that human behavior is as predictable as a chemical reaction in a test tube.

William McDougall (1871–1938), who came to America from Great Britain, was a sort of behaviorist, though he chose to emphasize purpose (teleology) in describing psychological occurrences. He thought in terms of instincts and propensities. Roback called him the greatest American psychologist — one reason why Roback's book received from his neighbors in Cambridge this annotation: "By a conservative psychologist who polemizes against the behavioral positivistic American trend."[43] In a public debate, 1924, McDougall tangled with Watson and won by a small majority of the audience vote. Psychologists probably make good debaters. Pavlov was said to have been a terror to his opponents.

2. Psychoanalysis and Related Systems. This school was headed by Sigmund Freud (1856–1939), physician and neurologist. He used the analogy of the iceberg to describe the human mind — most of it is below the level of consciousness. Unpleasant memories and other materials are repressed into the unconscious; there they develop in disguised form, as dreams, compulsive activities, etc. The great driving force is the libido, which C. G. Jung later said took the place of God in Freud's thinking. The humanity and the fascinating character of the master are clearly seen even in translation: *The Standard Edition of the Complete Psychological Works. . . . ,* London: Hogarth Press, 1953–1964, 24 vols.) Freud has been subjected to an unusual amount of criticism and ridicule, to say nothing of a poor attempt at fictionalized biography by Irving Stone.

Alfred Adler (1870–1937) joined Freud in 1902, but broke with him nine years later. He formulated the idea of the inferiority complex and of compensation for defects (as when the stutterer becomes an orator). C. G. Jung (1875–1961), another early follower of Freud, veered sharply from him, and emphasized the idea of a great racial unconsciousness in the individual. He also spoke of introverts and extroverts, as well as of word association tests. His works too are available in an excellent English translation.

Others in this school worthy of attention are Otto Rank (1884–1939), who had some influence on Carl Rogers's non-directive counseling theory; Harry Stack Sullivan (1892–1949), who believed that social factors could contribute to mental health or illness; and Erik Erikson, author of a number of books on the stages of individual development.

3. Understanding, Gestalt, and Field Psychologies. The German word *gestalt* is usually translated as pattern, or configuration. This group of psychologists have shown that the whole is greater (in appearance) than the sum of its parts. Some pioneers

were Wolfgang Köhler (1887–1967), who wrote a great deal about apes, and Kurt Lewin (1890–1947).

Currently, many psychologists have studied the brain as a key to behavior and to the person's ability to control voluntarily certain physiological processes (with the aid, perhaps, of biofeedback). It is not quite fair, then, to credit the widely quoted saying that psychology first lost its soul, then its mind, then consciousness, and may even lose its body.

Though recent years have seen the differences among schools diminish in favor of various "approaches," with a greater tendency toward eclecticism, variations in points of view are still noticeable. There has been a growing split between academic psychologists (as research scientists) and practitioners, who work in industry, government, or clinics. This division is marked more decidedly in psychology than in the traditional social sciences, where there are fewer university-trained practitioners distinct from academics.

The American output for psychology and philosophy together is running around 1,300 new books (including new editions) per year. In view of the fact that many of its books are texts and collections of readings, psychology is one of the smaller fields in this respect, but its periodical literature is strong.

A wide-ranging, annotated list that can be used for selection in medium-sized and larger libraries has been provided by Robert I. Watson Sr.: *The History of Psychology and the Behavioral Sciences: A Bibliographic Guide* (New York: Springer Publishing Co., 1978, 241 p.). Still of some help also is *The Harvard List of Books in Psychology,* compiled and annotated by the psychologists in Harvard University, 4th ed. (Cambridge, Mass.: Harvard University Press, 1971, 108 p.), bearing "the idiosyncratic stamp of the Harvard psychologists who chose the books and wrote the annotations" (preface). The 744 titles arranged by 31 topics are intended for "students, librarians, and the reading public."

Aware that many works in this field are preoccupied with conditioning of rats and are filled with big words, Ivan McCollom gives a short list of titles about human beings, written in good prose: "Psychological Thrillers: Psychology Books Students

Read When Given Freedom of Choice," *American Psychologist* 26 (October 1971): 921–927.

The American Psychological Association publishes about a dozen journals, but its reviews are collected in *Contemporary Psychology,* which began in 1956, one of the first of the special scholarly-review–type periodicals. It is excellent, though a study of 180 reviewed books indicated some tendency for reviewers to favor the works written by members of their own sexes.[44]

When it comes to research in psychology, the periodical is extremely important, since "virtually everything an author uses for research bibliography has been published recently, is about to be published, or is just reaching the writing stage."[45] Consulting *Social Sciences Citation Index,* two professors compiled a list of journals ranked by number of citations (per published article) received from other journals. The top ten were (in descending order):

> *American Psychologist*
> *Journal of Experimental Social Psychology*
> *Journal of Mathematical Psychology*
> *Journal of Verbal Learning and Verbal Behavior*
> *Psychological Bulletin*
> *Journal of Experimental Child Psychology*
> *Child Development*
> *Journal of Comparative and Physiological Psychology*
> *Developmental Psychology*
> *Journal of Applied Behavior Analysis*[46]

For the general reader, *Psychology Today: The Magazine of Human Experience* provides a simplified though overly clever approach. Among the NICEM guides is an *Index to Psychology (Multimedia).*

EDUCATION

Who was the first person to make a conscious attempt to instruct another? Whoever it was and wherever it happened, that was one of the decisive steps in history. Undoubtedly human culture was transmitted spontaneously for centuries, after which certain persons were appointed for the responsibility. In *Saber-tooth Curriculum, Including Other Lectures in the History of Paleolithic Education* [47] it is reported playfully that the first "subjects" taught were fish-grabbing-with-the-bare-hands, woolly-horse-clubbing, and saber-tooth-tiger-scaring-with-fire, but that, like most later curricula, this one became outmoded by changing conditions. The Bible, especially the Old Testament, has several observations on instruction, and Plato presents a clear picture of the wise teacher Socrates. Also important in the history and theory of the field are Quintilian (ca. 30–96 A.D.), John Locke (1632–1704), Jean Jacques Rousseau (1712–1778), Heinrich Pestalozzi (1746–1827), Friedrich Froebel (1782–1852), and Maria Montessori (1870–1952).

Everyone is being educated all the time by family, church, club, television, work, or just meditation, and Henry Adams used the right word when he called his autobiography *The Education. . . .* A good thirty percent of the American people are associated with institutional schools more or less full-time as students, teachers, or administrators. Estimates of the total adult population engaged in some sort of formal or informal educational activities range up to seventy-five percent. The bill runs well over a hundred billion dollars annually.

For these reasons, the educational enterprise attracts widespread interest. Parents are anxious for their children to have the "best opportunities." Along with others who are taxed heavily for public schools, they often have definite ideas about what should be taught, how it should be taught, and what should be avoided. They feel, rightly or wrongly, that the future of the individual and of the nation depend in considerable measure on what is learned in school.

The questions raised by this field are as fundamental as, and more numerous than, the issues encountered in any other of the social sciences: Should tax revenues go to non-public schools? How much money do schools really need in order to do a good job? Should schools impart knowledge or develop character?

Should they give more attention to the gifted or to the backward? Should they emphasize marketable skills or "richness?" Is physical education important? How should minority groups be portrayed in textbooks? Should homosexuals be employed to teach the young? The list of issues is hardly begun. Lawrence Cremin, speaking of the teaching process, calls it one which is "fraught with irony and contradiction,"[48] adding that what is learned may not be the same as what is taught and vice versa.

Thus, like most other establishments, that in education is under attack, and in recent years the artillery fire has become quite heavy. Everybody who has been through any formal education (and about every person has, of course) knows a little something about it, and thus has a toehold for making comment. After World War II, during the McCarthy era, there were searches for subversive teachers, and more lately attacks have been focused on methods of organizing schools, teaching itself, and ways of preparing teachers. For instance, Charles E. Silberman, in his *Crisis in the Classroom: The Remaking of American Education* (New York: Random House, 1970, 552 p.) was highly critical of schools and of teacher training, while the title of Ivan Illich's *Deschooling Society* (New York: Harper & Row, 1971, 116 p.) would seem self-explanatory. Smith and Cox may be too optimistic in the view that "somehow and somewhen the society's preferences and likes will emerge. Gradually and painfully they will be accommodated in school districts throughout the country."[49]

Traditionally, education has been related to philosophy and especially to psychology, in that it has studied what to teach and how to teach it. In more recent years, sociology also has furnished background materials, as studies are made about the relationships between schools and other institutions in their influence on the learning process.

Books are produced, not only for educators themselves but for the general public also. The subject is frequently touched on in popular magazines and in newspapers. Counting new editions, over a thousand new titles are issued by American publishers each year in the Dewey Decimal classification 370–379. For some reason, there is a widespread tendency to depreciate books in this field. As early as 1886, teachers were being urged to "assiduously cultivate the robust moral power of ignoring the great mass of petty, under-vitalized and worthless reading matter that is printed for them, which makes real knowledge impossible."[50] Christopher Jencks and David Riesman have remarked that "academic prejudice against educationists, being nonethnic, does not seem to cause even twinges of guilt among those who indulge themselves in it. Like most enduring prejudices, it embodies part of the truth, and this is thought to excuse missing part of it."[51]

Though the literature of education, like that of most other fields, includes a goodly measure of triviality, it also contains works that have been researched intelligently and many that embody outstanding theories, such as those of John Dewey and Alfred North Whitehead, not to mention those of contemporaries like Lawrence Arthur Cremin.

Reference books are numerous, the most important being *The Encyclopedia of Education,* Lee C. Deighton, editor-in-chief (n.p.: Macmillan & Free Press, 1971, 10 vols.) with its long sweeping articles. *The Encyclopedia of Educational Research,* with a new edition about every decade, reviews research studies by topic.

This field is another in which government documents are important. On the international scale, valuable works are available from UNESCO. The U. S. Department of Education, gathering innumerable statistics and other facts, has published reports on most of the problems and subjects in the field. State and municipal governments also issue bulletins and studies, many of them having use in the general library.

The United States has about three thousand institutions of higher education. Catalogs of those most likely to interest the local clientele are needed in public, high school, and college libraries. In many cases a set on microfiche is the best buy. Most libraries also need one or more of the reference works which periodically summarize information about colleges, universities, and their course offerings; for example, *The College Handbook* (New York: College Entrance Examination Board, frequently updated). Yearbooks are common in this field, among the best being those of the National Society for the Study of Education.

Among the selective bibliographies, two are especially suitable for medium-sized, perhaps even smaller, general libraries: W. Kenneth Richmond's *The Literature of Education: A Critical Bibliography 1945–1970* (London: Methuen, 1972, 206 p.) combines witty bibliographic essays with enumerative lists. *A Guide to Sources of Educational Information* (Washington: Information Resource Press, 1976, 371 p.) gives more of an American slant for both print and nonprint sources.

A periodical devoted largely to book reviews in the field is *Educational Studies: A Journal in the Foundations of Education,* a quarterly which began in 1970. It is needed in medium-sized and larger libraries. Smaller ones depend on the extensive review sections in the standard educational journals.

22. ARTS AND HUMANITIES — GENERAL

Here we deal with a rich, varied, amorphous body of materials — many of them quite old — which may have some value in the schizophrenic, sadistic, masochistic world of the latter twentieth century. If it is true that "the ultimate problem of modern American society is not so much conformity but the bureaucratic compulsion to fit unique human individuals into standardized molds like so many pieces of machinery,"[1] then works in the humanities and arts are of tremendous import. Before discussing this, however, we need to set some things in order.

PROBLEMS OF DEFINITION

The conundrums of definition, delimitation, and structure found in all areas of knowledge are, if anything, more troublesome in the humanities than in either the social or the natural sciences.

"The arts" may include all that human beings have done or achieved, but in this context, the term is generally taken to mean painting, sculpture, music, literature, theatre, dance, film, and certain minor topics or activities. "The humanities" are the study, the history, and the criticism of these arts, plus philosophy and theology, which involve thought and creativity but are not directed toward the production of any tangible objects (books being a byproduct in these fields). The National Endowment for the Humanities adds certain social sciences "concerned with questions of value and not with quantitative matters."[2] The editor of the new quarterly *Humanities in Society* says that the journal "will be devoted to the systematic interpretation of human behavior."[3] If definition becomes too confusing, it is always possible to simply follow Professor Crane, of the University of Chicago, when, in a facetious mood, he spoke of "the people who teach in the Humanities Division and eat lunch at a certain table in the faculty club."[4]

Like the social sciences, then, the humanities have to do with human beings and their activities; yet the approaches really are quite different. This area emphasizes those achievements that demonstrate characteristics which seem distinctively human. Whereas social scientists are more often seeking generalizations about behavior, humanists usually are interested in unique and outstanding works. Even the social studies of micropolitics and microeconomics (descriptions of the particular, as opposed to macrostudies — generalizations based on aspects of large groups of people) tend to lay stress on typical behavior rather than unique occurrences; therefore their approach differs clearly from that of the humanities.

In their search for the unusual, the humanists naturally value the old (more than do the scientists), while at the same time always seeking the new, the novel. To the scientist *qua* scientist, the old is of interest usually because it can help explain or solve a present-day problem. To the humanist the old is valuable because it is different and/or has not been improved upon. "Humanist scholars have therefore a special responsibility in that the past is their natural domain."[5]

This question of definition and scope can be clarified further by a consideration of the purposes of the humanists.

VALUE OF THE HUMANITIES

Scholars in this area, more than in the others, seem anxious about the worth of their profession. One can hardly read about the humanities without first being told that they are "adrift," "at bay," "in crisis" or facing some awful future. This anxiety is manifested particularly in the United States, and as David Daiches has remarked, "One of the features of the American academic scene that the European visitor finds most striking is the strenuous defense of the humanities that seems to go on all the time."[6] Europeans rather take these values for granted. Toronto professor Northrop Frye further chides some defenders for a "querulous and self-righteous air, like that of a strip-tease performer who informs a newspaper reporter that while all the other girls just take off their clothes, she is an authentic artist."[7] The Commission on the Humanities was especially extravagant in its claims as to the usefulness of this area of knowledge.[8] Some of these justifications need to be reviewed, even though humanists themselves are by no means in agreement about them.

First, the humanities may be called good simply because they bring enjoyment. The French Catholic Philosopher Jacques Maritain has spoken of two traditional assumptions in the humanistic tradition: the invincibility of the inner world and the superiority of delightfulness over usefulness. People derive satisfaction from paintings. They take pleasure in literature and in music. They even like, some of them, to mull over the ideas of the great thinkers. One interest leads to another. Having contemplated a work of art, one naturally wishes to know what others think of it, and to learn something of the creator; thus one is led to critical and biographical works. To speak of the enjoyable effect of the humanities is not to deny the very real difference between art and entertainment. For the library, however, this difference is not crucial. The fact that one patron looks at a book of art reproductions on the simplest level while another uses it for more serious purposes should not be too upsetting.

Again, the humanities and arts are valued because they lead to truth. Some would say that they reveal more truth about human nature than do the sciences. Sir Richard Livingstone once declared that fields like psychology, economics, and anthropology show only a fragment of man, and "not the best or most characteristic part. If we wish to see man full in the face, it is to religion, literature, and history that we must turn."[9] Dorothy Thompson somewhere said that one could learn more about American small-town life from the novel *Main Street* than from the sociological study *Middletown* (though she was prejudiced, perhaps, by marriage to Sinclair Lewis).

By revealing the diversity of human personalities and actions, many of them far from normal or average, the humanities and arts show possible options for the individual who reads, sees, or hears. The counterpart is that people with odd quirks or habits can see that others are different from them. The rich lady who brushes her teeth with champagne needs to realize that many people don't.[10]

No one should assume that the evaluation and use of ideas derived from the humanities is easy. Some argue rather convincingly, that works of art merely elaborate, refine, or perhaps explain certain truths that really have been discovered by science, or by the observation of "real life." In either event, though, a painting or novel is excellent for stimulating thought in the direction of a finer understanding. Holbrook puts it well:

> Humanistic learning aims to enrich human existence by placing before it a vision of the heights and depths of the human spirit. It offers no ready-made philosophy of life; the interplay among alternatives is too vigorous for that. It can deepen and broaden man's self-awareness and sense of values by confronting him with variant forms of the ways in which men past and present discover or deny the human possibility.[11]

This statement suggests a similar value of the humanities: they may bring wisdom; show what we ought to do; they may *humanize*. Some deny such possibilities and say that these studies certainly don't humanize humanists. Can't a scientist be humane and wise; a professional humanist, cruel and foolish? The force of humanistic disciplines, however, is to lead people to explore areas that lead to their own highest development. As Howard Mumford Jones once stated: "Books ripen readers in ways that those other admirable enterprises the laboratory and the market place cannot. . . . The wisdom of the man of learning is wisdom about Man as he might be, and this is quite as important as his knowledge or lack of knowledge about men as today they are."[12] Jorge Luis Borges expresses it: "Few things have happened to me, and I have read a great many. Or rather, few things have happened to me more worth remembering than Schopenhauer's thought or the music of England's words."[13]

The humanities afford us the best experiences of the past as a background for judging the actions of the present. They allow people, all of whom are limited to a small space in the world for a minimal stretch of time, to be tempered by a huge inheritance of culture.

Can the humanities guide human conduct and provide a constructive influence on public policy? To many, the answer is: Yes, in spite of the dangers inherent in politicizing these works and studies. There is some ground for believing that the humanities have restrained the Western world and saved it from the excesses of industrialization. Perhaps they are needed also by developing nations. "Can we infect . . . the whole world with this demon of industrial and material progress and then knock away the moral and ethical support which the humanities represent?"[14] George Sarton, the great historian of science, probably was right in his assertion that "the humanities are not useful, but they are necessary. They are essential to the good life even of the humblest people, who may be themselves too poor in any sense to cultivate them, for the fate of these people will not be as pleasant if their masters, however just, are less humane."[15] At their best these endeavors humanize society, lead to wise public policies, and produce the finest possible result: free and responsible persons.

Despite their obvious value, the humanities, in addition to being defensive about their proper place in relation to other studies, have suffered considerable discontent within. Advanced programs for the preparation of teachers, especially, have come under attack. It is urged that for this area the teacher's main qualifications should be sound aesthetic judgment and excellence as a person; that counting the commas in the Deuteronomic Code does the teacher no good and adds very little to anybody's appreciation of the code. Such detailed, exhaustive studies may even raise barriers between the reader and the ideas in the text.

Sometimes these precise scholarly activities of humanists are contrasted bitterly with their failure to work toward the solution of crucial social problems — a criticism loosely paralleled by the complaints of some social scientists about their own programs. Opinion is not unanimous, however. The piling up of numerous small facts may be tedious to some and the results boring to others, but it is possible to look upon such work as generally useful in view of the final accomplishments.

> Only the professional workers in humanistic disciplines know how slow and methodical must be the advance toward goals of scholarship. The meaningful end product is often a result of scores of investigations. A definitive edition of an early poet and even passages of Biblical text, most familiar to all, are fair copies from hundreds of studies that lay scattered over centuries of time before these classical forms came into being.[16]

It may be that a worker who does not take an oath for the glorious claims of the humanities can nevertheless contribute something to the ultimate aims of scholarship by patient labor in a small domain. That such painstaking attention to detail produces valuable products is amply illustrated by the unabridged dictionary — composed of nothing much but hundreds of thousands of minute bits of information.

Some have charged that the humanists, obsessively looking backward, have failed to come to terms with present realities; that they snobbishly favor aristocracy rather than democracy; and that they often are associated with narrow nationalism or with the promotion of particular political or economic ideas (for example, fascism or Marxism). Others, while admitting that all of these charges are more or less true in one circumstance or another, ask whether the possible abuses should interfere with the legitimate enjoyment of humanist studies, or with whatever influence they may have toward making a better world.

It may be well to pause here and draw a couple of conclusions about selection. Recognizing the contribution made by the humanities to the individual and to society, the library will collect many general works because of their value: because they lead to truth or favorably influence behavior; because they are rich in ideas; because they offer aesthetic stimulation. On the demand theory, the library will collect materials that furnish enjoyment, and also some volumes containing small facts, even though those facts be trivial, because they are wanted by some users, both scholars and general readers.

A 1977 survey of nineteen American public libraries found that the humanities, including history, accounted for twenty-two percent of all adult nonfiction books, and that, in general, selection was in harmony with the judgments of knowledgeable critics.[17]

THE STRUCTURE OF THE HUMANISTIC ENTERPRISE

Professor Jones[18] gives such a good outline of the humanistic structure that it will serve as a frame for consideration by librarians. He points out that the beginning of any humane outlook is a human experience — a thought, song, vision, or even a single word. These experiences, as recorded in durable physical form, make up the foundations of humanistic study. The records (monuments) may be artifacts (as paintings, tablets, buildings), or documents (as poems, music scores, written prayers). To be useful, these monuments must be (1) discovered, (2) identified, (3) preserved and if possible duplicated, and (4) studied and restudied. Usually the results of such investigations are made available to others in the forms of periodical articles, books, and pictures.

These publications are reworked, combined, and sifted to produce descriptions (and histories) of paintings, music, literature, religion, and even of science. More particular topics or objects, such as novels, silver bowls, classical music, Impressionist paintings, or Buddhism, also are described in minute detail. Another task is the compilation of huge "bodies" like the *Corpus Vasorum Antiquorum* (begun in various countries in the 1920s and still in the process of publication). Its numerous volumes contain photographic details and verbal descriptions of ancient vases. Scholars also have compiled and edited bodies of texts, for example, the theological writings of the church fathers. On a different level there are reference books, such as encyclopedias and dictionaries, devoted to art, music, philosophy, and other fields, singly or in combination. Further analysis, collection, sifting, and writing leads to such publications as indexes and bibliographies.

The goal of all this activity, at least in idealistic terms, is humane learning, which, properly assimilated and used, may lead in turn to wisdom.

GENERAL CHARACTERISTICS OF THE LITERATURE

That libraries are necessary to the humanistic enterprise should be clearly apparent. They collect artifacts or reproductions (for example, books of paintings) as well as music scores and literary works (sometimes the original manuscripts of the writer or composer) and critical publications of scholars. Sometimes they produce catalogs and bibliographies, which further organize humanistic studies. Thus the humanities, more than either of the other two great areas of knowledge, depend on library materials. The Commission on the Humanities was not out of line in declaring that "scholars in nearly all humanistic fields deal amost entirely with information preserved and organized in book form, and they therefore need large and complex libraries."[19]

There are needs also for sound recordings and projected visual images. Color slides of paintings in the Uffizi Gallery in Florence are used by an art historian in New York. A modern musicologist may well demand recordings of medieval song. In addition to supplying primary information, such "newer media" serve also an educational purpose for the humanities, as they do for the social and natural sciences.

Humanists use library materials in a greater variety of ways than do scholars in other areas. In Jones's classification, a book or film may be an artifact as well as a document. It may be treasured for its own sake (as for its wood cuts or photographic technique) while considered valuable also as a record of human experience. Thus, in the words of Carl H. Kraeling, then director of the University of Chicago's Oriental Institute, the scientist uses printed materials as a repository of information; to the humanist, they are "part of his flesh and blood."[20] Over a quarter of a century later, another humanist expresses it: "Humanists are probably the most book-bound creatures in the world of scholarship. . . . Their appetite for books is insatiable. They simply feel better by being surrounded by books."[21] Perhaps it should be noted again that these remarks are made in general terms; there are exceptions.

Because of the nature of the materials studied by humanists, and because of their appreciation of the outstanding and unique in all ages, they use more older library materials more often than do students in the other broad areas of knowledge. This generalization is substantiated by citation analyses in the humanities, though such studies are less numerous here than in the sciences. Whereas roughly half the sources used by social scientists are ten years old or less, for the various fields of the humanities the proportions are more like one third, one fourth, or even smaller. Literary critics in particular are occupied with older materials in the form of original texts or early editions. Some refinements in these generalizations are needed, but they will be discussed in connection with the individual fields.

Humanists tend to use far more sources written in foreign languages than do the social scientists, and, all things considered, more even than do the natural scientists. Here the differences among the humanistic fields are quite marked, however. Classicists, musicologists, and art historians make heavy use of foreign-language materials. Scholars in literature, of course, tend to use the languages of the literatures in which they specialize, with historians of German literature generally consulting German language sources and critics of American literature using English predominantly (even though some criticism of American literature is published in German and vice versa). As with social sciences, use of a particular language is related to the locus of the "thing" studied. In the humanities, though, locus of the subject (or object) investigated is less likely to be the same as the place in which the scholar works. That is, whereas American sociologists tend to study American society (and so use English language sources), American historians of art are relatively more likely to study Italian paintings or sculpture and hence need Italian publications. In the realm of letters, Americans may study English, German, or any other national literature. All in all, therefore, foreign-language materials are quite important for humanistic research collections in American libraries.

There is another significant characteristic of the materials used by humanists, traceable also to the fact that they deal with the unique and outstanding. This literature is, or seems to be, more difficult to describe bibliographically. For one thing, lists of works are not easily divided into exclusive subtopics. The point is expressed well by an authority on the nature of scientific writings:

> In science one paper can be laid on top of a set of papers, then another paper over that, and so on. Because of this property it is quite common to regard each scientific field as a sort of pyramid of bricks. To use another analogy, depicting the connexions between papers, the cumulating structure of science has a texture full of short-range connexions like knitting, whereas the texture of a humanistic field of scholarship is much more of a random network with any point being just as likely to be connected with any other.[22]

Furthermore, while abstracts are highly useful in the sciences and even in the social sciences, they are less valuable in the humanities. Faulkner's novel *Light in August,* for example, loses practically everything in an abstract. Even a criticism of the novel can be abstracted with only limited success. The same is true, more or less, for other fields in the humanities. Because they are concerned with concrete (sometimes unique) artifacts or records, any kind of generalization — summary, abstract, or statistical analysis — is for most purposes inadequate.

On the whole, works in the humanities are relatively easy to understand. Exceptions are found frequently, of course, in such topics as theology, esoteric criticism, and current philosophy, but most of the masters can be comprehended by the "intelligent layperson," and a sampling of this quarter's scholarly journals in science and in art will demonstrate the difference. The humanities "can transact their business in the language of ordinary discourse. Not in simple language, mind you, but . . . language at once clear and fertile."[23] As the director of the Folger Shakespeare Library expresses it: "Clerk Maxwell's thermodynamic equations are intrinsically beautiful, but to appreciate their beauty you need at least two years of calculus. You do not, however, need to know marble from granite to appreciate Michelangelo's *David,* or how to play the scales to enjoy a Mozart trio."[24]

SOME GENERAL AIDS

Good guides to the humanities as a whole are very few, again undoubtedly due to the nature of the literature. The best for library use is A. Robert Rogers's *The Humanities: A Selective Guide to Information Sources,* 2nd ed. (Littleton, CO: Libraries Unlimited, 1980, 355 p.) The bulk of this work is made up of annotated topical bibliographies for the various disciplines. Also of value in spite of its age, *The Humanities and the Library: Problems in the Interpretation, Evaluation and Use of Library Materials* by Lester Asheim and associates (Chicago: American Library Association, 1957, 278 p.) describes the work being done at the time in religion, philosophy, fine arts, music, and literature, with emphasis on problems of selection and reference. Betty Maurstad has edited a nice little book, *The Library and the Contemporary Arts* (n.p., 1977, 98 p.), with short lists for several fields. In view of the shortage of current tools, librarians may resort to late editions of syllabi compiled for courses in library school, for example, Antje B. Lemke's *The Humanities: Resources and Information Systems* (Syracuse) and *Reference Books on the Social Sciences and Humanities,* by Rolland E. Stevens and Donald G. Davis Jr. (Illinois and Texas).

23. RELIGION

With this subject we enter one of the most confusing fields of study and activity to deal with some of the most complex issues in selection of materials for the general library.

> Few terms conjure up so many different ideas as does the term *religion*. It is associated with institutions such as churches, synagogues, and temples; with attitudes such as devotion, faith, belief, and prayer; with traditions and systems of thought such as Protestantism, Buddhism, Judaism, Thomism, and Lutheranism; with objects such as a supernatural being, the ultimate one, gods, and natural entities.[1]

How shall we sort out these elements? One attempt at clarification takes up the "basic religious questions":

> What are the fundamental characteristics of human beings and the chief problems they face?
> What are the characteristics of nonhuman reality that are of greatest significance for human life?
> Given the nature of man and the universe, how should men try to live?
> Given answers to the first three questions, what practices will best develop and sustain in men an understanding of the nature of human and nonhuman reality, and a dedication to the ideal of human life?
> In seeking true answers to the first four questions, what method or methods should we use?

Religious beliefs are the answers to these questions. A definite set of beliefs, together with the attitudes and practices which they determine, constitutes a "religion."[2]

Anthropologists and other social scientists start with human behavior. "The late Edwin Goodenough used to say that if we wish to understand what religion is about, we must study man praying, not what he is praying to."[3] Anthony Wallace, searching for the essence of religion as it is manifest in all practices, begins with the natural conflict between entropy and organization. People see disintegration on every hand: metals rust to powder, plants and animals die and decay, groups of people splinter into parts. A great part of human energy is spent in an attempt to organize, and to prevent disintegration. "This dialectic, the 'struggle' . . . between entropy and organization is what religion is all about."[4] There seems to be a basic need to reach "wholeness," though the attempts take varying forms.

An extensive Gallup Poll in 1977 found a high level of religious concern in America, with people searching for deeper meanings to life, despite some disillusionment with churches, especially on the part of young adults.[5] The fact that radio preachers can raise millions of dollars a year points up further the widespread interest.

Religious behavior, which has taken so many forms in different parts of the world over the course of history, has been changing in the western world. Those institutions that once stressed the "eternal verities" are now often more interested in such practical problems as environmental pollution, war, overpopulation, the energy crisis, and racial injustice — representing a religious point-of-view on secular issues. At the same time, conservative religious bodies continue their gains over the more liberal ones. (When the Memphis Public Library polled the community's clergy, it found that moderates and liberals were better pleased with the library's holdings than were conservatives, probably because of the review media used in selection.[6])

In the general library, traditional materials on theology (a term often used to designate speculation about God, investigation of religion as an activity, or the description of a particular religious system) and on religious beliefs, theories, practices, and experiences still constitute the staples of the collection. Much of the background material used for discussion of practical current issues necessarily is borrowed from other disciplines.

PROBLEMS OF SELECTION

There are four elements which make selection of religious materials unusually difficult for the general library. All four revolve around the fact that religion has been so largely concerned with institutions, and that in the absence of a national "church," these many institutions all have status.

1. The large volume of publication means that in most libraries, great numbers of religious books cannot be purchased. The United States produces each year about 2,000 new books, including new editions, in the Dewey Decimal 200s. Many other works, including those in art, music, and fiction have religious themes, and religion is a subject often investigated by social scientists. In addition to this continuing production, older books are important and widely sold. A prime example is the Authorized (King James) version of the Bible, translated in 1611.

2. There seems to be a wider variation in quality here than in any other field — perhaps with the exception of fiction. Not only are there numerous profound works; the cheapest, most useless religious ideas also seem to have a way of getting into print. It should not be forgotten, however, that any book that is published seems important to some person — though it may not be to the taste of anyone else. Raymond P. Morris, while Librarian of the Yale University Divinity School, referring to the fact that religion by its very nature is subject to abuse and misuse, added that poor books here are especially "grotesque because in our minds we associate with religion that which is high and holy and which is lifted up above the failures of human limitations."[7] In somewhat the same vein, Holbrook speaks of

> . . . the distilled traces of scholarship found in popular paperbacks which appear on the literature racks in the entries of churches. Since the church expects to be talked down to and written down to, there are always authors, who might otherwise produce scholarly works, who are ready to meet these expectations. This type of journalistic writing has not been without value to churchmen, but it has also abetted the erroneous impression that whatever there is of importance can be presented in digest form.[8]

The noted theologian Karl Rahner declares that the religious book of the future must begin with "work, love, death and all the well-worn and familiar matters with which human life is filled" and then go into the "deeper truths."[9]

3. Much writing in religion is polemical — implicitly or explicitly. It is more likely to have a flavor of prosecuting or defending than is writing in most other fields. Obviously there is less plain mud-slinging in religious books today than there was four hundred years ago, or even fifty, what with the current emphasis on ecumenicity, but the spirit of "friendly competition" is not entirely dead either.

The polemical nature of the field and of its publications contribute also to the problem of censorship. People feel strongly about these issues and ideas. The librarian may refuse to purchase certain books because, being mere uninformed diatribes against others, they simply are not of sufficient value to justify their prices, but there is a difference between this kind of rejection and any attempt to protect the innocent or guilty from the effects of print. However, the issue, being partly a question of taste, is not resolved easily. A book which attacks a religion may meet either the demand or the value criterion, or both. A decision not to buy it would be a disservice to the community. The fact that a work is controversial certainly should not mean that it is to be rejected by a general library. A good book in any field is likely to be controversial to some extent — at least if it says something new.

Books in other fields, also, may receive pressure because of their religious ideas. Such was the fate of Kurt Vonnegut's *Slaughterhouse Five*.[10]

On the other hand, the Charlotte-Mecklenburg (North Carolina) Public Library was sued on the complaint that it did *not* take atheist magazines.

4. In the same way, books on religion tend to be more narrowly parochial than those in science, or even art. Wallace, speculating about the number of separate religions which have existed on earth, comes up with an astounding figure: "If we say that one religion, as an entity, is distinct from another when its pantheon, its ritual, its ethical commitments, and its mythology are sufficiently different for its adherents to consider that the adherents of other religions are, in a general sense, 'unorthodox' or

'pagans' or 'nonbelievers,' then we must conclude that mankind has produced on the order of 100,000 different religions."[11] In the United States there are about 250 active, separate religious denominations, each with some interest in explaining and/or propagating its particular faith. When the general editor of the series *Humanistic Scholarship in America* entered into plans for the volume on scholarship in religion, "we came upon a peculiar difficulty — peculiar that is to the field of religion scholarship. A number of American scholars maintain that religion is not a scholarly discipline like art history or musicology or classical studies because religion demands of its students creedal commitments incompatible with free scholarly inquiry."[12]

The difficulty created for general libraries was pointed up by a 1960 editorial in *Library Journal:* "In no other field also is it so difficult to draw a clean line between what is propaganda and what an exposition of the elements of a particular faith or creed. In some subject fields the librarian often cannot do better than seek outside advice; in dealing with religious books this can often be the most dangerous course of action, for almost everyone is partisan."[13] Again, a modifying statement may be in order. The spirit and practice of cooperation are apparent. The production of numerous works representing scholars from different faiths testifies to it. *The Anchor Bible* (Garden City, NY: Doubleday, 1964–) to be completed in 39 volumes, and *The Bible Reader: An Interfaith Interpretation . . .* (Milwaukee: Bruce, 1969, 995 p.) are cases in point. However, it is true also that practically every form of communication has been used (in some cases exploited) by religious groups to further their own particular causes: fiction, drama, periodicals, pamphlets, recordings, filmstrips, films — even, to some extent, poetry and reference books.

Though these problems are due in large measure to the institutional character of much religious belief and practice, there are difficulties also in selecting materials to represent current movements that are independent of traditional religious organizations. In fact, these publications, being more obscure and irregular, require close attention if the library is to obtain the ones most suitable.

What shall be the librarian's attitude toward these voluminous writings? In the first place, "off-brand" religious books and periodicals may serve a good purpose. The economist Boulding makes the point that "if socialist culture and free-market culture can develop side by side without fatal conflict, their constant interaction may be beneficial to both parties. Similarly even the development of religious sects and subcultures which are isolated from the world by what may seem a nonrational ideology may turn out to be extremely useful devices for preserving the diversity of mankind." [14] Though public and most other general libraries will not purchase out-and-out propaganda, such works when donated may well be accepted. The public library makes no pretense of being free of propaganda, nor does it refuse to take gifts of many kinds of books. It should be slow to reject materials that claim virtues for minority groups.

The general library can render a fine service by offering good religious materials. They are interesting in many ways, and they have some effect on behavior. Especially important is provision for the clergy, for they frequently pass on to others the things learned from books. In a study of Lutheran ministers, Huseman found that the average one spent twenty-three hours a week reading books and periodicals. A good many ministers can scarcely afford to purchase the materials they need. Of those who had access to public libraries, about 53 percent made use of them. [15]

OUTLINE OF THE FIELD

It has been traditional to divide religion/theology curricula, along with books in the field, into four parts. That arrangement is convenient for considering library materials.

Historical

Many religions tend to be oriented toward the past, deriving from it authority, belief, and practice. Histories, therefore, are of high importance. One of the best known scholars on the topic (and on others in the field) is Mircea Eliade, the first volume of whose *History of Religious Ideas* was published in English translation by the University of Chicago Press in 1978. Louis Finkelstein has edited three volumes entitled *The Jews . . .* (4th ed., New York: Schocken Books, 1970–1971). Also devoted to a single world religion, though a different one, is Kenneth Scott Latourette's *A History of the Expansion of Christianity* (New York: Harper, 1937–1945, 7 vols.), a long, detailed, heavily documented set with a topical emphasis on missions. Histories may stress institutions, the development of doctrine, or other matters. William Warren Sweet emphasized the influence of the frontier in his works on religion in America. There are histories which cover religion in a given country; there are histories of one denomination in one state. An entire volume may be devoted to a single local congregation.

Another great work mentioned previously which deserves attention here, though it is not, strictly speaking, a history of religion, is Sir James G. Frazer's *The Golden Bough, A Study in Magic and Religion,* 3rd ed. (London: Macmillan, 1911–1915, 12 vols.). A one-volume illustrated edition was published by Doubleday in 1978. Of similar scope but different in arrangement is *Mythology of All Races* (Boston: Marshall Jones Co., 1916–1932, 12 vols. plus index). Each volume represents the work of an authority and deals with the mythology of a certain people.

Recently there has been a revival of interest in major world religions, with attempts to speak fairly and appreciatively rather than merely to point out the deficiencies of those which differ from one's own.

Turning to biography: with the exceptions perhaps of Shakespeare and Napoleon, more books have been written about Jesus Christ than about any other person in history. The number is amazing in view of the fact that the four extant original sources which say anything much at all about Jesus (the gospels of Matthew, Mark, Luke, and John) mention only about one hundred separate days of his life. The varying points of view among religious writers are reflected vividly in their approaches to Jesus. Ernest Renan's classic *Life of Jesus* (first published in French,

1863, with many editions in English) treated him as a great reformer but as not necessarily divine.* Another classic, making more of Jesus' divinity, was by Canon Frederic W. Farrar, of the Church of England: *Life of Christ,* first published in the 1870s, and offered in many editions since, including one in 1976. A popularized approach by a noted scholar is *Jesus and His Times,* by Daniel-Rops (New York: E. P. Dutton, 1956, 479 p.). Bruce Barton, an advertising man, treated Jesus as a busy, harassed executive in *The Man Nobody Knows* (Indianapolis: Bobbs-Merrill, 1925, 210 p.). And so they go, down to the journalistic details of *The Day Christ Was Born* and *The Day Christ Died,* both written by Jim Bishop. Especially colorful is William Barclay's book, *Jesus of Nazareth,* based on a filmscript by Anthony Burgess (London: Collins, 1977, 287 p.), a highly fictionalized account redeemed by beautiful plates.

Then there are biographies of popes, cardinals, bishops, rabbis, reformers, theologians, martyrs, television preachers, missionaries, ministers, circuit-riders, gurus, and other kinds of "holy" men and women.

Interpretative and Doctrinal

Statements of doctrine and practice form another recognizable group of books. These works may be written from a general standpoint, as are James H. Leuba's *A Psychological Study of Religion: Its Origin, Function and Future* (New York: Macmillan, 1912, 371 p.), and William James's *Varieties of Religious Experience: A Study in Human Nature* (London: Longmans, 1902, 534 p.). Representing more specific religious points of view, the better-known writings of the great theologians such as Thomas Aquinas, Paul Tillich, and Karl Barth are appropriate in most general libraries, at least those of any size, though many of these works are not easy for the laity to understand. Reinhold Niebuhr's two-volume *Nature and Destiny of Man: A Christian Interpretation* (New York: Scribner, 1941–1943) has proved one of the most influen-

*In Aldous Huxley's *Eyeless in Gaza,* Mrs. Foxe reads to the children from this book, in place of their attending Easter church services.

tial theological works ever produced by an American. The Jesuit Pierre Teilhard de Chardin's profound books have been translated into English from the French, and are widely quoted. Hans Küng's *On Being a Christian,* translated by Edward Quinn (New York: Doubleday, 1976, 720 p.) was a Book-of-the-Month Club selection. The Vienna-born Jewish philosopher-theologian Martin Buber's most representative work is *I and Thou,* translated by Walter Kaufman (New York: Scribner, 1970, published in German, 1923).

In this same grouping, the sacred writings of the various religions should come in for consideration. A fundamental set is *The Sacred Books of the East,* edited by Max Müller (Oxford: Clarendon Press, 1879–1910. [A warning: There is a poor quality set with the same title.]) The fifty volumes are based on anthropological and linguistic studies. The Koran has been published in several English translations, as have the Bhagavad-Gita and many other sacred writings.

Among the English translations of the Bible, these are notable: The Authorized Version (King James, 1611 [revised in 1979 to remove the thees, thous, and some other expressions]); the American Standard, 1901; the Revised Standard, 1946 and 1952, with Roman Catholic adaptations. The Douay is a traditional Catholic favorite and the Jerusalem Bible (Doubleday, 1966) is a Catholic translation based on the original Greek and Hebrew languages. The New English Bible was published jointly by the Oxford and Cambridge University Presses, in three volumes, 1961–1970. The New American Bible (Catholic Press, 1971, 1,066 p.) is a translation by fifty-one scholars. The American Bible Society published in 1976 the Good News Bible: The Bible in Today's English Version.

Needed also in connection with texts of the Bible are basic reference tools. Among the commentaries are *The Interpreter's Bible* (New York: Abingdon-Cokesbury, 1951–1957, 12 vols.), also offered in a "completely new and up-to-date" single-volume edition in 1971, and the *Anchor Bible* (previously mentioned) now nearing completion. There are concordances to various parts and translations; for instance, *Young's Analytical Concordance* (first published in 1880) is for use with the King James version. Incidentally, *Subject Guide to Books in Print* has over sixty entries under Bible — Concordances. Those under Bible — Commentaries are too numerous to count. Of the many dictionaries of terms used in the Bible, a representative example is *The Interpreter's Dictionary of the Bible* (New York: Abingdon, 1962, 4 vols., with a supplementary volume, 1976).

Devotional and Inspirational

Many people have been inspired or consoled by books of the nature of *The Imitation of Christ,* written by Thomas à Kempis, presumably, in the early fifteenth century, and by modern counterparts of a sort, like *Peace of Soul* (New York: Whittlescy House, 1949, 292 p.), by Fulton J. Sheen, and *How To Be Born Again,* by Billy Graham (Waco, Texas: Word Books, 1977, 187 p.). Of course if demand is a strong factor, *The Power of Positive Thinking* (New York: Prentice-Hall, 1952, 276 p.), by Dr. Norman Vincent Peale, must not be overlooked; it has gone well over the two-million mark in sales. The variation in quality among books in religion is quite evident in this group; some of them seem merely to exploit human need. It is true that religion seeks to help solve the great problems of life, but those books which promise more solutions than they can deliver are not exactly fair. A content analysis was made for forty-six best sellers in the realm of religious inspirational literature published in the United States between 1875 and 1953. Six of the books sold over a million copies each. The results of the analysis were a not-encouraging indication of the quality of inspirational reading demanded by the American people.[16]

Practical

Books on church administration, preaching, church organization, and methods for activities such as Sunday school teaching also have a place in the general library.

Another way of analyzing religious scholarship is suggested by

Holbrook, in the fine work quoted previously: technical, perspectival, and pivotal.[17] Technical scholarship means an intensive, usually narrow, study, which gives new information (as Millar Burrow's *The Dead Sea Scrolls* [New York: Viking, 1955, 435 p.] or in a wider sense the *New Catholic Encyclopedia* [New York: McGraw-Hill, 1967, 15 vols.]). Perspectival scholarship builds on these foundations and gives broad principles or interpretations (for example, Nels Ferré, *Christianity and Society* [New York: Harper, 1950, 280 p.], or Paul Ramsey, *War and the Christian Conscience: How Shall Modern War Be Conducted Justly?* [Durham, NC: Duke University Press, 1961, 331 p.]). Pivotal studies are those which are powerful enough to turn the thought of the field into different directions, or so stimulating as to provide a fresh starting point (for example, H. Richard Niebuhr's *Christ and Culture* [New York: Harper, 1951, 259 p.]). The best in each of these types are needed by the general library.

Magazines range from the small denominational weeklies through scholarly quarterlies (for example, *Theology Today*), and include such learned periodicals as *Journal of Religion, Religious Studies,* and *Zygon* (the latter devoted to the relationship between religion and science).

AIDS IN SELECTION

The comments made in connection with the topic "Problems in Selection" are borne out in part by the fact that in religion there are few selective bibliographies that may be termed useful to all general libraries. Best overall is *A Reader's Guide to the Great Religions,* edited by Charles J. Adams, 2nd ed. (New York: Free Press, 1977, 521 p.). This group of bibliographic essays, each by an authority, is especially good for medium-sized and larger libraries. "Mainly for undergraduate students as well as the general public" is Leszek M. Karpinski's annotated *Religious Life of Man: Guide to Basic Literature* (Metuchen, NJ: Scarecrow Press, 1978, 399 p.). More specialized in subject, *American Religion and Philosophy: A Guide to Information Sources* (Detroit: Gale, 1978, 377 p.) lists recent "secondary literature."

Religious Book Review, with its advertisements and notes, is an aid to keeping abreast of the current output in this field, but is short on evaluative information. *The New Review of Books and Religion* carries both long reviews and short notes. Articles such as Douglas Marsh's "Popular Religious Books for Public Libraries," with its bibliography (*Library Journal* 102 [1 June 1977, 1243–1250]), are better for small libraries.

NONPRINT MATERIALS

Recordings and motion pictures are used widely to teach religious concepts; especially favored are filmstrips. Many religious groups invest heavily in these teaching media, which present facts about the Bible, raise ethical questions, and otherwise promote discussion. Some of the collections which have been developed are extensive. The significance of such formats is indicated further by the attention given new titles by journals in religion and religious education, for example, the "Audio Visual Reviews" section of *Religious Book Review*. Even feature films are valuable in this respect, and it has been urged that theologians both learn and teach through discussions of commercial motion pictures.[18] An extensive multimedia package, the *New Media Bible,* proposes to give details of all the books of the Bible.

24. PHILOSOPHY

This fundamental discipline is in its traditional sense the ground of almost all other subjects, dealing with such basic questions as:

> What is the good life? What is happiness, and is it attainable? How?
>
> Is there such a thing as freedom of the human will, or is every action and thought the result of causes which themselves have been caused, and so on back to the first move in the universe?
>
> Does the universe have some purpose toward which it is moving; or is there merely a series of events that happen by "pure chance"?

Philosophy usually is described as being conceptual, reflective, meditative. Somehow it often has been associated with sad and pessimistic people. As Oliver Edwards said to Dr. Johnson: " 'I have tried too in my time to be a philosopher; but I don't know how, cheerfulness was always breaking in.' "[1] Really the popular idea is questionable, as is the notion that philosophy is only for old folks. It is not out of place in high schools, or even for children.[2] Karl Popper declares that "all men and all women are philosophers; or, let us say, if they are not conscious of having philosophical problems, they have, at any rate, philosophical prejudices."[3]

Academic, professional philosophers are criticized — perhaps more than are other humanists — for a tendency to draw back from sweeping, fundamental issues. Professor Jones complains that "the present tendency of many philosophers to direct their energy and their skill toward small-scale problems is indeed the philosophic form of escapism."[4] Oxford philosopher A. J. Ayer has referred to previous eras as being dominated by the "pontiffs," while the present era is that of the "journeymen."[5] Philosophers, therefore, have tended to lose influence with the general public, and even in the academic community, while historians, scientists, artists, and novelists have taken over their traditional province. Using an analogy to law, however, Professor Maynard Adams writes convincingly that philosophers operate at the level of constitutional law — not concerned with everyday squabbles, but with fundamental issues; that this is the reason they have become highly technical; but that "no individual nor the culture at large can ignore philosophy and hope to come to grips with the basic problems of life in our time."[6]

DEFINITION OF THE FIELD

In view of its wide-ranging interests, it is no wonder that philosophy means (going back to the original Greek) the love of wisdom. Brand Blanshard thinks of it as "part of an older and wider enterprise, the enterprise of understanding the world."[7] The person who termed it "the search by a blind man in a dark cellar for a black cat which isn't there" was very cynical.

Philosophers, even more than most other thinkers and scholars, disagree on their task, so this discipline is quite elusive. An article entitled "What Is Philosophy?" points out that there is no study called "philosophy of philosophy," though we do have the "philosophy of science" and of many other pursuits.[8] The problem is apparent in the Dewey Decimal Classification, where "Specific philosophical viewpoints" such as Pragmatism and Utilitarianism are in the 140s, and modern Western philosophy in the 190s — a space once allotted to individual philosophers.

By general agreement, though, there are five main branches of philosophy: ethics (the considerations of good conduct; what is right; obligations toward other people, animals, and things); aesthetics (the study of beauty; what makes a thing sublime); logic (reasoning, evidence, language); epistemology (related to logic; the question of whether we can have knowledge, and if so, how); and metaphysics (the investigation of first principles — the ultimate character of things; the science of being). Some philosophers say that it is impossible to study metaphysics satisfactorily; that we therefore would do better not to fool with it; others, pointing out that questions such as these are the most basic, conclude that they deserve more time and vigorous thought than the others.

SOME CURRENT PHILOSOPHICAL VIEWS

Though philosophies tend to be built around the works of individual thinkers, there have been numerous recognizable groups or schools. A brief resume of each of three contemporary schools will serve to illustrate.

1. *Pragmatism* is an American philosophy whose main root is a series of articles published in *Popular Science Monthly* (quite a different journal in those days) by Charles S. Peirce in 1877 and 1878. Superficially, this school may be thought of as teaching that truth is what works. A phrase often associated with the viewpoint (perhaps a bit unfairly) is the "cash value of ideas." Its greatest proponents were William James, who wrote a little book entitled *Pragmatism,* and John Dewey (unless Dewey is thought of more specifically as an Instrumentalist). The latter published thirty-eight books and 815 articles, including pamphlets, ". . . a pile twelve feet, seven inches high — but if he ever wrote one quotable sentence it has got lost in the pile," or so Max Eastman declared.[9]

2. *Analytical philosophy,* abstract and academic, closely related to logical positivism or logical empiricism, is represented by the great three-volume work *Principia Mathematica,* by Bertrand Russell and Alfred North Whitehead (Cambridge: At the University Press, 1910–1913), which shows how communication and meaning can be analyzed, and the universe examined, with the tool of pure logic. Rudolf Carnap, who came to the United States from Vienna, and Ludwig Wittgenstein, who went from there to England, are other big names in this movement. For the last half-century, analytical philosophy has been powerful in British and American universities, especially, but its influence has been felt in other areas as well.

3. *Existentialism,* whose forerunner was Søren Kierkegaard, the Danish philosopher and theologian, includes also the work of

Martin Heidegger, and, of course, Jean-Paul Sartre. For human beings, existence is more important than essence, says this school. Since man is free to develop, he cannot be defined. It is this responsibility for personal freedom which brings apprehension and despair.

In addition to these movements, the thought of the Oriental philosophers is receiving more and more attention in the United States, and it is fortunate that so many of their works have been translated.

THE LITERATURE OF PHILOSOPHY

The earlier editions of the Decimal Classification took cognizance of the importance of persons as a way of dealing with philosophic thought, and in the Library of Congress Classification, the sections of schedule B which pertain to philosophy have hundreds of names of individual philosophers. Many of these are minutely subdivided. Immanuel Kant, for instance, is given two full pages in the scheme. By contrast, the LC schedule BF (psychology) mentions no individuals by name. In the previous chapter, it was pointed out that selection in religion is made difficult by the fact that the subject is institution-centered; philosophy, on the other hand, is simplified, at least slightly, by this relation to persons. Will Durant successfully used a biographical approach in his *Story of Philosophy* (1926), but when Professor Charles F. Potter, in a book called *Story of Religion as Told in the Lives of Its Leaders,* published in 1929, tried a similar presentation, the result was a failure.[10]

The fact that philosophy tends to be person-centered suggests that great philosophers' names offer one way of looking at the literature of this field. General libraries need the best editions or translations of the principal works of philosophers on the level of Aristotle, Plato, Aquinas, Spinoza, Berkeley, Locke, Hume, Kant, Hegel, Nietzsche, Schopenhauer, James, Russell, Wittgenstein, Sartre, et al. True, they will be read deeply by few, but from the standpoint of value, they are among the most important books in the library. More contemporary trends are presented in such works as Marjorie Grene's *Philosophy In and Out of Europe* (Berkeley: University of California Press, 1976, 169 p.).

Passmore, incidentally, notes the tendency of American scholars to deal with relatively unimportant philosophers. "For a modern edition of a minor writer, one naturally looks first to America. On the other hand, one does not turn to America for a classical edition of a major writer."[11]

Very small libraries have to settle for selections culled from major works, though many authorities agree with Passmore when he speaks against "truncated selections (often from great and readily available works). . . . For inevitably, such selections will reflect a particular, usually a fashionable, interpretation of the mutilated text."[12] The warning is necessary, but Passmore does feel that some volumes of selections and readings are useful. For a small library, such works may have to suffice. Surely there are few of its clientele who read the complete works of even the most noted philosophers.

Also needed are histories and criticisms. Durant's *Story of Philosophy: The Lives and Opinions of the Great Philosophers* (Simon and Schuster, 1926, 577 p.; New revised ed., 1933) is a delightful exposition of important philosophical thought — less likely to lead the average reader astray than some of its critics have feared. Though it can't claim the popularity of McDonald's hamburgers, its publishers do advertise "Over One Million Sold." Bertrand Russell, whose *History of Western Philosophy, and Its Connection with Political and Social Circumstances From the Earliest Times to the Present Day* (New York: Simon and Schuster, 1945, 898 p.) has been called the "rich man's Durant," relates philosophy to social and political concerns. Russell, who wrote this book after attaining his three score and ten, could be biased when he took a notion, but his wit and clarity of explanation are fabulous. A long work by Frederick C. Copleston, SJ, *A History of Philosophy* (New rev. ed., Westminster, MD: Newman Press, 1945–74), has reached nine volumes.

Coming to contemporary philosophy, an extremely important series for the more advanced student is the *Library of Living Philosophers,* edited by Paul A. Schilpp (various publishers,

1939–). The fourteenth in the series (on Karl Popper) was published in 1974. Previous volumes have been devoted to John Dewey, George Santayana, Alfred North Whitehead, G. E. Moore, Bertrand Russell, Ernst Cassirer, Albert Einstein, Sarvepalli Radhakrishnan, Karl Jaspers, C. D. Broad, Rudolf Carnap, Martin Buber, and C. I. Lewis. The typical volume includes a brief biography (or autobiography), criticism of the philosopher by expert colleagues and opponents, and then rejoinders by the subject. How much we would give for similar compilations of the great philosophers of previous ages!

Unlike the field of religion, philosophy is a relatively easy subject in which to choose books and periodicals — this in spite of the fact that it is hard to define, and that many of its publications make difficult reading. Though argument and debate are characteristic of its practitioners, there is usually a fair amount of agreement on what constitutes a good book. Furthermore, this body of literature is compact. Not only does philosophy constitute a very small percentage of the holdings of most libraries, but the annual rate of publication is low. In the United Kingdom, 1974–1975, only 0.83 percent of the new adult nonfiction books were classified here.[13] (Figures for the United States are not available.)

Reference books are few, partly because not many reference questions are asked in philosophy; this being due in turn, probably, to the fact that reference questions are difficult to formulate in this subject. The *Encyclopedia of Philosophy* (New York: Macmillan and Free Press, 1967) in eight volumes is an excellent work which should be in practically every library of high school level and above.

Two notable aids to selection are: *Philosophical Books,* a British journal devoted almost entirely to new books, which carries medium to long reviews, and *Bibliographie de la Philosophie,* published quarterly in Paris, which is made up of short reviews and abstracts of books from many countries and is useful for larger collections.

It is interesting to note the growing number of American periodicals in this field, where the book once reigned supreme. In

1930, there were only four professional journals, according to Stevens;[14] by 1960 the number was 39, and it reached 91 in 1975.[15] Possibly this is another reflection of professional philosophers' increasing concern with smaller issues. Frankel notes (with disapproval) the tendency of graduate students to spend more time on articles published since 1970 than on Plato or Kant,[16] but Vickery reports a strong demand for older periodicals and classic texts.[17]

25. ART

In this chapter we take up one of the most delightful fields in which to collect library materials. Not that it is especially easy to make judgments on these publications — in fact, selection is more difficult here than in many other subjects. But if any part of the library collection brings immortality to the selector, it surely is this one. Most of the books, periodicals, and other media in art provide use or pleasure for a long time, and many of them are beautiful productions.

Art activities go back to earliest times, perhaps to "the moment man awoke to consciousness through language and thought."[1] In fiscal year 1971–1972, over 43 million visits were made to American art museums. Museums devoted to art *and* history received another 17.5 million.[2]

SOME DEFINITIONS

If we could back up and look at all the things in the world at a glance, we would note a distinction between natural objects on the one hand, and those articles made by human beings on the other. It is in the latter province that we find works of art. However, nature is not exactly in opposition to art, for, as Hans Arp declared, "art is of natural origin and is sublimated and spiritualized through the sublimation of man."[3]

Among the Greeks, the word nearest in meaning to our "art" was *techne* — a skill or aptitude; the capacity to achieve something. There is, however, a distinction to be made between the useful and the fine arts. The former result in products that have utilitarian value, such as compost grinders or contact lenses, or even chocolate cakes. The latter produce forms that communicate some essential truth which the artist has analyzed or distilled from experience. This essence may be conveyed by physical things such as paintings, statues, sonnets, or concertos. A painting and a poem may say much the same thing despite the different media in which the message has been composed.

Obviously there is a relationship between the useful and the fine arts. A bridge may give aesthetic pleasure though its basic purpose is to provide a way for people to go from one side of the river to the other. Beautiful designs have been carved on such "useful" implements as weapons.[4] Sometimes a work is hard to classify. In the 1920s, U.S. Customs officials refused to recognize as a work of art Constantin Brancusi's "Bird in Space" (one of them), claiming it a mere object of manufacture. That photography is both a useful and a fine art is shown by the fact that it is classified by the Dewey Decimal system in 770 (Fine Arts), while the Library of Congress places it in the T (Technology) section.

This chapter deals with one group of the fine arts, those commonly known as visual arts (the term "spatial art" also is used), as opposed to literature, music, and other activities or products. Included here are painting, drawing, sculpture, architecture, graphics, and certain minor arts.

THE PLACE OF LIBRARY MATERIALS IN THE PRESENTATION OF ART

Libraries, by collecting reproductions of paintings, buildings, sculpture, and other objects, make an especially important contribution to the study and enjoyment of visual arts. The oft-quoted declaration of the author and connoisseur Bernard Berenson (1865–1959) is apropos: "Photographs, photographs, photographs! In our work we can never have enough of them."[5] Though a picture of a mob scene is worth a good deal to the student of sociology, a picture of Michelangelo's "David" does much more for the student of art. The *Encyclopedia of World Art* notes that "the making of reproductions is one of the most significant phenomena in the history of art."[6] André Malraux, in *Museum Without Walls*, which is the first part of his famous *Voices of Silence*, declares that "for the last hundred years (if we except the activities of specialists) art history has been the history of that which can be photographed."[7] In some instances, the photograph suggests more than the work itself. It may offer a close-up of details hard to see directly, as the crown of a gothic column, and "in isolating the fragment the art book sometimes brings about a metamorphosis (by enlargement); sometimes it reveals new beauties."[8] Photographs also preserve objects which have been lost or which have changed over the years.* They can be of great help in the restoration of damaged works and of historic buildings.

The study of art history has been facilitated by the development of photography. In a few visits to a good library, a student can see and compare a Grand Tour's worth of paintings and sculptures. Color plates and slides can be used both to instill the fundamentals of the subject and to assist the expert, although a dedicated art historian will always want to see the original, if possible, as well. Occasionally, photographs have suggested the solution to a mystery, as when the scholar Lotte Brand Philip saw a picture of a medieval reliquary and realized that the panels of the Ghent Altarpiece, whose curious shifts in scale had long puzzled experts, would fit with dramatic coherence into just such a sculptural framework.[9]

This potential of photography for the study and appreciation of works of art has been enhanced with the development of better techniques for reproducing color in printed books. The newer technology of the printing industry, producing finer art books at relatively moderate prices, is of great significance to libraries. Of course, this is not to say that all fine printed works of art are recent. Magnificent effects were achieved by the laborious hand methods of the nineteenth century, for instance Albert Charles Auguste Racinet's *Le Costume Historique* (Paris: Librairie de Firmin-Didot et Cie., 1888, 6 vols.). The illustrations were reproduced by chromolithography, a process which involved drawing

---

*The art critic Maurice Raynal deplored the impermanence of artists' colors. "We are assured by those who saw the Impressionist pictures when they were new that their colors have faded badly. An earlier instance is that famous pink horse in "The Justice of Trajan" for whose preposterous color Delacroix was so often blamed; it now is yellow, while the dapple-grey horse beside it has turned green. And, speaking of Seurat's pictures, J. E. Blanche remarked that only a few years after their making they had lost their pristine brightness" (*Modern Painting*, translated by Stuart Gilbert [Geneva, Switzerland: Skira, 1960] p. 237). In some cases, he suggested, a good print might prove more faithful to the original than the original itself.

by hand on lithographic stones or plates. The important modern achievement is the production of high quality plates at fairly reasonable prices. Astounding advances have been made not only in the techniques of making plates, but also in printing. Efforts at further improvement are most promising.[10]

Perhaps a word of warning is in order here. It should not be inferred that the reproduction can ever be absolutely satisfactory. The reduced size, as well as the slight imperfections found in even the best of printing, make the book less accurate than we might wish. Any reproduction is in one sense an interpretation of the original and fails to preserve all its characteristics. Some authorities even question whether the term "reproduction" should be applied to such attempts. Strauss recognizes that "neither color transparencies nor most painted originals can be reproduced in such a manner that a trained eye, or even the eye of a merely attentive though untrained observer, could not point out many differences between the original image and the image presented by the very best of reproductions."[11] These remarks merely serve as a warning that high quality is not the same as perfection.

The book (or other reproduction), then, is a way of making widely scattered works of art available in one place for the study of the scholar. May it be said further that for the common viewer, reproductions of paintings in a book sometimes afford greater satisfaction than do the originals in an art museum? Anyone who has stood in line to see a special exhibit need not be reminded of the long wait, the foul air, the jostling for position before each painting the crunch of mashed toes, the howls of unappreciative infants, the banal remarks of the mob, and the smart-aleck observations of reluctant schoolchildren freshly unpacked from yellow buses. How much better to have a book with good reproductions so that each painting can be enjoyed at leisure, with notes and comments to be read along with the viewing. Not that museums are always unpleasant; even the "Mona Lisa" is interesting and beautiful when seen in the Louvre. It's just that on occasion the book seems preferable.

THE PRODUCTION OF ART BOOKS

Typically the process of making reproductions for the art book begins with a photograph of a painting, building facade, interior, piece of sculpture, or other subject. To obtain a good likeness requires patience and skill, especially if the object is three-dimensional. A piece of sculpture, for instance, may have to be moved from its usual spot in a museum to an area where the lighting is more favorable. From the photograph, which may be a large transparency, printing plates are made by other competent craftsmen using intricate machinery. Several plates, for use with different colors of ink, are prepared for each finished picture.

The presswork must be done by skilled technicians who are willing to strive for perfection. If the register is to be satisfactory (that is, if the plate carrying the black ink is to be in exactly the same spot on the page as the plate carrying ycllow), not only must the press be adjusted to a fine point, but the temperature and moisture content of the paper must not vary.

There are three principal methods of printing: letterpress, offset, and gravure. In letterpress printing (until recently the most common method), ink is applied to the plate's raised surfaces and transferred directly to paper. For reproductions of oil paintings, this process is excellent. Offset printing, which usually employs plates without depressions (hence is known as planographic), transfers the image from the plate to another surface, usually a roller; thence to paper. It is also now making some superb art books, especially those reproducing pastels and watercolors. Overall, probably the best means of printing a color picture is by gravure. Plates for this method look like tiny egg crates—covered with squares of almost microscopic size, etched to varying depths. Each square depression is filled with ink, the surplus is wiped off, and the plate applied to paper. The deeper depressions have more ink to deposit, and give that part of the picture a greater opacity with a hint of "thickness." The process is difficult and rather expensive, but the finished reproduction has a richness and depth not possible by other methods; however, words of text (type) printed in this way do not have the same sharpness as found in other methods. There is some evidence that for printing as a whole, gravure is increasing and planographic levelling off.[12]

An excellent treatise on the problems and methods for this area of photographing and printing is: *Reproducing Art: The Photography, Graphic Reproduction and Printing of Works of Art,* by John Lewis and Edwin Smith, (New York: Praeger, 1969, 143 p.). An unusual feature of this book is that it includes actual examples of reproductions printed by the various methods, so that comparisons may be made easily.

Even with modern technology, excellence in reproduction is not achieved easily. When proofs are pulled, they ought to be compared with the original art object photographed so that adjustments in color can be made. The process usually has to be repeated, and sometimes a third proof is required. This routine is expensive, especially for paintings located in other cities. Albert Skira, the European publisher, planned his books in minute detail, with attention to paper, ink, and type styles, as well as to engravings. He might build scaffolding as high as fifty feet in order to photograph a work at the most favorable range and angle. He once went to Georges Rouault (then eighty-two years old) to let the venerable painter examine the reproduction proof of a late painting. Since the original was still there in the studio, the artist compared the two versions closely; then took up a brush and changed a detail of the original to make it match the reproduction.

In short, the best books still cost money, but the important point is that with plates perfected and made more economical, with the use of new devices such as electronic color scanners, and with improvements in quality of inks and papers, it is possible to get rich, almost true colors.

Since World War II, the production of art books has assumed huge proportions, owing to better methods of printing and to an increase in the size of market. American publishers offer fourteen to seventeen hundred new art books a year, including new editions. Because color plates and their printing are still relatively expensive as compared with plain text, some firms have used the same reproductions for separate publications. Each of these may have its own text in English, French, German, Italian, Spanish, or some other language. Thus one large printing of color pages will serve several books with sales in different countries, and the cost of the individual copy can be reduced.

SOME TYPES (AND EXAMPLES) OF LIBRARY MATERIALS IN ART

Books

In his doctoral dissertation, Wesley C. Simonton made a citation analysis of the references in six art periodicals, each from a different country: England, France, Germany, United States, Italy, and Spain. He found that among the sources of information for those writing serious articles in the field, books were extremely important, 71.4 percent of the citations being to this form,* whereas only 28.6 percent were to periodicals. The seven books (sets) most often cited (in descending order of frequency) were:

Vasari, Giorgio. *Le Vite de Più Eccellenti Pittori, Scultori ed Architettori* (first edition, 1550, frequently translated with the title, *Lives of the Most Eminent Painters, Sculptors, and Architects,* or similar, with a varying number of volumes.)

Thieme, Ulrich, and Felix Becker. *Allgemeines Lexikon der Bildenden Künstler von der Antike bis zur Gegenwart,* 1907–1949, 37 vols.

Venturi, Adolfo. *Storia dell' Arte Italiana,* 1901–1940, 11 vols. in 25.

Marle, Raimond van. *The Development of the Italian Schools of Painting,* 1923–1928, 19 vols.

Migne, J. P. *Patrologiae Cursus Completus . . .* (Series Latina) Prima. 1844–1864, 221 vols. (This set usually is classified in religion rather than in art.)

*Diane Nelson points out that, because of the sources from which Simonton drew his citations, his study may be interpreted in such a way as to underrate seriously the value of catalogs of art collections ("Methods of Citation Analysis in the Fine Arts," *Special Libraries* 68 [November 1977]: 390–395).

Post, Chandler. *A History of Spanish Painting,* 1930–1966 14 vols. in 20.[13]

Wilpert, Josef. *Die Römischen Mosaiken der Kirchlichen Bauten vom. IV–XIII Jarhundert.* 1916, 4 vols.

These sets, therefore, would seem of considerable importance to large, and to some medium-sized libraries.

One convenient way to consider books in art is by the following commonly used fourfold breakdown:

1. *Historical and critical.* The earliest form of art historical literature was biographical,[14] Vasari's work being a good example. Since art, like the other humanities, is concerned with the unique and individual, the biographical approach is natural. In 1764, the German scholar Johann Winckelmann published the first work of art history which was not basically a collection of lives.[15] In the many histories which have followed can be found biographical, historical, social, stylistic, and technical themes. Some examples of general historical works are H. W. Janson's *History of Art: A Survey of the Major Visual Arts from the Dawn of History to the Present Day,* 2nd ed. (Englewood Cliffs, NJ: Prentice-Hall and New York: Abrams, 1977, 767 p.) and Helen Gardner's *Art Through the Ages,* 6th ed. by Horst de la Croix and Richard G. Tansey (New York: Harcourt Brace Jovanovich, 1975, 959 p.). The magnificent *Pelican History of Art,* begun in 1953 under the general editorship of Nicolaus Pevsner, runs to some fifty volumes.

To make brief mention of some more specialized histories: There are such works as Sir Herbert Read's *Concise History of Modern Painting,* new ed. (New York: Oxford University Press, 1974); *Sir Banister Fletcher's A History of Architecture on the Comparative Method,* 18th ed. revised by J. C. Palmes (New York: Scribner's 1975, 1,390 p.); *Chinese Carved Jades,* by S. Howard Hansford (Greenwich, CT: New York Graphic Society, 1968, 131 p. plus plates); Norman Feder's *American Indian Art* (New York: Abrams, 1971, 445 p.); and *Two Centuries of Black American Art,* by David C. Driskell (New York: Knopf, 1976, 222 p.). Also available in profusion are histories of furniture, glass, iconography, antiques, silver, wood carving, porcelain, coins, and many other art subjects.

2. *Theoretical works.* Many philosophers as well as other writers, have struggled with the theory of aesthetics and related topics. Some of the classics here are Immanuel Kant's "Critique of Aesthetic Judgment" (the first major part of his *Critique of Judgment,* first published in German in 1790); John Dewey's *Art as Experience* (New York: Minton, Balch & Co, 1934, 355 p.); and *The Sense of Beauty: Being the Outlines of Aesthetic Theory,* by George Santayana (New York: Scribner, 1896, 275 p.). Among the contemporary works of theory are E. H. Gombrich's *Art History and the Social Sciences* (Oxford, Eng.: Clarendon Press, 1975, 60 p.) and his *Art and Illusion: A Study in the Psychology of Pictorial Presentation,* 3rd ed. (London: Phaidon, 1968, 388 p.).

3. *Practical and technical works.* With the need on the part of so many people to create their own works of art, there is moderate to heavy demand for how-to-do-it materials. A wide assortment is available: books on painting, leatherwork, embroidery, paper sculpture, flower arrangement, knitting, macrame, rug hooking — uses for every kind of raw material from eye of newt to toe of frog.

4. *Reference works.* The *Encyclopedia of World Art* (New York: McGraw-Hill, 1958–1968, 15 vols) is still a highly valuable set for most libraries. Though it lists at $750, its fifteen volumes cover far more territory in an authoritative way than could be accomplished with the same expenditure on a number of individual books. Phaidon is producing an encyclopedia of which each volume covers a school or movement, for instance, *Phaidon Encyclopedia of Surrealism,* by René Passeron (New York: Dutton, 1978, 288 p.). Biographical compilations are numerous for this field. Books giving current market values of antiques, paintings, and other objects are popular.

Periodicals

While there is some dispute about the matter, probably the first real art periodical appeared in Germany near the middle of the eighteenth century, the first one in America about a hundred years later.[16] Now, journals are, along with exhibition catalogs, "the prime agent . . . for the transmission worldwide of new art."[17] So far as heavy research is concerned, this form is relatively unimportant as compared with other publications, but Simonton found that the three titles cited most frequently were *Burlington Magazine, Gazette des Beaux-Arts,* and *Art Bulletin.*[18]

The general library needs some good all-around art magazines, like *Art in America;* one or two that emphasize current events, activities, and exhibits, like *Art News* or *Arts Magazine;* representations of contemporary trends, as in *Artforum* and *Art International;* and perhaps regional coverage, as in *Art Voices South.* Most general libraries also need periodicals on specialized topics. Covering art history in a scholarly way are such journals as *Art Bulletin* and *Art Quarterly.* Photography is handled by *Camera: International Magazine for Photography* and (for the amateur) *Popular Photography.* Other specialties are treated in periodicals like *Craft Horizons, Architectural Record, Journal of Glass Studies, Graphis (International Journal for Graphic and Applied Art), Feminist Art Journal,* and *Journal of Jewish Art.*

Exhibition Catalogs

It may seem strange, but considerable information about art and reproductions of works is often best found in the catalogs prepared in connection with special exhibits at art museums. For this reason, a collection of such catalogs is essential for most libraries, even relatively small ones. These catalogs naturally are a bit elusive. One of the most helpful continuing lists is *The Worldwide Art Catalogue Bulletin* (Boston: Worldwide Books, Inc., 1963– , quarterly with annual index.)

Slides and Other Materials

In spite of their size, photographic slides may cost up to three dollars each and so represent a considerable investment. Color fidelity is a major consideration. An original slide costs more and is more satisfactory than a copy made from it. Two series interesting because they include slides with the printed books are: *Color Slide Program of the Great Masters* and *Color Slide Program of Art Enjoyment,* both published by McGraw-Hill.

There are numerous catalogs issued by producers of slides, but general bibliographic coverage is not satisfactory. The larger part of the NICEM *Index to Educational Slides,* is devoted to the fine arts. Still valuable is *The American Library Compendium and Index of World Art: Architecture, Sculpture, Painting and the Minor Arts as Compiled From the Archives of the American Library of Color Slides,* issued by the American Color Slide Company, Inc. (New York: American Archives of World Art, 1961, 465 p.). It lists over 60,000 slides "derived from 30,000 works of art," and includes recommendations on basic sets of slides for library purchase. Several publishers are exploring the possibility of producing books on microforms.[19]

Motion pictures also are a most satisfactory way of experiencing and presenting art. They may center on a museum (such as the Louvre), a theory of art, or a period in its history. Some of the most interesting films deal with the lives and works of individual painters or sculptors. The Canadian Centre has compiled for the American Federation of Arts *Films on Art* (New York: Watson-Guptill, 1977, 220 p.).

Many libraries provide a fine service by loaning framed reproductions for extended periods. For selection of these pictures some feeling is required for the tastes of various segments of the community, together with a knowledge of what is available. Of the several guides to reproductions of paintings, the best is a pair of books published in Paris by UNESCO: *Catalogue of Colour Reproductions of Paintings Prior to 1860,* 1979, 346 p., and *Catalogue of Reproductions of Paintings — 1860 to 1973,* 1974, 341 p.; and the New York Graphic Society's *Fine Art Reproductions of Old & Modern Masters . . .* (Greenwich, CT: The Society, 1976, 572 p.).

SELECTION CRITERIA

In choosing art books and periodicals, evaluations often must be made both for text and for quality of printing or reproduction. The charge has been made that many art books printed in color are purposely not true to the original, that they are deliberately made garish to appeal to the eye of the uninformed. A shopper in a bookstore, picking up a book which is true to the colors of Rembrandt may think it less interesting or less "beautiful" than one which makes the colors gaudily bright. Even Skira (whose fine work has been noted previously in this chapter) was so accused by David Wright, of the Institute for Advanced Study: "perhaps every reader . . . has at some time cursed [Skira's color plates] . . . for their inaccuracy, yet returned to them for their usefulness. . . . As usual in Skira's plates the colors are generally exaggerated in brilliance."[20]

In spite of these remarks, Skira must be considered one of the few outstanding publishers in the field. Among the others are Harry N. Abrams, The New York Graphic Society, McGraw-Hill, Thames and Hudson, Frederick A. Praeger, G. P. Putnam's Sons, Phaidon Press, Crown Publishers, and the Princeton and Harvard University Presses.

General selection tools in the arts are rather scarce. The traditional authority, Mary W. Chamberlin's *Guide to Art Reference Books* (Chicago: American Library Association, 1959, 418 p.), is still of use, and the promised new edition should be excellent. Planned for the general reader and the university student, Donald Ehresmann's *Fine Arts: A Bibliographic Guide to Basic Reference Works, Histories and Handbooks* 2nd ed. (Littleton, CO: Libraries Unlimited, 1979, 349 p.), is general in the sense of listing only those works which deal with two or more of the three topics: architecture, sculpture, and painting. With its descriptive and often evaluative annotations, it is an important tool, along with Ehresmann's *Applied and Decorative Arts: A Bibliographic Guide to Basic Reference Works, Histories, and Handbooks* (Littleton, CO: Libraries Unlimited, 1977, 232 p.). Lois Sevan Jones has a well-annotated bibliography as the major part of her *Art Research*

Methods and Resources: A Guide to Finding Art Information (Dubuque, IA: Kendall/Hunt Publishing Co., 1978, 243 p.). The topical selective bibliographies published regularly in *Art Libraries Journal* are for specialized collections, but are worth perusal by selectors for general libraries.

26. MUSIC

Music may well be the art that comes closest to being universal. It is practiced by tribes which we are pleased to call primitive, yet also cultivated by the civilizations we consider highest. Insects have a kind of music; the sounds of termites are regular and rhythmic. The noted philosopher Charles Hartshorne has discussed the musical qualities of bird songs, calling some of them "astonishingly sophisticated, considering the limitations of the bird brain."[1] Who can define the place of music in human life? As Percy Scholes once put it, "Beethoven and the barrel-organ are but differing manifestations of the same desire. . . . The bringing in of sinners is best accomplished (so specialists tell us) to the accompaniment of the brass and the big drum."[2] War calls for music. So do the football game, the graduation exercise, the marriage ceremony, and finally the funeral rite. Music may be played in the background to create moods. It may be used also for blatant propaganda,[3] but according to a biologist, "we are only saved by music from being overwhelmed by nonsense."[4]

How all this began we probably shall never know, but from some first act have come the symphonies of Mozart, the masses of Palestrina, the jazz of New Orleans, the country music of Nashville, the rock beat, the electronic compositions, the aleatoric performances. Bands, orchestras, singers, pianists, flutists, drummers — all are part of this same current.

In the United States, about thirty million persons play some musical instrument. Some fifteen million sing in choirs or other groups.[5] Countless millions merely listen. Attendance at concerts in the United States was up from 4,900,000 in 1955 to 11,769,000 in 1974.[6]

Music has been the subject of extensive philosophical thought and of investigation by scientific method. The procedures and the resulting body of systemized knowledge are termed musicology. The work of the scholar is quite different from the activity of the musician. (The same division occurs, of course, in the other fields of humanities. We use such words as theology and philology.) Musicology contributes both to composition and to performance of music, as well as to its understanding. It serves further to discover what musical thought can teach about human beings themselves. Not that all concerned are enthusiastic about musicology. Some think that it creates a gap between scholar and layman, or that it tends to kill feeling and insight. There is also the question of how scholarly a work must be in order to qualify as true musicology.

This field, like most others, has had to face the question of where to draw its own limits. Should it encompass acoustics, psychology, physiology, and the sociology of music? Are teaching, aesthetics, and theory of music included? There is some doubt. In a long survey, historical and theoretical, of the meaning of musicology, Palisca pictures it as made up of various strands which have the characteristics of humanistic scholarship, excluding topics which employ the methods of the sciences. "The musicologist is concerned with music that exists, whether as an oral or a written tradition, and with everything that can shed light on its human context."[7] More recently, psychological, social, and political considerations often have been taken into account.

LIBRARIES AND MUSIC

Libraries are primarily or traditionally related to the eye; music typically is for the ear. What does one have to do with the other? In some early unknown time, the idea came that musical sounds could be indicated by written signs of some sort (as was done for the sounds of speech), so music began to have a relationship to the eye. Later came words about musical sounds, and finally the library began to work with aural materials directly by collecting sound recordings. It is interesting to note how far this relationship has gone. Enumerative bibliography is well developed for scores and recordings as well as for books. How many fields can boast a library-centered periodical as sophisticated as *Notes,* the journal published by the Music Library Association? (*Art Libraries Journal* is a start, but so far is hardly comparable.)

In many respects, music is a challenging and difficult field for libraries to collect in, not merely because of the varying forms of material (including scores and recordings) but also because values are so disparate. Tolerance for opposing tastes and views can reach the vanishing point. For example, the scholarly T. W. Adorno, referring to serious, not popular, music, speaks of "a type of musical composition — feigning unabashed pretensions of 'modernity' and 'seriousness' — which has adjusted to mass culture by means of calculated feeble-mindedness."[8] Leonard Bernstein then calls Adorno's work "a fascinating, nasty, turgid book."[9] To choose a less scholarly example, there is the casual description, in a Margery Allingham mystery novel, of a "song which had captured the great hairy ear of the unfastidiously musical."[10] Nicolas Slonimsky has dealt with the extremes of criticism over the years.[11]

Perhaps the reason for such dogmatic views is that the ear — being, unlike the eye, impossible to close or focus — is as annoyed by unwanted sounds as the nose by disgusting stenches. In any event, decisions about what to select for a general library are more controversial here than in many other subject fields.

TYPES OF LIBRARY MATERIALS

Of the four major kinds of music materials, it is difficult to say that any is unimportant. Each type makes a distinct contribution to both the scholar and the amateur.

Books

Jacques Barzun says that the general public started reading about music by looking over the comments on the jackets of long-playing records, and thus learned that words could contribute to the experience of listening.[12] While the number of new books for the field of music is relatively small — about 350 to

400, counting new editions, for the United States each year — one has the impression that most of them are of high quality. (Scores and recordings may be another thing.)

Perhaps the best way to get a closer look at books in this field is to approach them according to traditional divisions. (The usual caveat about classification should be understood.)

1. *History and criticism.* These works range in size and level from single-volume popular approaches to multi-volume scholarly treatises. That remarkable year in publishing history, 1776, saw the start of modern music historiography, with the first volume of "the great Doctor" Burney's *General History of Music,* and of a four-volume history by Sir John Hawkins. In our day, Marion Bauer's introductions to music history and the numerous works of David Ewen fall into this section, showing the various kinds of treatment which are possible. The *New Oxford History of Music,* under the general editorship of Jack Allan Westrup (London: Oxford University Press, 1954–) will be a monumental set if its eleven volumes are ever completed, though some of its chapters are said to be "spotty and irregular."[13] The excellent series of scholarly musical histories published by the W. W. Norton Company has individual volumes by such competent researchers as Alfred Einstein, Curt Sachs, Gustave Reese, Manfred Bukofzer, Donald J. Grout, and Paul Henry Lang. The newer series, Norton Introduction to Music History, is to be complete in six volumes, the first of which is Richard H. Hoppin's *Medieval Music* (New York: 1978, 566 p.).

Biographies of composers and performers are interesting to the common reader, but, as is true in many other parts of the humanities, the authorities are ambivalent about their contribution to real understanding. Herbert Weinstock, who has written biographies of Chopin, Verdi, Tchaikovsky, and Donizetti, along with other books, said, "I stand by the belief that a musical performer can and should find valuable aids to a proper performance in first-rate musical biographies."[14] (B. H. Haggin had written that the performer should study the composer's printed score and hear other performances of it, but he could not see knowledge of the composer's life contributing much to all this.[15]) Biographies are wanted by the public, however, as well as by many who are concerned with serious scholarship.

2. *Theory.* There is a small body of literature which relates music to aesthetic principles. Some of these works are written by philosophers and psychologists; others, by musicians and musicologists. Aaron Copland's *What to Listen for in Music,* rev. ed. (New York: McGraw-Hill, 1957, 307 p.) is an example. Other themes include the psychology, aesthetics, and style of music.

3. *Reference.* These works, fairly numerous in music, generally are edited with care. *Baker's Biographical Dictionary of Musicians,* 6th ed. edited by Nicolas Slonimsky (New York: Schirmer Books, 1978, 1,955 p.) is a fine example of the genre. The long-awaited *New Grove Dictionary of Music and Musicians,* ed. Stanley Steele (Washington: Grove's Dictionaries of Music, Inc., 1980, 20 vols.) is the world's greatest work for this scope, but its price tag of $1,900.00 presents the smaller library with a dilemma. A point to be noted is that so much information in separate works would cost two or three times as much; yet some libraries have to settle for the one huge volume of Oscar Thompson's *International Cyclopedia of Music and Musicians,* 10th ed., edited by Bruce Bohle (New York: Dodd, Mead, 1975, 2,511 p.). Willi Apel's *The Harvard Dictionary of Music,* 2nd ed., rev. and enl. (Cambridge, MA: Belknap Press of Harvard University Press, 1969, 935 p.), "to be consulted (somewhat like a dentist) in case of emergency only" is one of the better one-volume reference works in any field. Ewen's popular reference books are remarkably reliable in spite of the author's rate of production. Biographical handbooks abound. (In a passage of interest to librarians, Barzun and Graff describe the use of reference works to establish the exact date of Joseph Haydn's birth.)[16]

Reference books in music are reviewed, sometimes at length and in depth, by the periodicals in the field. Nyal Williams is right in saying that *Notes* is the most systematic and exhaustive for this purpose.[17]

Periodicals

The scholarly journals in music are not extremely difficult to understand, but, as with other learned publications, the articles they contain usually are devoted to small topics. Most of these journals carry reviews of books, scores, and recordings; critical comments have been severe on occasion. Examples of scholarly periodicals are the *Musical Quarterly* (edited for many years by Paul Henry Lang), and *Music Review,* started, surprisingly, in England in 1940, during the early part of World War II.

Ethnic and folk music, a relatively new but fast-developing specialty, is represented by *Ethnomusicology.* Regrettably the fascinating if sometimes irritating avant-garde journal *Source* is no longer published, though it may be revived. For librarians, a most important periodical is *Notes,* the Quarterly Journal of the Music Library Association. Among its regular lists are record reviews and catalogs issued by music publishers. Featured are extensive reviews of both music and books. *Fontes Artis Musicae,* published by the International Association of Music Libraries, has articles in several languages. For educators, *Journal of Research in Music Education* on the one hand, and *Music Educator's Journal* on the other are representative. Specialties like church music and opera are covered by such journals as *The Hymn* and *Opera News.* Periodicals devoted to particular instruments are exemplified by *Guitar Player Magazine* and *American Harp Journal.*

Music and Music Scores

In the western world about a quarter of a century after the first use of movable type, the printing of musical notes was accomplished (probably in 1473). A landmark in publication of scores was a critical edition of all the works of Bach, started in 1851, and requiring about three-quarters of a century for its forty-seven volumes to be completed.

Since about 1800, a good deal of attention has been paid to the bibliography of scores. They are prime sources for study by musicologists, and as Krummel observes, "musical editions have a visual and technical interest all their own."[18] The systematic analyses of music texts, to determine what the composer actually wrote, parallel similar studies in literature and related fields. They seek to reverse the mistakes and other changes which have been made by printers and editors over the years. Commenting on the present-day printing of music, Ernst Roth, after a lifetime in the business, said, "There are very few if any music copies or prints without a host of mistakes, and this has always been so. . . . On the occasion of a new revision of Stravinsky's *Rite of Spring* in 1952 about seven hundred mistakes were found and corrected."[19] The building of complete, accurate texts requires patience and intelligence. Not only has this analytical bibliography been an important activity, but enumerative bibliography for this form of publication also has been extensive and productive, so that now we have many, many lists for various kinds and periods of music.

The printing and publishing of music is a highly specialized business. "Selling music and no more has been his [the publisher's] traditional business since the day in about 1503 when Ottaviano Petrucci of Venice offered the first printed sheets of music for sale."[20] One reason for the specialized knowledge and skill needed in this sort of publishing is suggested by the distinctive requirements of the sheet of music: "Whereas in a verbal text the letters forming a word represent a concept to be conveyed by the eye to the brain, in music the note, whether accompanied by a text or not, is primarily an instruction to bring into action lungs or fingers, or both combined, in order to produce a sound at a certain pitch and of a certain duration."[21] Designing and spacing the printed elements of music is much more complex than stringing together a series of letters to make a word.

For music scores, sizes of printings usually are small, numbered in the hundreds (rather than in the thousands as is the case with books). This fact together with the technical difficulties of production keeps the number of firms at a minimum. Some of the outstanding publishers of music are G. Schirmer, Inc.; Boosey and Hawkes; Carl Fischer, Inc.; Broude Brothers, Inc., and Theodore Presser Co. J. W. Edwards, of Ann Arbor, Michigan, has reprinted in large sets the complete works of such great composers as Bach, Brahms, and Mozart.

Since musical works are often available in several different editions, libraries select them according to format and editorial treatment.[22] For use in performance, full-size clearly printed scores are essential. Miniature scores (sometimes called pocket or study scores) are good for individual perusal, while listening to a performance, for instance, live or recorded. The quality of paper should be high because of the use received. Cloth binding is preferable, and it is very important that the score lie flat when opened. If there is a text, the original language is desirable. Foreign texts should have an English translation as well.

Of the thousands and thousands of musical pieces composed, most are performed publicly only a few times, if at all. It may take a century for a work to reach its full volume of appreciation.[23] The violent disagreements over quality make it difficult to select scores for the small library, but two useful aids are *A Basic Music Library: Essential Scores and Books,* compiled by the Music Library Association, and edited by Pauline Shaw Bayne (Chicago: American Library Association, 1978, 173 p.) and *Canadian Music: A Selected Checklist, 1950–73,* edited by Lynne Jarman (Toronto: University of Toronto Press, 1976, 170 p.).

Both these works deal with books as well as music. Most of the better music periodicals carry reviews of published scores.

Recordings

In 1889, an American ethnologist made a phonograph recording of the music of the Passamaquoddy and Zuñi Indians.[24] Other "folk" music was soon captured in the same manner. Further impetus was given when Franz Boas, the great anthropologist, became interested in this kind of material. Such recordings in the Library of Congress, in universities, and in museums have provided invaluable sources for study. They serve some of the same functions for music that photographic reproductions do for art, preserving the exotic and bringing home the far-off. On a more sophisticated level, they allow one to compare different performances that originally took place thousands of miles apart. Replaying gives the opportunity to concentrate on details. A person may listen in the home or library without the fuss of obtaining tickets, gasoline, and parking space. Sound recordings have been for a century a source of pleasure and "instruction." Neither radio nor television have infringed seriously on their popularity.

It must not be thought, of course, that listening to records is as satisfactory as being at the scene of performance: Roth complains that "music which is summoned by turning a knob is as far away from the living sound as preserved fruit is from the tree upon which it grew,"[25] but the quality of sound obtainable on the best modern equipment is remarkably good.

Of the three forms in which musical recordings are available, most libraries still find it preferable to stock discs rather than reel-to-reel tapes or cassettes, though the latter are gaining in popularity.

Many compositions, especially the famous classics, have been recorded by different performers and producers. For these, choice by the library can be made primarily on the bases of quality of performance and technical perfection. The reproducing of sound involves the acoustical qualities of the hall in which the music was played originally, requires a precarious balance among microphones, and demands great engineering skill if the sound is to be transferred from tape, say, to disc. It is possible for recordings to be too clear and brilliant, thus distorting the true overtones of the original performance. European firms traditionally have been highly reputable in terms of technical perfection.

Judging the competence of a given conductor, orchestra, soloist, or other musician is the task of the music critic, and those who review recordings generally do not hesitate to voice their judgments. Fortunately most of the critics have ears alert also to technical quality.

Because musical recordings are produced in such large quantities and appeal to so many different tastes, the problem of what kinds of music to select is one of the most fundamental. Since the 1820s, a distinction has been made between popular and serious music, and the former, as the term suggests, accounts for the larger share of the market — by far. New hits constantly appear, then fade away. When it comes to serious music, however, new (contemporary) compositions are not interesting to most people, compared with the older ("classical") music. Roth, who was mainly concerned with the commercial aspects of music, nevertheless offered some facts which bear on selection for libraries: "It is almost common-place to say that our musical life in every part of the western world is a museum of antiquities. We live on the musical diet of our predecessors, on pre-classical, classical, romantic, neo-romantic and neo-classical music. . . . This is all the more remarkable at a time when music is ubiquitous and has become an integral part of our daily life."[26] The sour comment of Sigmund Spaeth may be noted also: "The number of those who honestly enjoy the established masterpieces is a limited one, representing perhaps less than one per cent of the population. There are even fewer who manifest a sincere interest in contemporary composition, although their ranks are swelled by various hypocrites and snobs who are secretly bored to death with the modern idiom."[27]

Most people, then, seem to prefer the popular melodies that require no mental discipline or the classical works made familiar by repetition. Whatever the reason, there is a clear indication of the kinds of "serious" music and recordings most likely to be requested by typical patrons in a general public library. The library has some obligation to make available avant-garde works, which a minority of patrons, after a fair trial, may learn to like, but in terms of the demand theory of selection, the older works have the stronger claim.

As for contemporary popular music, there is every reason why the library should offer a fair representation. Rock, for instance has been called "*the* basic medium of expression and communication for the majority of the population, the pre-thirty group,"[28] but some general libraries have been slow to accept it.

Another thought on selection of materials in music: There is some advantage in choosing scores, recordings, and books about music to go together.[29] While both the authors cited are writing of fairly specialized collections, it would seem that for a smaller library, other things being equal, a recording of Mozart might suggest a score of the same composition (provided scores are purchased) and might in turn make more urgent the purchase of a Mozart biography. This is not a hard-and-fast rule, of course.

Aids in Selection of Recordings

Since there are relatively few companies which produce recordings (as compared with books), the catalogs of these firms tend to cover a relatively large proportion of the output, hence are useful as bibliographies (or discographies) — more so than catalogs of individual book publishers. An example is *Treasury of Great Music,* published by the Musical Heritage Society, whose new releases are listed in *Musical Heritage Review,* eighteen times a year.

Schwann-1 Record & Tape Guide lists each month about 45,000 stereo LP records, in addition to tapes and cassettes, for stores and consumers. Included are classical, pop, country, soul, and other kinds. The semi-annual supplement, *Schwann-2 . . .* does not duplicate Number 1, but covers non-current popular and other recordings. The *Schwann Artist Issue,* about every three years, lists classical recordings by performer (person or group). Schwann's little publication *A Basic Record Library* is good for its selectivity.

NICEM has both an *Index to Educational Audio Tapes* and an *Index to Educational Records.*

Limited discographies, many of them devoted to the work of a single composer, are legion, as shown by Michael H. Gray and Gerald D. Gibson in their *Bibliography of Discographies,* Volume 1, *Classical Music, 1925–1975* (New York: Bowker, 1977, 163 p.).

A general selective guide has been produced by Richard Sweeney Halsey. His *Classical Music Recordings for Home and Library* (Chicago: American Library Association, 1976, 340 p.) has been both praised and soundly thrashed by critics, but it is very helpful for the general library. Also to be watched for are such lists as "The Best Classical Recordings in 1978" by Kenyon C. Rosenberg, published in *Library Journal* 103 (15 December 1978): 2490–2493, and "Rock: The Best Recordings of 1979," by Thomas N. Jewell, in the same journal, 105 (15 February 1980): 473–480.

To name only a few of the periodicals which list and/or review recordings, we have: *High Fidelity, Fanfare, American Record Guide, Stereo Review, Gramophone, Musical Quarterly,* and *Ethnomusicology.* There are many guides to reviews of recordings, for example, "Index to Record Reviews," a regular feature of *Notes,* cumulated and published in book form by G. K. Hall.

27. LITERATURE

We need a word to denote that large body of imaginative, "creative" writing whose primary purpose is not to convey information. The term *literature* (from the Latin *littera*—letter) is commonly employed, though in its widest sense it still includes (as it has since the eighteenth century) virtually all writing. (We speak of "campaign literature," and the "literature of mathematics.")

Even considered in its narrow scope, much "literature" is not especially creative, and it does convey information in considerable quantities. Indeed, the term is not easily definable, as witnessed by the essays making up the volume *What Is Literature?* [1] Reichert says that it is "fruitless" to "search for the proper or real or essential nature of literature." [2] Marcus Klein's statement is in order, however: "Imaginative literature generally is a way in which human beings talk to one another when they admit that the area of their special knowledge is humanity, rather than pharmacy or the law or parenthood or youth or any other such fragment." [3]

The term *belles lettres,* if a bit pretentious, suggests the relationship of literature to the fine arts. Susan Sontag avers that "language is the most impure, the most contaminated, the most exhausted of all materials out of which art is made. . . . something corrupted, weighed down by historical accumulation," [4] but the ingredients in artists' paints must rank second.

The generally recognized forms of creative literature are poetry, drama, fiction, letters (of many kinds), public addresses (as written), essays (some of them), and satire. Northrop Frye points out that libraries sometimes cause a bit of confusion by treating criticism as a subdivision of literature itself, whereas the relationship is really the same as that between history and events (or, it could be added perhaps, musicology and music): "Art, like nature, has to be distinguished from the systematic study of it, which is criticism. It is therefore impossible to 'learn literature': one learns about it in a certain way, but what one learns, transitively, is the criticism of literature."[5] The point is well made, but in this chapter we revert to the common library practice of treating together the primary creative literature itself and the writings *about* it. The latter include works on the theory of literature, as well as on its history, analysis, criticism. The two types may as well be together in the library, for it is natural for a person reading a book to want to know something of who wrote it, the conditions of its writing, and what others (preferably persons of good judgment) think about its meaning or even its value.

The size of this field is indicated by the output of American publishers. About 3,000 to 3,300 new titles, counting new editions, are offered each year in the Dewey Decimal 800s, plus over 3,500 volumes of fiction.

As to the values of literature in the library, it would be enough to say that people read it, find it interesting, and like it. Beyond that, through a poem or play readers may relive, and perhaps reinterpret, events in their own lives. Observing a field of daffodils is a richer, more satisfying experience to the person who has studied Wordsworth's poem. In addition to providing aesthetic pleasure, literature instructs. From it comes knowledge of many subjects, especially of human nature and behavior. More important, people learn about themselves as individuals. To follow with sympathy and understanding a character in Mark Twain or William Faulkner may lead even to wisdom.

Many authorities have acknowledged this power of literature. For examples, consider the following words coming from three separate disciplines: (1) Harvard psychologist Gordon W. Allport has written, "It *is* true that the giants of literature make psychologists, who undertake to represent and to explain personality, seem ineffectual and sometimes a bit foolish in comparison. Only a pedant could prefer the dry collections of facts that psychology can offer regarding an individual mental life to the glorious and unforgettable portraits that the gifted novelist, dramatist, or biographer can give."[6] (2) Historian Samuel Eliot Morison recognizes the fact that his tribe also can be instructed by literary people. From Henry James, he says, "you will learn more about the top layers of American and European society in the second half of the nineteenth century than you can ever glean from the works of social historians."[7] (3) To choose one example for social science: the use of James T. Farrell's *Lonigan Trilogy* to explain life on the Chicago South Side during the 1920s is well known. But an endless number of works could be cited, illustrating the instructive value of poetry, drama, satire, and public address. A sociologist views literature as "a primary source of knowledge about man. . . . Humanity's central concerns have been most faithfully delineated over the centuries by painters, sculptors, and writers."[8]

Graham Dunstan Martin, commenting on the number of creative literary works which are banned or burned despite the fact that they are not written primarily to convey information, goes on to speculate:

> There is perhaps something in the nature of literature . . . that stimulates the hostility of bigots and fanatics. And I believe that this something is literature's tendency to militate against simple answers, against hasty judgments, and against rigid systems of thought. For literature is both complex and ambiguous: it is hostile to preordained frameworks of thought; and in this respect it is like science, in which new discoveries tend to build up increasing pressure on the old ways of thinking.[9]

PROBLEMS AND PRINCIPLES IN THE SELECTION OF LITERATURE

Of first importance in literature for the general library are the primary works. It is better to have a copy of Shaw's *Saint Joan* than a criticism of it, or even (perhaps — the decision may be close) a biography of GBS. However, at some point not easy to make explicit, the library should prefer a history or criticism of drama to copies of more drama texts. All such choices involve consideration of who uses the particular library and with what interests and purposes. The literary historian Douglas Bush expresses a widespread feeling: "There is already far too much to know, in literature itself, without taking account of scholarship and criticism at all. We are in a perpetual rat race, neglecting original works because we must keep up with new knowledge and opinions."[10]

Creative Literature

Many informed people think that the English-speaking people are the greatest producers of literature, partly because of the language itself: "That docile and spacious hybrid of the Germanic and Latin stocks, a language with a synonym for everything, and a grammatical flexibility that permits every kind of music to be struck from it."[11] For this reason, if for no other, original writings should occupy a considerable place in British, Canadian, Australian, and American libraries.

Naturally, many libraries also collect literature in foreign languages, as well as English translations thereof. American public libraries have an unusual obligation in this regard because of the large numbers of immigrants and their descendants who wish to retain parts of their native heritages. Saul Bellow in his novel, *The Adventures of Augie March,* draws a sketch of the old Russian-born grandmother in Chicago, ruling the house and cheating the charities:

> Still the old lady had a heart. I don't mean to say she didn't. She was tyrannical and a snob about her Odessa luster and her servants and governesses, but though she had been a success herself she knew what it was to fall through susceptibility. I began to realize this when I afterward read some of the novels she used to send me to the library for. She taught me the Russian alphabet so that I could make out the titles. Once a year she read *Anna Karenina* and *Eugene Onegin.* Occasionally I got into hot water by bringing a book she didn't want. "How many times do I have to tell you if it doesn't say *roman* I don't want it? You didn't look inside. Are your fingers too weak to open the book? Then they should be too weak to play ball or pick your nose. For that

you've got strength! *Bozhe moy!* God in Heaven! You haven't got the brains of a cat, to walk two miles and bring me a book about religion because it says Tolstoi on the cover.[12]

The selection of primary works of literature involves two major problems: first, judgments have to be made on the merits of the various authors and their creations; second, because many of these works are available in multiple texts and editions, decisions are necessary as to which of them are most suitable for the library's own clientele.

1. *Works.* In creative literature, the problem of what authors to select is more troublesome than in any other field, with the exception of religion. A part of the difficulty lies in attempts to assess the "truth" of literature. How shall we measure its authenticity? Another factor is that tastes vary so widely, even among those who are informed. (If the library collects original works of art on a wide scale, the same issues come up; they arise in music where scores are bought in large quantities.)

The reality of this problem is indicated by George Orwell's notion of "Good Bad Books" (a phrase borrowed from G. K. Chesterton). No one pretends that these things are great works of literature, but, eminently readable, they remain popular after some of the so-called serious works have been forgotten by all except scholars. Some of these writers are natural storytellers and their apparent sincerity is due in part to the fact that "they are not inhibited by good taste."[13] Able to identify with their characters, these authors can "feel with them and invite sympathy on their behalf, with a kind of abandonment that cleverer people would find it difficult to achieve."[14] While escapist literature may not be the highest type, who can deny its utility as long as the conditions of life are such that people feel the need for distraction? Poetry and the other forms of literature involve similar questions about interest and value. Many years ago, D. B. Wyndham Lewis and Charles Lee edited a volume called *The Stuffed Owl: An Anthology of Bad Verse* (London: J. M. Dent & Sons, Ltd., 1930, 264 p.) in which they distinguished between *good* bad verse and *bad* bad verse.

Again, since the assessment of a literary production, or of any other artistic creation, is based not only on the work itself but also on the characteristics of the judge, the librarian should not be overly dogmatic. Here is another situation in which analysis of the community must be used to obtain essential information on users' backgrounds and values. Selection is made in terms of the sociology of clientele as well as evaluations by literary critics.

This tenuous and indefinite quality in literary taste also adds perplexity in the interpretation of reviews, for the selector has to consider the possible cantankerousness of literary critics. They sometimes do strange things. It has been charged, with some truth, that though the initial evaluations of James Gould Cozzen's 1957 novel *By Love Possessed* were favorable, the critics reversed themselves when they saw how popular it was.

Another problem is that of the thousands of creative works which each year are produced in English and other languages, none can be eliminated automatically on the basis of specificity. In other fields, a book may be rejected because its scope is too narrow for the interests of the library's users. To take books in history, for example, the small library may buy a comprehensive treatment of a given country, but consider a volume devoted to one city as too limited in scope. A book on dogs may be needed but one on Rottweilers may be too highly specialized for the budget. In creative literature, since subject is unimportant, there is no such handy measurement. The choice is wide and users of the general library sometimes cannot understand why their own favorites are not heavily represented.

Because of such difficulties and controversies as these, the library cannot be concerned exclusively with literary masterpieces, but must endeavor to obtain also the best and the most likely to endure of the current crop.

The general guides offer help in selecting authors and works. In a more specialized vein, a book worth perusal by selectors is Jay B. Hubbell's *Who Are the Major American Writers? A Study of the Changing Literary Canon* (Durham, NC: Duke University Press, 1972, 344 p.) Hubbell bases his selections on polls, literary histories, reviews, and similar evidence. *World Literature Today* (formerly *Books Abroad*) carries a long section "World Literature in Review," which covers current works from many countries.

2. *Editions.* The other problem peculiar to the selection of creative literature has to do with the variety of editions (and texts) available. Not all printings of a given work are anything like "accurate." When a play, poem, or novel has been issued dozens of times with different printers copying from previous texts, numerous errors inevitably creep in (sometimes by intention), and the words of the author are distorted or partly lost. Many of these errors are inconsequential; some make a significant difference. A classic example on this point is Herman Melville's *White Jacket,* in which the novelist described "some inert, soiled fish of the sea." A competent twentieth-century critic, F. O. Matthiessen, referred to this expression as a twist of imagery "of the sort that was to become peculiarly Melville's. . . . Hardly anyone but Melville could have created the shudder that results from calling this frightening vagueness some *'soiled* fish of the sea.' " Later, a professor at Ohio State found that Melville originally had written "coiled" fish. "Soiled" was a typographical error, presumably made by a printer whose literary talent was unworthy of enthusiasm.[15]

One branch of bibliographic scholarship (analytical bibliography) is devoted to the study of variant readings and to the reconstruction of accurate texts. Some readers and critics feel that the tedious job is not worth the trouble; others believe the works so precious that finding the author's exact words is worth months or years of painstaking research. For the use of scholars, definitive editions of great writers are essential — worth the great cost. General readers, of course, are about as well satisfied by one edition as another, though Fredson Bowers makes a case for the best editions here also.[16]

The Modern Language Association's Center for Editions of American Authors, which was in operation during the years 1963–1976, produced definitive editions of over 140 volumes by twelve American writers: Mark Twain, Stephen Crane, John Dewey, Ralph Waldo Emerson, Nathaniel Hawthorne, William Dean Howells, Washington Irving, Henry David Thoreau, Walt

Whitman, William James, Herman Melville, and William Gilmore Simms. Nearly two hundred scholars and eleven university presses were involved. Special care was given to selection of type, to proofreading, and to presswork. (See, for one example, Stephen Crane, *Works,* University of Virginia edition, edited by Fredson Bowers [Charlottesville: University of Virginia Press, 1969–1976], 10 vols.) Since 1976, the Modern Language Association has supported the Center for Scholarly Editions, whose scope is broader than that of the CEAA.

Even for the general reader and the less-than-perfect text, typography is important. It is a disgrace that in some libraries important writers are represented only by editions with small, inappropriate type and uncomfortably cramped margins. This curse is greater in literature than in any other field.

The librarian has a few works to aid in choice among texts in creative literature. Good, though somewhat dated, notes about editions of important American authors are given in the Bibliography volume of the *Literary History of the United States,* edited by Robert E. Spiller and others (4th ed., Macmillan, 1974, 1,466 p.). For British writers, the venerable if cranky F. W. Bateson discusses and evaluates editions in his *Guide to English Literature* (2nd ed., Garden City, NY: Anchor Books, 1968, 261 p.). A. E. Dyson has edited specialized works which include excellent discussions of texts: *English Poetry: Select Bibliographical Guides* (London: Oxford University Press, 1971), 378 p.), and *The English Novel: Select Bibliographical Guides* (London: Oxford University Press, 1974, 372 p.). Bibliographies devoted to individual authors generally specify standard or definitive texts. British scholar David Daiches declares that American scholars are especially busy in such endeavors: "There is scarcely an important (or even unimportant) writer whose bibliography has not been painstakingly compiled in the United States."[17]

A fine example of the use of both analytical and enumerative bibliographic method is *Bibliography of American Literature,* compiled by Jacob N. Blanck for the Bibliographical Society of America (New Haven, CT: Yale University Press, 1955–   ). Six volumes were completed before Blanck's death, and they are marvels of thoroughness and bibliographic skill, though they do not indicate definitive editions.

Secondary Materials

After the primary works, libraries need biographies, histories, and criticisms of literature. (Sometimes "criticism" subsumes the other two.) Such publications are produced in abundance and at varying levels of quality. The good critic or historian needs an eye for minute detail, as well as a long-range understanding of sociology, philosophy, psychology, linguistics, aesthetics, and many other fields.

Literary criticism usually is thought to have started with Plato, and since his time there have been so many brands that they cannot all be discussed here. There are several ways to classify critical approaches. We may think, for instance, of the main categories as: moral, psychological, sociological, formalistic, and archetypal.

If "what we read becomes part of us," [18] then it is valid to criticize literature in terms of its influence on the reader. What effects are desirable and what undesirable? While such evaluations have fallen into disrepute, Reichert suggests that critics not be victimized by "fashionable skepticism about the making of value judgments." [19] Among those using this framework have been F. R. Leavis and Yvor Winters.

The psychological approach to criticism uses facts and theories from that science to explain the process of creative writing, to interpret the behavior and thought of fictitious characters, or to relate the work in question to the life of its author. Associated with this movement are such names as Kenneth Burke and Leslie Fiedler. It is a fruitful approach, but has seen some of the same abuses as those discussed in the chapter on biography.

The relation of literature to society has occupied many critics in the nineteenth and twentieth centuries — especially during the Depression era. Marxists, for instance, have been inclined to consider a work good if it promotes desirable social effects. Others with different social goals have measured literature against them.

Such an approach, then, is similar to the moral one. Vernon L. Parrington and Joseph Wood Krutch were identified largely with this general category. In a variation on the sociological approach, the critic may interpret the work of art as an expression of contemporary social forces.

Formalistic criticism has received great attention in this century. It involves the close study of texts themselves — their form, or structure — as aesthetic entities. Outstanding among these "New Critics" have been I. A. Richards, T. S. Eliot, John Crowe Ransom, and Cleanth Brooks.

The archetypal approach stresses the notion of a great unconscious mind in the human race. Thus themes in literature are likely to reflect the ancient myths or the cultural patterns of a given people. Archetypal criticism is largely concerned with explaining these patterns and meanings. Three representative practitioners are Fiedler, Kenneth Burke, and Northrop Frye.

Some works about literature combine history and criticism; indeed it is difficult to keep them apart. A long, cooperative venture, *Cambridge History of English Literature,* edited by A. W. Ward and A. R. Weller (Cambridge: At the University Press, 1907–1927, 15 vols.), though published before the advent of the recent critical theories, is readable and in many ways instructive. More recent (in fact still incomplete) is the *Oxford History of English Literature* (Oxford: Clarendon Press, 1945– , of which twelve volumes are promised). Bibliographic notes are excellent. The Frederick Ungar Publishing Company's series, A Library of Literary Criticism, including, for example, *Modern Black Writers,* compiled and edited by Michael Popkin (New York: 1978, 519 p.), gives excerpts from critical works about various authors and is handy for the general library, as are the series offered by the Gale Research Company, such as *Twentieth-Century Literary Criticism . . .* (Detroit: 1978–).

Reference works have to do with facts about particular books, fictitious characters, authors' lives, and literary terms. *Readers' Encyclopedia of American Literature,* by Max J. Herzberg (New York: Crowell, 1962, 1,280 p.), is an example of the minutely factual book — a contrast with *Princeton Encyclopedia of Poetry and*

Poetics, enlarged edition, edited by Alex Preminger (Princeton, NJ: Princeton University Press, 1974, 992 p.), which has long sweeping articles on history, theory, technique, and criticism. The Oxford Companions to American, English, and other literatures are standard in most libraries. Handbooks to Faulkner, Milton, and other authors are practical, as are books explaining literary allusions. Concordances are especially useful in literature because the field is word-centered.

Periodicals are now the most important vehicles for literary history and criticism. The number of American scholarly journals devoted to English and American literature rose from 39 in 1960 to 114 in 1975.[20] *American Literature, Publications of the Modern Language Association of America* (*PMLA*), and *ELH* (for *English Literary History*) are examples of heavy (but interesting) periodicals devoted to the topic.

POETRY

This form of literature originated very early, perhaps as oral incantation for the purpose of influencing gods or nature, perhaps as accompaniment to group movements such as dancing, rolling logs, or paddling canoes.[21] It reached a high degree of perfection among the ancient Greeks, Hebrews, Romans, and others, and has been over the centuries a favorite form for writers in English.

Usually it is said that poetry is the most moving kind of literary art, giving delight because it packs so much meaning into such a small volume of words. "Semantic density" is an expression often used. The poet loves language, takes pleasure in working with it, and lets it lead where it will.

> There is first the elaborate, almost playful skill with words; the love of their plasticity, and pride at mastering the complicated rhythms one can impose on them. But there is also the second, more unruly pleasure: the poet's surprise at the unnamed shapes he has entangled in his net, the dark language, the unmanageable

love he dredges up from that part of his experience where opposites coincide, and where his word and some higher Word may be the same; that strangely "impersonal" mood.[22]

"My own feeling," says Fred Inglis, "is that the poem which tells no story but offers an experience and its evaluation is the most finished and powerful work of art of which language is capable — of which, I would be prepared to say, all art is capable."[23] The many uses and values of poetry have frequently been celebrated.[24] It helps ease emotional pressure. It dispenses truth to society. It heals the soul which is sick. The audience for modern serious poetry, however, like that for modern serious music, is comparatively small, at least in this country. (In Russia the story is quite different.) Here, "the slender volume that doesn't sell" is made up of poems. If such a book finds buyers for as many as a thousand copies, it is doing well — a fact bemoaned by Professor Frye in observing that a poet's "manuscript excreta," when sold to libraries, may bring in more money than royalties on the finished printed work.[25]

The small general library needs the works of the great poets — those recognized as having made a lasting contribution. Preferably these writers are represented by good editions of their complete (or at least principal) output. The English essayist Robert Lynd once said that the general reader wants a chance to see all of a poet's works, "barren as well as fertile, choked with weeds as well as rich with grain. He does not really lose much time in discovering the good among the bad. As a reader he has instincts like those of a bee searching for honey in a garden."[26] In our time this seems a bit optimistic, but things may change again.

The greater problem in selection arises in the case of new, relatively unknown, untested poets. Eric Moon, agreeing with Dan Lacy's complaint that book selection manuals and library school courses advise librarians to buy only recognized anthologies and the collected works of standard poets, urges more reliance on personal taste as a guide for library selection.[27] This advice is not so good for those whose taste is bad or uncertain.

A practical dilemma is: Shall we buy this new 96-page work

of a promising but generally unrecognized poet, or shall we wait a few years and see? The already-obscure work may pass into complete oblivion, or a few of the poems may be included in a later anthology, or the poet may be published in a collected edition at a far lower price per page. In many ways the present little volume is more attractive. The poetry is fresh, and the format of the book may well be suitable to poet and meaning. Some interest certainly will be lost by the time a duller-looking anthology appears. In many instances, then, the slender volume is worth the price, but the decision is hard to make for particular cases. Basic anthologies are recommended by William Cole in the article "Poets & Anthologies," *American Libraries* 5 (June 1974): 294–297.

Much good verse is produced by very small publishing houses: some also by the larger ones. An interesting phenomenon is the continued publication of the magazine *Poetry,* founded by Harriet Monroe in 1912. Some businessmen who possibly had never voluntarily read a poem made financial contributions in the early days. The journal has published the first works of a number of poets who later have become famous.

Nonprint materials are important here, as well as for drama, speech, fiction, and even essays. This fact relates to literature's oral beginnings. To the ancient Greeks, especially in the time before Plato, the written word held a less significant place than it does in our time. Then, it was impermanent and secondary, a kind of script for speaking, whereas the oral word was of primary importance. This orientation toward the ear has never been lost entirely.

Among the many series of sound recordings is an eighteen-disc set, Treasury of 100 Modern American Poets, issued by Spoken Arts, Inc. Eight years were needed to find old tapes and discs of the poets reading their own works. Included are such well-known writers as Sylvia Plath, John Updike, and Allen Ginsberg, along with the less acclaimed.

For keeping up with the current output, there are the spoken records sections of *Schwann-2.*

DRAMA

The origins of drama most likely go back to religious ritual — tragedy having to do with propitiation of the hidden powers; comedy with festivals and celebrations. The word *drama* stems from the Greek term for "action." Drama is commonly assumed to involve three essentials: impersonation, dialogue, and action itself. Since practically all plays are written to be performed on stage, the best primary records of them are motion pictures or video records. Sound recordings of complete plays or of selected passages also are used for study and enjoyment. The general guides to nonprint media are filled with examples.

The library is concerned too (perhaps mainly) with the printed texts of plays, plus works on theory, history, and criticism. Printed dramas have been called playbooks of literary quality. Such authors as Eugene O'Neill and George Bernard Shaw considered their writings to be far more than acting scripts. They wrote plays as literature (though in O'Neill's case the stage presentations — complete with masks and so forth — are not fully realized by reading the texts). Their stage directions represented vivid writing — sometimes difficult for the actors to carry out.

For many plays, the printed text offers meanings that are not apparent in the actual performance. As Charles W. Cooper observed, "Playreading brings you into most direct possible contact with the mind of the playwright. . . . No interpretative artists stand in the way. No actors serve as intermediaries to add their flourishes and inflections based upon their own personal understanding or misunderstanding of the script." [28]

As in the case of poetry, the general library always faces a problem with regard to printed texts of plays: should it buy copies of current hits, or wait for cheaper anthologies? There is certainly much more interest in new plays than in new poetry. Broadway productions receive such publicity that the demand for texts is substantial. Nevertheless, for each library there is a point at which buying the current edition is not the better course. Fortunately the series, *Best Plays of* [the season] (edited at various times by Burns Mantle, John Chapman, Louis Kronenberger, Otis L. Guernsey, Jr., and others, with varying imprints and titles) is available to help fill the gap. Though the plays are condensed, the books are enhanced by facts about the production and by illustrations. Regrettably, many libraries do not have good editions of the great dramatists; they may have an over-abundance of old textbooks or anthologies cast aside by erstwhile students.

Related to books of drama and criticism are "how-to" books on such subjects as the oral interpretation of literature, puppetry, stagecraft, acting, and the dance. Each of these topics has a small body of historical and critical literature also. Among histories of the theatre is the elephantine work by George C. D. Odell, *Annals of the New York Stage* (New York: Columbia University Press, 1927–1949), whose 15 volumes are written in interesting if dated style, carrying the story into the 1890s. By contrast, there is the severely factual, skeleton-like work, *The London Stage, 1660–1800, A Calendar of Plays, Entertainments, and Afterpieces* . . . (Carbondale, IL: Southern Illinois University Press, 1960–1968, five parts, each in several volumes), with added volumes giving lists of performances and of other persons.

ESSAYS

The form of literature least bound by conventions, the essay had its beginning (at least in name) with Michel de Montaigne, who spent nine years, off and on, producing two volumes of papers which were published in 1580. John Florio's translation into English appeared twenty-three years later. Montaigne wrote in rambling, conversational fashion, and since his time the word "essay" has been applied not only to the paper written in brilliant style without particular concern for subject matter, but also to the more formal, concise, polished, tightly-reasoned effort. An essay which has been well researched and skillfully written gives the reader a rich concentration of thought. By its compression in style it compares with the short story, though it is less compact than most poetry. Not that such a work is short, necessarily; sometimes an entire book is labeled an essay.

Associated with this genre are Francis Bacon, John Locke,

Ralph Waldo Emerson, Henry David Thoreau, William Hazlitt, Charles Lamb, John Ruskin, George Santayana, H. L. Mencken, E. B. White, and, obviously, many others. George Bernard Shaw's prefaces are really essays, and so are most pieces of literary criticism. Addison and Steele, writing in *The Spectator,* and Samuel Johnson, in *The Rambler,* illustrate the connection between essays and journalism. *Time* and *Newsweek* usually carry short essays; *Atlantic* and *Harper's* offer more.

At the present time United States publishers have in print about a thousand works whose titles begin with the word "Essai," "Essay," or "Essays." Many another has such a word in its subtitle. Since the reader can't make use of essays without finding them, the library should give preference in selection to books listed in *Essay and General Literature Index,* 1900-   (New York: Wilson, 1934-   , semi-annual, with annual and five-year cumulations), which lists authors, subjects, and some titles for articles found in collections of essays and other composite works, especially those having reference value, with particular emphasis on the humanities and social sciences. Fortunately, a list of books indexed here over a seventy-year period is available in one volume: *Essay and General Literature Index: Works Indexed, 1900–1969* (New York: Wilson: 1972, 437 p.).

SPEECH

Another kind of work, public address with its related forms, may as well be considered a part of literature. The speech is in one sense a work of art, transmitting information and emotion about any number of topics and issues. This form has been significant in political, and even intellectual, history. Its usual overall purpose is what sociologists call "social coordination." (Social policies do not gain acceptance from statements of fact, but from the use of rhetoric [or force]).[29]

In the ancient Athenian democracy, public speaking was of crucial importance in handling issues facing the state and in legal matters — a citizen might be called upon to defend himself before a jury of hundreds. Aristotle's *Rhetoric* (available in several good translations) is a fundamental treatise on this subject,* and the speeches of Demosthenes (notably "On the Embassy" and "On the Crown," found in the Loeb Classical Library and other places) rank among the greatest of all time.

Periods of crisis have produced the greatest oratory: the Reformation, the French Revolution, the eighteenth century in Britain, the American Civil War, and World War II. Today, via television, speakers such as the President of the United States are subject to evaluation by large audiences.

In judging public address, the critic uses standards which differ from those by which excellence is measured in other forms of communication, but there is some relation to the sociological approach employed in literary criticism. The main question is: was the speech effective in accomplishing the speaker's purpose? Were the long-range results beneficial? There are several considerations involved in making these judgments, but the real issue is whether the speaker (in Aristotle's terms) used all the available means of persuasion. Were the ideas sound? Was there a skillful appeal to emotions? Were the speaker's own character and reputation such as to inspire confidence? Were structure (arrangement) and style (wording) of the speech best for the situation? Was the oral delivery effective?[30] These factors also suggest some criteria for selecting written speeches in a library.

Accurate texts of speeches are very hard to reconstruct. If they are pieced together from separate reports by members of the audience, they may bear very little resemblance to the originals. Who knows now what Pope Urban II actually said at Clermont in 1095 as he inspired people to go on the Crusades? Even if a speaker later writes out an address for publication, there is the temptation to make changes. For these reasons anthologies of public speeches contain some badly mangled texts, though they do convey something of what actually was said. Stenographic reports and sound recordings, fortunately, give us accurate reproductions of contemporary public addresses.

*Mortimer Adler, training people to sell *Great Books of the Western World,* based his approach on Aristotle's principles of persuasion (*Philosopher at Large: An Intellectual Autobiography* [New York: Macmillan, 1977], p. 282).

Two publications made up almost entirely of the texts of current speeches are *Vital Speeches of the Day,* 1934– twice a month, and *Representative American Speeches,* 1937/38– (New York: Wilson, 1938– annually).

In the area of history and criticism, two older works are of outstanding merit. Chauncey A. Goodrich's *Select British Eloquence . . .* (Harper, 1852, reprinted later) is an amazingly perceptive evaluation of orators, particularly those of the eighteenth century, such as Charles James Fox, Edmund Burke, the Earl of Chatham, and his son, William Pitt. The Speech Association of America has sponsored *A History and Criticism of American Public Address* (McGraw-Hill [and others] 1943–1955, 3 vols., also reprinted). It gives an analysis of the style and background of each of about forty leading speakers of our history, each chapter written by an authority.

Obviously sound recordings and motion pictures — the latter especially — are important for preserving speeches as history and as models for study. The contrast between the delivery of Franklin D. Roosevelt and of his successors, for instance, can be perceived more clearly by this means than by any other. As a different example: to see an old film of the evangelist Billy Sunday with bared teeth threatening the liquor interests is quite instructive.

28. PROSE FICTION

The long-predicted (anxiously-awaited?) death of the novel has not yet come to pass. The American output for fiction was 3,836 titles, counting new editions, in 1976; 3,681 in 1977; 3,693 in 1978; and 3,264 in 1979. (Some forty to fifty percent of these titles are paperbacks.)

There has been an old if not venerable notion, perhaps more pronounced in the United States than in other countries, that novel-reading is worthless, to say the least, or downright wicked. Those wanting to depict the idle, no-good person have sometimes indicated that he (more often she, really) is reading a novel. Oberlin College students, among others, were warned in the 1840s, "Put down that novel! It will ruin your soul." One way the novel was regarded in the latter part of the century is illustrated by an 1872 book called *The Truth About Love,* whose author said that the parents of the young ought to encourage any gratification short of intercourse: "kissing, embracing, waltzing, and even novel-reading." [1]

Esther Jane Carrier, in her book *Fiction in Public Libraries 1876–1900,* uses this quotation from the periodical *Outlook* of April 21, 1900, to summarize America's developing attitude toward fiction at the turn of the century:

> It is not many years since serious-minded people were earnestly questioning whether the novel was a real form of literature, or simply a literary device for wasting the time of a host of readers. To a great many good people the novel was something even worse than this; it was a source of demoralization, if not of corruption. The novel . . . has touched on many forbidden topics, has often clothed vice in the garments of virtue, and has separated sin from its punishment. A host of other novels have been mere wasters of time — written without conviction, knowledge of life, or literary skill, for the sole purpose of making money, and read by the multitude who care neither for veracity, quality, nor knowledge, but who simply wish to be entertained. But, against

the drift of serious opinion, and in spite of constant misuse and abuse, the novel as a literary form has steadily made its way until it has become pre-eminently the literary form of our time; the form, that is, which most deeply, intimately, and frankly records the passion, the emotion, the questioning and the aspiration of the age.[2]

In our day, moving pictures, periodicals, and even telecasts have shaken fiction's preeminent role in the world of sin, but it is not giving up the field without a fight; its moral effects and defects continue to make good conversation.

For reasons such as these, censorship has been a greater problem, at least traditionally, in the area of fiction than in most others. Attacks on the novel as immoral, coupled with the real difficulty of choosing between good writing and poor, have caused librarians to face some very difficult decisions. Let us say that a given piece of fiction is disgusting to most people in the community, and that as a result the overall estimate of the work's value is extremely low. May not the librarian legitimately refuse to buy the book? Such a decision is quite different from the ones advocated by the famous Indian librarian, S. R. Ranganathan, who (though claiming not to favor censorship) declared that public libraries should not acquire fiction having "anti-social suggestions."[3]

The old suspicion that fiction is a waste of time helps explain why its acceptance as an object of serious study has occurred only recently. When William Lyon Phelps began to offer a course in the contemporary novel at Yale University in 1895, he was strongly criticized by some of the older professors, who insisted that either the course or the professor be dropped.[4] Now, the catalogs of American colleges and universities show how fashions have changed.

British writer Colin Wilson goes so far as to claim that novels have "altered the consciousness of the civilised world," and have been of greater influence than Darwin, Marx, and Freud together, more powerful than "the torture chambers of the Inquisition or the armies of Frederick the Great."[5] To limit ourselves to the testimony of one practitioner, there is D. H. Lawrence's somewhat extravagant estimate: "Being a novelist, I consider myself superior to the saint, the scientist, the philosopher and the poet, who are all great masters of different bits of man alive, but never get the whole hog."[6]

THE SHORT STORY

There seems to have been a tendency for works of fiction to get shorter since the multi-volume efforts of Samuel Richardson in the middle of the eighteenth century, and the rise in popularity of the short story represents, perhaps, a furtherance of that trend. Henry Seidel Canby once put it: "In a time of much writing, tastes are quickly jaded, and the short story because it is terse, striking, highly-colored, and somewhat new, meets with quick applause. Its brevity is of advantage, for many people can be made to swallow good literature in a pill who reject it in larger doses."[7] British writer Anthony Burgess, however, referring to James Jones's works, cracked: "But sheer size is a commodity the Americans purvey easily."[8] The many trilogies and tetrologies as well as long sequences such as C. P. Snow's *Strangers and Brothers* (British) all testify that the lengthy work is still here.

The short story may be thought of in several ways. It is not of course just a short novel or tale. Though less compact than the poem, it does tend to leave a vivid, sharp impression, and draws its interest from description of persons or situations more than from recital of events. Unlike the novel, it usually has no character with whom the reader can really identify.[9] Its graphic presentations engage the reader in a brief, intense experience. Appearing less intellectual than a formal essay, it can still be an effective, penetrating criticism of life.

The short story may be said to have a long history dating back two or more millennia before Christ. After slow and sporadic growth, it developed rapidly in the early nineteenth century, with Nikolai Gogol in Russia and Edgar Allen Poe in America, both born in 1809. Poe's theory of the short story (1842) was a landmark. This form of writing was facilitated further by the rise of the periodical. (It is worth noting that in science also the short paper — as opposed to the book — was accommodated by the periodical.) Perhaps its early association with mass-circulation journals caused the short story to be regarded as a second-class form of literature.[10] Today, The *New Yorker, Atlantic,* and a few other general magazines (along with the literary journals) publish excellent stories, though periodical fiction has, in general, declined.

If a list of the typically great writers of the genre is needed, here are a few samples: Mark Twain, Stephen Crane, Anton Chekhov, Graham Greene, Joseph Conrad, Sherwood Anderson, Ambrose Bierce, Honoré de Balzac, Guy de Maupassant, Ernest Hemingway, and William Faulkner. Like poetry and plays, short stories are a favorite for anthologists, and the library sometimes finds better buys in collections.

Much of the comment given below about the novel applies also to the short story.

An excellent reference tool, useful also in selection, is *The Short Story Index: An Index to 60,000 Stories in 4,320 Collections,* compiled by Dorothy E. Cook and Isabel S. Monroe (New York: Wilson, 1953, 1,553 p.), with annual supplements, cumulated at five-year intervals. The same firm has published also a list of the collections that have been analyzed since the beginning of this service: *Short Story Index: Collections Indexed, 1900–1978* (New York: 1979, 349 p.).

THE NOVEL

Usually distinguished among books of fiction by its length, the novel is a work of "considerable extent" or more specifically of over 50,000 words, novellas and novelettes being shorter. When and where did this form begin? The answers include the France of Louis XIV, seventeenth-century Spain (*Don Quixote*), the Babylon of 2000 B.C. (the Gilgamish epic), and several others. More commonly, the modern novel is considered to have arisen in the eighteenth century with Samuel Richardson's *Pamela: A Study of the Female Heart,* published in 1740, or perhaps

The Adventures of Robinson Crusoe, by Daniel Defoe twenty-one years earlier. Thus while narrative is ancient, the novel as we know it is rather young. "The most slattern of literary forms stumbled, ambled, swaggered into view" at this point, says Goldknopf, because power in the novel centers upon the main character and this age in the western world placed great stress on the individual.[11]

There are several ways to classify novels (as romantic, psychological, social, realistic) but one work may have so many aspects that it does not fit well in any category.

How shall we evaluate the novel with reference to library collections? The words of Henry James, nearly a century ago, are still relevant: "The only obligation to which in advance we may hold a novel without incurring the accusation of being arbitrary, is that it be interesting. . . . The ways in which it is at liberty to accomplish this result (of interesting us) strike me as innumerable, and such as can only suffer from being marked out, or fenced in, by prescription."[12] This standard holds up well today, for even if a work is only a blob, without sequential plot or realistic characters, it at least ought to be interesting.★

Another standard is verisimilitude: like other literary forms, the novel substitutes for "real-life" experience, but really,

> it is quite different in this respect from poetry, where we expect . . . drastic reassessment of reality; different from the drama where verisimilitude is conveyed by actual human beings supported by the elaborate apparatus of the theater, and where dramatic conventions sanction numerous departures from realism. The novel engages life much more frankly, intimately, and particularly.[13]

The novel is better, then, if it is plausible and gives the reader a slice of life. True, even the best work gives only one person's

---

★It is said that the great philosopher Kant failed only one time to take his daily walk by which people set their watches. He became too absorbed in Rousseau's 1760 novel, *The New Héloise* (Colin Wilson, *The Craft of the Novel* [London: Victor Gollancz Ltd., 1975], p. 42).

understanding, but it can suggest how reality may be perceived. A novel about a slum family may paint a more accurate portrait than a case history by a social worker. One about a delinquent boy may be more "realistic" than a clinical report. Even a gothic may describe genuine human emotions. To quote Henry James again, "Humanity is immense and reality has a myriad forms; the most one can affirm is that some of the flowers of fiction have the odour of it, and others have not." [14] Dr. Sigmund Freud, who in 1907 published the first psychoanalytic study of a novel (Wilhelm Jensen's *Gradiva*), said, "Creative writers are valuable allies and their evidence is to be prized highly, for they are apt to know a whole host of things between heaven and earth of which our philosophy has not yet let us dream. In their knowledge of the mind they are far in advance of us everyday people, for they draw upon sources which we have not yet opened up for science." The author "experiences from himself what we learn from others — the laws which the activities of this unconscious must obey." [15] This judgment has been questioned by some, and it is possible that Freud was speaking playfully or ironically, but many other students of the human mind have made similar declarations. One psychiatrist said, "Literature can present as living actuality that which the textbook petrifies in jargon." [16]

The kinds of truth presented in the novel may be factual — the techniques of bell-ringing in Dorothy L. Sayers's detective story, *The Nine Tailors* (New York: Harcourt, Brace, 1934, 331 p.), or the conditions and verbal expressions of Victorian England in Michael Crichton's *The Great Train Robbery* (New York: Knopf, 1975, 266 p.), or New York City in the late 1960s as reflected in some of the details of *Mr. Sammler's Planet* by Saul Bellow (New York: Viking, 1970, 313 p.). Less satisfactory by this criterion is Jack Higgins's book *The Eagle Has Landed* (New York: Holt, Rinehart and Winston, 1975, 353 p.), which at the start makes the claim that at least half is "documented historical fact." The basis of the count is not given. Far worse are works which deal with recent historical events and living, recognizable persons, mangling the truth to make the story more "interesting."

The writer may suggest truth about people's minds, as William Faulkner does in teasing out the layers of thinking and motivation in such characters as Mink Snopes, Gavin Stevens, and young Charles Mallison. The novel may stimulate the reader to think on deep theological or philosophical issues, as do some works of Thornton Wilder. But there is a difficulty here: as a novel tries to deal with the more profound questions it becomes less likely that readers will agree on the truth of its assumptions. In *Moby Dick* the facts about ships and whales are more easily understandable and are subject to less disagreement than are the psychological and theological implications.

Wilson suggests that the good novel is at base an exploration of human freedom; "therefore, a successful novel is one that builds up tension, and then allows it to be discharged, like a bursting thunderstorm." The greatest novelists, he says, are those who "have been able to suggest the human spirit's indestructible capacity for freedom." [17] Elements of tension and conflict often provide the main interest for the reader.

Other considerations in judging the novel have to do with literary qualities, such as unity and style. These factors should not be passed over by the library selector who examines books or reviews, but we still come back to interest and truth as the chief criteria.

Some mention has been made of the "good bad book." There is also a category perhaps best labeled "poor bad" (or, since "bad" carries some positive connotation, the "poor no-good book"). I have in mind that series of literary clones perpetrated by Horatio Alger Jr., repeating the same theme and plot over and over — they are worth mentioning only because of their uncanny popularity in the late nineteenth and early twentieth centuries. Perhaps they were popular, ironically, because they were not true to life. "Holy Horatio" just never grew up, and according to Frederick Lewis Allen, it was his "singular fortune to have just that simplicity, that elementary directness of approach to fiction-writing, which would make his books a joy to immature minds." [18] Beginning with *Ragged Dick* in 1868, Alger, or someone using his name, published more than a hundred novels, whose unrealistic characters each saw virtue finally rewarded by wealth. The modern counterparts of these works — the "days of pleasure, nights of passion" concoctions, for instance — must, in the modern library, be given some place, the size of that place depending on the strength of demand theory of selection. Some libraries believe that these works also give an opportunity for studying the psychology of writers and readers. One can hope that some money is saved to buy the "better" current works, and that even "classics" are not ignored.

Nonprint media are fairly important in connection with fiction. Moving pictures are used to present analyses of the novel or short story, to explain how a work has been written, or to recreate the story itself. Feature films and videorecords which have been based on fictional works are often sought in conjunction with the printed versions. Filmstrips and sound recordings bring out particular aspects of the originals.

A BIBLIOGRAPHICAL NOTE

One of the great authorities on the bibliography of fiction was Ernest A. Baker (1869–1941), the director of the University of London School of Librarianship. He wrote a ten-volume *History of the English Novel* (London: H.F. & G. Witherby, 1924–1939), as well as other notable books on the subject, and with James Packman completed the *Guide to the Best Fiction, English and American, Including Translations from Foreign Languages* (New and Enlarged edition, London: Routledge, 1932, 634 p.) with good annotations for over 10,000 titles. The most serviceable of the many lists of recommended titles is *Fiction Catalog,* 9th ed. (New York: Wilson, 1976, 797 p.) with its annual supplements. The titles (4,734 in the main volume) have been selected by committees representing the Public Library Association and the Reference and Adult Services Division, both parts of the American Library Association. Including novels and short stories for adults, it is a companion set to the *Public Library Catalog.* Dorothy M. Broderick once called a previous edition the "bug-a-boo" of what is suitable for the small library, but like all good selection tools, it has a place of value, especially for the beginner.

SPECIAL KINDS OF FICTION

There are several sorts of novels and stories (in addition to those mentioned above) which seem to inspire loyalty or contempt in unusual measure. The librarian must form some general guidelines for selecting these types, as well as making yes/no decisions on individual works.

Confessions — True and Fabulous

A type of fiction with very little redeeming value is the confession story. The first issue of *True Story* magazine appeared in 1919, and the editors declared that acceptable manuscripts should not only be true to life but also teach a strong moral lesson. Not all such productions, however, hold to a lofty standard of veracity, and even their moral lessons may not be very impressive. An anonymous author who during the Great Depression made his living by creating one "true" yarn after another told of instructions received from his editor:

> The formula is simple: Sex and success. A girl loves not wisely but too well. Her lover betrays her. She suffers. She struggles. Either she raises herself from the mud by her own efforts, or she marries a splendid man, preferably rich, and thus accomplishes the same thing. You can let her have a baby or not. The Big Boss thinks it is a good idea for betrayed heroines to have babies. Some of the rest of us don't think so. Use your own judgment. You can ring up all the changes you want to on the above theme.[19]

The cynic might say of these stories that they are so true to life that they have nothing new to reveal about it. In any case, most people rapidly tire of the same sorts of people going through similar actions in ways which are virtually identical. And yet, the very fact that such stories exist is itself of interest to scholars, and perhaps Manchester, years ago, was right: "While Catholics have their confessional, Protestants have their purge literature."[20]

Westerns

The term *western* applies to a wide variety of stories which (most say) began with James Fenimore Cooper's novels in the first half of the nineteenth century. Attempting to define the genre, says Richard Etulain, is "like trying to shovel fleas through a barn door — more escape than are captured."[21] The influence of the land on the character and actions of a hero is the western's most distinctive element.[22]

Prolific writers such as Max Brand (1892–1944) and Louis L'Amour have sold millions of copies (using one name or another) and have produced dozens of movie scripts. Western movies seem to have a perennial appeal, and they whet the public's appetite for western novels.

To some readers, the plots and characters of westerns are a bit repetitious, but other people, including presidents of the United States, read them avidly. Adolf Hitler was among the European boys who read works about the American Wild West by the German author Karl May. *Der Führer* apparently thought his generals would have profited from these thrilling stories.[23] And then there was the college student who wrote an essay to prove the superiority of Zane Grey over William Shakespeare, citing the former's knowledge of the human heart, beautiful descriptions, realistic characters, and charming style.[24] A few more sophisticated critics have managed to find merit in these works.[25] Of this type of writing in general, Professor George R. Stewart comments:

> Eventually, I suppose, all justification of the study of literature must rest upon a belief that it makes the individual a better citizen and a happier person. It seems to me that I have observed instances in which the study of regional literature has achieved this result, when perhaps the study of a more distant literature would not have done so.[26]

Detective Stories and Mysteries

The realms of Sherlock Holmes, Lord Peter Wimsey, Hercule Poirot, Perry Mason, and Lew Archer have received a curious mixture of disdain and (growing) approval in libraries. Though included in most of the standard guides to collection building, they often have been frowned upon or apologized for. Detective novels, however, the most popular form of entertainment reading — perhaps of any reading — are consumed in great numbers by many intellectuals* (and by university presidents). Abraham Lincoln loved to read Edgar Allen Poe, sometimes considered the father of the genre. Dean Shailer Mathews, of the University of Chicago Divinity School, spoke of detective stories as "good for mental chewing gum"; a noted New York clergyman expressed suspicion of those among his parishioners who did not read them. When Archibald MacLeish was made Librarian of Congress in 1939, he obtained a collection of these books for the White House.

What is the fascination of the detective novel? In the classic works, the main interest centers around the coolly rational sleuth who uses pure intelligence to analyze evidence and reach a solution. In a certain sense, "watching the detective is like watching a skillful artist who is able to take a few odd patches of color and wiggly lines and make a face or a landscape emerge from them."[27] Furthermore, we all like to be challenged by puzzles, then to be told whether we have discovered the answers. While this sort of fiction is really not very true to life, it does build up tension in the reader and provide for release by revealing the identity of the murderer.

The classic detective novel has been encumbered more in recent times by explicit sex scenes, attempted humor, and irrelevant violence, to say nothing of the meandering meditations of Travis McGee. Such themes may have an interest of their own, but they usually prove to be a hindrance to the pace of the essential story.

---

*It has been suggested that one of the most important ideas of the historian R. G. Collingwood had its genesis in an Agatha Christie (Joseph M. Levine, "The Autonomy of History," *Clio* 7 [Winter 1978]: 254).

Many unnecessary defenses have been made for detective stories. It has been claimed that they promote good government by showing that only guilty people are convicted; that they teach a moral by warning the killer of sure punishment; that they short-circuit readers' murderous impulses and so prevent crime. It may be said also that such stories extend the mind by showing that the unexpected and least predictable sometimes happens (the most unlikely person turns out to be the murderer). This way of thinking is not exactly useless in our world. We are trained by science and common sense to act according to statistical probabilities. "The stock market more than likely will go down because of the President's State of the Union message"; "Probably it will rain today — I see a black cloud — so I'll get the umbrella." Even baseball managers and football coaches are prone to play the percentages. We need to be reminded that the unexpected, the unusual, even the outlandish, sometimes can happen.* It is claimed also, with some reason, that detective stories can "train one to be a careful and observant reader — no small benefit." [28] If these points seem to be rationalizations, books of this kind still may be bought because they are interesting.

Perhaps it is well to emphasize also that the variation in quality of detective fiction is great, though some tend to lump all such books together, as many people once did novels. G. K. Chesterton, author of the famous Father Brown stories, pointed out also that "the mere absence of artistic subtilty does not make a book popular. Bradshaw's Railway Guide contains few gleams of psychological comedy, yet it is not read aloud uproariously on winter evenings." [29] As with other writing, popularity is not always a sign of poor quality.

Of the bibliographies and other reference works devoted to this specialty, the best yet for selection purposes is *A Catalogue of Crime* by Jacques Barzun and Wendell Hertig Taylor (New York:

*Derek J. de Solla Price, noting that the various types of intelligence seem to have little relationship to achievement in science, says that for the scientist one important quality is "a certain gift that we shall term *mavericity*, the property of making unusual associations in ideas" (*Little Science, Big Science* [New York: Columbia University Press, 1963], p. 107).

Harper & Row, 1971, 831 p.). Written by a former university administrator and a science professor, the volume lists about 3,500 entries on factual and fictitious crime. The authors do not hesitate to give their own definite opinions about these books, and more often than not they are "right." Even the absence of running heads (see above, p. 96) does not destroy the bibliography's usefulness.

Science Fiction

Having long since outgrown its reputation for trashiness, science fiction has been studied seriously in universities since the early 1960s and claims great numbers of learned people as readers. Says astronomer Carl Sagan, "I find that science fiction has led me to science."[30] Like the other arts, observes James Blish, it adds to our knowledge of reality, "but unlike any other art, science fiction also evokes for the nonscientist the basic scientific emotions: the thrill of discovery, the delight in intellectual rigor, and the sense of wonder, even of awe, before the order and complexity of the physical universe."[31]

Four major classifications of science fiction have been delineated: imaginary voyages (to planets, stars, the center of the earth, or prehistoric time); future predictions (of what could happen tomorrow or in a million years); remarkable inventions (of many sorts); and social satires (à la *Gulliver's Travels* or *1984*).[32] Related to this genre are weird tales about the supernatural and pure fantasy, whose subjects are entirely imaginary. Science fiction proper, says Darko Suvin, is "continuous with a body of already existing cognitions" and is "based on cognitive logic."[33] Suvin attaches a negative bibliography — books which are *not* to be considered as belonging to the true body.

A "critical guide to science fiction" aimed at school, public, and academic libraries is Neil Barron's *Anatomy of Wonder: Science Fiction* (New York: Bowker, 1976, 471 p.). There is a *Science Fiction Book Review Index, 1923–1973,* edited by H. W. Hall (Detroit: Gale Research Co., 1975, 438 p.), and numerous short lists of recommended sf titles have been published in magazines.

29. SCIENCE AND TECHNOLOGY

The third of the major divisions of knowledge, with a body of literature which is distinct in several ways, is considered rather less important in the average general library. Nevertheless, this literature is extensive, it has a direct effect on human life, and a good deal of it is highly interesting.

ON THE NATURE AND VALUE OF SCIENCE

There is no purpose to be served here by rehearsing the numerous attempts to define *science*. Very simply, the term is derived from the Latin word *scire* (to know), and according to the *Oxford English Dictionary*, *scientist* was coined by the British writer William Whewell, who in 1840 produced a learned work called *The Nature of the Inductive Sciences*. "We need very much," he said, "a name to describe a cultivator of science in general. I should incline to call him a Scientist." Now the words are used all too commonly and carelessly.

In one respect, science may be thought of as a method — a logical and imaginative search for order. It attempts to provide, as the result of asking questions, a systematic understanding of the phenomena in nature. James Bryant Conant (a chemist and a former president of Harvard), along with the noted physicist J. Robert Oppenheimer and others, liked to think of science as having something to do with the extension of common sense. All of us explore our own environments; organized science investigates a wider area, by more and more elaborate methods, based on detailed constructs in the mind. Perhaps, then, it is fair to say that science really develops when, in order to understand the world, someone develops a new theoretical framework. For instance, Galileo, explaining the fall of a stone as an event, had to fashion a concept different from Aristotle's notion that the rock was merely undergoing a change in state.[1]

Science is also considered a corpus of knowledge — the record of human investigations. This information is embodied largely in the materials which are gathered and preserved by librarians.

The breadth of scientific interest can be illustrated by a couple of measures: it studies the nucleus of the atom, at something like 1/10,000,000,000,000 of an inch, and the billion galaxies, some of which are five billion light years out in space. Encompassed within biology are bacteria weighing 3/10,000,000,000,000,000 of an ounce, more or less, and blue whales at 150 tons each. The infinite variety of phenomena are a continuing cause for astonishment.

Science seems somehow modern and Western, but its roots must go back as far as humanity. In fact, George Sarton (1884–1956), the great Belgian-born historian, took 4,000 pages to describe science through the fourteenth century.[2] Early human beings had to recognize basic "scientific" facts if they were to survive at all. At least, they needed some knowledge of plants and animals in order to obtain food. They began the cultivation of crops (probably first in the Middle East and China) and the extraction of metals from ores. Observation of the moon, sun, and stars led to generalizations about their movements and calculation of times and seasons. Foremost in the ability to formulate principles from observed phenomena were the ancient Greeks.

After the decline (relatively speaking) of "science" during the Middle Ages, great steps forward were taken with the Renaissance of the fourteenth, fifteenth, and sixteenth centuries, a notable year being 1543, which saw the publication of Copernicus' *Revolutions of the Heavenly Spheres* and of Vesalius' *Fabric of the Human Body*. The case for inductive investigation (another of the key characteristics of science) was fortunate in having such a spokesman as Sir Francis Bacon (1561–1626). "The great landmark in the history of science as a social institution"[3] was the establishment of the Royal Society of London, in 1662.

Though science has been cultivated on most parts of the globe, it has flourished more freely in the Western world, and Max Lerner even went so far as to say of America that it "is a civilization founded on science and rooted in its achievements. . . . The whole atmosphere surrounding the settlement and peopling of America was an atmosphere of scientific beginnings."[4] Why in

America? "Presumably, some blend of the frontier democracy, primitive capitalism and the entrepreneurial talents of a handful of inventors were involved."[5] The remarkable growth of scientific organizations in the United States is illustrated by the American Chemical Society. Started in the year of the nation's centennial (1876) with 133 members, it had 110,000 members a century later.

We find it difficult to recognize the pervasive influence of science in our own age and civilization because we have scarcely known any other climate; hence we have no basis for objective comparison. "As architecture was the great imaginative triumph of one age, and music of another, and poetry of another, the greatest achievement both of the human intellect and of the human imagination during the past hundred years has been that of natural science. It is because science is a triumph of the imagination as well as of the intellect, a thing of beauty as well as of utility."[6] Even this was written before the expenditure for scientific research and development had reached its present level of tens of billions of dollars annually.

Why the long-term, widespread interest in science? Why do people choose careers of this kind? The purposes of individual investigators are not easily discerned, and apparently are mixed. Some authorities have pictured the scientific spirit arising from pessimism, unhappiness, and self-repression. Feuer, however, thinks the seventeenth-century movement toward science was due not to "asceticism, but satisfaction; not guilt, but joy in the human status; not self-abnegation, but self-affirmation; not original sin, but original merit and worth; not gloom, but merriment; not contempt for one's body and one's sense, but delight in one's physical being; not the exaltation of pain, but the hymn to pleasure."[7]

One of the rewards of the scientific approach is aesthetic, as expressed in a classic statement by the French physicist and mathematician, Henri Poincaré (1854–1912), where he described the delight in understanding the profound beauty of nature — a beauty which is the product of the harmonious order of parts as grasped by a pure intelligence. Bertrand Russell considered the proportions of mathematics to be similar to the cold beauty of sculpture.

Again, to discover things is fascinating; to find new truth is exciting. Understanding the processes of nature is reason enough for hard work in research. Thomas describes scientists as, "despite their efforts at dignity, rather like young animals engaged in savage play. When they are near to an answer their hair stands on end, they sweat, they are awash in their own adrenalin."[8]

Science, then, has a charisma, which is "subtly blended with the charisma of the aesthetic, as the repeated evidence of the importance of elegance in science testifies. . . . The best science is most esteemed because it combines the charisma of great transforming and explanatory power with that of great beauty. Perhaps only thus can we fully explain the motivation of the most creative scientists."[9]

The scientist has other incentives also. The financial rewards of the research scientist usually are satisfactory. Doubtless some are spurred by desire for the recognition and distinction to which science provides so direct a path.

To the laity, possibly more than to researchers, the phenomena described by scientists are terribly interesting — even such "simple" things as the "radar" system of the bat, the periodic table of chemical elements, the way a tree conveys moisture from roots to leaves.

Another reason for the study of science (and for building library collections in the area) is that it helps human beings become oriented to their environment. How can we understand our place in the order of nature without some knowledge of what things are really like? Some introductions to philosophy, therefore, (for example, Bertrand Russell's *Philosophy,* published in 1927) have started by explaining the essentials of what has been learned about the universe. Most people find fascinating, or even highly inspirational, this basic knowledge about the world in which they live. (But then there was Sherlock Holmes, who, told by Dr. Watson that the earth is spherical, said that having learned the fact he would try to forget it, because he couldn't see that it had any use.)

To many, science's practical value for society is its most important aspect. Knowledge provides a means of control. It confers power. Without tools, some of them quite sophisticated, the earth could not support its present number of people, even if all accepted the minimum for subsistence.

Consider the sources of energy made available by technology. In the early days people drew on such primary energy sources as animals, slaves, the wind, and moving water. Technology has made it possible to use steam, gasoline, electricity, and finally nuclear power. It is said that now each man, woman, and child in the United States can command energy sources equivalent to the power of two hundred strong men. There is no need to comment on the ability of computers to do routine mental tasks at a tremendous saving of time and labor. To cite a couple of other examples: much of the credit for doubling human life expectancy over the past two centuries must go to the science of medicine, and the huge increases in farm productivity are due to agricultural science (including animal and plant breeding).

It would be excessive to say (though some scientists have) that only through science and technology have we become distinguished from the lower animals and taken on those characteristics which are clearly human; such exaggeration accomplishes nothing. But in terms of physical power, the achievement of the scientific enterprise is almost beyond one's ability to comprehend.

In view of these accomplishments, it is regrettable that words like *science* have been degraded by hucksters trying to sell products like deodorants, toothbrushes, and children's toys. "Turn all problems, petty and grand, over to science for a solution." Furthermore, something of the quality of primitive magic has become associated with this kind of activity, as if repeating the word would produce results. These false pretensions should not be held against genuine scientific enterprise, any more than the abuses of religiosity can be charged to religion itself.

Perhaps the overwhelming power that science has unlocked is the cause of its being castigated in so many quarters. The love-hate relationship of the public to science continues to grow, as does the serious concern that science, or more accurately, technology, is ruining the quality of human life. In a spiritual sense, this ruination is brought about (so the charge goes) by the great value placed on material things and processes, and by the denigration of emotions and subjectivity. The emphasis on cause and effect relationships, typical of science, has a way of being applied to human beings, thus robbing them of spontaneity. To many, it is time to give more attention to those processes in the world that are not considered strictly predictable. The efficiency and smooth regularity necessary in technological efforts may be against nature.

There are more direct and telling accusations. The poisoning of the environment can be charged in large measure to technology, or at least to the abuse of it. Factories pollute air and stream; landscapes are mutilated by grotesque machines; flying planes and motor scooters ruin the ear with intolerable noise. Even great dams across rivers — engineering feats that they are — destroy animal life and displace human beings. Dangers are increased by shoddy automobiles, defective nuclear power plants, and overcrowded air corridors.

Has not technology, then, brought on more evils than benefits? The answer must be a tentative "Perhaps," but, as many competent authorities have pointed out, the technology that has achieved such spectacular results on so many fronts can most surely find a way to remove its own contaminants and reduce its own dangers. It is people who determine how the tools are to be used. And if the solution depends not on reversion to ignorance, but on the cultivation of greater understanding, the place of science materials in all kinds of libraries will become even more important.

GENERAL NATURE OF SCIENTIFIC LITERATURE

Publications in science tend to fall into two categories: those *of* science and those *about* science. *The McGraw-Hill Encyclopedia of Science and Technology* represents the former; thus it does not include history and biography except "as required in the natural and factual development of technical subjects. Philosophical considerations are presented only if needed for the basic understanding of a scientific concept or its technical application." (Preface to edition 4.) *The Handbook of Chemistry and Physics*, with its brief no-nonsense lines of data, and *The Journal of the American Chemical Society,* reporting investigations on the frontiers of knowledge, are even more clearly *of* science. Works like Sarton's *Introduction to the History of Science* and Freeman Dyson's autobiography, *Disturbing the Universe* (New York: Harper & Row, 1979, 283 p.) are more *about* than *of* science, describing scientific ideas in their historical and personal settings.

In time, we may come to make this same distinction for books and periodicals in the social sciences — perhaps even in the humanities — but it is much sharper in the sciences.

Related somewhat to this division of the literature is another — that between materials for professional scientists and those for the laity. Again, in no other area of knowledge is this distinction so clear, and it may be worthwhile to speculate on the reasons why such lines exist. Two factors suggest themselves: (1) the nature of the things studied by science, and (2) the purposes to which these studies are put.

What Science Investigates

First, many of the materials and processes studied by scientists are repeated with little change from century to century, and from country to country. Consider two facts: Alexander the Great died in 323 B.C.; lithium has three protons in its nucleus. Both facts are still "true" (though many scientists are shy of this word). The fact studied by history is a unique event; not repeated. The one studied by science is with us to this day, repeated over and over. Science explores in project after project the nature of atoms; hence is able to use ever more sophisticated methods for measuring and understanding them. Alexander's death, having happened once, can be studied only from very limited records, and the possible methods for this investigation are soon exhausted. Even in meteorology, where results are not as predictable as they are in chemistry or physics, the processes at work are still more regular than those of the social sciences or the humanities.

Because scientists study groups of things that are similar, and processes that are repetitive, such as atoms, or rocks, or electricity, and because so many individuals are engaged in similar research projects, they have been able to develop an extraordinary degree of refinement in their methods and to discover a tremendous amount of detailed information. Whenever a group of people are interested in the same phenomena, they develop shortcuts in terminology which are meaningless to outsiders, who refer to them as "mere jargon." Moreover, since much of science deals with data which can be expressed by numbers, mathematical expressions are a natural way of communicating. Thus it becomes feasible to use one new term or a mathematical formula in place of a whole page of common words. In these ways the concepts of science and the terms used in its communication soon go beyond the understanding of the laity.

The social sciences, on the other hand, study typically those things and relationships that are changing in significant ways. The quality of the contacts made between people of different races is in flux. The economy is changing. Political behavior shifts and moves. Thus social scientists can't very well focus on such minute details as scientists do; they are not able to develop methods and terminology quite so far in advance of the common person's understanding, and hence their works are accessible to more people—a few more, at least.

In the humanities there is also something protean about the subject matter. Not only are new objects being produced constantly, but the older ones are reinterpreted according to the changing ideas of the age. Even the fact that a work of art is "finished" does not mean that activity or knowledge in this area is cumulative as it is in science. The humanities, then, somewhat like the social sciences, are more often limited to producing materials within the range of the intelligent general reader. Exceptions may be theology and philosophy, both of which involve some topics which are studied over and over, so that terminology, and perhaps methods, become too hard for the laity to understand.

The Uses of Scientific Research

The second factor explaining why the literature of science is difficult has to do with the use for which it is intended. The main purpose of humanistic writing is to provide material for the minds of other human beings. To a large extent this is true also of the social sciences. When scholars write, the ultimate goal is understanding. Papers in science, and especially technology, on the other hand, result largely in activities (like checking the experiment described) and in practical applications. The findings of technology often do not stop in the human mind; they go on to bring about changes in physical things. "Papers are not the end-product of technology, but only an epiphenomenon."[10] The end product may be a machine or a drug. To illustrate further: a humanistic criticism of an Egyptian vase is intended for appreciation by human minds. It has little to do with proposing new ways for vases to be made or even decorated. A survey of the economic conditions in the Appalachians may result in action, but only if that survey is understood by a sizable number of people who, though not specialists in economics, assume the responsibility (as voters or administrators) for making such changes. A piece of research on metal alloys, however, may result in improved engines for motor cars, which may be used by thousands of people who do not understand the change or who do not even know that it has been made.

Thus we can understand why science has the reputation of being, in Fritz Machlup's words, "almost by definition, what the layman cannot understand."[11] The intelligent layman is able to read a sizable proportion of the articles in anthropology, literature, music, and even in economics and the other social sciences or humanities, but not in the pure sciences.

Because of this fact, it is appropriate that selection tools for the literature of science be graded, as they so often are, to the level of the intended reader.

THE LITERATURE *OF* SCIENCE

Plainly, scientists do not make use of the printed word in the same way or to the same extent as humanists do. Direct observation and experiment followed by meticulous recording and reporting of results are science's traditional activities; yet, as a professor of theoretical physics has observed, "A scientific laboratory without a library is like a decorticated cat: the motor activities continue to function, but lack coordination of memory and purpose."[12] There is evidence to show that the better scientists (especially those engaged in "pure" research) spend ample time with the published writings.

Over the decades, a large, constantly changing body of literature has been formed — the work of thousands of people — each part having some relationship to the whole. "One cannot observe . . . [the process of scientific communication] from the outside as long and intimately as we have without marveling at the elegance of this complex social system which man consciously created to establish and protect knowledge. The checks and balances which keep the process orderly and uncontaminated are ubiquitous."[13]

The literature *of* science, to repeat, is about things and processes which fundamentally change rather little. As facts are discovered, they are "comprehended within, and therefore in a sense annihilated by, general statements of steadily increasing explanatory power and compass — whereupon the facts may be forgotten."[14] For this reason the literature is cumulative, with one research person building on the findings of others. This systematic procedure means that the scientist seldom feels a need to go all the way back to the foundations; usually it can be assumed that for a particular problem only very recent publications are necessary. Citation studies completed over the years have demonstrated that for most experimental sciences the typical published materials referred to are not more than ten years old.

This body of literature is huge, even in terms of the number of books published annually. Including new editions, United States publishers send forth each year eight to ten thousand new books in science (of and about), including such related subjects as technology, agriculture, and medicine. The amount of writing produced by some individual scientists and mathematicians is amazing. For instance, *The Mathematical Papers of Isaac Newton,* edited by D. T. Whiteside (Cambridge, Eng.: At the University Press, 1967–) consists of large, magnificent volumes, the seventh of which was issued in 1976.

The more common unit of publication in science is the short paper — one reason why the periodical is so important. Citation studies seem to demonstrate that for research in science, 75 to 90 percent of the materials come from journals, as compared, for instance, with American history, where, according to one analysis, only 9 percent come from this format. These findings are substantiated, in general, by facts of library use. In the pure sciences, it is not uncommon for periodicals to account for 80 percent of the total uses of materials.

In Ziman's estimation, the most valuable of all the activities of the great scientific academies was their sponsorship of the learned journals, in the 1660s.[15] Conditions were right for such enterprises. The rejection of ancient and scholastic opinions made place for a new body of writings, while the then-new emphasis on observation and experiment produced short papers. These same conditions account for the ubiquitous scientific periodical today. "The general form of a scientific paper has changed less, in nearly three hundred years, than any other class of literature except the bedroom farce."[16]

Another reason for the scientific journal is that it usually offers relatively quick publication and wide distribution, as compared with the book. The advantages are particularly significant in view of the fact that one important purpose of the scientific paper is to stake the author's claim to discovery of a bit of new knowledge. Unfortunately the lag between acceptance of a formal article and its actual appearance in print has become excessive, so that some journals have arranged for "letters" from scientists to be published swiftly, without editing or other niceties. One example of this type is *Physical Review Letters.*

The total number of science journals is in some doubt, and

there have been estimates running as high as 100,000. Some ob-
servers even say that by the end of the century there will be a
round million of them. K. P. Barr, after a careful survey in 1967,
took a more conservative view: "It is concluded that the number
of currently available scientific and technical periodicals which
contain material of interest to practising scientists and technolo-
gists is 26,000." [17] Of this number about 6,000 were produced in
the United States. Numerous journals in this area, as in others,
have ceased publication, but the back files of these titles are
sometimes sought by research libraries trying to build exhaustive
collections.

Houghton offers a three-fold classification of scientific and
technical periodicals: (a) Learned society and professional journals, including those which publish original research, which announce research in progress, which serve the general purposes of
the organization, or which review the research of others. (b)
Commercially published journals, which also may disseminate
original research, or repackage information for the trade. These
controlled circulation journals, usually made up largely of advertisements, are aimed at potential purchasers. (c) House journals,
issued by organizations wishing to enhance their images either to
the outside public or to their own employees. [18]

Government publications are a prime source of information
here. They give data about the physical aspects of the jurisdiction, producing, for example, surveys of soils, weather, and geology. They report discoveries made in connection with projects
sponsored by the military establishment. In these and other
ways, governments provide scientific information of benefit to
industry and to the individual. The periodical *Science & Government Report* frequently mentions documents which are of general
interest.

Medium-sized and some smaller general libraries can use a
compilation by Philip A. Yannarella and Rao Aluri, *U.S. Government Scientific and Technical Periodicals* (Metuchen, NJ: Scarecrow Press, 1976, 263 p), which gives, for each entry, full bibliographic information and a long annotation.

Another form of publication, the technical report, which dates back to the early part of the century, has received wide use in recent years. A paper of, say, ten to twenty pages, the report is distributed as a separate publication to a small group having a special interest in the topic. It may show the progress made on a project financed through a government grant or may pertain to some other matter. Despite poor bibliographic control over them, these reports are used and quoted frequently, for they are issued quickly and allow an author to go into detail if necessary. Their total number may approach 500,000 a year.[19] Attention is being given to the problem of improving access to this and other "grey" literature.[20]

The body of scientific materials, considered as a whole, is so large as to be almost unmanageable, and no one has time to read more than a small fraction of it. Therefore summaries and reviews of literature are most helpful. Librarians may be forgiven if they look with some relief on the indicators that the overall rate of growth is slowing. A minor tragedy is that much of this material is repetitious and/or trivial, a fact which led the editor of *Science,* P. H. Abelson, to say in 1964, "Science is doing more research, and is publishing more, but it is accomplishing less in some of the classical disciplines than at any time during the last 100 years."[21] If this estimate remains accurate, the need for knowledgeable selection is all the more urgent.

Notes on a Few Titles

For historical perspective on the literature of science, a most instructive compilation is Harrison D. Horblit's *One Hundred Books Famous in Science,* based on an exhibition held at the Grolier Club (New York: The Club, 1964, 449 p.). For each entry complete bibliographic information is given, with a short annotation and a facsimile of the title page. Authors go from A (Agassiz's *Études sur les glaciers,* 1840) to W (Wilhelm Wundt's *Grundzüge der Physiologischen Psychologie,* 1874).

There are some books of science that should be found in almost all general libraries. Among them is the famous *CRC Handbook of Chemistry and Physics; A Ready-Reference Book of*

Chemical and Physical Data (West Palm Beach, FL: CRC Press, 1913– , publisher varies). Another is the larger *McGraw-Hill Encyclopedia of Science and Technology,* 4th ed. (New York: McGraw-Hill, 1977, 15 vols.) with its *Yearbook of Science and Technology,* 1962– . *Van Nostrand's Scientific Encyclopedia,* whose 5th edition is edited by Douglas M. Consident (New York: Van Nostrand Reinhold Co., 1976, 2,370 p.) presents a massive amount of information in one volume.

LITERATURE *ABOUT* SCIENCE

For the general library, materials about science are the more important of these two classes, for such works are more often within the reach of the nonscientist's understanding. Biographies and histories are particularly interesting to the general reader, though they should not be considered outside the concern of the research specialist. For instance, most of the essays in Loren Eiseley's *Darwin and the Mysterious Mr. X* (New York: Dutton, 1979, 278 p.) "were written for scientific and scholarly publications or prepared to be delivered before a gathering of scientists."[22] The importance of such materials is suggested by Louis N. Ridenour, once professor of physics and dean of the Graduate College, University of Illinois, who said, "I feel that it's important for libraries, even quite specialized libraries, to pay first attention to the acquisition of books about science, rather than scientific books as such."[23]

Until the latter part of the nineteenth century, the writings of scientists could be understood by the intelligent layperson. Darwin's *On the Origin of Species* (London: J. Murray, 1859, 502 p.), for example, was widely read by nonscientists. In the twentieth century, we have had books written by research scientists for the express use of people outside the profession. Sir James Jeans and Sir Arthur S. Eddington, British mathematicians and astronomers wrote, respectively, such books as *The Mysterious Universe* (New York: Macmillan, 1930, 163 p.) and *The Nature of the Physical World* (New York: Macmillan, 1929, 361 p.). Both were good literary stylists and adept at using clear analogy. In our own time Isaac Asimov, professor of biochemistry in the Boston University School of Medicine, has written two hundred books, including science fiction, detective novels, history, mathematics, and a number devoted to the explanation of science in understandable terms. *Asimov's Guide to Science* (New York: Basic Books, 1972, 945 p.) is a masterly exposition of the subject in general. As John Updike has remarked: "A class of essayists has grown up . . . that . . . makes 'sense' of the surreal scientific facts that loom beyond our lives like Oz, a benevolent kingdom ever receding into strangeness, but one that now and then deigns to send us in whimsical emissions, a new immunity, or photographs of other planets."[24] Fortunately, popularizing by top-notch research people has become respectable, though Eiseley, now recognized as one of the most capable interpreters of science, once said that he wrote in secret, almost as a vice, for nearly fifteen years. "If I had let any of my colleagues know that I wrote for a general audience, or what they called a popular audience, it would have ruined me academically, and I would never have gotten ahead in my chosen profession."[25] By contrast, scholars are now coming to think that the public must be educated about the consequences of scientific research, and "some of the nation's most prestigious organizations" are supporting programs to improve communication skills in this area.[26]

And yet, there are dangers to society if scientists themselves are the only ones to speak for their establishment, explaining their needs and making pronouncements about bombs and the social utility of nuclear power. The problem is parallel to that raised in George Bernard Shaw's comment about surgeons: If the doctor's wife is demanding a new coat, how can he be objective in deciding whether to amputate your leg and collect a big fee? To refer to our previous discussion about science not being understood by the general reader, public policy in regard to scientific matters should be decided only after the facts have passed through the minds of the laity. De Solla Price has advocated a "science of science" — a study involving the "history, philosophy, sociology, psychology, economics, political science and operations research (etc.) of science, technology, medicine (etc.);"[27]

thus giving people outside the establishment a certain authority over it, based on objective understanding.

It would be grossly unfair, of course, not to point out that scientists generally work for the well-being of society. The marine biologist Rachel Carson, in 1962, published the highly controversial *Silent Spring* (Boston: Houghton Mifflin, 368 p.), which, though attacked vigorously by the pesticide industry, proved so influential that it was listed, along with the discovery of the neutron and the development of stannous floride toothpaste, as one of the great "chemical events" of the century.[28] The journal *Science,* published by the American Association for the Advancement of Science, is frank in reporting news. *The Bulletin of the Atomic Scientists,* devoted to "Science and Public Affairs" has taken a position of social responsibility since its founding, in 1945. In recent years a number of books have been written on the theme of science's relation to the public.

Among the publications about general science are some good annuals, such as *Science News Yearbook . . . ,* compiled and edited by Science Service (New York: Scribner, 1969–) and *Yearbook of Science and the Future . . .* (Chicago: Encyclopaedia Britannica, 1969–).

Several periodicals are good candidates for the lists of general libraries. *Science, Science News,* and *Scientific American* are essential for most. *New Scientist* gives a British view. *Science Digest,* in spite of its small format and gaudy composition, carries articles by reputable authors. *American Scientist* is more sedate but readable. *Nature,* a large weekly journal both *of* and *about* science, is a likely choice for medium-sized and larger general libraries. *Science* [year], a colorful new journal sponsored by the American Association for the Advancement of Science, bridges "the distance between science and citizen."

CRITERIA FOR JUDGING MATERIALS IN SCIENCE

Recency and up-to-dateness obviously are important for materials of science. Another major standard for deciding on whether or not to buy an item on any subject is truth, and the librarian would prefer to apply this measure to works of science, though to some it may sound a bit old fashioned. Ridenour's observation that science by its very nature, "enjoys the property of having an agreed body of discipline and an agreed storehouse of objective information, which is shared by scientists the world around"[29] is generally true, and as a matter of practicality, the librarian, especially one who is building a general collection, has to settle for the consensus of the scientific establishment as to truth in books *of* science. There is no other way to turn. Even these judgments are not easy to come by, and may involve reading reviews in specialized journals. The selector may remember with some apprehension also the many times when a new discovery was rejected, then accepted later. For instance, when Roentgen discovered x-rays, Lord Kelvin, at the time perhaps the leading authority in that field, called the thing an elaborate hoax. Thomas S. Kuhn, in his *Structure of Scientific Revolutions,* has described how the admission of new discoveries or theories may involve breaking of accepted paradigms.[30]

For materials *about* science, the approval of practicing researchers also is the best standard for testing reliability, but when social questions are at stake, the librarian may seek the opinion of those who have a reputation for defending the public interest.

Iwaschkin urges that though a public library may have to obtain pseudoscientific books because of patron demand, it should make "things at least a little difficult for the intellectual charlatans" by stocking such works as Lawrence Kusche's *The Bermuda Triangle Mystery — Solved* (New York: Harper & Row, 1975, 302 p.).[31]

A criterion of special significance in judging books about science (and even those *of* science) is rhetoric. A writer for the *New York Times Book Review* gives as the first question to be asked about a science book: "Does the author understand his audience's limitations, and is he willing to work within them? If scientists want to communicate with nonscientists, I expect them to take the trouble to answer the 'stupid' questions that the intelligent reader is likely to ask."[32]

Style of writing is important here also. André Maurois was

right in saying that "a scientific book, perfectly constructed, is a work of art."[33] It is true that in this area content is by far the most significant factor, but even here the value of the descriptions is partly a matter of arrangement and style. One critic goes so far as to say that the scientific textbook is in one sense aesthetic — an object of literary criticism.[34]

Even in books *of* science, style is a notable standard. Perhaps the reason Gregor Mendel, the nineteenth-century pioneer in genetics, was ignored for so long was that his literary style was terrible, compared with that of his contemporaries in the field.[35] Alvin Weinberg, an expert on scientific communication, once said that the style of American scientific writing (he was speaking here about materials *of* science) took a turn for the worse about the time of World War I, perhaps because of the increase of government influence. "Government institutions are necessarily impersonal and rigid, and their style of communication tends to be correspondingly impersonal, rigid, and unclear."[36] John Maddox has decried the fact that "language used to describe what may be, after all, the highest achievements of the twentieth century is matched in inelegance only by the more tedious forms of civil service composition."[37] It has not always been thus. A professor of English (Howard Mumford Jones) and an expert in the history of science (I. Bernard Cohen) have collaborated to edit *A Treasury of Scientific Prose; A Nineteenth-Century Anthology* (Boston: Little, Brown, 1963, 372 p.). But if good style is important in books *of* science, how much more highly is it to be valued in those *about* science?

One shortcoming of popularizers is the inability to inject humor successfully. Its use is seldom skillful, and such attempts almost always detract from the message. In this respect, science writing is like detective fiction and perhaps for the same reason.

A strong criterion for judging works of science is up-to-dateness, but as suggested in the chapter on social sciences, it can be overrated. Authors who are too anxious to incorporate last week's astounding discoveries are more likely to miss a certain perspective, which discussions about science ought to have.

SOME AIDS IN SELECTION

Guides to library materials in this area frequently include those both *of* and *about* science. For the general library, a tool of first importance is the *AAAS Science Book List Supplement* (Washington: American Association for Advancement of Science, 1978, 457 p.). It continues the Association's third edition, published in 1970, and lists works for high school and college students, as well as for teachers and nonspecialists. Annotations are descriptive, evaluative and readable. Arranged by the Dewey Decimal classification, it includes books in related fields such as psychology and anthropology.

Ching-Chih Chen's *Scientific and Technical Information Sources* (Cambridge, MA: MIT Press, 1977), 519 p.), though primarily for science and engineering librarians, has a place also in the general library. It is selective, and for most entries gives a brief annotation and references to reviews. Other works of interest here are Denis Grogan's *Science and Technology: An Introduction to the Literature*, 3rd ed., rev. (London: Clive Bingley, 1976, 343 p.); and John L. Thornton and R.I.J. Tully's *Scientific Books, Libraries and Collectors: A Study of Bibliography and the Book Trade in Relation to Science*, 3rd ed. (London: Library Association, 1971, 508 p.), with a supplement for 1969–1975, published in 1978.

Technical Book Review Index, a monthly which began in 1935, is a kind of *Book Review Digest* for science and technology (including medicine and agriculture), giving excerpts from published reviews.

The Technology Department of the Carnegie Library of Pittsburgh has a good series, *Science and Technology: A Purchase Guide for Branch and Small Public Libraries* — annotated lists for service to students and nonspecialists. An excellent monthly bibliography, *New Technical Books; A Selective List with Descriptive Annotations* has been published by the New York Public Library since 1915. It covers pure and applied physical sciences, mathematics, engineering, industrial technology, and related areas as published (mainly) in the United States. For each entry, there is a contents note plus a brief description, usually giving the level of the material and the kind of library or audience for which it is appropriate.

An unusually fine reviewing medium is *AAAS Science Books & Films,* issued four times a year by the American Association for the Advancement of Science. For each entry the level of difficulty is indicated, kindergarten through professional. Annotations are extensive, usually informal. Recommendations are clear.

Books about science frequently are reviewed by the general periodicals. *The New Yorker,* for instance, has published some excellent reviews.

NONPRINT MATERIALS

Facts both of and about science are preserved and communicated well by the nonprint media. Photography has become one of the major tools of research for physicists, astronomers, and biologists, who use the camera to record not only what can be seen by the human eye but also much more, via such instruments as the electron microscope. Sound recordings hold primary data like the sounds of the animal world. Such organizations as the American Chemical Society produce recordings of speeches and symposia which reveal the latest research findings. (These particular materials are for large and/or specialized collections.)

Nonprint media are important too for purposes of teaching. Not only do they present well the facts of science, but they deal with its history and demonstrate laboratory techniques. The motion picture is unusually advantageous for instruction of this kind. Visual materials in general have been shown to be effective, but sound films "were found to be more than twice as effective as filmstrips in providing learning in a general science course."[38]

Educators Guide to Free Science Materials (Randolph, WI: Educators Progress Service, 1960– , annually) includes both print and nonprint items. A list of considerable value is *AAAS Science Film Catalog* (Washington: American Association for the Advancement of Science, and New York: Bowker, 1975, 398 p.), an annotated and graded list, though not necessarily selective or evaluative. One section is for junior high through adult levels; the other, for elementary students.

SUBDIVISIONS OF SCIENCE

Here we give attention to several of the major fields of science and to their practical applications, concentrating on those of interest to the general library. Notice is given a few representative titles which are suitable for nonspecialists.

Biological Sciences

Biology is currently one of the two or three most exciting fields for high-level research, and the study of life is of obvious interest to the public, relating to everyday observations that can be made by anyone. Books and journals that describe and picture mammals, birds, reptiles, insects, trees, flowers, fishes, and other objects in the natural world are among the more interesting. The publications of the Sierra Club are especially notable; many of them are examples of fine color printing. Edwin Way Teale wrote superb nature books, for example, *North With the Spring; A Naturalist's Record of a 17,000-Mile Journey with the North-American Spring* (New York: Dodd, Mead, 1951, 366 p.). Rachel Carson's *The Sea Around Us* (New York: Oxford University Press, 230 p.) came out the same year.

Among the current popularizers in biology, the best known is Dr. Lewis Thomas, of the Memorial Sloan-Kettering Cancer Center in New York City. In 1974, Viking Press published an anthology of his short articles, *The Lives of a Cell: Notes of a Biology Watcher* (153 p.), and in 1979, *The Medusa and the Snail: More Notes of a Biology Watcher* (175 p.). Thomas does not hesitate to criticize aspects of his discipline, but James D. Watson's *The Double Helix; A Personal Account of the Discovery of the Structure of DNA* (New York: Atheneum, 1968, 226 p.), describing experimental work on the structure of genes, included a far more uncomplimentary version of how scientists work and contend. *The Case of the Midwife Toad* by Arthur Koestler (New York:

Random House, 1971, 187 p.) is an exciting and disheartening account of a tragic clash between an eminent biologist and his more orthodox colleagues.

Here may be classed also the great flood of materials about the crucial topic of preserving the environment. Conditions and ideas change fast, and so it is fortunate that the library periodicals make a special point of keeping selectors abreast of the times with articles like George H. Siehl's "Environment Update" (*Library Journal* 104, 1 May 1979, p. 1003–1007), and Daniel Coyle's "The Feds and the Environment" (Ibid., p. 1008–1011). NICEM has a catalog: *Index to Environmental Studies — Multimedia*.

Materials on medicine and health are becoming more important in the general library, owing to interest stimulated by newspapers, popular periodicals, and television. The "health industry" in the United States now grosses billions of dollars annually, and though Thomas speaks of this obsession as "fundamentally, radically unhealthy,"[39] the demand for materials is in many respects legitimate. If patients come to be treated more as thinking, responsible individuals, the need for such information will increase. The widespread interest in activities like running has resulted in works appropriate for general libraries. (There is even a *Runner's Index*.) Books of medical advice for the laity, though generally acknowledged as suitable for public libraries, do create an unusual problem, since misinterpretation of them can lead to unfortunate results. Still, in this field, as in most others, a little learning, though dangerous, probably is less hazardous than none at all.

In 1977, the Encyclopaedia Britannica Corporation began publication of the *Medical and Health Annual,* a well-illustrated serial which includes feature articles and reviews of recent developments. An example of a medical guide is *The Book of Health: A Medical Encyclopedia for Everyone,* 3rd ed., (New York: Van Nostrand Reinhold, 1973, 974 p.) with a "Quick Guide to Emergencies" inside its back cover. Old standbys like *Gray's Anatomy,* which has undergone numerous revisions, are needed in almost all general libraries.

Marilyn McLean Philbrook has compiled a good list for the

general public seeking medical information: *Medical Books for the Layperson: An Annotated Bibliography* (Boston: Boston Public Library, 1976, 113 p.). It can be updated by lists which appear in the library periodicals.

Producers, publishers, and distributors are listed by Joan Ash and Michael Stevenson in *Health: A Multimedia Source Guide* (New York: Bowker, 1976, 185 p.). A smaller compilation of practical use is Patricia A. Hamilton's *Sources of Free or Low Cost Health Education Materials for Consumers* (Piscataway, NJ: Rutgers Medical School, 1978, 13p.).

Among the guides to nonprint media are NICEM's *Index to Health and Safety Education — Multimedia* and the annual catalog issued by the National Medical Audiovisual Center (Washington: Government Printing Office).

Agriculture and gardening are topics of interest even to apartment and condominium dwellers, to say nothing of suburbanites. The *Yearbook* of the U.S. Department of Agriculture is still one of the most interesting of all government series. Though some recent volumes deal with topics other than plants and animals, the 1977 annual, *Gardening for Food and Fun* (392 p.) is good for a wide audience. Also hard to beat are the books by Thalassa Cruso.

Mathematics and Physical Sciences

Astronomy, perhaps the oldest of the sciences, called upon by early kings to foretell the future, still has power to bring awe to the mind of the amateur. Conventional telescopes have become larger and larger. X-ray telescopes mounted on satellites have detected more and more.

Materials about how to make telescopes, about star charts, about space exploration, and about the nature of the physical universe usually get a ready response from general readers. In this field also, photographs, charts, and diagrams are used with great skill, as in, for instance, *Catalog of the Universe,* by Paul Murdin and David Allen (New York: Crown Publishers, 1979, 256 p.). In 1977, Crown also brought out the *Cambridge Encyclo-*

pedia of Astronomy (495 p.). Carl Sagan, in his *Broca's Brain: Reflections on the Romance of Science* (New York: Random House, 1979, 347 p.) has demonstrated again how much interest this field holds for the general reader. Fred Hoyle's popularizations (most of them) are splendid examples of the art. *A Guide to the Literature of Astronomy,* by Robert A. Seal (Littleton, CO: Libraries Unlimited, 1977, 306 p.) annotates works mostly for students and amateurs.

The field of mathematics has produced some good popularizations as well as materials totally beyond the common person. A new journal, *The Mathematical Intelligencer,* proposes to publish readable articles written by specialists for non-specialists. William L. Schaaf's *The High School Mathematics Library,* issued in a new edition about every three years by the National Council of Teachers of Mathematics, is helpful in selection. A companion series is prepared for elementary grades and junior high schools.

The literature on the computer is growing fast, with theoretical, technical works and practical manuals standing beside those about its effects on careers, society, and human values.

The American Chemical industry has moved in a century "from the days of salt, bleach, and sulfuric acid to a complex of industries that produce some $100 billion worth of chemical and allied products each year,"[40] and there has been a commensurate growth in its body of literature. Martin Sherwood has given a readable survey of the field in *The New Chemistry* (New York: Basic Books, 1974, 322 p.), but his concluding words "now read on" remind us that we could use more books in this vein.

Works about the care and repair of automobiles, motorcycles, bicycles, and other vehicles are becoming more important as the public takes a turn toward conservation. The names of Chilton, Audel, and Glenn are prominent here.

People are also expressing interest in the construction and maintenance of houses, walls, and patios. Fortunately, works on this general topic have improved significantly in recent years — for example *The Reader's Digest Complete Do-It-Yourself Manual* (New York: Reader's Digest Press, 1973, 600 p.).

Cookbooks continue to be produced at a fast rate, and a couple of thousand are in print with American publishers. Representative specialties: *Dumpling Cookbook, Fine Arts Cookbook,* and *Zucchini Cookbook.* There are recipe books for most nationalities and for most religious groups, as well as for every physical condition and means of cooking. David Riesman, in his famous work *The Lonely Crowd,* said that inner-directed (gyroscope-type) people favor staid old works such as the *Boston Cooking School Cookbook* (Fanny Farmer's) while use of more exotic recipes is a sign of the other-directed (radar-type) personality.[41]

Still holding its own is *Joy of Cooking,* by Irma Rombauer and Marion R. Becker (rev. ed., Indianapolis: Bobbs-Merrill, 1975, 915 p., plus other editions). Theodora Fitzgibbon has written about eatables from thirty-four countries in *The Food of the Western World: An Encyclopedia of Food from North America and Europe* (New York: Quadrangle/New York Times Book Co., 1976, 519 p.). A related work of high interest and practical use is *The Cooks' Catalogue: A Critical Selection of the Best, the Necessary and the Special in Kitchen Equipment and Utensils* (New York: Harper & Row, 1975, 566 p.).

CONCLUSION

Practical considerations aside, there is no inherent reason why this book should be coming to an end. For one thing, some topics have not yet been covered, and others have been treated less fully than they deserve. More important, learning about the carriers of information is a lifetime task, and anyone who expects to master anything like the entire field is doomed to frustration. But almost everything a person reads or experiences, whether book, review, guide, bibliographic note, film, or conversation, adds to the ability to select wisely, and serves to make that person a better librarian in other respects as well.

I have tried to explore the areas of present knowledge at least, with an attempt to illuminate the principles and problems of selection in each. While stressing the need for meeting users' demands for the materials they think they prefer, I have not ignored the importance of presenting matter of high quality. It is not good to underestimate either aspect of selection.

Looking ahead, just about the only thing prognosticators agree upon is that, whatever its physical embodiment, we shall have more information, not less. Selection, therefore, will gain in importance. Over the years, the world of books will alter, perhaps rapidly. Different subjects will become fashionable. Guides will go out date and be replaced. Reviewers' styles will change. Conceivably the book itself (and maybe the film, disc, and tape) will be replaced by better media of some sort. Such possibilities are interesting to contemplate and certainly are no cause for alarm. The librarian who learns the job well and who is flexible in mind need not worry. There will always be a place for those who know how to handle information on the one hand, and who, on the other, have a good understanding of people, so that they may mediate between the two.

NOTES: CHAPTER 1 Introduction

1. *Book Selection in a Siege Economy: The LIBTRAD Holborn Conference 1975,* ed. B. H. Baumfield for the Working Party on Library & Book Trade Relations (Radlett: The Working Party, 1976), 46 pp.

2. "Editorial," *Library Journal* 85 (1 January 1960): 58.

3. John Cotton Dana, "Selection and Rejection of Books," *Public Libraries* 13 (May 1908): 178.

4. Eric Moon, Introduction to his *Book Selection and Censorship in the Sixties* (New York: Bowker, 1969), p. 9.

5. Augustine Birrell, "Book-buying," in his *Obiter Dicta,* Second series (New York: Charles Scribner's Sons, 1887), p. 289.

6. John P. Dessauer, "The 1977 U.S. Census of Book Publishing Reveals Significant Industry Expansion," *Publishers Weekly* 216 (9 July 1979): 36.

7. Charles R. Cook, "The Overall Market for Graphics, 1970–1990," *Publishers Weekly* 198 (2 November 1970): 39–40.

8. Daniel Bell, Introduction to Peter S. Jennison and Robert N. Sheridan, eds., *The Future of General Adult Books and Reading in America* (Chicago: American Library Association, 1970), p. 7.

9. *The Role of Libraries in America* (Frankfort, KY.: Kentucky Department of Library and Archives, 1976), p. 21.

10. "Who Reads Books and Why: Washington Meetings Examine Consumer Survey," *Publishers Weekly* 214 (6 November 1978): 16.

11. William Saroyan, "Myself Upon the Earth," *American Mercury* 33 (October 1934): 211.

12. Chandler B. Grannis, "Statistical Update — Domestic and Foreign," *Publishers Weekly* 218 (26 September 1980): 92.

13. Harold K. Guinzburg, "Free Press, Free Enterprise, and Diversity," in Harold K. Guinzburg, Robert W. Frase, and Theodore Waller, *Books and the Mass Market* (Urbana: University of Illinois Press, 1953), p. 15–16.

14. The best source of such information is: United Nations Educational, Scientific and Cultural Organization, *Statistical Yearbook* (Paris: The Organization, Annually).

15. See Jesse H. Shera, *Foundations of Education for Librarianship* (New York: Becker and Hayes, Inc., 1972), p. 48.

16. John W. Senders, "Information Storage Requirements for the Contents of the World's Libraries," *Science* 141 (13 September 1963): 1068.

17. Bolt, Beranek, and Newman, Inc., *Toward the Library of the 21st Century; a Report on Progress Made in a Program of Research Sponsored by the Council on Library Resources* (Cambridge, MA: Bolt, Beranek, and Newman, 1964), p. 6.

NOTES: CHAPTER 2 The Library in Its Environment

1. Ralph P. Davidson, "Letter From the Publisher; Time, Inc. Library," *Time* 103 (8 April 1974): 2.

2. "Collecting Resources for Historic Preservation," Supplement to *Preservation News*

27 (March 1977) [4p.]. This article refers to 6,000 books and 30,000 files, but the Trust has since altered its collection.

3. See, for instance: David O. Lane, "The Selection of Academic Library Materials, A Literature Survey," *College and Research Libraries* 29 (September 1968); 364–72; Note also: Fritz Veit, *The Community College Library* (Westport, CT: Greenwood Press, 1975. Contributions in Librarianship and Information Science, No. 14) p. 78.

4. William E. McGrath, "A Pragmatic Book Allocation Formula for Academic and Public Libraries With a Test for Its Effectiveness," *Library Resources and Technical Services* 19 (Fall 1975): 356–369.

5. S. K. Goyal, "Allocation of Library Funds to Different Departments of a University — An Operational Research Approach," *College and Research Libraries* 34 (May 1973): 220.

6. Jasper G. Schad, "Allocating Materials Budgets in Institutions of Higher Education," *Journal of Academic Librarianship* 3 (January 1978): 328–332.

7. See: Veit, *The Community College Library,* p. 4.

8. Ira J. Peskind, "The Junior College Library," *Library Trends* 23 (January 1975): 386.

9. "Statement on Quantitative Standards for Two-Year Learning Resource Programs," *College & Research Libraries News* 40 (March 1979): 71. (Endorsed by the ACRL Board of Directors, June 1979).

10. Doris Cruger Dale, "The Community College Library in the Mid-1970s," *College and Research Libraries* 38 (September 1977): 405.

11. Association of College and Research Libraries, "Standards for College Libraries," *College and Research Libraries News* 36 (October 1975): 279.

12. See the periodical, *Learning Today* (formerly *Library-College Journal*), 1968–

13. William Miller and D. Stephen Rockwood, "Collection Development From a College Perspective," *College and Research Libraries* 40 (July 1979): 319.

14. J. Periam Danton, *Book Selection and Collections: A Comparison of German and American University Libraries* (New York: Columbia University Press, 1963), 188 p.

15. Wilmer H. Baatz, "Collection Development in 19 Libraries of the Association of Research Libraries," *Library Acquisitions: Practice and Theory* 2 (No. 2, 1978): 85–121.

16. Albert Perdue, "Conflicts in Collection Development," *Library Acquisitions: Practice and Theory* 2 (No. 2, 1978): 123; John N. DePew, "An Acquisitions Decision Model for Academic Libraries," *Journal of the American Society for Information Science* 26 (July–August 1975): 237–246.

17. Robert B. Downs, "Doctoral Degrees and Library Resources," *College and Research Libraries* 30 (September 1969): 418.

18. Association of College and Research Libraries, "Standards for University Libraries," *College and Research Libraries News* 40 (April 1979): 102, 107.

19. Allen Kent, *et al., Use of Library Materials: The University of Pittsburgh Study* (New York: Marcel Dekker, Inc., 1979), p. 12–13.

20. Norman Higham, "The State of the Argument: United Kingdom," in Colin Steele, ed., *Steady-State, Zero Growth and the Academic Library* (London: Clive Bingley, 1978), p. 39.

21. See Michael K. Buckland and Anthony Hindle, "Acquisitions, Growth and Performance Control Through Systems Analysis," in Daniel Gore, ed., *Farewell to Alexandria: Solutions to Space, Growth, and Performance Problems of Libraries* (Westport, CT: Greenwood Press, 1976), p. 44–61.

22. B. J. Enright, "Bibliochlothansia: Library Hygiene and the Librarian," in Keith

Barr and Maurice Line, eds., *Essays on Information and Libraries* (London: Clive Bingley, 1975), p. 61–78.

23. David A. Kronick, "Preventing Library Wastelands: A Personal Statement," *Library Journal* 107 (15 February 1980): 485.

24. Charles B. Osburn, *Academic Research and Library Resources: Changing Patterns in America* (Westport, CT: Greenwood Press, 1979), p. 142.

25. See, for instance, an excellent review which covers a large segment of them: Rose Mary Magrill and Mona East, "Collection Development in Large University Libraries," in Michael H. Harris, ed., *Advances in Librarianship,* Vol. 8 (New York: Academic Press, 1978), p. 1–54.

26. Quoted by: Marilyn L. Miller, "Collection Development in School Library Media Centers: National Recommendations and Reality," *Collection Building* 1 (No. 1, 1978): 30.

27. American Association of School Librarians, American Library Association, and Association for Educational Communication and Technology, *Media Programs, District and School* (Chicago and Washington: The Associations, 1975), p. 70.

28. Lowell A. Martin, *Students and the Pratt Library: Challenge and Opportunity,* Deiches Fund Studies of Public Library Service No. 1 (Baltimore: Enoch Pratt Free Library, 1963), p. 50.

29. Kay E. Vandergrift, "Selection: Reexamination and Reassessment," *School Media Quarterly* 6 (Winter 1978): 103–111.

30. Ellen Nemhauser, "Book Selection Parties," *Library Journal* 99 (15 February 1974): 551.

31. AASL, ALA, and AECT, *Media Programs,* p. 62.

32. Lillian L. Shapiro, "Quality or Popularity? Selection Criteria for YAs," *School Library Journal* 24 (May 1978): 24.

33. Mark Weber, "Back to Basics: Its Meaning for School Media Programs," *School Library Journal* 24 (October 1977): 83–85.

34. Miller, "Collection Development in School Library Media Centers," 33.

35. Lee Burress, "A Brief Report of the 1977 NCTE Censorship Survey," in James E. Davis, ed., *Dealing with Censorship* (Urbana, IL: National Council of Teachers of English, 1979), p. 16–17.

36. Vandergrift, "Selection: Reexamination and Reassessment," p. 111.

37. See, for instance: R. Kathleen Molz, "The American Public Library: Its Historic Concern for the Humanities," in Robert N. Broadus, ed., *The Role of the Humanities in the Public Library* (Chicago: American Library Association, 1979), p. 30–49.

38. Francis K. W. Drury, *Book Selection* (Chicago: American Library Association, 1930), p. 1.

39. For instance: Marvin Scilken, "Solving Space and Performance Problems in a Public Library," in Gore, ed., *Farewell to Alexandria,* p. 63; Kenneth C. Davis, "The Selling of the Library," *Publishers Weekly* 216 (13 August 1979): 26–28.

40. David W. Davies, *Public Libraries as Culture and Social Centers: The Origin of the Concept* (Metuchen, NJ: Scarecrow Press, 1974), 167 p.

41. Pauline Wilson, *A Community Elite and the Public Library: The Uses of Information in Leadership* (Westport, CT: Greenwood Press, 1977), p. 26.

42. *1979 American Library Directory,* 32nd ed., ed. Jaques Cattell Press (New York: Bowker, 1979), p. 297.

43. Lowell A. Martin, *Library Response to Urban Change: A Study of The Chicago Public Library* (Chicago: American Library Association, 1969), p. 57.

44. American Library Association, Public Library Association, *The Public Library Mission Statement and Its Imperatives for Service* (Chicago: The Association, 1979), 16 p.

45. Ann Bender, "Allocation of Funds in Support of Collection Development in Public Libraries," *Library Resources & Technical Services* 23 (Winter 1979): 45.

NOTES: CHAPTER 3 Fundamental Principles

1. Philip H. Ennis and Floyd N. Fryden, "The Library in the Community: Use Studies Revisited," *Library Quarterly* 30 (October 1960): 253–265.

2. Mollie Shapiro, "What Food and Oxygen is to the Body, Reading Means to Me," *Wilson Library Bulletin* 45 (January 1971): 469.

3. Marie Zielinska and Irena Bell, "Selection and Acquisition of Library Materials in Languages Other than English: Some Guidelines for Public Libraries," *Collection Building* 2 (No. 1, 1980): 11.

4. William F. Newberry, "The Last Unserved," *American Libraries* 11 (April 1980): 218–220.

5. Herbert J. Gans, "The Public Library in Perspective," in Ralph W. Conant, ed., *The Public Library and the City* (Cambridge, MA: MIT Press, 1965), p. 67. (Italics in original.)

6. Francis K. W. Drury, *Book Selection* (Chicago: American Library Association, 1930), p. xi.

7. Ibid., p. 35.

8. Lionel Roy McColvin, *The Theory of Book Selection for Public Libraries* (London: Grafton & Co., 1925), p. 35–36.

9. M. B. Line, "On the Design of Information Systems for Human Beings," *Aslib Proceedings* 22 (July 1970): 333.

10. Quoted by Sir Charles Petrie, "The Unattractive Mr. Stanley" (a review) *Illustrated London News* 263 (January 1975): 67.

11. James R. Squire, Roger K. Applebee, and Robert A. Lucas, "Student Reading and the High School Library," *School Libraries* 16 (Summer 1967): 11–19.

12. F. M. Crunden, "Selection of Books," *Library Journal* 19 (December 1894): 41.

13. Charles A. Cutter, "Should Libraries Buy Only the Best Books or the Best Books That People Will Read?" *Library Journal* 26 (February 1901): 71.

14. Richard Burgin, *Conversations with J. L. Borges* (New York: Holt, Rinehart and Winston, 1969), p. 122–123.

15. Kenneth C. Davis, "The Selling of the Library," *Publishers Weekly* 216 (13 August 1979): 26.

16. Sidney Rosen, "Reader Interest in Science: Children," in Illinois, University, Library School, *Collecting Science Literature for General Reading* (Champaign, IL: Illini Union Bookstore, 1961), p. 44.

17. See his *Books and the Teen-age Reader: A Guide for Teachers, Librarians, and Parents,* rev. and updated (New York: Harper & Row, 1971), 247 p.

18. United Kingdom, Parliament, House of Commons, Select Committee on Public Libraries, *Report . . . ,* together with the Proceedings of the Committee, Minutes of

Evidence, Appendix and Index (London: House of Commons, 1849), sec. 1273–1275, p. 83.

19. Deirdre Boyle, "Personal Cinema Comes to the Library," *American Libraries* 8 (January 1977): 39.

20. Bill Katz, "Statistical Wailing Wall: A Nation Wide Survey," *Library Journal* 93 (1 June 1968): 2208.

21. Ralph A. Ulveling, "The Public Library — An Educational Institution?" *Library Resources and Technical Services* 3 (Winter 1959): 15.

22. Jesse H. Shera, "The Public Library in Perspective," in Ralph W. Conant and Kathleen Molz, eds., *The Metropolitan Library* (Cambridge, MA: MIT Press, 1972), p. 108.

23. Edward C. Banfield, "Some Alternatives for the Public Library," Ibid., p. 95.

24. Rinaldo Lunati, *Book Selection: Principles and Procedures,* trans. Luciana Marulli (Metuchen, NJ: Scarecrow Press, 1975), p. 140.

25. American Library Association, Public Library Association, *Minimum Standards for Public Library Systems, 1966* (Chicago: The Association, 1967), p. 9.

26. See Alice Payne Hackett and James Henry Burke, *80 Years of Best Sellers, 1895–1975* (New York: Bowker, 1977), 265 p.

27. Salvador de Madariaga, *Spain: a Modern History* (New York: Praeger Publishers, 1958), p. 76.

28. Eric Moon, "The View From the Front," *Library Journal* 89 (1 February 1964): 574.

29. Jerome Cushman, "The Adult Book Collection," in Illinois, University, Library School, *The Nature and Development of the Library Collection* (Champaign, IL: Illini Union Bookstore, 1957), p. 19.

30. Charles Frankel, "A Humanistic Scholar Looks at the Public Library," in Robert N. Broadus, ed., *The Role of the Humanities in the Public Library* (Chicago: American Library Association, 1979), p. 104.

31. Edgar H. Schein, *Professional Education: Some New Directions* (New York: McGraw-Hill, 1972), p. 9.

32. Frankel, "A Humanistic Scholar . . . ," p. 104.

33. T. Saracevic, W. M. Shaw Jr., and P. B. Kantor, "Causes and Dynamics of User Frustration in an Academic Library," *College and Research Libraries* 38 (January 1977): 7–18.

34. Rita Hoyt Smith and Warner Granade, "User and Library Failures in an Undergraduate Library," *College and Research Libraries* 39 (November 1978): 467–473.

35. John A. Urquhart and J. L. Schofield, "Measuring Readers' Failure at the Shelf," *Journal of Documentation* 27 (December 1971): 274.

36. For instance: John C. Swan, "Librarianship Is Censorship," *Library Journal* 104 (1 October 1979): 2040–2043.

NOTES: CHAPTER 4 Objective Evidence on Use

1. Maurita Peterson Holland, "Serial Cuts vs. Public Service: A Formula," *College and Research Libraries* 37 (November 1976): 543–548.

2. William E. McGrath and Norma Durand, "Classifying Courses in the University Catalog," *College and Research Libraries* 30 (November 1969): 533–539.

3. William E. McGrath, "The Significance of Books Used According to a Classified Profile of Academic Departments," *College and Research Libraries* 33 (May 1972): 212–219.

4. J. L. Schofield, A. Cooper, and D. H. Waters, "Evaluation of an Academic Library's Stock Effectiveness," *Journal of Librarianship* 7 (July 1975): 207–227.

5. Michael K. Buckland, "An Operations Research Study of a Variable Loan and Duplication Policy at the University of Lancaster," *Library Quarterly* 42 (January 1972): 97–106.

6. T. Saracevic, W. M. Shaw Jr., and P. B. Kantor, "Causes and Dynamics of User Frustration in an Academic Library," *College and Research Libraries* 38 (January 1977): 7–18.

7. Paul Metz, "The Use of the General Collection in the Library of Congress," *Library Quarterly* 49 (October 1979): 415–434.

8. Derek J. deSolla Price, "Networks of Scientific Papers," *Science* 149 (30 July 1965): 512.

9. Julie A. Virgo, "A Statistical Procedure for Evaluating the Importance of Scientific Papers," *Library Quarterly* 47 (October 1977): 415–430.

10. Stephen D. Gottfredson, W. D. Garvey, and J. Goodnow II, *Quality Indicators in the Scientific Journal Article Publication Process* (Baltimore: Center for Research in Scientific Communication, Department of Psychology, Johns Hopkins University, 1977), 114 leaves.

11. Murray J. White and K. Geoffrey White, "Citation Analysis of Psychology Journals," *American Psychologist* 32 (May 1977): 301–305.

12. A. E. Cawkell, "Evaluating Scientific Journals with *Journal Citation Reports* — A Case Study in Acoustics," *American Society for Information Science Journal* 29 (January 1978): 41–46.

13. See James C. Baughman, "Some of the Best in Sociology: A Bibliographic Checklist Created by the Unusual Technique of Citation Counting," *Library Journal* 98 (15 October 1973): 2977–2979.

14. Maurice B. Line and Alexander Sandison, "Practical Interpretation of Citation and Library Use Studies," *College and Research Libraries* 36 (September 1975): 393–396.

15. Robert N. Broadus, "The Applications of Citation Analyses to Library Collection Building," in Melvin J. Voigt and Michael H. Harris, eds., *Advances in Librarianship,* Vol. 7 (New York: Academic Press, Inc., 1977), p. 302–307.

16. Ibid., p. 322–328.

17. James C. Baughman, "A Structural Analysis of the Literature of Sociology," *Library Quarterly* 44 (October 1974): 293–308.

18. But for fair warning, see Maurice B. Line and Alexander Sandison, " 'Obsolescence' and Changes in the Use of Literature With Time," *Journal of Documentation* 30 (September 1974): 283–350.

19. William Miller, *Collection Development in the Literature of the Humanities: Can Citation Analysis Provide a Rational Guide?* (Beaverton, OR: Blackwell North American, Inc., 1976), unpaged, nearprint.

20. Harry M. Kriz, "Subscriptions vs. Books in a Constant Dollar Budget," *College and Research Libraries* 39 (March 1978): 105–109.

21. Robert N. Broadus, "Use Studies of Library Collections," *Library Resources and Technical Services* 24 (Fall 1980): 317–324.

22. David A. Kronick, "Preventing Library Wastelands: A Personal Statement" *Library Journal* 107 (15 February 1980): 483–487.

NOTES: CHAPTER 5 Book Publishers and Publishing

1. John P. Dessauer, *Book Publishing, What It Is and What It Does* (New York: Bowker, 1974), p. 17.

2. Herbert S. Bailey Jr., *The Art and Science of Book Publishing* (New York: Harper & Row, 1970), p. 4.

3. John O. Stevens, "How I Succeeded as a Small Publisher by Breaking All the Usual Rules," *Publishers Weekly* 210 (18 October 1976): 32–34.

4. John Farrar, "Securing and Selecting the Manuscript," in Chandler B. Grannis, ed., *What Happens in Book Publishing,* 2nd ed. (New York: Columbia University Press, 1967), p. 32.

5. Herbert S. Bailey Jr., "The Decision to Publish: Economic Factors," in Weldon A. Kefauver, ed., *Scholars and their Publishers* (New York: Modern Language Association of America, 1977), p. 23.

6. Nancy Evans, "Line Editors, The Rigorous Pursuit of Perfection," *Publishers Weekly* 216 (18 October 1979): 24

7. Curtis G. Benjamin, *A Candid Critique of Book Publishing* (New York: Bowker, 1977), p. 48. Another hypothetical analysis is given by Benjamin M. Compaine, *The Book Industry in Transition, An Economic Study of Book Distribution and Marketing* (White Plains, NY: Knowledge Industry Publications, Inc., 1978), p. 16.

8. Cass Canfield, "Reflections on Reaching the Age of 150," *Harper's Magazine* 234 (June 1967): 18, 21.

9. Bennett Cerf, *At Random* (New York: Random House, 1977), p. 40, 41.

10. Bennett Cerf, [essay] in Gerald Gross, ed., *Publishers on Publishing* (New York: Bowker, 1961), p. 473.

11. Paul D. Doebler, "The Statistics of Concentration," *Publishers Weekly* 214 (31 July 1978): 30.

12. John Fischer, "Myths about Publishing," *Harper's Magazine* 227 (July 1963): 14, 16.

13. Jason Epstein, "A Criticism of Commercial Publishing," *Daedalus* 92 (Winter 1963): 63.

14. Maurice Temple Smith, "The General Publisher," in Raymond Astbury, ed., *Libraries and the Book Trade in Britain* (Hamden, CT: Archon Books, 1968), p. 45.

15. Elliott Shore, "The Alternate Press and Libraries," *Collection Building* 1 (No. 3, 1979): 10.

16. Lewis A. Coser, "Publishers as Gatekeepers of Ideas," *Annals of The American Academy of Political and Social Science,* Vol. 421 (September 1975): 14–22.

17. Jesse H. Shera, *The Foundations of Education for Librarianship* (New York: Becker and Hayes, Inc., 1972), p. 108.

18. Virginia H. Mathews and Dan Lacy, *Response to Change: American Libraries in the*

Seventies. Indiana Library Studies, Report Number One. (Bloomington, IN: 1970), p. 18.

19. By Barbara C. Campbell, *School Library Journal* 25 (September 1978): 42–43.

20. John Tebbel, *A History of Book Publishing in the United States*, Vol. II (New York: Bowker, 1975), p. 23.

21. Margaret L. Weeks, "Their Books Rejected by Others, Scholars Turn to 'Subsidy' Presses," *Chronicle of Higher Education* 13 (14 February 1977): 3.

22. Edward Uhlan, *The Rogue of Publishers Row, Confessions of a Publisher* (New York: Exposition Press, 1956), p. 16.

23. Irving Louis Horowitz, "The Tripartite World of the University Press," *Chronicle of Higher Education* 19 (7 January 1980): 80.

24. Daniel Melcher, "When is a Book Really O/P?" *Library Journal* 91 (1 October 1966): 4577.

NOTES: CHAPTER 6 How to Judge a Book

1. Brian Alley and Jennifer S. Cargill, "Inventory and Selection Techniques for Large Unorganized Collections." *Library Acquisitions: Practice and Theory* 2 (No. 1, 1978): 23–28.

2. Julian Critchley, "Now Read on . . . ," *Illustrated London News* 263 (August 1975): 69.

3. Samuel Eliot Morison, *By Land and By Sea* (New York: Knopf, 1953), p. 291.

4. Charles Scribner Jr., "Confessions of a Book Publisher." *Publishers Weekly* 211 (6 June 1977): 48.

5. Kathryn Crane, "Questions on New Editions," *RQ* 9 (Spring 1970): 227–231.

6. Scott R. Bullard, "When is a New Edition Not a New Edition?" *Library Acquisitions: Practice and Theory* 3 (No. 2, 1979): 63–64.

7. G. R. Price, "Science and the Supernatural," *Science* 122 (26 August 1955): 359–367.

8. R. A. McConnell, "ESP and Credibility in Science," *American Psychologist* 24 (May 1969): 532.

9. Ibid., 535.

10. Denys Hay, "The Historical Periodical: Some Problems," *History* 54 (June 1969): 167.

11. "Introduction," p. x–xi.

12. Daniel J. Boorstin, "Twenty-five Issues Programmed for Retrieval," *Saturday Review* 52 (9 August 1969): 35.

13. Manfred Kochen and Renata Tagliacozzo, "Book-Indexes as Building Blocks for a Cumulative Index," *American Documentation* 18 (April 1967): 59.

14. S. R. Ranganathan, assisted by M. A. Gopinath, *Library Book Selection*, 2nd ed. (Bombay: *Asia Publishing House*, 1966), p. 100.

15. George Selement, "Perry Miller: A Note on his Sources in *The New England Mind: The Seventeenth Century*," *William and Mary Quarterly*, 3rd Series, 31 (July 1974): 453–464.

16. Mary W. George, review of Louis Shores, *The Generic Book*, in *College and Research Libraries* 39 (January 1978): 68.

17. James R. Squire, Roger K. Applebee, and Robert A. Lucas, "Student Reading and the High School Library," *School Libraries* 16 (Summer 1967): 17.

18. R. Hunter Middleton, "Exhibition Review," *Journal of Typographic Research* 1 (July 1967): 329.

19. Quoted in: John Lewis, *Typography: Design and Practice* (New York: Taplinger Publishing Co., 1978), p. 48.

20. (Cambridge: At the University Press, 1951), p. 5.

21. Quoted in: Middleton, "Exhibition Review," 328.

22. James B. Meriwether, "Notes on the Textual History of *The Sound and the Fury*," *The Papers of the Bibliographical Society of America* 56 (Third Quarter 1962): 295.

23. James Shand, "Author and Printer: G.B.S. and R. & R.C.: 1898–1948," *Alphabet and Image* 8 (Winter 1948): 14.

24. Ranganathan, *Library Book Selection*, p. 80.

25. Curtis G. Benjamin, *A Candid Critique of Book Publishing* (New York: Bowker, 1977), p. 86.

26. Kenneth C. Davis, "The Cinderella Story of Paperback Originals," *Publishers Weekly* 217 (11 January 1980): 43.

27. Benjamin, *A Candid Critique of Book Publishing*, p. 86–87.

28. Paul Little, "The Effectiveness of Paperbacks," *Library Journal* 104 (15 November 1979): 2411–2416.

NOTES: CHAPTER 7 General Aids and Guides

1. Frank E. Howard, "A Survey of the Circulation of Books in Nine of the Subjects included in the Shaw *List*, 1931–38" (Master's Thesis, Kent State University, 1954), 111 p.

2. Eleanor H. Broadus, "A Study of the Relationship Between Book Reviews and the Circulation of Books in a University Library" (Master's paper, Northern Illinois University, 1966), 34 p.

3. Herbert Goldhor, "Are the Best Books the Most Read?" *Library Quarterly* 29 (October 1959): 251–55.

4. Jesse Shera, "Without Reserve, Standard Lists—An Unstandardized View," *Wilson Library Bulletin* 41 (February 1967): 615.

5. Ibid.

6. Rinaldo Lunati, *Book Selection: Principles and Procedures,* trans. Luciana Marulli (Metuchen, NJ: Scarcrow Press, 1975), p. 124.

7. Lewis Chester, Godfrey Hodgson, and Bruce Page, *An American Melodrama: The Presidential Campaign of 1968* (New York: Viking Press, 1969), p. 169.

8. David E. Pownall, *A Critique of "Books for College Libraries,"* 2nd ed. (Boulder, CO: Journal of Academic Librarianship, 1977), p. 36.

NOTES: CHAPTER 8 Book Reviews

1. American Library Association, Resources and Technical Services Division and Association of American Publishers/RTSD Joint Committee, *Numerical Results From Three Surveys on Book Marketing and Selection* (Chicago: American Library Association, 1975), p. [21].

2. Peter Berger, *Invitation to Sociology: A Humanistic Perspective* (Garden City, NY: Doubleday and Co., 1963), p. 11.

3. Karl E. Meyer, "Television, The Gulag of Reviewing," *Saturday Review* 5 (14 October 1978): 56.

4. Norman Podhoretz, *Making It* (New York: Random House, 1967), p. 160.

5. Richard Kluger, "What I Did to Books and Vice Versa," *Harper's Magazine* 233 (December 1966): 70–71.

6. Bill Moyers, "An American Editor's Odyssey," *Saturday Review* 50 (11 November 1967): 30.

7. American Library Association and Association of American Publishers, *Numerical Results,* p. [5].

8. Benjamin M. Compaine, *The Book Industry in Transition, An Economic Study of Book Distribution and Marketing* (White Plains, NY: Knowledge Industry Publications, Inc., 1978), p. 43.

9. Reported by Richard Ohmann, "The Social Definition of Literature," in Paul Hernadi, ed., *What is Literature?* (Bloomington: Indiana University Press, 1978), p. 94.

10. Louis Bromfield, "A Critique of Criticism," *Mirrors of the Year,* 1928, quoted by Helen Haines in her *Living with Books,* 2nd ed. (New York: Columbia University Press, 1950), p. 102.

11. LeRoy C. Merritt, "The Pattern of Modern Book Reviewing," in LeRoy C. Merritt, Martha Boaz, and Kenneth S. Tisdel, *Reviews in Library Book Selection* (Detroit: Wayne State University Press, 1958), p. 39.

12. Guy A. Marco, "An Appraisal of Favorability in Current Book Reviewing," Mimeographed (Urbana: University of Illinois, Graduate School of Library Science, *Occasional Papers,* No. 57, 1959), p. 20.

13. Elizabeth Hardwick, "The Decline of Book Reviewing," *Harper's Magazine* 219 (October 1959): 138.

14. Dean J. Champion and Michael F. Morris, "A Content Analysis of Book Reviews in the *AJS, ASR,* and *Social Forces,*" *American Journal of Sociology* 78 (March 1973); 1261.

15. "Advertisement to the First Issue," *Political Science Reviewer* 1 (Fall 1971): iii.

16. Richard Mayne, "Ishmael and the Inquisitors," *Times Literary Supplement* (12 November, 1976): 1413.

17. John B. Putnam, "The Scholar and the Future of Scholarly Publishing," *Scholarly Publishing* 4 (April 1973): 209.

18. Rita James Simon and Linda Mahan, "A Note on the Role of Book Review Editor as Decision Maker," *Library Quarterly* 39 (October 1969): 353.

19. See: Dwight MacDonald, "New York Times, Alas," *Esquire* 59 (April 1963): 55–57, and (May 1963): 104.

20. "Neglected Books," *The American Scholar* 39 (Spring 1970): 318–345, and following numbers.

21. S. I. Hayakawa, *Language in Thought and Action,* 2nd ed. (New York: Harcourt, Brace & World, 1964), p. 97–98.

22. Henry Regnery, "Bias in Book Reviewing and Book Selection," *A.L.A. Bulletin* 60 (January 1966): 62.

23. Richard Kostelanetz, *The End of Intelligent Writing: Literary Politics in America* (New York: Sheed and Ward, 1974), p. 39–59.

24. "All for One, One for All," *Time* (29 December 1967): 31.

25. Norval D. Glenn, "On the Misuse of Book Reviews," *Contemporary Sociology* 7 (May 1978): 254–255.

26. Stanley Edgar Hyman, *Standards: A Chronicle of Books for Our Time* (New York: Horizon Press, 1966), p. 280.

27. Described by Lewis Coser, *Men of Ideas, a Sociologist's View* (New York: Free Press, 1965), p. 333.

28. René Wellek, *Concepts of Criticism* (New Haven, CT: Yale University Press, 1963), p. 344.

29. C. S. Lewis, "On Criticism," in his *Of Other Worlds; Essays and Stories,* edited by Walter Hooper (New York: Harcourt, Brace & World, 1966), p. 46.

30. John Updike, *Picked-up Pieces* (New York: A. A. Knopf, 1975), p. 12.

31. Edmund Wilson, *The Shores of Light* (New York: Farrar, Straus and Young, 1952), p. 599.

32. Walter B. Hendrickson, "A Review of Reviews of Douglas Freeman's *Young Washington,*" *Library Quarterly* 21 (July 1951): 173–182.

33. Ed Zern, "Exit Laughing," *Field & Stream* 64 (November 1959): 142.

34. *The Bowker Annual of Library and Booktrade Information* (New York: Bowker, annually) publishes such statistics for several leading review journals.

35. Daniel Ream, "An Evaluation of Four Book Review Journals," *RQ* 19 (Winter 1979): 150.

36. Philip Nobile, "A Review of the New York Review of Books," *Esquire* 77 (April 1972): 103.

37. Ibid., p. 209.

38. Victoria E. Hargrave, "A Comparison of Reviews of Books in the Social Sciences in General and in Scholarly Periodicals," *Library Quarterly* 18 (July 1948): 216–217.

NOTES: CHAPTER 9 Free and Inexpensive Materials

1. Charles A. Cutter, "Common Sense in Libraries," *Library Journal* 14 (May–June 1889): 151, reprinted in Francis L. Miksa, ed., *Charles Ammi Cutter, Library Systematizer* (Littleton, CO: Libraries Unlimited, 1977), p. 103.

2. See: Lester Condit, *A Pamphlet About Pamphlets* (Chicago: University of Chicago Press, 1939), p. 1–8.

3. Ibid., p. 19.

4. (Cambridge, MA: Harvard University Press, 1930), p. 7.

5. (New York: Viking Press, 1953), p. 69–70.

6. "PAIS Selection Policy," *Public Affairs Information Service Bulletin* 63 (1977), p. vii.

7. Shirley Miller, *The Vertical File and Its Satellites: A Handbook of Acquisition, Processing and Organization,* 2nd ed. (Littleton, CO: Libraries Unlimited, 1979), p. 15–18.

8. Randolph G. Adams, "Librarians as Enemies of Books," *Library Quarterly* 7 (July 1937): 330.

NOTES: CHAPTER 10 Public Documents

1. Dale Lockard Barker, "Characteristics of the Scientific Literature Cited by Chemists of the Soviet Union" (Ph.D. dissertation, University of Illinois, 1966), p. 90.

2. Quoted by Larry Van Dyne, "The Adventures of I. F. Stone," *Chronicle of Higher Education* 17 (5 February 1979): Supplement, R-6.

3. Bernard M. Fry, *Government Publications: Their Role in the National Program for Library and Information Services* (Washington: National Commission on Libraries and Information Science, 1978), p. 1.

4. Peter Hernon and Sara Lou Williams, "University Faculty and Federal Documents: Use Patterns," *Government Publications Review 3* (No. 2, 1976): 103.

5. Arthur Hailey, *The Moneychangers* (Garden City, NY: Doubleday, 1975), p. 375.

NOTES: CHAPTER 11 Periodicals

1. Theodore Peterson, *Magazines in the Twentieth Century,* 2nd ed. (Urbana: University of Illinois Press, 1964), p. 103.

2. For a list of journals in library science and their refereeing policies, see: Daniel O'Conner and Phyllis Van Orden, "Getting Into Print," *College and Research Libraries* 39 (September 1978): 394.

3. Peterson, *Magazines in the Twentieth Century,* p. 441–442.

4. Frank Luther Mott, *A History of American Magazines,* vol. 2, (Cambridge, MA: Harvard University Press, 1938), p. vii.

5. Ruari McLean, *Magazine Design* (London: Oxford University Press, 1969), p. v. This book, filled with photographs of covers as well as inside pages of magazines, is an interesting study of various formats.

6. "Use of Scientific Journals by Psychologists and the Readership of Current Journal Articles," *Reports of the American Psychological Association's Project on Scientific Information Exchange in Psychology,* Vol. 1 (December 1963), p. 258.

7. Christine M. Oldman and Donald Davinson, *The Usage of Periodicals in Public Libraries* (Leeds, Eng.: Leeds Polytechnic, 1975), 112 p.

8. Peterson, *Magazines in the Twentieth Century,* p. 119.

9. Edmund Wilson, *The Shores of Light* (New York: Farrar, Straus and Young, Inc., 1952), p. 593.

10. Henry Brandon, " 'Everybody is Getting Very Serious,' " *New Republic* 138 (26 May 1958): 16.

11. Clay S. Felker, "Life Cycles in the Age of Magazines," *Antioch Review* 29 (Spring 1969): 7.

12. James Playsted Wood, *Magazines in the United States,* 3rd ed. (New York: Ronald Press Co., 1971), p. 164.

13. Bill Katz, *Magazine Selection: How to Build a Community-Oriented Collection* (New York: Bowker, 1971): p. 42.

14. Andrew D. Osborn, *Serial Publications: Their Place and Treatment in Libraries* 2nd ed., rev. (Chicago: *American Library Association,* 1973), p. 73.

15. Donald Davinson, *The Periodicals Collection* rev. and enl. ed. (London: Andre Deutsch, 1978), p. 1973.

16. Katz, *Magazine Selection,* p. 65, 73–79.

17. Robert N. Broadus, "The Application of Citation Analyses to Library Collection Building," *Advances in Librarianship,* vol. 7 (New York: Academic Press, 1977), p. 302–308.

18. See, for example, O'Conner and Van Orden, "Getting Into Print," p. 390–392.

19. D. O. Hotaling, "Those Bound Newspapers," Letter to the Editor, *Library Journal* 76 (1 September 1951): 1254, 1256.

NOTES: CHAPTER 12 Reference Works

1. Pauline Wilson, *A Community Elite and the Public Library, The Uses of Information in Leadership* (Westport, CT: Greenwood Press, 1977), p. 147.

2. Allan Nevins, "A New Horizon for Who's Who: A Proposal," *Who's Who in America,* vol. 30 (Chicago: A. N. Marquis Co., 1959), p. 7.

3. Patrick Wilson, *Public Knowledge, Private Ignorance; Toward a Library and Information Policy* (Westport, CT: Greenwood Press, 1977), p. 105.

4. Raymond L. Kilgour, "Reference and Subscription Book Publishing," *Library Trends* 7 (July 1958): 140–141.

5. "How Columbia Produced Its New Gazetteer of the World," *Publishers' Weekly* 161 (1 March 1952): 1066.

6. "The Art of Making a Gazetteer," *Library Journal* 77 (1 May 1952): 756–57.

7. Nicolas Slonimsky, (preface to) *Baker's Biographical Dictionary of Musicians,* 5th ed. (New York: G. Schirmer 1958), p. vii. The sixth edition (1978) has a few other interesting cases.

8. Peter Sutcliffe, *The Oxford University Press, An Informal History* (Oxford: At the Clarendon Press, 1978), p. 222.

9. John F. Baker, "A New Britannica is Born," *Publishers Weekly* 205 (14 January 1974): 64.

10. Edward Tripp, "The Man Behind the Book, The Reference Editor," *RQ* 4 (November 1964): 8.

11. Clement E. Vose, "Reference Materials and Books," *International Encyclopedia of*

the Social Sciences (Macmillan and Free Press, 1968), vol. 7, p. 318. Unfortunately, the writer does not give specific examples.

12. Discussed in terms of the late 1960s by Alma A. Covey, *Reviewing of Reference Books* (Metuchen, NJ: Scarecrow Press, 1972), 142 p. See also: Ken Kister, "Wanted: More Professionalism in Reference Book Reviewing," *RQ* 19 (Winter 1979): 144–148.

NOTES: CHAPTER 13 Out-of-Print Materials

1. Felix Reichmann, "Purchase of Out-of-Print Material in American University Libraries," *Library Trends* 18 (January 1970): 329.

2. Ibid.

3. William L. Williamson, *William Frederick Poole and the Modern Library Movement* (New York: Columbia University Press, 1963), p. 124.

4. Lawrence Clark Powell, *A Passion for Books* (Cleveland: World Publishing Co., 1958), p. 25–26. Read the rest for more adventures.

5. C. Edward Wall, "Budget Stretching: Remainder Books for Libraries," *American Libraries* 9 (June 1978): 367–370.

NOTES: CHAPTER 14 Nonprint—Nature and Use

1. Susan Sontag, *On Photography* (New York: Farrar, Straus and Giroux, 1977), p. 24.

2. Charles Morris, *Signs, Language and Behavior* (New York: Prentice-Hall, 1946), p. 190–201.

3. Marshall McLuhan, *Understanding Media; The Extensions of Man* (New York: Mc-Graw-Hill, 1964), p. 12.

4. Ben Bagdikian, "Is Print Dying?" in Robert Disch, ed. *The Future of Literacy* (Englewood Cliffs, NJ: Prentice-Hall, 1973), p. 164.

5. Ron Powers, "The Medium and Three Messages: Perception of a Televised Debate," *Library Quarterly* 45 (January 1975): 27–33 (Italics in original).

6. Lester Asheim, "Introduction," *Library Quarterly* 45 (January 1975): 3.

7. John I. Goodlad, "Education and Technology," in Sidney G. Tickton, ed., *To Improve Learning; an Evaluation of Instructional Technology*, Vol. 2 (New York: Bowker, 1971), p. 89.

8. David Riesman in collaboration with Reuel Denney and Nathan Glazer, *The Lonely Crowd, A Study of the Changing American Character* (New Haven, CT: Yale University Press, 1950), p. 340n.

9. Estelle Jussim, "The Research Uses of Visual Information," *Library Trends* 25 (April 1977): 765.

10. James W. Brown, "New Media in Public Libraries," *Wilson Library Bulletin* 51 (November 1976): 232.

11. Sterling M. McMurrin, "Technology and Education," in Tickton, ed., *To Improve Learning,* vol. 2, p. 7–8.

12. American Library Association, Public Library Association, Audiovisual Committee, *Recommendations for Audiovisual Materials and Services for Small and Medium-sized Public Libraries* (Chicago: American Library Association, 1975), p. 14.

13. _____, *Guidelines for Audiovisual Materials & Services for Large Public Libraries* (Chicago: American Library Association, 1975), p. 15.

NOTES: CHAPTER 15 Nonprint—Principles and Guides

1. Sara I. Fenwick, "Summary," *Library Quarterly* 45 (January 1975): 71.

2. Francis M. Dwyer, "The Effect of IQ Level on the Instructional Effectiveness of Black-and-White and Color Illustrations," *AV Communication Review* 24 (Spring 1976): 60.

3. Ibid., 59–60.

4. C. Dan Wright, "Film Collection Evaluation," *Audiovisual Instruction* 23 (November 1978): 46.

5. C. J. Duncan, "A Survey of Audio-Visual Equipment and Methods," in Derick Unwin, ed., *Media and Methods, Instructional Technology in Higher Education* (London: McGraw-Hill, 1969), p. 14–15.

6. George Rehrauer, *The Film User's Handbook, a Basic Manual for Managing Library Film Services* (New York: Bowker, 1975), p. 124.

7. Richard E. Clark, "Five Promising Directions for Media Research," in James W. Brown, ed., *Educational Media Yearbook, 1978* (New York: Bowker, 1978), p. 101.

NOTES: CHAPTER 16 Nonprint—Selection

1. Melvil Dewey, "Our Next Half-Century," *Library Journal* 51 (15 October 1926): 889.

2. James L. Limbacher, "Feature Films in Public Libraries," *Previews* 4 (September 1975): 5.

3. _____, *Feature Films on 8mm, 16mm, and Videotape,* 6th ed. (New York: Bowker, 1979), p. vii.

4. William Sloan, "Broadening the Access to Information," *Film Library Quarterly* 11 (Nos. 1 & 2, 1978): 3.

5. Goldstein, Seth. *Video in Libraries, A Status Report, 1977–78.* (White Plains, N Y : Knowledge Industry Publications, 1977), 104 p.

1. James Clifford, " 'Hanging Up Looking Glasses at Odd Corners:' Ethnobiographical Prospects," in Daniel Aaron, ed., *Studies in Biography* (Cambridge, MA: Harvard University Press, 1978), p. 43.

2. R.W.B. Lewis, "Washington Irving and Friends," *New York Times Book Review,* 30 December 1979, p. 9.

3. Gaston Bonheur, "Napoleon," *Paris-Match* No. 1029 (25 January 1969): 42.

4. *The Rambler,* No. 60 (13 October 1750), in *The Works of Samuel Johnson,* Connoisseurs' Edition (Troy, N Y : Pafraets Book Co., 1903), vol. 2, p. 32–33.

5. Richard D. Altick, *Lives and Letters, A History of Literary Biography in Europe and America* (New York: Knopf, 1965), p. xiii.

6. "Authorized Biography and Its Discontents," in Aaron, ed., *Studies in Biography,* p. 22.

7. André Maurois, "The Ethics of Biography," *English Institute Annual* 1942, Reprinted in James L. Clifford, ed., *Biography As An Art, Selected Criticism 1560–1960* (New York: Oxford University Press, 1962), p. 168.

8. Catherine Drinker Bowen, *The Writing of Biography* (Boston: The Writer, 1950), p. 18–19.

9. Bernard DeVoto, "The Skeptical Biographer," *Harper's Magazine* 166 (January 1933): 184.

10. Virginia Woolf, "The New Biography," in her *Granite and Rainbow; Essays* (London: Hogarth Press, 1958), p. 149.

11. John A. Garraty, *The Nature of Biography* (New York: Knopf, 1957), p. ix.

12. Altick, *Lives and Letters,* p. 337.

13. DeVoto, "The Skeptical Biographer," 185.

14. Sigmund Freud and William C. Bullitt, *Thomas Woodrow Wilson, Twenty-eighth President of the United States; A Psychological Study* (Boston: Houghton Mifflin, 1966), 307 p.

15. Arthur S. Link, "The Case for Woodrow Wilson," *Harper's Magazine* 234 (April 1967): 86.

16. Robert Gittings, *The Nature of Biography* (Seattle: University of Washington Press, 1978), p. 38.

17. Michael Holroyd, *Lytton Strachey; A Critical Biography* (New York: Holt, Rinehart and Winston, 1967), 2 vols.

18. Kenneth S. Lynn, "History's Reckless Psychologizing," *Chronicle of Higher Education* 15 (16 January 1978): 48.

19. Lewis Mumford, "The Task of Modern Biography," *English Journal* 23 (January 1934): 5.

20. Thomas Carlyle, *The Life of John Sterling* (New York: Scribner, 1897), p. 267. Originally published in 1851.

21. Geoffrey Wolff, "Minor Lives," in Marc Pachter, ed., *Telling Lives: The Biographer's Art* (Washington: New Republic Books, 1979), p. 59. (Original in italics.)

22. Altick, *Lives and Letters,* p. ix.

23. Maurice G. Baxter, Robert H. Ferrell, and John E. Wiltz, *The Teaching of American History in High Schools* (Bloomington: Indiana University Press, 1964), p. 93.

24. Arthur M. Schlesinger Jr., "On the Writing of Contemporary History," *Atlantic Monthly* 219 (March 1967): 69–74.

25. Gittings, *The Nature of Biography,* p. 59.

26. William H. Herndon and Jesse W. Weik, *Herndon's Lincoln* . . . (Springfield, IL: The Herndon's Lincoln Publishing Co., [1888]), vol. 3, p. 437n.

27. Stanley Walker, *Dewey: An American of this Century* (New York: McGraw-Hill, 1944), p. 1, 3.

28. James Keogh, *This Is Nixon* (New York: G. P. Putnam's Sons, 1956), p. 190.

29. Leon Edel, "Biography: A Manifesto," *Biography* 1 (Winter 1978): 1.

30. Catherine Drinker Bowen, *Biography: The Craft and the Calling* (Boston: Little, Brown, 1969), p. 43.

31. David Donald, "General in Gray," *New York Times Book Review* (28 November 1965): 60.

32. Amy Lowell, *John Keats* (Boston: Houghton Mifflin, 1925), vol. 1, p. 3–4.

33. Frederick A. Pottle, *The Literary Career of James Boswell* . . . (Oxford: Clarendon Press, 1929), p. xix.

34. Barbara W. Tuchman, "Biography as a Prism of History," in Marc Pachter, ed., *Telling Lives, the Biographer's Art,* p. 142.

35. David S. Muzzey, *Thomas Jefferson,* quoted in Garraty, *Nature of Biography,* p. [vii].

36. See: Barbara Conaty, "Biography," *Serials Review* 3 (April–June 1977): 30–31.

NOTES: CHAPTER 18 History

1. José Ortega y Gasset, *The Revolt of the Masses* (New York: W. W. Norton, 1932), p. 63.

2. American Library Association, Public Library Association, *The Public Library Mission Statement and Its Imperatives for Service* (Chicago: American Library Association, 1979), p. 1–2.

3. "General Introduction, A Definition of History," in Peter Gay and Gerald J. Cavanaugh, eds., *Historians at Work,* vol. 1 (New York: Harper & Row, 1972), p. xiii.

4. J. H. Plumb, *The Death of the Past* (Boston: Houghton Mifflin, 1970), p. 134.

5. Henry Steele Commager, *The Study of History* (Columbus, OH: Charles E. Merrill Books, Inc., 1966), p. 4.

6. Ibid., p. vii.

7. See Robert B. Downs, *Books That Changed the World* 2nd ed. (Chicago: American Library Association, 1978), p. 258–260.

8. Quoted in John Kirtland Wright, *Human Nature in Geography* (Cambridge, MA: Harvard University Press, 1966), p. 196.

9. Centenary Edition (New York: Scribner, 1897–98), Lecture I, p. 13.

10. Fernand Braudel, *The Mediterranean and the Mediterranean World in the Age of Philip II,* trans. from the French by Siân Reynolds (New York: Harper & Row, 1973), vol. 2, p. 1,237.

11. Hayden White, "The Discourse of History," *Humanities in Society* 2 (Winter 1979): 2 (White is the Professor of "History of Consciousness.")

12. Lawrence Stone, "History and the Social Sciences in the Twentieth Century," in Charles F. Delzell, ed., *The Future of History* (Nashville: Vanderbilt University Press, 1977), p. 11.

13. Daniel J. Boorstin, "Twenty-five Issues Programmed for Retrieval," *Saturday Review* 52 (9 August 1969): 27.

14. John Higman, with Leonard Krieger and Felix Gilbert, *History*, Humanistic Scholarship in America, The Princeton Studies (Englewood Cliffs, NJ: Prentice-Hall, 1965), p. 147.

15. See J. H. Hexter, "Historiography: The Rhetoric of History," *International Encyclopedia of the Social Sciences*, (New York: Macmillan and Free Press, 1968) Vol. 6, p. 369.

16. Sheldon Vanauken, "Froude: A Collision of Principles," in Albert Prior Fell, ed., *Histories and Historians: A Selection of Articles from* History Today . . . (Edinburgh: Oliver & Boyd, 1968), p. 102–103.

17. Samuel Eliot Morison, *By Land and By Sea* (New York: Knopf, 1953), p. 292.

18. George M. Trevelyan, *Clio, a Muse; and Other Essays Literary and Pedestrian* (London: Longmans Green, 1913), p. 14.

19. Louis Gottschalk, "The Evaluation of Historical Writings," in Louis R. Wilson, ed., *The Practice of Book Selection* (Chicago: University of Chicago Press, 1940), p. 110.

20. Noted by Kieran Egan, "Progress in Historiography," *Clio* 8 (Winter 1979): 217.

21. Plumb, *The Death of the Past*, p. 133.

22. Denys Hay, "The Historical Periodical: Some Problems," *History* 54 (June 1969): 167.

23. Maurice G. Baxter, Robert H. Ferrell, and John E. Wiltz, *The Teaching of American History in High Schools* (Bloomington: Indiana University Press, 1964), p. 91–92.

NOTES: CHAPTER 19 Geography, Maps, Travel

1. Kenneth E. Boulding, *The Impact of the Social Sciences* (New Brunswick, N J : Rutgers University Press, 1966), p. 108.

2. Jan O. M. Broek, *Geography: Its Scope and Spirit* (Columbus, OH: Charles E. Merrill Books, Inc., 1965), p. 13.

3. Translated by G. H. Smith (New York: D. Appleton, 1892), vol. 1, p. 149.

4. John Kirtland Wright, *Human Nature in Geography* (Cambridge, MA: Harvard University Press, 1966), p. 165.

5. Edward F. Bergman, "The Geography of the New York Business Lunch," *Geographical Review* 69 (April 1979): 235–238.

6. Preston E. James, "Continuity and Change in American Geographic Thought," in Saul B. Cohen, ed., *Problems and Trends in American Geography* (New York: Basic Books, 1967), p. 3.

7. T. W. Freeman, *The Geographer's Craft* (Manchester, England: At the University Press, 1967), p. 4.

8. Alan Sillitoe, "Maps, and the Geography of Consciousness," *Antaeus* 21/22 (Spring/Summer 1976): 76.

9. *The New York Times Atlas of the World in Collaboration with the Times of London* (New York: Times Books, 1978), p. 5.

10. For instance: J.E.G. Craig Jr., "Characteristics of Use of Geology Literature," *College and Research Libraries* 30 (May 1969): 230–236.

11. Walter W. Ristow, "Map Librarianship," *Library Journal* 92 (15 October 1967): 3612.

12. Arthur H. Robinson, Joel L. Morrison, and Phillip C. Muehrcke, "Cartography 1950–2000," *Institute of British Geographers Transactions,* new series, vol. 2 (1977): 6.

13. Kenneth E. Boulding, *The Image; Knowledge in Life and Society* (Ann Arbor: University of Michigan Press, 1956), p. 68.

14. Robinson, Morrison, and Muehrcke, "Cartography 1950–2000," p. 10.

15. Walter W. Ristow, "The Emergence of Maps in Libraries," *Special Libraries* 58 (July–August 1967): 403.

16. "At the School of Design (sic.), Computers Map the Demography of Cancer," *Harvard Magazine* 80 (March–April 1978): 81.

17. Mary Larsgaard, *Map Librarianship, An Introduction* (Littleton, CO: Libraries Unlimited, 1978), p. 235–236.

18. H. W. Wind, "The House of Baedeker," *New Yorker* 51 (22 September 1975): 42–44+.

NOTES: CHAPTER 20 Social Sciences—General

1. (New York: Macmillan, 1930–35), vol. 1, p. 3.

2. (Macmillan & Free Press, 1968), vol. 1, p. xxii.

3. Bernard Berelson, "Behavioral Sciences," *International Encyclopedia of the Social Sciences,* vol. 2, p. 41–42.

4. Salomon Bochner, *Eclosion and Synthesis, Perspectives on the History of Knowledge* (New York: W. A. Benjamin, Inc., 1969), p. v–vi.

5. Max Lerner, "Important Books of the Last One Hundred Years — Political Science, Economics, and Sociology," in Louis Round Wilson, ed., *The Practice of Book Selection* (Chicago: Unibersity of Chicago Press, 1940), p. 40.

6. Thomas S. Kuhn, *The Essential Tension, Selected Studies in Scientific Tradition and Change* (Chicago: University of Chicago Press, 1977), p. 229.

7. C. P. Snow, *Recent Thoughts on the Two Cultures,* Bilbeck Foundation Oration 1961, quoted in T. S. Simey, *Social Science and Social Purpose* (London: Constable, 1968), p. 8.

8. Maurice B. Line, "Information Requirements in the Social Sciences: Some Preliminary Considerations," *Journal of Librarianship* 1 (January 1969): 2.

9. See Robert N. Broadus, "The Literature of the Social Sciences: A Survey of Citation Studies," *International Social Sciences Journal* 23 (No. 2, 1971): 236–243; reprinted in C. D. Needham, ed., *Reader in Social Science Documentation* (Englewood, CO: Information Handling Services, 1976), p. 215–220.

10. Peter H. Mann, *Methods of Sociological Inquiry* (New York: Schocken Books, 1968), p. 78.

11. Bernard Berelson and Gary A. Steiner, *Human Behavior, An Inventory of Scientific Findings* (New York: Harcourt, Brace & World, 1964), p. 11n.

12. Arthur M. Doerr, "The Social Sciences — Origins and Trends," in *The World of Ideas, Essays on the Past and Future,* Introduction by George L. Cross (Norman: University of Oklahoma Press, 1968), p. 60.

13. Robert S. Lynd, *Knowledge for What? The Place of Social Science in American Culture* (Princeton, N.J.: At the University Press, 1939), p. 181.

14. T. S. Simey, *Social Science and Social Purpose* (London: Constable, 1968), p. 4.

15. Orlando Patterson, "The Moral Crisis of the Black American," *The Public Interest* No. 32, (Summer 1973): 52–53.

16. James L. McCartney, "On Being Scientific: Changing Styles of Presentation of Sociological Research," *American Sociologist* 5 (February 1970): 30.

17. Karl W. Deutsch, John Platt, and Dieter Senghaas, "Conditions Favoring Major Advances in Social Science," *Science* 171 (5 February 1971): 450–59.

18. R. P. Cuzzort and E. W. King, *Humanity and Modern Social Thought,* 2nd ed. (Hinsdale, IL: Dryden Press, 1976), p. 326.

19. Donald Fleming, "Big Science Under Fire," *Atlantic* 226 (September 1970): 98.

20. Philip W. Semas, "How Influential Is Sociology?" *Chronicle of Higher Education* 15 (19 September 1977): 4.

21. Kenneth E. Boulding, *The Image; Knowledge and Life in Society* (Ann Arbor: University of Michigan Press, 1956), p. 80.

22. Kenneth E. Boulding, *The Impact of the Social Sciences* (New Brunswick, N.J.: Rutgers University Press, 1966), p. 108.

23. Keith Monroe, "The New Gambling King and the Social Scientists," *Harper's Magazine* 224 (January 1962): 35–41.

24. Thomas S. Kuhn, *The Structure of Scientific Revolutions,* 2nd ed., enl. (Chicago: University of Chicago Press, 1970), p. viii.

25. David J. Gray, "American Sociology: Plight and Promise," *American Sociologist* 14 (February 1979): 35.

26. Malcolm G. Scully, " 'Striking Change' Seen in Reshaping Social Sciences," *Chronicle of Higher Education* 16 (15 May 1978): 7.

27. Harry Alpert, "The Growth of Social Research in the United States," in Daniel Lerner, ed., *The Human Meaning of the Social Sciences* (New York: Meridian Books, Inc., 1959), p. 73.

28. Edward A. Shils, quoted in Simey, *Social Science and Social Purpose,* p. 18.

29. James West [pseud.], *Plainville, U.S.A.* (New York: Columbia University Press, 1945), p. xiv.

30. Line, "Information Requirements in the Social Sciences," p. 6.

31. Patrick Wilson, "Limits to the Growth of Knowledge: The Case of the Social and Behavioral Sciences," *Library Quarterly* 50 (January 1980): 11.

32. Robert K. Merton, *On Theoretical Sociology; Five Essays Old and New* (New York: Free Press, 1967), p. 35.

33. Broadus, "The Literature of the Social Sciences," 240.

34. Julia S. Brown and Brian G. Gilmartin, "Sociology Today: Lacunae, Emphases and Surfeits," *American Sociologist* 4 (November 1969): 287.

35. Robert N. Broadus, "A Citation Study for Sociology," *American Sociologist* 2 (Feb-

ruary 1967): 19. Martin Guha, "Literature Use by European Sociologists," *International Library Review* 3 (October 1971): 451.

36. Gloria B. Levitas, "Introduction," to her *Culture and Consciousness, Perspectives in the Social Sciences* (New York: George Braziller, 1967), p. 2.

37. Edward O. Wilson, "The Lyric Poet of Evolution," *Saturday Review,* n.s. 3 (3 April 1976): 27.

38. Irving Louis Horowitz, "An Introduction to *The New Sociology,*" in his *The New Sociology, Essays in Social Science and Social Theory in Honor of C. Wright Mills* (New York: Oxford University Press, 1964), p. 23.

39. David E. Pownall, *A Critique of* Books for College Libraries, 2nd ed. (Boulder, CO: Journal of Academic Librarianship, 1977), p. 31.

NOTES: CHAPTER 21 Social Sciences—Fields

1. William P. McEwen, *The Problems of Social-Scientific Knowledge* (Totowa, NJ: Bedminster Press, 1963), p. 24.

2. Robert K. Merton, *On Theoretical Sociology; Five Essays, Old and New* (New York: Free Press, 1967), p. 2n.

3. Francis E. Merrill, *Society and Culture, An Introduction to Sociology,* 3rd ed. (Englewood Cliffs, NJ: Prentice-Hall, 1965), p. 9.

4. Summarized by Albert Reiss, Jr., "Sociology, The Field," *International Encyclopedia of the Social Sciences* (Macmillan and Free Press, 1968), vol. 15, p. 2–3.

5. Richard Herbert Franke and James D. Kaul, "The Hawthorne Experiments: First Statistical Interpretation," *American Sociological Review* 43 (October 1978): 623–643.

6. Edmund H. Volkart, ed. *Social Behavior and Personality, Contributions of W. I. Thomas to Theory and Social Research* (New York: Social Science Research Council, 1951), p. 20–25.

7. Julius Gould, "In Defence of Sociology," in his *Penguin Survey of the Social Sciences 1965* (Baltimore: Penguin Books, 1965), p. 14.

8. Rochelle Girson, "Mutations in the Body Politic," *Saturday Review* 47 (29 August 1964): 76.

9. Norval D. Glenn, "American Sociologists' Evaluations of Sixty-three Journals," *American Sociologist* 6 (November 1971): 300–301.

10. David C. Marsh, *The Social Sciences: An Outline for the Intending Student* (London: Routledge and Kegan Paul, 1965), p. 125.

11. David Easton, "Political Science," *International Encyclopedia of the Social Sciences,* vol. 12, p. 285. (Original in italics.)

12. I Samuel 8.

13. Easton, "Political Science," p. 282.

14. Donald M. Freeman, "An Assessment of Future Trends," in *Foundation of Political Science; Research Methods, and Scope,* ed. Donald M. Freeman (New York: Free Press, 1977), p. 702.

15. William Keech and James W. Prothro, "American Government," in Marian D.

Irish, ed., *Political Science, Advance of the Discipline* (Englewood Cliffs, NJ: Prentice-Hall, 1968), p. 152.

16. Frank J. Sorauf, *Perspectives on Political Science* (Columbus, OH: Charles E. Merrill Books, Inc., 1966), p. 25.

17. Bernard R. Berelson, Paul F. Lazarsfeld, and William N. McPhee, *Voting: A Study of Opinion Formation in a Presidential Campaign* (Chicago: University of Chicago Press, 1954), p. 314.

18. Robert Q. Kelly, "State of the Art Survey of Legal Reference Sources," *Reference Services Review* 6 (January/March 1978): 13.

19. Harry W. Jones, "Law and Politics," in Malcolm B. Parsons, ed., *Perspectives in the Study of Politics* (Chicago: Rand McNally, 1968), p. 71.

20. Philippians 4:11.

21. Kenneth E. Boulding, *The Impact of the Social Sciences* (New Brunswick, NJ: Rutgers University Press, 1966), p. 38.

22. Harry G. Johnson, *On Economics and Society* (Chicago: University of Chicago Press, 1975), p. 143.

23. Bert F. Hoselitz, ed., *A Reader's Guide to the Social Sciences*, Rev. ed. (New York: Free Press, 1970), p. 239.

24. Joseph H. Greenberg, "Anthropology: The Field," *International Encyclopedia of the Social Sciences*, vol. 1, p. 305.

25. Boulding, *The Impact of the Social Sciences*, p. 108.

26. James Deetz, *Invitation to Archaeology* (Garden City, NY: Natural History Press, 1967), p. 3.

27. Carlton S. Coon, "The Knowledge Explosion and Society," in Francis Sweeney, S. J., ed., *The Knowledge Explosion, Liberation and Limitation* (New York: Farrar, Straus & Giroux, 1966), p. 124.

28. Eliot D. Chapple, "The Science of Humanics: Multidisciplinary Renaissance of General Anthropology," *American Anthropologist* 80 (March 1978): 44.

29. Pertti J. Pelto, *The Study of Anthropology* (Columbus, OH: Charles E. Merrill Books, Inc., 1965), p. 57.

30. Margaret Mead, "More Smoke than Fire," *Film Comment* 7 (Spring 1971): 34.

31. Emilie de Brigard, "The History of Ethnographic Film," in Timothy H. H. Thoresen, ed., *Toward a Science of Man: Essays in the History of Anthropology* (The Hague: Mouton Publishers, 1975), p. 33–34.

32. Larry Van Dyne, "A Titan of Anthropology," *Chronicle of Higher Education* 16 (13 March 1978): 7.

33. Susan Sontag, *Against Interpretation, and Other Essays* (New York: Farrar, Straus & Giroux, 1966), p. 70.

34. R. B. Joynson, "Critical Notice: Contemporary Prospects in Psychology," *British Journal of Psychology* 59 (February 1968): 73–74.

35. Boulding, *The Impact of the Social Sciences*, p. 107.

36. J. Robert Oppenheimer, "Science and the Human Community," in Charles Frankel, ed., *Issues in University Education; Essays by Ten American Scholars* (New York: Harper, 1959), p. 54.

37. Jean Piaget, "What Is Psychology," trans. Constance Kanii, *American Psychologist* 33 (July 1978): 651.

38. For instance, Leonard Krasner, "The Future and the Past in the Behaviorism-Humanism Dialogue," *American Psychologist* 33 (September 1978): 799–804.

39. John Beloff, *Psychological Sciences: A Review of Modern Psychology* (New York: Barnes & Noble, 1973), p. 3.

40. "CP Speaks," *Contemporary Psychology* 12 (October 1967): 488.

41. Ruth Mehrtens Galvin, "Psychology: There Are Other Therapists at Work," *New York Times,* 14 August 1977, Section 4, p. 7.

42. (New York: Library Publishers, 1952), p. 225–243.

43. *Harvard List of Books in Psychology,* Compiled and annotated by the Psychologists in Harvard University, 3rd ed. (Cambridge, MA: Harvard University Press, 1964), p. 11.

44. Michael Moore, "Discrimination or Favoritism? Sex Bias in Book Reviews," *American Psychologist* 33 (October 1978): 936–938.

45. Robert S. Daniel, "Psychology," *Library Trends* 15 (April 1967): 672.

46. Murray J. White and K. Geoffrey White, "Citation Analysis of Psychology Journals," *American Psychologist* 32 (May 1977): 301–305.

47. Attributed to Harold Benjamin (New York: McGraw-Hill, 1939), p. 29.

48. Lawrence A. Cremin, *Public Education* (New York: Basic Books, 1976), p. 43.

49. Frederick R. Smith and C. Benjamin Cox, *Secondary Schools in a Changing Society* (New York: Holt, Rinehart and Winston, 1976), p. 177.

50. G. Stanley Hall and John M. Mansfield, *Hints Toward a Select and Descriptive Bibliography of Education* (Boston: Heath, 1886), p. viii.

51. Christopher Jencks and David Riesman, *The Academic Revolution* (Garden City, N.Y.: Doubleday, 1968), p. 488.

NOTES: CHAPTER 22 Arts and Humanities—General

1. Philip Olson, *The Study of Modern Society: Perspectives From Classic Sociology* (New York: Random House, 1970), p. 167.

2. *National Endowment for the Humanities, Program Announcement* (Washington: The Endowment, 1977), p. 1.

3. "Editors Note" *Humanities in Society* 1 (Winter 1978): n.p.

4. Ronald S. Crane, *The Idea of the Humanities, and Other Essays Critical and Historical* (Chicago: University of Chicago Press, 1967), vol. 1, p. 4.

5. Commission on the Humanities, *Report* (New York: Sponsored by The American Council of Learned Societies, Council of Graduate Schools in the United States, and United Chapters of Phi Beta Kappa, 1964), p. 3.

6. David Daiches, *English Literature,* Humanistic Scholarship in America, The Princeton Studies (Englewood Cliffs, NJ: Prentice-Hall, 1964), p. 153.

7. Northrop Frye, "Speculation and Concern," in Thomas B. Stroup, ed., *The Humanities and the Understanding of Reality* (Lexington: University of Kentucky Press, 1966), p. 33.

8. Commission on the Humanities, *Report,* p. 4–5.

9. Sir Richard Livingstone, "The Essentials of Education," *Atlantic Monthly* 189 (January 1952): 47.

10. Charles Frankel, "A Humanistic Scholar Looks at the Public Library," in Robert

N. Broadus, ed., *The Role of the Humanities in the Public Library* (Chicago: American Library Association, 1979), p. 99.

11. Clyde A. Holbrook, *Religion, A Humanistic Field,* Humanistic Scholarship in America, The Princeton Studies (Englewood Cliffs, NJ: Prentice-Hall, 1963), p. 42.

12. Howard Mumford Jones, *One Great Society: Humane Learning in the United States* (New York: Harcourt, Brace, 1959), p. 99.

13. Jorge Luis Borges, "Epilogue," in his *Dreamtigers,* trans. Mildred Boyer and Harold Morland (New York: E. P. Dutton, 1964), p. 93.

14. Michael Scammell, informal remarks in *The Contemporary Humanities in an International Context: Critical Issues and Prospects* (New York: The Rockefeller Foundation, 1976), p. 32.

15. George Sarton, "Preface to Volume Thirty-eight, a Tribute to Gilbert Murray and a Plea for Greek Studies," *Isis* 38 (November 1947): 3–4.

16. David H. Stevens, *The Changing Humanities, An Appraisal of Old Values and New Uses* (New York: Harper, 1953), p. xii.

17. Herbert Goldhor, "US Public Library Adult Non-Fiction Book Collections in the Humanities," *Collection Management* 3 (Spring 1979): 31–43.

18. Jones, *One Great Society,* p. 102–117.

19. Commission on the Humanities, *Report,* p. 13.

20. Carl H. Kraeling, "The Humanities: Characteristics of the Literature, Problems of Use, and Bibliographic Organization of the Field," in Jesse H. Shera and Margaret E. Egan, eds., *Bibliographic Organization* (Chicago: University of Chicago Press, 1951), p. 111.

21. Karl J. Weintraub, "The Humanistic Scholar and the Library," *Library Quarterly* 50 (January 1980): 25.

22. Derek J. DeSolla Price, "The Scientific Foundations of Science Policy," *Nature* 206, No. 4981 (17 April 1965): 235.

23. Joseph Duffy, "The Social Meaning of the Humanities," *Change* 12 (February-March, 1980): 41–42.

24. O. B. Hardison, Jr., *Toward Freedom & Dignity: The Humanities and The Idea of Humanity* (Baltimore: Johns Hopkins University Press, 1972), p. 156.

NOTES: CHAPTER 23 Religion

1. Clyde A. Holbrook, *Religion, A Humanistic Field,* Humanistic Scholarship in America, The Princeton Studies (Englewood Cliffs, NJ: Prentice-Hall, 1963), p. 27.

2. Elizabeth Lane and Monroe C. Beardsley, "Two Forms of Religion," *Religious Humanism* 3 (Summer 1969): 119.

3. Ward H. Goodenough, "Toward an Anthropologically Useful Definition of Religion," in Allan W. Eister, ed., *Changing Perspectives in the Scientific Study of Religion* (New York: John Wiley & Sons, 1974), p. 165.

4. Anthony F. C. Wallace, *Religion, An Anthropological View* (New York: Random House, 1966), p. 38.

5. *Religion in America, The Gallup Opinion Index, 1977–78* (Report No. 145, 1977): p. 1–4.

6. Douglas S. Marsh, "Religious Book Selection in the Public Library: Principles and Problems," *Catholic Library World* 49 (November 1977): 174–175.

7. Raymond P. Morris, "The Good Book in Religion," *A.L.A. Bulletin* 47 (September 1953): 341.

8. Holbrook, *Religion,* p. 262.

9. Karl Rahner, "The Future of the Religious Book," *The New Review of Books and Religion* 3 (February 1979): 6.

10. William J. Banach, "Intellectual Freedom and the Community," *School Media Quarterly* 1 (Winter 1973): 125.

11. Wallace, *Religion, An Anthropological View,* p. 3.

12. Richard Schlatter, Foreward to: Paul Ramsey, ed., *Religion,* Humanistic Scholarship in America, The Princeton Studies (Englewood Cliffs, NJ: Prentice-Hall, 1965), p. vii.

13. "Balance in Boom-Time," *Library Journal* 85 (1 January 1960): 58.

14. Kenneth E. Boulding, *The Meaning of the 20th Century; the Great Transition* (New York: Harper & Row, 1964), p. 20.

15. Dwight A. Huseman, "Books, Periodicals and the Pastor," *Drexel Library Quarterly* 6 (January 1970): 7, 10.

16. Louis Schneider and S. M. Dornbusch, *Popular Religion; Inspirational Books in America* (Chicago: University of Chicago Press, 1958), 173 p.

17. Holbrook, *Religion,* p. 242–250.

18. Cark Skrade, "Theology and Films," *Journal of the University Film Association* 22 (No. 1, 1970): 16–27.

NOTES: CHAPTER 24 Philosophy

1. W. Jackson Bate, *Samuel Johnson* (New York: Harcourt Brace Jovanovich, 1977), p. 100.

2. See: Merrill Sheils with Frederick V. Boyd, "Philosophy for Kids," *Newsweek* 88 (20 September 1976): 85–86.

3. Karl R. Popper, "How I See Philosophy," in Charles J. Bontempo and S. Jack Odell, eds., *The Owl of Minerva: Philosophers on Philosophy* (New York: McGraw-Hill, 1975), p. 48.

4. W. T. Jones, *The Sciences and the Humanities: Conflict and Reconciliation* (Berkeley: University of California Press, 1965), p. 25.

5. Charles Harvey Arnold, "Philosophy and Religion," *Library Trends* 15 (January 1967): 461.

6. E. M. Adams, *Philosophy and the Modern Mind, A Philosophical Critique of Modern Western Civilization* (Chapel Hill: The University of North Carolina Press, 1975), p. 58.

7. Brand Blandshard, "The Philosophic Enterprise," in Bontempo and Odell, eds., *The Owl of Minerva,* p. 163.

8. Joseph C. Flay, "What Is Philosophy?" *The Personalist* 47 (Spring 1966): 207.

9. Max Eastman, "America's Philosopher," *Saturday Review* 36 (17 January 1953)'; 23.

10. Edward H. O'Neill, *A History of American Biography, 1880–1935* (Philadelphia: University of Pennsylvania Press, 1935), p. 261.

11. John Passmore, "Philosophical Scholarship in the United States," in Roderick M. Chisolm, et al., *Philosophy,* Humanistic Scholarship in America, The Princeton Studies (Englewood Cliffs, NJ: Prentice-Hall, 1964), p. 17.

12. Ibid., p. 13.

13. J. E. Vickery, "Philosophers, Libraries and the BLLD," *BLL Review* 4 (July 1976): 80.

14. David H. Stevens, *The Changing Humanities: An Appraisal of Old Values and New Uses* (New York: Harper, 1953), p. 140.

15. *Scholarly Communication: The Report of the National Enquiry* (Baltimore: Johns Hopkins University Press, 1979), p. 40.

16. Charles Frankel, "A Humanistic Scholar Looks at the Public Library," in Robert N. Broadus, ed., *The Role of the Humanities in the Public Library* (Chicago: American Library Association, 1979), p. 78.

17. Vickery, "Philosophers, Libraries and the BLLD," p. 79, 81.

NOTES: CHAPTER 25 Art

1. Joseph Chiari, *Art and Knowledge* (New York: Gordian Press, 1977), p. 46.

2. National Endowment for the Arts, *Museums USA* (Washington: Government Printing Office, 1974), p. 48.

3. Hans Arp, *Collected French Writings,* ed. Marcel Jean (London: Calder and Boyars, 1974), p. 241. Quoted in Chiari, *Art and Knowledge,* p. 93.

4. See: Johannes Schöbel, *Fine Arms and Armor; Treasures in the Dresden Collection,* trans. M.O.A. Stanton (New York: Putnam's, 1975, 255 p.).

5. Oreste Ferrari, "Reproductions," *The Encyclopedia of World Art* (New York: McGraw-Hill, 1958–1968), Vol. 12, p. 173.

6. Ibid., p. 167.

7. André Malraux, *The Voices of Silence,* trans. Stuart Gilbert (Garden City, NY: Doubleday, 1953), p. 30.

8. Ibid., p. 27.

9. Jon Swan, "The Mystery of the Ghent Altarpiece," *Saturday Review* 5 (4 March 1978): 37.

10. For instance: Alan Stephenson, "Recreating the Original," *Penrose: International Review of the Graphic Arts* 70 (1977–1978): 121–128; Tony Johnson, "Tone Reproduction Objectives in Colour Printing," Ibid., 151–156.

11. Victor Strauss, "A Publisher's Guide to Color Printing — 2," *Publishers Weekly* 194 (2 December 1968): 42.

12. M. H. Bruno, "The Status of Printing in the U.S.A. — 1975," in W. H. Banks, ed., *Advances in Printing Science and Technology* (London: Pentech Press, 1977), p. 23.

13. Wesley C. Simonton, "Characteristics of the Research Literature of the Fine Arts During the Period 1948–1957" (Ph.D. dissertation, University of Illinois, 1960), p. 10.

14. Wolfgang M. Freitag, "Art Libraries and Collections," *Encyclopedia of Library and Information Science* Vol. 1 (New York: Marcel Dekker, 1968), p. 572.

15. Ibid., p. 574.

16. Anthony Burton, "Nineteenth Century Periodicals," in Trevor Fawcett & Clive Phillpot, eds. *The Art Press: Two Centuries of Art Magazines* (London: The Art Book Company, 1976), p. 3, 8.

17. Trevor Fawcett, "Illustration and Design," in Ibid., p. 58.

18. Simonton, "Characteristics of the Research Literature of the Fine Arts . . . ," p. 14.

19. See the entire issue of *Microform Review* 8 (Summer 1979).

20. David Wright, [Review of:] André Grabar and Carl Nordenfalk, *Early Medieval Painting . . .* , *Art Bulletin* 43 (September 1961): 245–246.

NOTES: CHAPTER 26 Music

1. Charles Hartshorne, "The Aesthetics of Birdsong," *Journal of Aesthetics and Art Criticism* 26 (Spring 1968): 312.

2. Percy Scholes, *Everyman and His Music, Simple Papers on Varied Subjects,* 1917, (Reprinted: Freeport, N.Y.: Books for Libraries Press, 1969), p. 1.

3. Joseph Agee Mussulman, *The Uses of Music; An Introduction to Music in Contemporary American Life* (Englewood Cliffs, NJ: Prentice-Hall, 1974), p. 93–102; 126–129.

4. Lewis Thomas, *The Lives of a Cell: Notes of a Biology Watcher* (New York: Viking Press, 1974), p. 20.

5. National Research Center of the Arts, Inc. *Americans and the Arts: A Survey of Public Opinion* (New York: The Center, 1975), p. 51.

6. U.S. Bureau of the Census, Social Indicators 1976, *Selected Data on Conditions and Trends in the United States.* (Washington: Government Printing Office, 1977), p. 516.

7. Claude V. Palisca, "American Scholarship in Western Music," in Frank Ll. Harrison, Mantle Hood, and Claude V. Palisca, *Musicology,* Humanistic Scholarship in America, The Princeton Studies (Englewood Cliffs, N.J.: Prentice-Hall, 1963), p. 116 (Original in Italics).

8. T. W. Adorno, *Philosophy of Modern Music,* trans. Anne G. Mitchell and Wesley V. Blomster (New York: Seabury Press, 1973), p. 6.

9. Leonard Bernstein, *The Unanswered Question; Six Talks at Harvard* (Cambridge, MA: Harvard University Press, 1976), p. 270.

10. Margery Allingham, *Dancers in Mourning* (London: W. Heinemann, 1937), p. 30.

11. Nicolas Slonimsky, *Lexicon of Musical Invective, Critical Assaults on Composers Since Beethoven's Time* 2nd ed. (New York: Coleman-Ross Co., Inc., 1965), 325 p.

12. Jacques Barzun, ed., *Pleasures of Music: An Anthology of Writing about Music and Musicians from Cellini to Bernard Shaw* (Chicago: University of Chicago Press, 1977), p. ix.

13. Charles Warren Fox [Review of *New Oxford History of Music,* vol. 2], *Musical Quarterly* 41 (October 1955): 547.

14. Herbert Weinstock, "Speaking of Musical Biography," *Music Library Association Notes* 22 (Winter 1965–1966): 863.

15. B. H. Haggin, "Music," *Nation* 165 (23 August 1947): 189.

16. Jacques Barzun and Henry F. Graff, *The Modern Researcher,* rev. ed. (New York: Harcourt, Brace & World, Inc., 1970), p. 104–106. (Lamentably absent from the third edition.)

17. Nyal Williams, "Music Reference Materials: An Examination of the Reviews," *RQ* 17 (Fall 1977): 38.

18. D. W. Krummel, *English Music Printing, 1553–1700* (London, The Bibliographical Society, 1975), p. 1.

19. Ernest Roth, *The Business of Music: Reflections of a Music Publisher* (New York: Oxford University Press, 1969), p. 72.

20. Ibid., p. 84.

21. A. Hyatt King, *Four Hundred Years of Music Printing,* 2nd ed. (London: The British Museum, 1968), p. 7.

22. See Walter Gerboth, "Acquisitions: College Library," in Carol June Bradley, ed. Manual of Music Librarianship (Ann Arbor, MI: Music Library Association, 1966), p. 16.

23. Rebecca Green, "The Use of Music and Its Literature Over Time," *Music Library Association Notes* 35 (September 1978): 55.

24. Lewis Foreman, *Systematic Discography* (Hamden, Conn.: Linnet Books, 1974), p. 11.

25. Roth, *The Business of Music,* p. 11.

26. Ibid., p. 236–237.

27. Sigmund Spaeth, *The Importance of Music* (New York: Fleet Publishing Corp., 1963), p. 33.

28. John Voigt, "Rock Music," *Wilson Library Bulletin* 46 (October 1971): 130–131.

29. Gerboth, "Acquisitions: Public Library," in Bradley, ed., *Manual of Music Librarianship,* p. 15, 24.

NOTES: CHAPTER 27 Literature

1. Paul Hernadi, ed., *What Is Literature* (Bloomington: Indiana University Press, 1978), 257 p.

2. John Reichert, *Making Sense of Literature* (Chicago: University of Chicago Press, 1977, p. 133.

3. Marcus Klein, "Books in the Field: American Fiction," *Wilson Library Bulletin* 42 (January 1968): 466.

4. Susan Sontag, "The Aesthetics of Silence," in her *Styles of Radical Will* (New York: Farrar, Straus and Giroux, 1969), p. 14–15.

5. Northrop Frye, *Anatomy of Criticism: Four Essays* (Princeton, NJ: Princeton University Press, 1957), p. 11.

6. Quoted in John A. Garraty, *The Nature of Biography* (New York: Knopf, 1957), p. 9.

7. Samuel Eliot Morison, *By Land and by Sea; Essays and Addresses* (New York: Knopf, 1953), p. 297.

8. Robert N. Wilson, *The Writer as Social Seer* (Chapel Hill: University of North Carolina Press, 1979), p. 5.

9. Graham Dunstan Martin, *Language, Truth and Poetry, Notes towards a Philosophy of Literature* (Edinburgh: At the University Press, 1975), p. 278.

10. Douglas Bush, "Literary History and Literary Criticism," in Leon Edel, ed., *Literary History and Literary Criticism, ACTA of the Ninth Congress, International Federation for Modern Languages & Literatures* (New York: New York University Press, 1965), p. 13.

11. John Updike, "The Plight of the American Writer," *Change* 9 (December 1977): 37.

12. (New York: Viking Press), 1953, p. 10–11.

13. George Orwell, "Good Bad Books," in his *Shooting an Elephant, and Other Essays* (New York: Harcourt, Brace, 1950), p. 183.

14. Ibid., p. 184.

15. John W. Nichol, "Melville's ' "Soiled" Fish of the Sea,' " *American Literature* 21 (November 1949): 338–339.

16. Fredson Bowers, "Recovering The Author's Intentions," *Pages, The World of Books, Writers, and Writing* (Detroit: Gale Research Co., 1976–   ), vol. 1, p. 219.

17. David Daiches, *English Literature,* Humanistic Scholarship in America, The Princeton Studies (Englewood Cliffs, NJ: Prentice-Hall, 1964), p. 143.

18. Fred Inglis, *An Essential Discipline; An Introduction to Literary Criticism* (London: Methuen Educational Ltd., 1968), p. 1.

19. Reichert, *Making Sense of Literature,* p. 173.

20. *Scholarly Communication; The Report of the National Enquiry* (Baltimore: Johns Hopkins University Press, 1979), p. 40.

21. Denys Thompson, *The Uses of Poetry* (Cambridge, Eng.: Cambridge University Press, 1978), p. 25.

22. Paul Zweig, "The American Outsider," *The Nation* 203 (14 November 1966): 517.

23. Inglis, *An Essential Discipline,* p. 120.

24. For instance: Thompson, *The Uses of Poetry,* p. 194–225.

25. Northrop Frye, *The Modern Century* (Toronto: Oxford University Press, 1967), p. 70.

26. Robert Lynd, *Books and Writers,* (London: J. M. Dent & Sons, Ltd., 1952), p. 330.

27. Eric Moon, "Blue Chip Book Selection," *Library Journal* 89 (15 June 1964): 2562, 2579.

28. Charles W. Cooper, *Preface to Drama, an Introduction to Dramatic and Theater Art* (New York: Ronald Press Company, 1955), p. 102.

29. R. P. Cuzzort and E. W. King, *Humanity and Modern Social Thought,* 2nd ed. (Hinsdale, IL: Dryden Press, 1976), p. 330–331.

30. Lester Thonssen, A. Craig Baird, and Waldo W. Braden, *Speech Criticism,* 2nd ed. (New York: Ronald Press Company, 1970), p. 387–534.

NOTES: CHAPTER 28 Prose Fiction

1. Quoted by Carl Bode, "Columbia's Carnal Bed," *American Quarterly* 15 (Spring 1963): 59.

2. (New York: Scarecrow Press, 1965), p. 12.

3. S. R. Ranganathan, *Library Book Selection,* 2nd ed. (Bombay: Asia Publishing House, 1966), p. 140.

4. William Lyon Phelps, *Autobiography, With Letters* (New York: Oxford University Press, 1939), p. 297, 301. One of his students was Clarence (*Life with Father*) Day.

5. Colin Wilson, *The Craft of the Novel* (London: Victor Gollancz Ltd., 1975), p. 30, 46.

6. D. H. Lawrence, *Selected Literary Criticism,* ed. Anthony Beal (London: Wm. Heinemann, Ltd., 1956), p. 105.

7. Henry Seidel Canby, "Introduction: Part I," in Henry Seidel Canby and Robeson Bailey, *The Book of the Short Story,* New and enl. ed. (New York: Appleton-Century-Crofts, 1948), p. 19.

8. Anthony Burgess [*pseud.*], *The Novel Now: A Guide to Contemporary Fiction* (New York: W.W. Norton, 1967), p. 52.

9. Frank O'Connor [*pseud.*], *The Lonely Voice: A Study of the Short Story* (Cleveland: World Publishing Co., 1963), p. 17.

10. William Peden, *The American Short Story: Continuity and Change 1940–1975,* 2nd ed. rev. & enl. (Boston: Houghton Mifflin, 1975), p. 2–3.

11. David Goldknopf, *The Life of the Novel* (Chicago: University of Chicago Press, 1972, p. 1–24 (Quotation, p. 17).

12. Henry James, "The Art of Fiction," *Longman's Magazine* 4 (September 1884): 507.

13. Goldknopf, *The Life of the Novel,* p. 92.

14. James, "The Art of Fiction," p. 509.

15. Sigmund Freud, *Standard Edition of the Complete Psychological Works,* translated from the German under the General Editorship of James Strachey . . . Vol. 9 (London: Hogarth Press, 1959), p. 8, 92.

16. Kenneth Gorelick, " 'Great Literature' as a Teaching Tool in the Education of Mental Health Professionals," *Libri* 25 (July 1975): 139.

17. Wilson, *The Craft of the Novel,* p. 88, 100.

18. Frederick Lewis Allen, "Horatio Alger, Jr.," *Saturday Review of Literature* 18 (17 September 1938): 4.

19. "Confessions of a Confession Story Writer," *Bookman* 72 (September 1930): 27. Techniques are discussed also by Dorothy Collett in her *Writing the Confession Story* (Boston: The Writer, Inc., 1969), 190 p.

20. Harland Manchester, "True Stories," *Scribner's Magazine* 104 (August 1938): 60.

21. Richard W. Etulain, "The Historical Development of the Western," in Richard W. Etulain and Michael T. Marsden, eds., *The Popular Western* (Bowling Green, OH: Bowling Green University Popular Press, 1974), p. 75.

22. John G. Cawelti, *Adventure, Mystery, and Romance; Formula Stories as Art and Popular Culture* (Chicago: University of Chicago Press, 1976), p. 192–193.

23. John Toland, *Adolf Hitler* (Garden City, NY: Doubleday, 1976), p. 13, 604.

24. James Cloyd Bowman, "Shakespeare and Zane Grey," *English Journal* 10 (November 1921): 533–534.

25. Gary Topping, "Zane Grey: A Literary Reassessment," *Western American Literature* 13 (Spring 1978): 51–64.

26. George R. Stewart, "The Regional Approach to Literature," in Gerald W. Haslam, ed., *Western Writing* (Albuquerque: University of New Mexico Press, 1974), p. 47.

27. Cawelti, *Adventure, Mystery, and Romance . . . ,* p. 89.

28. Donald A. Yates, "Locked Rooms and Puzzles: A Critical Memoir," in John Ball, ed., *The Mystery Story* (San Diego: University of California Extension in Cooperation with Publisher's Inc., Del Mar, CA: 1976), p. 193.

29. Gilbert K. Chesterton, "A Defense of Detective Stories," in his *The Defendant*, 2nd ed. (London: R. Brimley Johnson, 1902), p. 118.

30. Carl Sagan, *Broca's Brain: Reflections on the Romance of Science* (New York: Random House, 1979), p. 140.

31. James Blish, "The Tale that Wags the God: The Function of Science Fiction," *American Libraries* 1 (December 1970): 1033.

32. Donald A. Wollheim, *The Universe Makers: Science Fiction Today* (New York: Harper & Row, 1971), p. 16–17.

33. Darko Suvin, "On What Is and Is Not an SF Narration; With a List of 101 Victorian Books That Should Be Excluded from SF Bibliographies," *Science-Fiction Studies* 5 (March 1978): 45. (Original in Italics.)

NOTES: CHAPTER 29 Science and Technology

1. Stephen David Ross, *The Scientific Process* (The Hague: Martinus Nijhoff, 1971), p. 12–13.

2. George Sarton, *Introduction to the History of Science* (Baltimore: Published for the Carnegie Institution of Washington by the Williams & Wilkins Company, 1927–1948), 3 vols. in 5.

3. Lewis S. Feuer, *The Scientific Intellectual: The Psychological & Sociological Origins of Modern Science* (New York: Basic Books, 1963), p. 23.

4. Max Lerner, *America as a Civilization: Life and Thought in the United States Today* (New York: Simon Schuster, 1957), p. 209.

5. Philip Handler, "In Praise of Science," *Saturday Review* 6 (24 November 1979): 43.

6. Cyril Bibby, "Science: A Tool of Culture," *Saturday Review* 47 (6 June 1964): 51.

7. Feuer, *Scientific Intellectual*, p. 7.

8. Lewis Thomas, *The Lives of a Cell, Notes of a Biology Watcher* (New York: Viking Press, 1974), p. 101.

9. Bernard H. Gustin, "Charisma, Recognition, and the Motivation of Scientists," *American Journal of Sociology* 78 (March 1973): 1131.

10. Derek J. de Solla Price, "The Scientific Foundations of Science Policy," *Nature* 206, No. 4981 (17 April 1965): 235.

11. Fritz J. Machlup, "Are the Social Sciences Really Inferior?" *Southern Economic Journal* 27 (January 1961): 181.

12. John Ziman, *Public Knowledge; An Essay Concerning the Social Dimension of Science* (Cambridge, Eng.: At the University Press, 1968), p. 102.

13. S. D. Gottfredson, W. D. Garvey, and J. Goodnow 11, *Quality Indicators in the Scientific Journal Article Publication Process* (Baltimore, MD: Center for Research in Scientific Communication, Johns Hopkins University, and Washington: National Technical Information Service, 1977), p. ii (b).

14. P. B. Medawar, "Anglo-Saxon Attitudes," *Encounter* 25 (August 1965): 52.

15. John Ziman, The Force of Knowledge, *The Scientific Dimension of Society* (Cambridge, Eng.: Cambridge University Press, 1976), p. 99.

16. Ziman, *Public Knowledge*, p. 105.

17. K. P. Barr, "Estimates of the Number of Currently Available Scientific and Technical Periodicals," *Journal of Documentation* 23 (June 1967): 114.

18. Bernard Houghton, *Scientific Periodicals, Their Historical Development, Characteristics and Control* (Hamden, CT: Linnet Books, 1975), p. 32–40.

19. Auger, C. P., ed., *Use of Reports Literature* (Hamden, CT: Archon Books, 1975), p. 3, 4, 15.

20. J. M. Gibb and E. Phillips, "A Better Fate for the Grey, or Non-Conventional, Literature," *Journal of Research Communication Studies* 1 (1978/1979): 225–234.

21. P. H. Abelson, "Trends in Scientific Research," *Science* 143 (17 January 1964): 219.

22. Kenneth Heuer, "Editor's Preface," to Loren Eiseley, *Darwin and the Mysterious Mr. X* (New York: Dutton, 1979), p. x.

23. Louis N. Ridenour, "Science and Pseudo-Science," in American Library Association, Committee on Intellectual Freedom, *Freedom of Book Selection,* ed. Frederic J. Mosher (Chicago: The Association, 1954), p. 20.

24. John Updike, "A New Meliorism," in his *Picked-Up Pieces* (New York: Knopf, 1975), p. 481.

25. Quoted by Victor Cohn, "On Writing About Science," *Science* 140 (10 May 1963): 628.

26. Anne C. Roark, "Programs to Teach Science Writing Gain on Campuses," *Chronicle of Higher Education* 18 (9 July 1979): 3.

27. Derek J. de Solla Price, "The Science," in Maurice Goldsmith and Alan Mackay, eds., *The Science of Science, Society in the Technological Age* (London: Souvenir Press, 1964), p. 200. (The Science of Science Foundation was established that year.)

28. "Chronology of Important Chemical and Related Events since 1876," *Chemical & Engineering News* 54 (6 April, 1976): 91–92.

29. Ridenour, "Science and Pseudo-Science," 12.

30. (2nd. ed., Chicago: University of Chicago Press, 1970), 210 p.

31. Roman Iwaschkin, "Pseudoscience and the Librarian," *Assistant Librarian* 71 (September 1978): 96.

32. Gerald Jonas, "The Art of Reviewing Science Books," *Sciences* 17 (September 1977): 14.

33. André Maurois, *Aspects of Biography,* Trans. from the French by S. C. Roberts (New York: D. Appleton, 1929), p. 38.

34. T. L. Cottrell, "The Scientific Textbook as a Work of Art," *Review of English Literature* 3 (October 1962): 7–16.

35. Jeremy Bernstein, "The Mystery of Life," *New Yorker* 50 (13 January 1975): 88–90.

36. Alvin M. Weinberg, *Reflections on Big Science* (Cambridge, MA: M.I.T. Press, 1967), p. 54.

37. John Maddox, "Is the Literature Worth Keeping?" *Bulletin of the Atomic Scientists* 19 (November 1963): 15.

38. Loran C. Twyford, Jr., "Educational Communications Media," *Encyclopedia of Educational Research,* 4th ed. (New York: Macmillan, 1969), p. 371.

39. Lewis Thomas, *The Medusa and the Snail; More Notes of a Biology Watcher* (New York: Viking Press, 1979), p. 47.

40. Albert F. Plant, "A Proud Heritage," *Chemical & Engineering News* 54 (6 April 1976) 7.

41. David Riesman, in Collaboration with Reuel Denny and Nathan Glazer, *The Lonely Crowd: A Study of the Changing American Character* (New Haven, CT: Yale University Press, 1950), p. 150–152.

INDEX